SPORT POLICY IN CANADA

SPORT POLICY IN CANADA

EDITED BY

Lucie Thibault, Brock University

and

Jean Harvey, University of Ottawa

Research Centre for Sport in Canadian Society
University of Ottawa

University of Ottawa Press
2013

u Ottawa

The University of Ottawa Press acknowledges with gratitude the support extended to its publishing list by Canadian Heritage through the Canada Book Fund, by the Canada Council for the Arts, by the Federation for the Humanities and Social Sciences through the Awards to Scholarly Publications Program and by the University of Ottawa.

Copy editing: Lisa Hannaford-Wong
Proofreading: Thierry Black
Typesetting: infographie CS
Cover design: Johanna Pedersen

Library and Archives Canada Cataloguing in Publication

Sport policy in Canada / edited by Lucie Thibault, Brock University; and Jean Harvey, University of Ottawa.

Includes bibliographical references and index.
Issued in print and electronic formats.
ISBN 978-0-7766-2126-5 (pbk.).--ISBN 978-0-7766-2095-4 (pdf).--
ISBN 978-0-7766-2097-8 (epub)

1. Sports and state--Canada. 2. Sports administration--Canada.
I. Thibault, Lucie, editor of compilation
II. Harvey, Jean, editor of compilation

GV706.35.S66 2013   796.06'9   C2013-907650-6
                                     C2013-907651-4

Printed in Canada

Table of Contents

List of Figures

List of Tables

Abbreviations

AAP	Athlete Assistance Program
AAU	Amateur Athletic Union of Canada
ABC	American Broadcasting Company
ASC	Aboriginal Sport Circle
AWAD	Athlete(s) with a disability
BASM	British Association of Sports Medicine
CAAWS	Canadian Association for the Advancement of Women and Sport and Physical Activity
CAC	Coaching Association of Canada
CAD	Canadian Dollars
CAN Fund	Canadian Athletes Now Fund
CBC	Canadian Broadcasting Corporation
CCES	Canadian Centre for Ethics in Sport
CEO	Chief Executive Officer
CFLRI	Canadian Fitness and Lifestyle Research Institute
CFTC	Children's Fitness Tax Credit
CGC	Commonwealth Games Canada
CGC IDS	Commonwealth Games Canada International Development through Sport
CICS	Canadian Intergovernmental Conference Secretariat
CIHR	Canadian Institutes of Health Research
COA	Canadian Olympic Association
COC	Canadian Olympic Committee
CODA	Calgary Olympic Development Association
COF	Canadian Olympic Foundation
CP-ISRA	Cerebral Palsy International Sport and Recreation Association

CPC	Canadian Paralympic Committee
CS4L	Canadian Sport for Life
CSC	Canadian Sport Centre
CSDP	Commonwealth Sport Development Program
CSI	Canadian Sport Institute
CSP	Canadian Sport Policy
CTV	Canadian Television Network
DMWG	Deputy Minister Working Group
FACE	Fuelling Athlete and Coaching Excellence
FCFA	Fédération des communautés francophones et acadienne du Canada
FIFA	Fédération internationale de football association
FINA	Fédération internationale de natation
FISU	Fédération internationale du sport universitaire
FPTSC	Federal-Provincial/Territorial Sport Committee
GSS	General Social Survey
HIV/AIDS	Human Immunodeficiency Virus/Acquired Immune Deficiency Syndrome
IAAF	International Association of Athletics Federation
IBSA	International Blind Sport Association
IDS	International Development through Sport
IF	International Sport Federation
IICGADS	International Intergovernmental Consultative Group on Anti-Doping in Sport
INAS-FID	International Sports Federation for Persons with Intellectual Disability
IOC	International Olympic Committee
IOSD	International Organizations of Sports for the Disabled
IPC	International Paralympic Committee
ISDO	Indigenous Sport Development Officer
ISRC	Interprovincial Sport and Recreation Council

IWAS	International Wheelchair and Amputee Sport Association
IWG	International Working Group on Women and Sport
LGBT	Lesbian, Gay, Bisexual, and Transgendered persons
LTAD	Long-Term Athlete Development
M&E	Monitoring and Evaluation
MSO	Multi-Sport/Service Organization
NAIG	North American Indigenous Games
NFC	National Fitness Council
NFL	National Football League
NGO	Non-Government Organization
NOC	National Olympic Committee
NSERC	Natural Sciences and Engineering Research Council
NSO	National Sport Organization
NWT	Northwest Territories
OCASI	Ontario Council for Agencies Serving Immigrants
OCOG	Organizing Committee of the Olympic Games
OCOL	Office of the Commissioner of Official Languages
OTP	Own the Podium
PAGS	Pan American Games Society
PARC	Federal-Provincial/Territorial Physical Activity and Recreation Committee
PASM	Physical Activity and Sport Monitor
P.A.Y.	Physically Active Youth
P.L.A.Y.	Promoting Life-Skills in Aboriginal Groups
PSO	Provincial Sport Organization
PTASB	Provincial/Territorial Aboriginal Sport Bodies
RTE	Road to Excellence
RTP	Right to Play
SCRI	Sport Canada Research Initiative

SDP	Sport for Development and Peace
SFAF	Sport Funding and Accountability Framework
SPARC	Sport, Physical Activity, and Recreation Committee
SPIN	Sport Programs in Inner City Neighbourhoods
SPRI	Sport Participation Research Initiative
SSHRC	Social Sciences and Humanities Research Council
UK Sport	United Kingdom Sport
UN	United Nations
UNESCO	United Nations Educational, Scientific and Cultural Organization
UNOSDP	United Nations Office on Sport for Development and Peace
USA	United States of America
USSR	Union of Soviet Socialist Republics
VANOC 2010	Vancouver Organizing Committee for the 2010 Olympic and Paralympic Winter Games
WAAF	Women's Amateur Athletic Federation
WADA	World Anti-Doping Agency
WOAW	Women Organizing Activities for Women
WWII	World War II
YMCA	Young Men's Christian Association
YWCA	Young Women's Christian Association

Acknowledgements

The editors and authors would like to acknowledge public servants from all levels of government involved in sport as well as leaders of various national, provincial and local non-profit sport organizations for their availability and their willingness to answer our questions about the policies that affect them and their organizations. We would especially like to recognize the assistance of Sport Canada and, in particular, Dan Smith, Joanne Kay, David McCrindle and Steve Findlay for their answers to our questions and their suggestions. The views expressed in this book however, are solely those of the authors.

We would also like to thank the Research Centre for Sport in Canadian Society, University of Ottawa. A number of authors presented versions of their chapters at workshops hosted by the Research Centre. To this end, we wish to thank the workshop participants for their constructive feedback. We would also like to acknowledge the Social Sciences and Humanities Research Council of Canada and Sport Canada's Sport Participation Research Initiative for the funds which made the research of many chapters included in this book possible.

Finally, we would like to acknowledge the universities and institutions to which we are affiliated. They provide the numerous resources that enable us to carry out our research. In alphabetical order, these are: British Columbia Centre of Excellence in Women's Health; Brock University; Loughborough University; Office of the Commissioner of Official Languages, Government of Canada; Queen's University; University of British Columbia; University of Michigan; University of Ottawa; University of Toronto; University of Windsor; Western University; and York University.

Introduction

Lucie Thibault, Brock University and
Jean Harvey, University of Ottawa

The purpose of this book is to provide a comprehensive overview of current Canadian sport policy. More than ever, in order to understand the role and meaning of sport in society, it is important to recognize the inter-relations between the sport system and the state, to realize that numerous sport issues are indeed also public policy issues in which the state has a key role to play. Given the current international trend toward devoting increasingly large sums of money to 'produce' Olympic medalists, to what extent should governments support high performance athletes, and through which channels? To what extent should municipalities provide access to sport infrastructures, free of charge or through user fees, to their citizens and community clubs? Should the federal government financially support national sport organizations (NSOs)? At what level? Under which conditions? Should governments establish public administrative bodies to control doping in sport, or should they mandate non-governmental organizations to do so? These are only a few examples of issues that first come to mind when one considers the role government plays in sport.

There have been prominent developments in sport in recent decades that reinforce government's central role in the field. Canadians remember the success of Canadian athletes at the Vancouver 2010 Olympic and Paralympic Winter Games, as well as the massive investments of the federal government, the province of

British Columbia and the city of Vancouver which made the hosting of these games successful. Canadian sport leaders, with funding from the government and sponsorships from the private commercial sector, launched the creation of Own the Podium, an initiative that continues to establish specific performance targets and strategies to achieve these targets for upcoming Summer and Winter Olympic and Paralympic Games. The Greater Toronto Area is preparing to host the 2015 Pan and Parapan American Games in 2015. As the lifespan of the 2002 *Canadian Sport Policy* was about to expire, a new Canadian Sport policy was adopted by sport ministers in June 2012. At the time of this book's writing, Canada is also preparing to host the Women's 2015 FIFA (Fédération internationale de football association) World Cup. Meanwhile, public health authorities are growing increasingly concerned over the alarming trend of Canadians' decreasing participation in sport, and as a result, a renewed vision of the role of community sport, as both a public good and a tool for social and economic development, has emerged as a central issue of the new 2012 *Canadian Sport Policy.*

The scene itself is rather commonplace: smiling politicians posing in front of media cameras alongside successful athletes in the hope of improving their own political capital; but there are various and more significant reasons why government should be involved in sport. As outlined by Harvey (2008, p. 227), governments perceive "sport as an instrument of social cohesion" whereby people from different backgrounds are brought together through sport's uniting force. As well, sport is considered "an instrument of economic development" where hosting international events, for example, is believed to contribute to the tourism sector and stimulate infrastructure development (e.g., transportation, technology, accommodations, sport facilities) in communities where events are held. Involvement in sport and sport policy are also considered to be important instruments of "foreign policy" and "international co-operation" (Harvey 2008, p. 227). Specifically, sport has often served as a strategy to foster economic and political relationships and generate goodwill among countries. Given sport's mass appeal and ability to transcend borders, culture, language, gender, race, religion and socio-economic status, sport may be considered an ideal medium to facilitate exchanges between various nations (Andrews & Grainger, 2007; Miller, Lawrence, McKay, & Rowe, 2001; Wertheim, 2004). Conversely, sport can be used as an instrument of political pressure against foreign governments, as was the case with the international boycott of the former apartheid regime in South Africa. Another reason why governments choose to invest in sport is based on its perceived contribution to "social development and the promotion of social inclusion" (Harvey, 2008, p. 228). Sport's connection to education and health and to the general well-being of individuals and communities would suggest that it serves an important function in society; however, as pointed out by Bloom, Gagnon and Hughes (2006, p. ii), "there is little evidence to support the anecdotal claims that high performance sport leads to social benefits such as building national pride, enhancing cultural awareness and encouraging healthy behaviours." Along similar lines, Grix and Carmichael (2012) have noted:

> isolated or (relatively) newly formed states, like Australia and Canada, have sought to use sport as a cornerstone of national identity creation, with the former often describing itself as a "sporting nation", despite exhibiting many of the problems of other advanced capitalist states, for example high levels of obesity and low mass sport participation. (p. 86)

In light of these issues and motives justifying government involvement and investment in sport, this book aims to provide a comprehensive overview of the multi-faceted public sport policies in Canada, more specifically at the federal level, which we will discuss in greater detail below. In this book, we are exclusively interested in government policies (or public policies) and programs. What do we mean exactly by government policies or public policies and programs? There is currently no consensus in the literature on the definitions of these terms. As Page (2006, p. 210) has stated, *"policies* can be considered as intentions or actions, or more likely a mix of the two."

Page (2006) argues that these intentions and actions can be viewed at four levels of abstraction. At the most general level, policy 'intentions' take the form of principles or general views about how to run public affairs. For example, in Western democratic countries, until the 1960s, the general view was that government should play a very limited role, if any, in what was then called amateur sports, while countries on the East side of the Iron Curtain were investing massively in their high performance system in order to demonstrate, through the Olympic Games, the superiority of their communist regime. The 'liberal' or non-interventionist vision of the state's role in sport has now overwhelmingly vanished from advanced indus-trialized countries. Indeed, the question is no longer should gov-ernment intervene in sport, but rather what are the best policies to support such intervention. At the next level, somewhat more specific intentions take the form of policy 'lines,' or strategies about how to manage specific issues or topics. For example, a significant section of Bill C-12 is dedicated to establishing and laying out the operating rules for the Sport Dispute Resolution Centre of Canada, which is in charge of mediating disputes within the sport system. Moving, then, to the sphere of actions, "*measures* are the specific instruments [or tools] that give effect to distinct policy lines" (Page, 2006, p. 211). Among the policy instruments used by governments are, for example, subsidies, exhortation, taxes, regulations, and licensing systems oper-ated by state agencies. Finally, "*practices* are the behavior of officials normally expected to carry out policy measures" (Page, 2006, p. 211).

Pal's (2010) definition of public policy is more encompassing than Page's insofar as it includes inactions as well as intentions and actions. Policies are "a course of action or inaction chosen by public authorities to address a given problem or interrelated set of problems" (Pal, 2010, p. 2). It is important to emphasize Pal's point that a decision by a government not to act on a specific issue is often, in itself, a policy. Finally, Pal (2010) argues that there is a fine line between programs and policies. Policies are mostly "guides to a range of related actions in a given field" (Pal, 2010, p. 2), while 'programs' are the specific courses of action taken in order to fulfill the goals of a policy. In summary, for the purpose of our work, 'public policies' are defined as intentions, actions, or inactions by public authori-ties. Therefore, the chapters included in this book address not only explicit policies, programs and actions taken by government, but also implicit ones.

This book is not the first to be published in the area of sport policy and Canadian government involvement in sport, but the existing literature tends to be limited and, for the most part, dated. In 1987, a book written by Donald Macintosh, Thomas Bedecki, and C.E.S. Franks entitled *Sport and Politics in Canada: Federal Government Involvement Since 1961* was published. This book was followed by other works such as: *Not Just a Game: Essays in Canadian Sport Sociology* (Harvey & Cantelon, 1988), *The Game Planners. Transforming Canada's Sport System* (Macintosh & Whitson, 1990), *Sport and Canadian Diplomacy* (Macintosh & Hawes, 1994), and *Taking Sport Seriously:*

Social Issues in Canadian Sport (Donnelly, 1997, 2000, 2011) as well as numerous book chapters and articles (e.g., Cantelon, 2003; Comeau, 2013; Harvey, 1988, 2002, 2008; Harvey, Thibault, & Rail, 1995; Macintosh, 1996; Semotiuk, 1994; Thibault & Babiak, 2005). These works and others have contributed to our understanding of the nature and scope of the Canadian government's involvement in amateur sport for a period of more than 50 years. But as noted earlier, given the developments that have taken place during the past decade, almost all of this literature is now outdated.

This book provides the most recent and most comprehensive examination of sport policy in Canada published to date. Questions steering the content of the book include: What roles do various levels of government play in high performance sport and sport participation in Canada? What are the major issues facing sport policy in this country? What are the strengths and weaknesses of Canada's sport system? and What policies have been developed to guide the actions of government in sport?

Moreover, it brings together contributions from the largest selection of the best Canadian scholars in the field, providing an unprecedented depth and breadth of expertise on the various topics covered. In addition, it examines the most recent developments in Canadian sport policy, including the 2012 *Canadian Sport Policy*, which is set to cover the next 10 years. As such, this book provides readers with the most relevant and contemporary perspective on sport policy in Canada.

As is the case for all projects of such magnitude, this book is not without its limitations. First, as stated above, although this book focuses predominantly on sport policy at the federal level, some chapters address the involvement of provincial/territorial and local governments. Chapter II, for example, examines the interrelationships in the sport policies of governments at the federal, the provincial/territorial, and local levels. Despite its comprehensiveness, however, a full account of sport policies at all levels of government was well beyond the scope of this project. To the extent that it focuses on public policies in sport, this book does not deal with the relationships between the state, professional sport and the commercial sport sector, primarily because these relationships are more relevant to industrial and labour policy rather than to sport policy. However, this delimitation does not prevent the authors in this book from making relevant observations on the impact of the private commercial sector on sport, most notably through sponsorship, endorsement and/or the financial support of athletes and non-profit sport organizations as it may relate to their topic. Some readers may notice the absence of a single, overarching framework that might provide a unified point of analysis for all the chapters. One could perceive this as a shortcoming; however, we prefer to see it as a strength in the sense that the absence of such an overarching framework gave the authors the freedom to discuss their areas of expertise in the most effective way, affording them the opportunity to go into greater depth in their policy analysis.

The book's 13 chapters are organized into three sections: in Section I, the first three chapters of the book give an overview of sport policy in Canada. The first chapter by Lucie Thibault and Jean Harvey provides an historical overview of government involvement covering the period from 1961 to the adoption and implementation of the latest *Canadian Sport Policy* in 2012. The second chapter by Jean Harvey addresses the various levels of government involved in Canada's sport system and the bilateral agreements that have been developed to manage collaboration among governments. The third chapter, authored by Bruce Kidd, examines sport, international relations and Canada's role in sport for development.

In Section II, the major features of the *Canadian Sport Policy* are discussed. Chapter IV by Lisa Kikulis examines high performance sport and sport excellence in Canada. The following chapter, Chapter V, by Lucie Thibault and Kathy Babiak, highlights programs and services involved in the development and support of athletes. Chapter VI by Peter Donnelly investigates sport participation within Canadian sport and the role governments play in this area.

The third section of the text addresses the various policies within Sport Canada as well as policy issues affecting sport. Chapter VII by Rob Beamish discusses the history of Canada's policy against doping in sport. The following chapter, Chapter VIII, by Cora McCloy and Lucie Thibault, presents and analyzes Canada's policy and program for hosting international single sport and multi-sport events. Chapter IX is authored by Janice Forsyth and Vicky Paraschak and covers Canada's policy on Aboriginal peoples and sport. The following chapter, Chapter X by David Howe, examines Canada's sport policy for persons with a disability. In Chapter XI, Parissa Safai investigates Canada's sport policy for girls and women, while in Chapter XII Graham Fraser addresses official languages in Canada's sport system. In Chapter XIII, Wendy Frisby and Pamela Ponic investigate the issue of inclusion in sport. In the last section of the book, we conclude with a synopsis and closing remarks and address future directions with regard to high performance sport and sport participation in the Canadian context. The book provides a comprehensive analysis of recent developments in Canadian sport policy. It also provides a solid foundation for understanding contemporary issues in Canada's sport system. We believe the current text fills an important gap in the existing literature on sport policy and provides an important overview of the involvement of both government and non-profit organizations in Canadian sport and the complex nature of the interactions between all sport stakeholders.

References

Andrews, D.L., & Grainger, A.D. (2007). Sport and globalization. In G. Ritzer (Ed.), *The Blackwell companion to globalization* (pp. 478–497). Malden, MA: Blackwell.

Bloom, M., Gagnon, N., & Hughes, D. (2006). *Achieving excellence: Valuing Canada's participation in high performance sport.* Ottawa, ON: Conference Board of Canada. Retrieved from http://www.sportmatters.ca/files/Groups/SMG%20Resources/Reports%20and%20Surveys/2006-CBOC%20Benefits%20HP%20Sport.pdf

Cantelon, H. (2003). Canadian sport and politics. In J. Crossman (Ed.), *Canadian sport sociology* (pp. 172–189). Toronto, ON: Thomson Nelson.

Comeau, G.S. (2013). The evolution of Canadian sport policy. *International Journal of Sport Policy and Politics, 5*(1), 73–93.

Donnelly, P. (Ed.) (1997). *Taking sport seriously. Social issues in Canadian sport.* Toronto, ON: Thompson Educational Publishing.

Donnelly, P. (Ed.) (2000). *Taking sport seriously. Social issues in Canadian sport* (2nd ed.). Toronto, ON: Thompson Educational Publishing.

Donnelly, P. (Ed.) (2011). *Taking sport seriously. Social issues in Canadian sport* (3rd ed.). Toronto, ON: Thompson Educational Publishing.

Grix, J., & Carmichael, F. (2012). Why do governments invest in elite sport? A polemic. *International Journal of Sport Policy and Politics, 4*(1), 73–90.

Harvey, J. (1988). Sport policy and the welfare state: An outline of the Canadian case. *Sociology of Sport Journal, 5*(4), 315–329.

Harvey, J. (2002). Sport and citizenship policy: A shift toward a new normative framework for evaluating sport policy in Canada? *ISUMA Canadian Journal of Policy Research, 3*(1), 160–165.

Harvey, J. (2008). Sport, politics, and policy. In J. Crossman (Ed.), *Canadian sport sociology* (pp. 221–237). Toronto, ON: Thomson Nelson.

Harvey, J., & Cantelon, H. (Eds.) (1988). *Not just a game: Essays in Canadian sport sociology.* Ottawa, ON: University of Ottawa Press.

Harvey, J., Thibault, L., & Rail, G. (1995). Neo-corporatism: The political management system in Canadian amateur sport and fitness. *Journal of Sport and Social Issues, 19*(3), 249–265.

Macintosh, D. (1996). Sport and government in Canada. In L. Chalip, A. Johnson, & L. Stachura (Eds.), *National sports policies. An international handbook* (pp. 39–66). Westport, CT: Greenwood Press.

Macintosh, D., Bedecki, T., & Franks, C.E.S. (1987). *Sport and politics in Canada. Federal government involvement since 1961.* Montreal, QC & Kingston, ON: McGill-Queen's University Press.

Macintosh, D., & Whitson, D. (1990). *The game planners. Transforming Canada's sport system.* Montreal, QC & Kingston, ON: McGill-Queen's University Press.

Macintosh, D., & Hawes, M.K. (1994). *Sport and Canadian diplomacy.* Montreal, QC & Kingston, ON: McGill-Queen's University Press.

Miller, T., Lawrence, G., McKay, J., & Rowe, D. (2001). *Globalization and sport. Playing the world.* London: Sage.

Page, E.C. (2006). The origins of policy. In M. Moran, M. Rein, & R.G. Goodin (Eds.), *The Oxford handbook of public policy* (pp. 207–227). Oxford, UK: Oxford University Press.

Pal, L.A. (2010). *Beyond policy analysis: Public issue management in turbulent times* (4th ed.). Toronto, ON: Nelson Education.

Semotiuk, D. (1994). Restructuring Canada's national sports system: The legacy of the Dubin inquiry. In R.C. Wilcox (Ed.), *Sport in the global village* (pp. 365–375). Morgantown, WV: Fitness Information Technology.

Thibault, L., & Babiak, K. (2005). Organizational changes in Canada's sport system: Toward an athlete-centred approach. *European Sport Management Quarterly, 5*(2), 105–132.

Wertheim, L.J. (2004, June 14). The whole world is watching. *Sports Illustrated, 100*(24), 72–86.

SECTION I

AN OVERVIEW OF SPORT POLICY IN CANADA

CHAPTER I

The Evolution of Federal Sport Policy from 1960 to Today

Lucie Thibault, Brock University and
Jean Harvey, University of Ottawa

As noted in the introduction to this book, contemporary analysis of government involvement in 'amateur' sport is not only warranted, it is essential given the significant changes that have occurred in Canadian sport and in federal government involvement in sport since the publications of Macintosh and his colleagues as well as others (cf. Cantelon, 2003; Harvey, 1988, 2002, 2008; Harvey & Cantelon, 1988; Macintosh, 1996; Macintosh, Bedecki, & Franks, 1987; Macintosh & Whitson, 1990). For example, since 1987, Canada has hosted two Olympic Winter Games (Calgary 1988 and Vancouver 2010), Ben Johnson was caught using a banned substance in the 1988 Seoul Olympic Games, and an inquiry investigating the use of banned performance-enhancing substances in Canadian sports (Dubin, 1990) was conducted. In addition, during this time period the sport system was put under close scrutiny as the very purpose and place of government in sport was reassessed (e.g., *Sport: The Way Ahead*; Mills Report) (Mills, 1998; Minister's Task Force, 1992). The position of Minister of State for Fitness and Amateur Sport was abolished in 1993, while at the same time, Sport Canada was moved to the newly created Department of Canadian Heritage. Canada hosted the Commonwealth Games in 1994 in Victoria and the Pan Am Games in 1999 in Winnipeg. Under the leadership of the new Secretary of State for Sport, Denis Coderre, an extensive pan-Canadian consultation process involving all major sport stakeholders was undertaken, which culminated in the *Report on the National Summit on Sport* (Government of Canada, 2001), the *Canadian Sport Policy* in 2002 (Sport Canada, 2002), and federal legislation in the form of an act to promote physical activity and sport (Bill C-12) in 2003 (Parliament of Canada, 2003). The original *Canadian Sport Policy* was subsequently renewed in 2012 (Sport Canada, 2012). Bill C-12 and the *Canadian Sport Policy* are part of a series of laws and policies developed by Sport Canada. Table 1.1 (below) provides a chronological outline of these laws and policies. For the most part, these will be examined in different chapters throughout this book. In the present chapter, we will provide a brief historical overview of federal government involvement in sport, where major features of increased government involvement in our sport system will be outlined.

In the late 1950s and early 1960s, the Canadian government started to consider a more direct involvement in our nation's sport system. Several events led politicians and bureaucrats down this path. For example, Canada's lack of gold medal performances in ice hockey during the 1956 and 1960 Olympic Winter Games, meager results at the 1960 Olympic Summer Games combined with poor levels of fitness among Canadians, led to increased pressure on politicians and the federal government to become directly involved in sport and fitness in the early 1960s. Giving further support

Table 1.1 Sport Canada Legislation and Policies

Year	Legislation or Policy
1985	*Federal Government Policy on Tobacco Sponsorship of National Sport Organizations*
1994	*National Sports of Canada Act*
1995	*Department of Canadian Heritage Act*
2002	*Canadian Sport Policy*
2003	Bill C-12: *An Act to Promote Physical Activity and Sport*
2005	*Sport Canada's Policy on Aboriginal Peoples' Participation in Sport*
2006	*Policy on Sport for Persons With a Disability*
2007	Bill C-47: *The Olympic and Paralympic Marks Act*
2008	*Federal Policy for Hosting International Sport Events*
2009	*Actively Engaged: A Policy on Sport for Women and Girls*
2011	*The Canadian Policy Against Doping in Sport*
2012	*Canadian Sport Policy*

for government involvement was the Prime Minister at the time, John Diefenbaker (Progressive Conservative government). As a young, aspiring politician who had attended the 1936 Olympic Games in Berlin as a spectator and then, as Prime Minister, the Pan American Games in Chicago in 1959, Diefenbaker experienced first-hand the power of sport to enhance national pride, identity and unity (Kidd, 2001; Macintosh et al., 1987). The Government of Canada would soon develop legislation that would secure its involvement for the future. In September 1961, the federal government passed Bill C-131, an *Act to Encourage Fitness and Amateur Sport*. In the years following Bill C-131, the nature of government involvement was predominantly in the form of grants to provincial governments to ensure the implementation of fitness programs as well as programs to enhance athletic performance in international competitions (Macintosh et al., 1987). In the mid-1960s, the federal government also created the Canada Games—a multi-sport national competition for youth held every two years (alternating between summer and winter games) where athletes represent their provinces and territories. The first games were held in 1967 in Quebec City (Macintosh et al., 1987).

The extent of government involvement took on greater propor-tion in the late 1960s and 1970s. In his electoral campaign for Prime Minister, Pierre Elliott Trudeau (Liberal government) made a promise to examine sport. Following his election in 1968, Trudeau honoured this promise and created a task force to examine the state of ama-teur and professional sport and explore the role of government and national and international sport organizations in promoting and developing Canadian sport (Macintosh et al., 1987). The task force included Nancy Greene,[1] a prominent downhill skier who won the inaugural World Cup in 1967 and won gold (giant slalom) and silver (slalom) medals at the 1968 Olympic Winter Games in Grenoble. In 1969, the *Report of the Task Force on Sports for Canadians* was pub-lished (Rae, 1969). Several of the task force recommendations would eventually be implemented by the Ministry of National Health and Welfare through a document presented by then Minister John Munro entitled *A Proposed Sports Policy for Canadians* (Munro, 1970). Several arm's-length agencies such as the Coaching Association of Canada, ParticipACTION, Hockey Canada and the National Sport and Recreation Centre were created during the early 1970s to support national sport organizations; office space was subsequently pro-vided to these organizations in Ottawa along with funding to hire one full-time employee (Macintosh, 1996; Macintosh et al., 1987). These government initiatives were well received by national sport organizations.

These initiatives were further sustained with the announcement in 1971 by the International Olympic Committee (IOC) that the 1976 Summer Olympic Games would be awarded to Montreal. The announcement provided the impetus for the federal government's emphasis on high performance sport (over the development of mass sport, fitness, or recreation). Several programs were initiated to prepare athletes for the Games. For example, athlete assistance programs (i.e., Game Plan, Game Plan 76) overseen by the Canadian Olympic Association (renamed the Canadian Olympic Committee in 2002) were developed to provide financial support to athletes preparing for the 1972 and 1976 Games. A lottery system (Loto-Canada) was created by the federal government to provide additional funding for the organization of the 1976 Games. National sport organizations benefited from greater federal funding in the years preceding the Games (Macintosh et al., 1987).

From an international perspective, the Montreal Games were considered a success, (particularly when compared to the 1972 Munich Olympic Games); however, from a fiscal perspective the 1976 Games were a financial disaster, with a reported deficit of CA$ 1B to CA$ 1.5B. It would take three decades to pay this deficit off—with funds originating mostly from taxation on tobacco products (Canadian Broadcasting Corporation, 2006). Of note, regarding our athletes' performances at these Games, Canada would become the first host-nation not to win a gold medal during the Games.

Shortly after the 1976 Montreal Games, the Liberal government created the position of Minister of State for Fitness and Amateur Sport (to work under the aegis of the Ministry of National Health and Welfare), with Iona Campagnolo appointed as its first minister. During her term, Campagnolo undertook a comprehensive review of Canada's sport and consulted with several stakeholders. In 1979, she released *Partners in Pursuit of Excellence—A National Policy on Amateur Sport*. Although this document was never tabled in the House of Commons, responsibilities regarding high performance sport would remain in the purview of the federal government while the responsibility for mass sport and recreation would be devolved to provincial and local governments. During Campagnolo's term, Canada hosted the 1978 Commonwealth Games in Edmonton and finished in first place overall, capturing 109 of 395 medals. This victory and Campagnolo's presence in the Games' closing ceremonies reaffirmed the involvement of the federal government in high performance sport (Macintosh et al., 1987).

In 1981, the IOC selected Calgary as host-city of the 1988 Olympic Winter Games. As was the case for the 1976 Games, the decision led to several government initiatives to prepare athletes for the event. One of these initiatives included Best Ever '88, a program wherein national sport organizations would receive federal funding to develop and implement four-year plans to enhance the preparation of their athletes (Macintosh & Whitson, 1990). The 1980s were marked by a high turnover rate in the ministers appointed to the sport portfolio (see Table 1.2 for a complete list of ministers responsible for sport since 1976). The 1980s were also marked by increasing levels of organization and bureaucracy within the Canadian sport system, with the hiring of more paid administrative and technical staff in most national sport organizations and in a number of provincial sport organizations. This led to the increased bureaucratization and professionalization of sport organizations as structures, policies, and systems were established and implemented (Macintosh & Whitson, 1990). But while the Games in Calgary were deemed successful, once again Canadian athletes failed to secure a gold medal for the country. By the 1990s, the increased bureaucratization and professionalization of sport organizations would lead to changes in governance in which paid executives took on greater responsibilities for the development of policies and strategies for their sport in shared leadership with volunteer executives.

The 1988 Summer Olympic Games in Seoul shook the foundation of Canada's sport system when Ben Johnson's win in the 100-metre race and his subsequent disqualification a few days later became the biggest story at the Games. The disqualification based on Johnson's positive drug test eventually resulted in the establishment by the federal government of an inquiry into the use of drugs and banned practices intended to increase athletic performance. This commission led by Justice Charles Dubin resulted in a comprehensive 1990 report entitled *Commission of Inquiry Into the Use of Drugs and Banned Practices Intended to Increase Athletic Performance*. Dubin's (1990) critical examination of Canada's high performance sport led to a new doping policy (*Canadian Policy on Penalties for Doping in Sport*) and several other reports, many of them also scrutinizing the Canadian

Table 1.2 Canadian Ministers/Secretary of State for Sport 1976–2013[2]

Term of Office	Minister	Political Party	Notes on Departments and Ministers/Prime Minister (PM) in Office
September 15, 1976–May 20, 1979	Iona Campagnolo	Liberal	Creation of Ministry of State for Fitness and Amateur Sport (FAS) under Ministry of Health and Welfare in September 1976 PM Pierre Elliot Trudeau
June 4, 1979–March 2, 1980	Steve Paproski	Progressive Conservative	Minister of State for FAS PM Joe Clark
March 3, 1980–September 22, 1982	Gerald Regan	Liberal	Minister of State for FAS PM Pierre Elliot Trudeau
September 30, 1982–August 11, 1983	Raymond Perrault	Liberal	Minister of State for FAS PM Pierre Elliot Trudeau
August 12, 1983–January 10, 1984	Céline Hervieux-Payette	Liberal	Minister of State for FAS PM Pierre Elliot Trudeau
January 10, 1984–June 30, 1984	Jacques Olivier	Liberal	Minister of State for FAS PM Pierre Elliot Trudeau
June 30, 1984–September 17, 1984	Jean Lapierre	Liberal	Minister of State for FAS PM John Turner
September 17, 1984–March 30, 1988	Otto Jelinek	Progressive Conservative	Minister of State for FAS PM Brian Mulroney
April 1, 1988–January 24, 1990	Jean Charest	Progressive Conservative	Minister of State for FAS PM Brian Mulroney
January 25, 1990–February 12, 1990	Perrin Beatty	Progressive Conservative	Minister of State for FAS PM Brian Mulroney

Table 1.2 (Continued)

Term of Office	Minister	Political Party	Notes on Departments and Ministers/Prime Minister (PM) in Office
February 13, 1990– April 22, 1991	Marcel Danis	Progressive Conservative	Minister of State for FAS PM Brian Mulroney
April 22, 1991– June 25, 1993	Pierre Cadieux	Progressive Conservative	Minister of State for FAS PM Brian Mulroney
June 25, 1993– November 3, 1993	Monique Landry[3]	Progressive Conservative	Minister of State for FAS eliminated by Progressive Conservative government Department of Canadian Heritage created under new PM Kim Campbell
June 25, 1993– November 3, 1993	Mary Collins[4]	Progressive Conservative	Minister of Amateur Sport PM Kim Campbell
November, 1993– January 1996	Michel Dupuy	Liberal	Minister of Canadian Heritage PM Jean Chrétien
July 12, 1996– August 2, 1999	Sheila Copps	Liberal	Minister of Canadian Heritage PM Jean Chrétien
August 3, 1999– January 14, 2002	Denis Coderre	Liberal	New Secretary of State for Sport is named PM Jean Chrétien
January 15, 2002– June 17, 2003	Paul DeVillers	Liberal	Secretary of State (Amateur Sport) PM Jean Chrétien
June 18, 2003– December 11, 2003	Paul DeVillers	Liberal	Secretary of State (Physical Activity & Sport) PM Jean Chrétien
December 12, 2003– July 19, 2004	Stan Keyes	Liberal	Referred to as Minister of State (Sport) PM Paul Martin

Table 1.2 (Continued)

Term of Office	Minister	Political Party	Notes on Departments and Ministers/Prime Minister (PM) in Office
July 20, 2004–February 5, 2006	Stephen Owen	Liberal	Referred to as Minister of State (Sport) PM Paul Martin
May 14, 2005–October 6, 2005	Paul DeVillers	Liberal	PM appoints Parliamentary Secretary to the PM to coordinate government programs for sport, recreation, fitness and active living PM Paul Martin
February 6, 2006–November 26, 2006	Michael D. Chong	Progressive Conservative	Minister for Sport PM Stephen Harper
November 27, 2006–January 3, 2007	Peter van Loan	Progressive Conservative	Minister for Sport PM Stephen Harper
February 6, 2006–October 14, 2008	David Emerson	Progressive Conservative	Minister of International Trade and Minister for the Pacific Gateway and the Vancouver Whistler Olympics PM Stephen Harper
January 4, 2007–October 29, 2008	Helena Guergis	Progressive Conservative	Secretary of State (Sport) PM Stephen Harper
October 30, 2008–May 17, 2011	Gary Lunn	Progressive Conservative	Minister of State for Sport and the 2010 Vancouver Whistler Olympics and Paralympics PM Stephen Harper
May 18, 2011–Present	Bal Gosal	Progressive Conservative	Minister of State for Sport PM Stephen Harper

government's (over)emphasis on international results for athletes and recommending an examination and adoption of 'ethical' sport practices (e.g., *Values and Ethics in Amateur Sport. Morality, Leadership, Education; Sport: The Way Ahead; The Status of the High Performance Athlete in Canada*). A list of these documents, including other sport-related documents published by the federal government and national non-profit organizations, is provided in Table 1.3. In addition to the publication of a number of reports, two organizations were created as a result of the Dubin inquiry: Fair Play Canada and the Canadian Centre for Drug-Free Sport. These two organizations eventually merged in 1995 to form the Canadian Centre for Ethics in Sport (Canadian Centre for Ethics in Sport, n.d.).

In 1993, amid a pre-election reorganization of government and efforts to cut government spending, Prime Minister Kim Campbell (Progressive Conservative government) eliminated the position of Minister of State for Fitness and Amateur Sport and restructured the Fitness and Amateur Sport Branch.[5] Sport Canada, then the primary unit in the branch, was subsumed by the new Department of Canadian Heritage, while Fitness Canada, the other unit, was moved to the Department of Health Canada. The mandate of sport and in particular high performance sport was perceived as a good fit in Canadian Heritage, as one of its main foci was to promote Canada both domestically and abroad (Harvey, Thibault, & Rail, 1995; Thibault & Kikulis, 2011).

In the 1990s, the Conservative government's emphasis on downsizing required all departments to assess their "core business." This resulted in a recommendation to fund selected national sport organizations (rather than funding all national sport organizations). In their quest to maximize the impact of funding, politicians and bureaucrats felt that money would be better invested in those sports in which athletes were doing well internationally. In this funding shift, the federal government would stop funding sport organizations with poor international performances. A change in government occurred before the Conservatives were able to implement this initiative; however, the funding of national sport organizations was reassessed by the Liberal government resulting in the adoption of the *Sport Funding and Accountability Framework* in 1996. This framework did in fact result in the selection of national sport organizations for funding based on assessments of high performance sport and sport participation and remains in effect as the process

Table 1.3 Sport-Related Publications by the Government of Canada and Other Organizations 1985–2012

Year	Report	Source/Author
1985	*Improved Program Delivery—Health and Sports. A Study Team Report to the Task Force on Program Review*	Government of Canada
1985	*High Performance Athlete Development in Canada*	Federal-Provincial/ Territorial Ministers of Sport
1987	*National Recreation Statement*	Interprovincial Sport and Recreation Council
1988	*Toward 2000: Building Canada's Sport System. The Report of the Task Force on National Sport Policy*	Fitness and Amateur Sport
1990	*Amateur Sport: Future Challenges*	Bob Porter and John Cole
1990	*Commission of Inquiry into the Use of Drugs and Banned Practices Intended to Increase Athletic Performance*	Charles L. Dubin
1990	*Discussion Paper Prepared for Consultation on the Dubin Report: Doping Related Matters*	Fitness and Amateur Sport
1991	*Values and Ethics in Amateur Sport: Morality, Leadership, Education*	Fitness and Amateur Sport (Marjorie Blackhurst, Angela Schneider and Dorothy Strachan)
1992	*Sport: The Way Ahead. Minister's Task Force on Federal Sport Policy*	Fitness and Amateur Sport
1992	*The Status of the High Performance Athlete in Canada*	Government of Canada
1993	*Foundation Themes for an Emerging Sport Plan for Canada*	Federal, provincial, territorial ministers responsible for sport and recreation
1994	*Report of the Core Sport Commissioner*	J.Cal Best
1994	*Sport Participation in Canada*	Statistics Canada
1994	*Athlete-Centred Sport—Discussion Paper*	Heather Clarke, Dan Smith, and Guy Thibault on behalf of the Federal-Provincial/Territorial Sport Policy Steering Committee
1995	*Sport Canada Sport Funding and Accountability Framework*	Sport Canada

Table 1.3 (Continued)

Year	Report	Source/Author
1995	*Federal-Provincial/Territorial Planning Framework for Sport*	Federal-Provincial/ Territorial Ministers of Sport
1997	*Physical Inactivity: A Framework for Action. Towards Healthy, Active Living for Canadians*	Federal-Provincial/ Territorial Advisory Committee on Fitness and Recreation
1997	*Governance of the Canada Games: 1997 Clear Lake Resolution*	Federal-Provincial/ Territorial Ministers Responsible for Sport Interprovincial Sport & Recreation Council
1997	*1996 Status of the High Performance Athlete Survey*	Sport Canada
1998	*Sport Canada Strategic Plan*	Sport Canada
1998	*Canadian Heritage Performance Report*	Canadian Heritage, Sheila Copps
1998	*Sport in Canada: Everybody's Business. Leadership, Partnership and Accountability*	Dennis Mills
1999	*National Sport Centres—Position Paper*	Sport Canada
1999	*Report of National Conference on Sport and Corporate Sector*	The Conference Board of Canada
1999	*1999–2000 Core Support Program Guidelines*	Sport Canada
2000–2001	*Sport Canada Documents for the Regional Conferences on Sport (1999–2000)*	Denis Coderre
2000	*A Win-Win Solution: Creating a National Alternate Dispute Resolution System for Amateur Sport in Canada. Report of the Work Group to the Secretary of State (Amateur Sport)*	Report of the Work Group on Alternate Dispute Resolution in Canadian Amateur Sport
2000	*Official Languages in the Canadian Sports System Volume 1*	Office of the Commissioner of Official Languages
2000	*Official Languages in the Canadian Sport System Volume 2—Athlete Survey— Compilation of Responses*	Office of the Commissioner of Official Languages
2001	*National Summit on Sport*	Denis Coderre

Table 1.3 (Continued)

Year	Report	Source/Author
2001	*London Declaration on Expectations for Fairness in Sport*	Provincial/Territorial-Federal Ministers of Sport
2002	Bill C-54 *An Act to Promote Physical Activity and Sport* [renumbered Bill C-12 in 2003]	Government of Canada
2002	*Canadian Sport Policy*	Canadian Heritage
2002	*Federal-Provincial/Territorial Priorities for Collaborative Action 2002–2005*	Federal-Provincial/Territorial Sport Ministers
2002	*The Canadian Strategy for Ethical Conduct in Sport*	Work group of Federal-Provincial/Territorial Sport Committee
2003	Bill C-12 *An Act to Promote Physical Activity and Sport*	Government of Canada
2003	*Report to the Secretary of State (Physical Activity and Sport) on Hosting International Sport Events in Canada— A Proposal for a Strategic Framework*	Jean-Pierre Blais, Strategic Hosting Work Group
2003	*Official Languages in the Canadian Sport System: Follow-Up*	Office of the Commissioner of Official Languages
2004	*Targets for Athlete Performance and the Sport System. Final Draft.*	Thérèse Brisson (F-P/T Work Group #4) submitted to InterProvincial Sport and Recreation Council
2004	*Own the Podium 2010. Final Report of the Independent Task Force*	Cathy Priestner Allinger and Todd Priestner
2004	*Investing in Sport Participation 2004–2008. A Discussion Paper*	Sport Canada
2005	*Status of the High Performance Athlete in 2004*	Ekos Research Associates
2005	*Sport Canada Sport Excellence Strategy*	Canadian Heritage
2005	*Long-Term Athlete Development: Canadian Sport for Life*	Sheila Robertson and Ann Hamilton (Eds.), Canadian Sport Centres
2005	*Strengthening Canada: The Socio-Economic Benefits of Participation in Canada*	Bloom, M., Grant, M. and Watt, D. Conference Board of Canada
2005	*Investing in Canada: Leveraging the Economic and Social Capital of Sport and Physical Activity*	Sport Matters Group

Table 1.3 (Continued)

Year	Report	Source/Author
2006	*Linguistic Barriers to Access to High Performance Sport Study—2005*	Mira Svoboda (Ekos) and Peter Donnelly
2006	*Achieving Excellence: Valuing Canada's Participation in High Performance Sport*	Bloom, M., Gagnon, N. and Hughes, D. Conference Board of Canada
2006	*Road to Excellence Business Plan for the Summer Olympic and Paralympic Sports*	Roger Jackson, Canadian Olympic Committee and Canadian Paralympic Committee
2007	*Federal-Provincial/Territorial Priorities for Collaborative Action 2007–2012*	Federal-Provincial/ Territorial Sport Ministers
2007	*Proposal Sport Canada 2008–12 Action Plan for Official Languages In Response to the Recommendations of the Report: Linguistic Barriers to Access to High Performance Sport Study—2005*	Canadian Heritage, Sport Canada
2008	*Sport Participation Strategy 2008–2012*	Canadian Heritage, Sport Canada
2008	*Raising Our Game For Vancouver 2010: Towards a Canadian Model of Linguistic Duality in International Sport*	Office of the Commissioner of Official Languages
2009	*A Report on the Status of Coaches in Canada*	Coaching Association of Canada; Coaching Research Group, University of Alberta; funded by Sport Canada
2009	*Raising Our Game For Vancouver 2010: Towards a Canadian Model of Linguistic Duality in International Sport—A Follow Up*	Office of the Commissioner of Official Languages
2009	*The 2010 and Beyond Panel Final Report and Recommendations*	David Zussman (Chair of panel), panel commissioned by Gary Lunn, Minister of Sport, Government of Canada
2010	*2009 Status of the High Performance Athlete*	Ekos Research Associates
2010	*Evaluation of the Canadian Sport Policy: Final Report*	The Sutcliffe Group

Table 1.3 (Continued)

Year	Report	Source/Author
2010	*Raising Our Game For Vancouver 2010: Final report on the Vancouver 2010 Olympic and Paralympic Winter Games*	Office of the Commissioner of Official Languages
2010	*Canada's Games: The Government of Canada and the 2010 Vancouver Olympic and Paralympic Winter Games*	Canadian Heritage
2010	*Environmental Scan 2010: Trends and Issues in Canada and in Sport*	Policy Research Group, Canadian Heritage
2010	*Canadian Sport Policy Renewal and Sport Participation*	Joanne Kay, Sport Canada
2010	*Canadian Sport Policy Renewal: Summary of Findings from the National Sport Community Engagement and Consultation Process*	The Sport Matters Group and Sport Canada
2010	*The Canadian Sport Policy: Toward a More Comprehensive Vision Discussion Paper*	Public Policy Forum
2010	*Canadian Sport Policy Renewal Workshop Summary Report*	Public Policy Forum
2011	*Community-Building Through Sport: Final Report of the Community Perspectives Project*	Public Policy Forum
2011	*Analysis of the Canadian Sport Policy Renewal Federal-Provincial/Territorial Government Consultations and e-Survey Data*	Conference Board of Canada
2011	*Towards a Renewed Canadian Sport Policy Discussion Paper*	Sport Canada
2011	*Canadian Sport Policy Renewal National Gathering Summary Report*	Groupe Intersol Group
2011	*Summary Report Canadian Sport Policy Renewal Consultations with the National Sport Community and Related Sectors*	Sport Canada, in collaboration with Sport Information Resource Centre, Sport Matters Group, Canadian Olympic Committee, and Own the Podium

Table 1.3 (Continued)

Year	Report	Source/Author
2011	*OTP [Own the Podium] Evaluation 2011 Full Report*	Kevin Lawrie & Rachel Corbett, Sport Law & Strategy Group Prepared for Own the Podium
2012	*Canadian Sport Policy 2012*	Sport Canada
2012	*Federal-Provincial/Territorial Priorities for Collaborative Action 2012*	Federal-Provincial/ Territorial Ministers for Sport, Physical Activity and Recreation

for funding national sport organizations (Harvey, 2008; Havaris & Danylchuk, 2007).

Greater concern for athlete support emerged in the 1990s. The creation of Canadian Sport Centres, training centres for athletes, was initiated with the collaboration of the federal government, the Canadian Olympic Committee and the Coaching Association of Canada. To date, there are seven centres/institutes serving different areas across the country: Atlantic Canada, Quebec, Ontario, Manitoba, Saskatchewan, Calgary and British Columbia/Pacific. As well, increases in funding levels to high performance athletes and in the number of athletes receiving this funding were made through the Athlete Assistance Program (in 1995–1996, in 2000–2001, and again in 2004–2005) (Thibault & Babiak, 2005).

In 1998, *Sport in Canada: Leadership, Partnership and Accountability. Everybody's Business* was published (Mills, 1998). This document is often referred to as the Mills Report (named after the Member of Parliament who chaired the committee responsible for its publication). Although the report addressed the social, cultural, economic and political significance of sport for Canadians, the media focus at the time was on proposed public subsidies for Canadian professional sport franchises, particularly National Hockey League teams. The subsequent announcement of subsidies by the Minister of Industry, John Manley, for Canadian National Hockey League teams in November 2000 was not well received by Canadians. Three days after the multi-million dollar aid package announcement, the Minister withdrew the offer (Harvey, 2008; Whitson, Harvey, & Lavoie, 2000).

The Mills Report and the favourable social, economic, and political contexts that gave rise to its publication were precursors to the most extensive pan-Canadian consultation process ever conducted involving all stakeholders in the system. This extensive consultation was led by Denis Coderre, the then Secretary of State for Sport within the Department of Canadian Heritage, and culminated in the National Summit on Sport, held in April 2001 (Government of Canada, 2001). These events eventually led to the development of the *Canadian Sport Policy,* issued in May 2002 (Sport Canada, 2002) and to new legislation, Bill C-12, enacted in March 2003, known as the *Physical Activity and Sport Act* (Parliament of Canada, 2003). Bill C-12 was to update and replace Bill C-131. The 2002 *Canadian Sport Policy* focused on four priorities: enhanced participation, enhanced excellence, enhanced capacity, and enhanced interaction. With these four priorities, the federal government acknowledged the importance of focusing on both sport participation and excellence. The priority of capacity and interaction provided support to participation and excellence. Capacity referred to putting in place the necessary systems (e.g., leadership, infrastructure, sport science and technology) to support participation and excellence, while interaction referred to increasing collaboration and communication among all stakeholders in sport (Sport Canada, 2002).

Several government initiatives were undertaken in the early 2000s. The *Sport Dispute Resolution Centre of Canada* was created in 2002 as a mechanism to address and resolve disputes and conflicts between athletes, coaches, and sport organizations (Thibault & Babiak, 2005). In July 2003, the IOC selected Vancouver as host of the 2010 Olympic Winter Games, a decision that led to more funding commitments on the part of the federal government. Collaboration among different sport stakeholders (e.g., the Canadian Olympic Committee, the Canadian Paralympic Committee, winter sport organizations, the Vancouver Organizing Committee, the federal government) led to the development of *Own the Podium—2010,* a strategy to be the best nation at the Vancouver Games. A similar collaborative strategy, *Road to Excellence—2012* (focus on summer sports), was developed for the 2012 Olympic Games in London. Although *Own the Podium—2010* and *Road to Excellence* are not federal government programs, they are fully endorsed by the government.

Concurrently, in the mid-2000s, leaders of the Canadian Sport Centre in Victoria, with Istvan Balyi at the helm, were preparing

Canadian Sport for Life (CS4L) also known as the Long-Term Athlete Development (LTAD) model, a seven-stage sport development program focused on guiding sport participants from the playground to lifelong participation by way of high performance sport for those athletes who show the necessary skills (Canadian Sport Centres, 2005). The model is designed to initiate Canadians in sport participation, training and competition based on development/maturation level rather than chronological age.

Several policies and strategies were developed or revised by Sport Canada from the mid-2000s to the early 2010s: These include a policy on Aboriginal people's participation in sport (2005); a policy on sport for persons with a disability (2006); a policy for hosting international sport events (revised in 2008); an action plan for official languages in the sport system (2008); a policy for women and girls in sport (revised in 2009); and a policy against doping in sport (revised in 2011). These policies are analyzed in various chapters of this book.

The federal government continues to be the primary financial supporter of Canada's sport system. In 2012–2013, the federal government invested CA\$ 210M in sport. These funds are divided among various government programs and national sport stakeholders: national and multi-sport organizations, Canadian Sport Centres/Institutes, the Athlete Assistance Program, sport participation initiatives, and hosting programs. In Table 1.4 and Figure 1.1, the level of funding for sport initiatives by the federal government since 1985 is provided.

In June 2012, in Inuvik (Northwest Territories), the renewed *Canadian Sport Policy* (CSP) was officially endorsed by federal, provincial and territorial ministers responsible for sport, physical activity and recreation. The new 2012 CSP document was the result of a process that was initiated in 2010. As outlined in the 2012 CSP:

> in 2010, a renewal process of unprecedented breadth, scope and transparency—involving governments, NGOs [non-government organizations] and communities—was launched. Its purpose was to build on the success of the 2002 *Canadian Sport Policy* and ensure an effective transition to its successor in 2012. (Sport Canada, 2012, p. 4)

In fact, the renewal of the 2002 *Canadian Sport Policy* was based on a number of background documents and an extensive pan-Canadian consultation process (cf. Sport Information Resource Centre, 2013). The process included feedback, survey results, position papers, and reports from individuals, sport organizations and governments across Canada. Feedback was also sought from five specific target groups: official-language minority communities; Aboriginal Peoples; persons with a disability; ethno-cultural populations; and women.

Table 1.4 Sport Canada's Contributions to Sport Since 1985[6]

Year	Sport Canada's Contributions to Sport (CA$)
1985–86	$ 58,102,493
1986–87	$ 50,558,340
1987–88	$ 51,145,460
1988–89	$ 57,200,576
1989–90	$ 55,580,000
1990–91	$ 68,776,000
1991–92	$ 68,255,000
1992–93	$ 72,162,084
1993–94	$ 75,801,000
1994–95	$ 64,219,000
1995–96	$ 47,234,004
1996–97	$ 51,583,915
1997–98	$ 64,601,465
1998–99	$ 57,526,127
1999–00	$ 52,895,586
2000–01	$ 82,060,618[7]
2001–02	$ 97,553,404
2002–03	$ 79,522,155
2003–04	$ 89,500,000
2004–05	$121,735,422
2005–06	$133,241,616
2006–07	$138,302,344
2007–08	$136,558,878
2008–09	$151,350,728
2009–10	$160,113,348
2010–11	$197,105,538
2011–12	$198,908,005
2012–13	$210,793,641

In addition, reports from six working groups centred on various top-ics relevant to sport and to the priorities of the 2002 CSP. The main focus of these six working groups centred on physical literacy, active for life, community building, interaction, capacity and excellence.

One of the documents that was instrumental in the CSP renewal was the evaluation of the 2002 CSP and its impact on Canada's sport system. The Sutcliffe Group (2010, p. 54), charged with the evaluation of the 2002 CSP, found that "three of the four Policy goals (Excellence, Capacity and Interaction) [had] been met ... Participation remains an area of weakness." Furthermore, as noted in the evaluation report:

> Somewhere along the way, either because of turn-over in lead-ership in government or within the sport sector, or because of change of governments, or because the products of the Policy such as the CS4L/LTAD became more attractive, immediate and tangible, the Policy itself moved onto a "back burner" in gov-ernments' dealings with the sport sector. (The Sutcliffe Group, 2010, p. 54)

This evaluation of the 2002 CSP, combined with the extensive con-sultation process with stakeholders and the numerous documents submitted for consideration for the CSP renewal process eventu-ally culminated in a national gathering in November 2011 (Groupe Intersol Group, 2011). A total of 184 delegates attended the national gathering and discussed the central elements that should shape the 2012 CSP. Concerns over the limited success achieved with sport

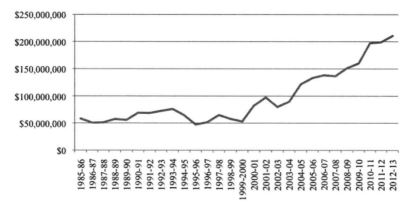

Figure 1.1 Sport Canada's Contributions to Sport 1985–2013 (CA$)[8]

participation led to the emergence of a number of themes at the CSP renewal national gathering. Attendees felt that physical literacy,[9] values and ethics, equity, access, inclusion and diversity should be foundational elements of the 2012 CSP. In addition, attendees believed that sport development as well as sport *for* development should be embraced (Groupe Intersol Group, 2011).

Based on the findings gathered during the renewal process, the 2012 CSP included a policy vision, policy values, policy principles and a policy framework to better address the five policy goals identified. The policy framework outlined in Figure 1.2 clearly addresses the complex nature of sport and the place it occupies in Canadian society. The 2012 CSP vision "is to have, by 2022, a dynamic and innovative culture that promotes and celebrates participation and excellence in sport" (Sport Canada, 2012, p. 5). The policy values include: "fun, safety, excellence, commitment, personal development, inclusion and accessibility, and respect, fair play and ethical behaviour" (Sport Canada, 2012, p. 5). The policy principles are based on the belief that quality sport requires the consideration of the following seven principles: that sport be "values-based, inclusive, technically

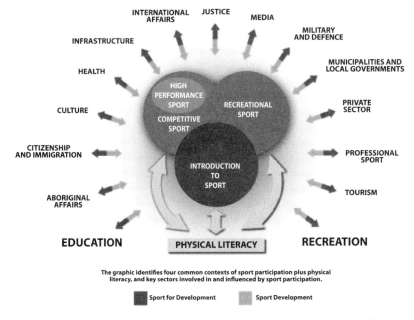

The graphic identifies four common contexts of sport participation plus physical literacy, and key sectors involved in and influenced by sport participation.

Sport for Development   Sport Development

Figure 1.2 *Canadian Sport Policy* 2012 Policy Framework[10]

sound, collaborative, intentional, effective and sustainable (Sport Canada, 2012, p. 6). The policy vision, values, principles and framework provide guidance to achieve the CSP's goals as these relate to each of the four contexts of sport participation identified in the policy in addition to physical literacy (see Figure 1.2). These four contexts are: introduction to sport, recreational sport, competitive sport, high performance sport. Introduction to sport states that Canadians should "have the fundamental skills, knowledge, and attitudes to participate in organized and unorganized sport" (Sport Canada, 2012, p. 8). Regarding recreational sport, it states that Canadians should "have the opportunity to participate in sport for fun, health, social interaction and relaxation" (Sport Canada, 2012, p. 8). Competitive sport refers to Canadians having "the opportunity to systematically improve and measure their performance against others in competition in a safe and ethical manner" while in high performance sport, "Canadians are systematically achieving world-class results at the highest levels of international competition through fair and ethical means" (Sport Canada, 2012, p. 8).

In addition to these four contexts, sport for development is woven into the framework (Sport Canada, 2012). Sport for development is more encompassing than the four contexts, perceiving sport "as a tool for social and economic development and the promotion of positive values at home and abroad" (Sport Canada, 2012, p. 8).

Similar to the 2002 CSP, federal, provincial and territorial ministers responsible for sport, physical activity and recreation identified a number of priorities for the implementation of the 2012 CSP (Federal and Provincial/Territorial Ministers Responsible for Sport, Physical Activity and Recreation, 2012). These priorities are addressed in the next chapter (Chapter II).

Federal, provincial and territorial governments have been instrumental in the development of Canada's sport system. Working with a number of non-profit organizations and stakeholders in the system, governments have been able to shape, through various sport policies, the level, nature and scope of sport participation and high performance sport. Given the ongoing federal government involvement in sport policy and funding, it is important to understand the relationships between the different levels of government and the various sport stakeholders (i.e., non-profit sport organizations, athletes/participants, coaches, officials and volunteers) to address the issues and challenges facing Canadian sport today.

Notes

1. Nancy Greene was recently appointed Senator in January 2009 by Prime Minister Harper (Senate of Canada, 2012).

2. Information for this table originated from the following sources: Canadian Heritage. (2000). Federal Ministers of Amateur Sport in Canada (1961 to Present). Retrieved from http://www.pch.gc.ca/SportCanada/SC_E/minister.htm
Government of Canada. (2007, January 15). Ministers of Amateur Sport in Canada. Retrieved from http://www2.parl.gc.ca/Parlinfo/Compilations/FederalGovernment/MinistersResponsible.aspx?Language=E&Ministry=&Responsability=a2570370-d959-47aa-b082-1516492eb99b Ministers of Amateur Sport in Canada. http://www.parl.gc.ca/ParlInfo/Compilations/FederalGovernment/MinistersResponsible.aspx?Ministry=&Responsability=a2570370-d959-47aa-b082-1516492eb99b&Language=E

3. According to the Government of Canada website [http://www.pco-bcp.gc.ca/mgm/dtail.asp?lang=eng&mstyid=25&mbtpid=1], Monique Landry was Minister of Communications [under Kim Campbell's tenure as PM] but the newspapers report her role as Minister of Canadian Heritage. See, for example, the *Toronto Star* June 26, 1993, page A8.

4. The Government of Canada's website [http://www2.parl.gc.ca/parlinfo/Compilations/FederalGovernment/WomenMinistry.aspx] refers to her as the Minister of National Health and Welfare and the Minister of Amateur Sport [under Kim Campbell's tenure as PM] but the newspapers report her role as Minister of Health. See the *Toronto Star* June 26, 1993, page A8.

5. The Fitness and Amateur Sport Directorate was upgraded to a 'Branch' in 1973 (cf. Houlihan, 1997; Macintosh et al., 1987).

6. Information obtained from Fitness and Amateur Sport Annual Reports and Sport Canada Annual Reports.

7. For fiscal years 2000–01 and 2001–02, Sport Canada contributed CA\$ 20M annually to the 2001 Edmonton World Championships in Athletics (IAAF). This explains the inordinate increase in Sport Canada contributions between 1999–00 and 2000–01. It also explains the decrease in contributions in 2001–02 and the ones in the following years.

8. Source: Data for this figure were obtained from Table 1.4.

9. Physical literacy is defined as the ability of an individual to "move with competence and confidence in a wide variety of physical activities in multiple environments that benefit the healthy development of the whole person" (Physical and Health Education Canada, 2010, paragraph 1).

10. Source: Sport Canada. (2012). *Canadian Sport Policy 2012*. Ottawa, ON: Canadian Heritage. Retrieved from http://sirc.ca/CSPRenewal/documents/CSP2012_EN.pdf, p. 7.

References

Canadian Broadcasting Corporation. (2006, December 19). Quebec's big Owe stadium debt is over. *CBC News*. Retrieved from http://www.cbc.ca/news/canada/montreal/story/2006/12/19/qc-olympicstadium.html

Canadian Centre for Ethics in Sport. (n.d.). *Elevating the conscience of Canadian sport*. Ottawa, ON: Author. Retrieved from http://www.cces.ca/files/pdfs/CCES-PUB-Story-E.pdf

Canadian Sport Centres. (2005). *Long-term athlete development. Resource paper v. 2. Canadian sport for life*. Vancouver, BC: Author. Retrieved from http://canadiansportforlife.ca/sites/default/files/resources/CS4L%20Resource%20Paper.pdf

Cantelon, H. (2003). Canadian sport and politics. In J. Crossman (Ed.), *Canadian sport sociology* (pp. 172–189). Toronto, ON: Thomson Nelson.

Dubin, C.L. (1990). *Commission of inquiry into the use of drugs and banned practices intended to increase athletic performance*. Ottawa, ON: Minister of Supply and Services Canada.

Federal and Provincial/Territorial Ministers Responsible for Sport, Physical Activity and Recreation. (2012). *Federal-provincial/territorial priorities for collaborative action 2012*. Ottawa, ON: Authors. Retrieved from http://sirc.ca/csprenewal.cfm

Government of Canada. (2001). *Towards a Canadian Sport Policy. Report on the National Summit on Sport*. Ottawa, ON: Minister of Public Works and Government Services Canada

Groupe Intersol Group. (2011). *Canadian Sport Policy renewal—National gathering*. Ottawa, ON: Author. Retrieved from http://sirc.ca/CSPRenewal/documents/Summary_National_Gathering.pdf

Harvey, J. (1988). Sport policy and the welfare state: An outline of the Canadian case. *Sociology of Sport Journal, 5*(4), 315–329.

Harvey, J. (2002). Sport and citizenship policy: A shift toward a new normative framework for evaluating sport policy in Canada? *ISUMA Canadian Journal of Policy Research, 3*(1), 160–165.

Harvey, J. (2008). Sport, politics, and policy. In J. Crossman (Ed.), *Canadian sport sociology* (pp. 221–237). Toronto, ON: Thomson Nelson.

Harvey, J., & Cantelon, H. (Eds.) (1988). *Not just a game: Essays in Canadian sport sociology*. Ottawa, ON: University of Ottawa Press.

Harvey, J., Thibault, L., & Rail, G. (1995). Neo-corporatism: The political management system in Canadian amateur sport and fitness. *Journal of Sport and Social Issues, 19*(3), 249–265.

Havaris, E.P., & Danylchuk, K.E. (2007). An assessment of Sport Canada's Sport Funding and Accountability Framework, 1995–2004. *European Sport Management Quarterly, 7,* 31–53.

Houlihan, B. (1997). *Sport, policy and politics: A comparative analysis.* London, UK: Routledge.

Kidd, B. (2001). *Essay. Canadians and the Olympics.* Library and Archives Canada. Retrieved from http://www.collectionscanada.gc.ca/databases/olympians/001064-1000-e.html

Macintosh, D. (1996). Sport and government in Canada. In L. Chalip, A. Johnson, & L. Stachura (Eds.), *National sports policies. An international handbook* (pp. 39–66). Westport, CT: Greenwood Press.

Macintosh, D., Bedecki, T., & Franks, C.E.S. (1987). *Sport and politics in Canada. Federal government involvement since 1961.* Montreal, QC and Kingston, ON: McGill-Queen's University Press.

Macintosh, D., & Whitson, D. (1990). *The game planners. Transforming Canada's sport system.* Montreal, QC and Kingston, ON: McGill-Queen's University Press.

Mills, D. (1998). *Sport in Canada: Everybody's business. Leadership, partnership and accountability.* Standing Committee on Canadian Heritage, Sub-Committee on the Study of Sport in Canada. Ottawa, ON: Government of Canada. Retrieved from http://www.parl.gc.ca/HousePublications/Publication.aspx?DocId=1031530&Mode=1&Parl=36&Ses=&Language=E

Minister's Task Force. (1992). *Sport: The way ahead. Minister's task force on Federal Sport policy.* Ottawa, ON: Minister of Supply and Services Canada.

Munro, J. (1970). *A proposed sports policy for Canadians.* Ottawa, ON: Department of National Health and Welfare.

Parliament of Canada. (2003). *Bill C-12. An Act to promote physical activity and sport* (S.C. 2003, c. 2). Retrieved from http://www.parl.gc.ca/Content/LOP/LegislativeSummaries/37/2/c12-e.pdf

Physical and Health Education Canada. (2010). *What is physical literacy?* Retrieved from http://www.phecanada.ca/programs/physical-literacy/what-physical-literacy

Rea, H. (Chair). (1969). *Report of the task force on sports for Canadians.* Ottawa, ON: Department of National Health and Welfare.

Senate of Canada. (2012). *Nancy Greene Raine Biography.* Retrieved from http://sen.parl.gc.ca/nraine/biography.htm

Sport Canada. (2002). *The Canadian Sport Policy.* Ottawa, ON: Department of Canadian Heritage. Retrieved from http://www.pch.gc.ca/pgm/sc/pol/pcs-csp/2003/polsport-eng.pdf

Sport Canada. (2012). *Canadian sport policy 2012.* Ottawa, ON: Canadian Heritage. Retrieved from http://sirc.ca/CSPRenewal/documents/CSP2012_EN.pdf

Sport Information Resource Centre. (2013). *Canadian Sport Policy renewal.* Retrieved from http://sirc.ca/csprenewal.cfm#

Sutcliffe Group, The. (2010). *Interprovincial Sport and Recreation Council. Evaluation of the Canadian Sport Policy. Final report.* Toronto, ON: Author. Retrieved from http://www.sirc.ca/CSPRenewal/documents/CSP_ Evaluation_Final_ReportEN.pdf

Thibault, L., & Babiak, K. (2005). Organizational changes in Canada's sport system: Toward an athlete-centred approach. *European Sport Management Quarterly, 5*(2), 105–132.

Thibault, L., & Kikulis, L.M. (2011). Canada. In M. Nicholson, R. Hoye, & B. Houlihan (Eds.), *Participation in sport. International policy perspectives* (pp. 268–293). Abingdon, UK: Routledge.

Whitson, D., Harvey, J., & Lavoie, M. (2000). The Mills report, the Manley subsidy proposals, and the business of major-league sport. *Canadian Public Administration, 43,* 127–156.

CHAPTER II

Multi-Level Governance and Sport Policy in Canada

Jean Harvey, University of Ottawa

A few years ago, I attended a reception at Ottawa's National Arts Centre in honour of recently appointed members of the Order of Canada. The reason for my presence was the nomination of the late Major Jan Eisenhardt, who was appointed for his work as the leader of British Columbia's Pro-Rec program in the 1930s, as well as for his presidency of Canada's National Fitness Council (NFC) between 1943 and 1946. As we were chatting about his past, he shared with me his recollection of the time when he met with the Honourable Maurice Duplessis, Premier of Quebec at the time, to discuss collaboration between the Commission and his province in order to co-establish physical fitness programs for Quebecois. "He greeted me in his office very kindly," Eisenhardt added, "and offered me a cigar, as well as a glass of a very good Scotch." Eisenhardt recalled that after several minutes of conversation on light generalities, Duplessis told him with a growing smile that in a few minutes as we leave the office, we will face the press waiting outside, and I will say loud and clear: "This is an unacceptable intrusion of the Federal government into the jurisdiction of this province which I will not tolerate as its Premier." Eisenhardt then explained how Duplessis "got up from his chair, warmly shook my hand smiling at me, thanked me for the visit, escorted me to the door of his office, opened the door and, with me by his side, did exactly what he had just told me he would do, while the cameras flashes blinded us from the row of journalists in front of us." Laughing at the recollection of the scene, Eisenhardt noted that from his perspective, the Premier behaved as a real gentleman. Needless, to say, the province of Quebec, like other provinces for that matter, never accepted any cost-sharing agreement with the short lived National Fitness Council.[1]

With this example of jurisdictional conflict in mind, one might think that, besides ice hockey, fighting over intergovernmental relations is one of the most popular sports in Canadian politics. Indeed, on many policy issues, the federal government and the provincial and territorial governments invariably clash over which one has jurisdiction to act in a variety of policy fields. Other examples of such intergovernmental conflicts over sport include Loto-Canada—put in place by the federal government in the early 1970s to finance the 1976 Montreal Olympic Games—and the funding of the Jeux du Québec. With regard to Loto-Canada, the position of the provinces was and still is that lotteries fall under the jurisdiction of the provinces.[2] Another example was the provisions set by the Province of Quebec in the 1990s to prevent the federal government from directly funding the Jeux du Québec, a creation of the province. However, besides these persistent frictions, there are also numerous instances of collaboration between these two levels of government, as shall be discussed in this chapter. Indeed, following Painter (1991), two forms of intergovernmental relationships have always existed in Canada: competitive federalism, in which each level of government fights to keep its jurisdictional prerogatives, and collaborative federalism, where the different levels of government negotiate their respective roles on a given dossier or a broad policy field. Sport is no different from other policy fields in this regard.

But, these federal-provincial/territorial interactions reflect only one aspect of the general picture of intergovernmental relationships in Canada, since cities and municipalities, although they are creations of the provinces according to section 92(8) of the *Constitution Act of 1867*, do form a *de facto* third order of government of great importance for sport. First, historically municipalities (i.e., local governments) were the first level of government to intervene in that field. At the end of the nineteenth century, long before provinces and the federal government became involved, cities such as Montreal and Toronto and many others started to intervene in sport, either positively by granting subsidies to local sport clubs and organizations like the YMCAs, or negatively, for example by passing by-laws preventing the practice of specific sports in their parks.[3] Second, currently, municipalities nearly always provide low-cost infrastructures as well as subsidies to local sport organizations, catering to a much greater proportion of Canadians' overall participation in sports in comparison to high performance sports. Consequently, in relation to overall expenditure, as well as in terms of total value of expenditure, collectively Canadian municipalities constitute the level of government that invests the most in sport. Although, to our knowledge, there are no recent figures available, in 1999 Statistics Canada published estimates of sport and recreation expenditures for fiscal year 1997–98 that aptly illustrate the weight of each level of government in terms of sport-related public spending. According to these estimates the federal government spent CA\$ 431.7M, the provinces CA\$ 551.2M and the municipalities CA\$ 3.615B during that year, representing 9.4%, 12%, and 78%, respectively, of all government sport expenditures (Luffman, 1999).

While they play an important role in sport, municipalities are not in a position of power in the game of intergovernmental relations, since, first, they are, as mentioned above, creations of the provinces which define what their prerogatives will be and, second, they are increasingly lacking the finances and other resources to fulfill their obligations (e.g., rising costs associated with sport infrastructures, shrinking tax-based sources of revenues). Central governments in federations like Canada are increasingly driven into intervening at the municipal level either directly or indirectly through the provinces and territories or through mechanisms that allow them to bypass second-tier levels of government (i.e., provinces/territories). It is notably the case in Canada with the federal power of the purse, which allows the federal government to spend money in fields that are not normally under its jurisdiction.

Finally, at each level of government, several social forces are present. Local clubs consistently rely on access to municipal infrastructures and subsidies to run their programs. Local boosters lobby their cities as well as higher levels of government to host numerous forms of sport events. At the provincial/territorial level, provincial/territorial sport organizations (P/TSOs) depend heavily on provincial/territorial government funding for their day-to-day operations. Such is also the case for national sport organizations (NSOs) at the national level, as well as organizations such as the

Canadian Olympic Committee (COC), which represents the IOC's interests on Canadian soil.

Given the above, one may be led to believe that it made sense that one of the four goals of the former *Canadian Sport Policy* (CSP) was "Enhanced Interaction." In the CSP, interaction meant collaboration and co-operation within the sport sector as well as among federal-provincial/territorial governments. As stated in the CSP, the goal was that by 2012, "the components of the sport system [become] more connected and coordinated as a result of committed collaboration and communications among stakeholders" (Sport Canada, 2002a, p. 19). In order to reach that goal, according to the CSP, governments were to undertake the following: increase collaboration within and among governments and between sectors, "foster stronger relations between national and provincial/territorial sport organizations," "foster stronger relations between sport organizations and educational institutions," "strengthen relations between governments and their sport communities," and "strengthen international strategies to promote Canadian sport values" (Sport Canada, 2002a, p. 19).

In the 2012 CSP, the former "Enhanced Interaction" has been replaced by the notion of a "Collaborative" policy (Sport Canada, 2012). In his book on public engagement as a new approach to policy making, Lenihan (2012) emphasizes the realization by the leaders in charge, right from the beginning of the CSP renewal process, of the complexity of the new policy environment. As a result, adds Lenihan (2012), collaboration among the different stakeholders in the mapping out of the policy space became the only possible way to develop the new policy in such a complex environment. So collaboration (as opposed to negotiations around competitive views) became the keyword right from the outset of the policy renewal process. Actually, as stated in the final version of the policy, the "collaborative" notion first appears within a new vision of "a dynamic and innovative culture" (Sport Canada, 2012, p. 5), that is, a policy that calls for "building collaborative partnerships and linkages within the sport system, as well as with other sectors such as education and health, with municipalities, local governments and community organizations, and within schools, recreation providers and the private sector" (Sport Canada, 2012, p. 5). Second, 'collaboration' is ranked as one of the seven overall policy core principles and therefore becomes "integrated into all sport-related policies and programs" (Sport Canada, 2012, p. 6). Visually, this policy principle is partially rendered in the 2012 CSP framework, through a series of arrows radiating from the contexts of sport participation and pointing to a wide range of sectors that might be involved in or influenced by sport participation (see Figure 1.2).

The principle is reiterated again in the section on policy implementation and action plans. First, the document stipulates that the eventual success of the 2012 CSP lies in the multiplication of 'linkages' involving stakeholders from within and from outside the sport system, some of them noteworthy: "among NSOs, P/TSOs, municipal clubs and community organizations; between the Sport, Education and Recreation sectors—among NGOs [non-government organizations] and within governments; and between, federal, provincial and territorial governments and their departments" (Sport Canada, 2012, p. 15).

Finally, section eight of the policy on the roles and key stakeholders is central to this chapter. In summary, first, it is stated that the federal government supports high performance athletes, the coaches and the sport system at the national level as well as the hosting of national and international sport events. Second, the federal government also supports sport participation through the funding of sport organizations and collaboration with provincial and territorial governments. Third, provincial/territorial governments' areas of focus according to the policy are the support for participation and volunteerism, athlete development, training of officials and coach education, and high performance sport up to the provincial and territorial levels. These governments also support the hosting of sport events. Finally, the document stipulates that the mutual roles of governments described above are in agreement with the National Recreation Statement of 1987, which will be discussed later.

In brief, the above excerpts from the 2002 CSP and the 2012 CSP point to the importance of intergovernmental relationships, as well as to the ideas of collaboration and linkages among various stakeholders from governments and civil society. The purpose of this chapter is precisely to focus on the intricacies of the relationships between all levels of government in the field of sport, while also taking into account the role of non-profit organizations active in sport. Rather than focusing solely on federal-provincial/territorial relations as most of the intergovernmental literature does, in this chapter, I also examine municipalities or more precisely, federal, provincial/territorial and municipal relationships, hence the reference to multi-level governance in this chapter. What are the respective roles of the federal, provincial/territorial and municipal governments in sport? What factors shape these relationships? How are the actions of each level of government in sport being co-ordinated? What are the social forces at play in this field? These are some of the questions addressed in this chapter. In order to answer them, I first examine the factors that shape current intergovernmental relationships in Canada broadly, as well as in the field of sport policy more specifically. I then turn my attention to the intricacies and challenges of multi-level governance of sport in Canada, with an emphasis on the evolution of the official mechanisms that have been put in place, especially for the delivery of policies and programs that involve more than one level of government. Finally, I conclude by identifying a series of challenges that sport public policy makers are now facing and will continue to face in the near future. But before doing so, I shall define the main concept: multi-level governance.

Nowadays, governance is a prominent notion in political science and in the management literature, as well as in other disciplines. Simply put, governance, according to Kooiman (1993), refers to the plurality of governing actors and to the interactions between political society (the sphere of the government and of its institutions) and civil society (the private, for-profit and non-profit sectors) in the contemporary government of public affairs. In other words, governance is a notion used in the context of a less central role played by contemporary governments and where civil society plays a larger role in decision making through a variety of arrangements such as partnerships, networks, private-public commissions, and so on. Accordingly, multi-level governance refers to:

> ... a system of continuous negotiations among nested governments at several territorial tiers [...] as a result of a broad process of institutional creation and decisional reallocation that has pulled some previously centralized functions of the state up to the supranational level and some down to the local/regional level. (Marks, 1993, p. 392)

In other words, first, multi-level governance refers to various mechanisms of public policy and decision making between different levels of governments. Second, multi-level governance refers to the interplay between governments and civil society and/or social forces.

Factors that Shape Multi-Level Governance

In this section, I review the main factors that shape multi-level governance in sport. At the highest level, the *Constitution Act of 1867* provides the earliest set of rules with regard to the respective roles of the different levels of government that are central to the topic. I have already referred above to section 98(2) of the Act, which stipulates that municipalities are creations of the provinces. That provision makes it extremely difficult for the federal government to interact directly with municipalities. In fact, the federal government cannot do so without the express consent of the provinces. On this specific issue, provincial/territorial governments have historically played different roles regarding federal-municipal relations: monitoring, advocacy, mediation, regulation or partnership (Garcea & Pontikes, 2006). For example, as I discuss later, in hosting major sport events, municipalities interact with the federal and provincial/territorial governments. In other instances, provincial/territorial governments may mediate or advocate for municipalities in order to obtain, on their behalf, federal financial assistance for specific sport infrastructure projects, for example. The case of the projected new arena in Quebec City is a good example of this type of provincial role. In providing up-front financing for the arena, the Quebec government became an advocate for the capital city of the province in its quest for federal funding, even though the federal government declined the invitation.

Concretely, these roles played by the provincial/territorial governments are also influenced by non-constitutional issues, such as the population and size of the city or the province/territory in question. On one end of the spectrum, since World War II, the biggest Canadian cities, such as Toronto, Montreal, and Vancouver, have evolved into major economic and cultural powerhouses, where significant portions of the Canadian population live. Therefore they carry important weight on the Canadian political scene. On the other end of the spectrum, the smallest provinces, both in size and in population, with their limited resources and political weight seldom have the luxury of resisting what could be seen as federal invasions of their jurisdiction.

Other major provisions of the *Constitution Act of 1867* outlining the role of government in sport are those dealing with the respective jurisdictions of the provincial/territorial governments in relation to those of the federal government. Provincial/territorial governments have exclusive jurisdiction over property and civil rights (S. 92(13)), and education (S. 93), as well as general matters of a local nature (such as, for example, community sport).[4] The Constitution is in fact silent on sport and physical activity for one good reason: At the time of the drafting of the Constitution, the fathers of the confederation did not have to care about sport since it was then in its infancy and nowhere on the political map. However, since then, sport has become generally associated with education and/or health, both of which fall under the jurisdiction of the provincial/territorial governments. As for the federal government's jurisdiction, as stated by Barnes (1996), several sections of the Constitution outline its jurisdiction. Its overall role mainly concerns matters of national and international affairs. As a result, the federal government has clear jurisdiction on matters that relate to national level sport as well as to international sport. Therein lies its main role. Section 91 of the *Constitution Act of 1867* touches on aspects that justify larger federal intervention in sport, as it relates to laws regarding peace, order and good government, as well as on commerce, taxes, immigration, citizenship and criminal law, for example (Barnes, 2010). One example of the initiatives that the federal government can take under these provisions is the Children's Fitness Tax Credit,[5] a measure that directly affects citizens, without the mediation of any other level of government. The exclusive federal jurisdiction over the army justified the first intervention of that level of government in what was then called physical fitness. Indeed, for example, in 1909, Lord Strathcona made a donation to the Government of Canada, which in turn created a trust that provided the Canadian army with funds to enter into partnership with provincial governments to finance physical education in schools (Guay, 1980). Finally, as stated above, the federal government may complement or support provincial/territorial governments in their respective jurisdictions, namely through grants or shared funding as a legitimate means of exercising its spending power "provided the intervention does not amount to a regulatory scheme relating to matters under provincial jurisdiction" (Barnes, 2010, p. 25). From this description of some of the provisions of the Constitution, one can conclude that there are as many clear delineations of government's roles as there are grey areas, a notable example being the extent to which the federal government can use its spending power to 'work its way' into community sport and recreation.

The second layer of factors that shape multi-level governance in sport is formed by legislation. At the federal level, three pieces of legislation had an important impact on one of the main points of contention between the federal and the provincial/territorial governments, that is, cost-sharing programs that deal with physical activity and mass sport participation at the local level. The first piece is the *National Physical Fitness Act* of 1943 that created the NFC.[6] As referred to in the introduction to this chapter, its provisions led to tensions between the NFC and several provinces. The second piece is Bill C-131, the *Fitness and Amateur Sport Act* of 1961, which also included cost-sharing provisions that several provincial government leaders resented (Macintosh, Bedecki, & Franks, 1987). Finally, section 7(1) of Bill C-12, the *Act to Promote Physical Activity and Sport* of 2003, the current federal legislation, stipulates that the minister may enter into agreements with the provinces and territories for the payment of contributions to programs to develop physical activity and sport (Parliament of Canada, 2003). I shall return to this provision of the act later on. While we find three main pieces of such legislation at the federal level, as pointed out by Barnes (2010), each province/territory has also enacted different pieces of sport legislations of their own, putting the list of total provisions beyond the scope of this chapter.

Administrative structures put in place to manage these policies by the different levels of government form a third layer of factors affecting multi-level governance of sport in Canada. At the federal level, two examples illustrate this point. With the creation by the federal government of Recreation Canada in 1972, increasing tensions erupted between the two higher orders of government with regard to their respective role in recreation and mass sport participation. The restructuring of Cabinet in 1993 under the Conservative government led by Kim Campbell resulted in the creation of the Department of Canadian Heritage, to which Sport Canada was reassigned, while Fitness Canada remained with the Ministry of Health (now part of the Healthy Living Unit within the Public Health Agency of Canada). Thus, this restructuring created a strong departmental barrier between the two major divisions of the federal government in charge of sport and physical activity.[7] In the case of Sport Canada, with its inclusion within Canadian Heritage, the use of sport as a tool for the promotion of national identity and unity became even more important.

While sport and physical activity fall under two different administrative structures at the federal government level, they normally fall under only one at the provincial and territorial level.[8] Indeed, as each province and territory has exclusive jurisdiction within its territory over significant aspects of sport, from initiation and recreation to high performance sport selection and development, each of them has the power to adopt its own policies and programs as it sees fit, as long as it does not infringe on the exclusive jurisdiction of the federal government. Table 2.1 shows under which ministerial portfolios sport, physical activity and recreation fell, as of September 2013, within provinces and territories. It varies from one constituency to another. The fact that sport is sometimes affiliated

Table 2.1 Provincial/Territorial Government Units Responsible for Sport, Recreation and Physical Activity[9]

Province/Territory	Ministry Responsible for Sport, Recreation and Physical Activity
Alberta	Ministry of Tourism, Parks and Recreation
British Columbia	Ministry of Community, Sport and Cultural Development
Manitoba	Department of Aboriginal and Northern Affairs (Sport Manitoba) Department of Children and Youth Opportunities (Recreation and Regional Services) Department of Healthy Living, Seniors and Consumer Affairs
New Brunswick	Department of Healthy and Inclusive Communities
Newfoundland and Labrador	Department of Tourism, Culture and Recreation
Northwest Territories	Department of Municipal and Community Affairs
Nova Scotia	Department of Health and Wellness
Nunavut	Department of Culture and Heritage
Ontario	Ministry of Tourism, Culture and Sport
Prince Edward Island	Department of Health and Wellness
Quebec	Ministère de l'éducation, du loisir et du sport
Saskatchewan	Ministry of Parks, Culture and Sport
Yukon	Department of Community Services

with education or with health promotion for example is one indication of the emphasis a particular constituency wants to place on sport. Moreover, whether or not the word "sport" appears in the title of a department or ministry is also an indication of the importance of this portfolio for the government in power. Indeed, from one election to another or from one cabinet shuffle to another, the sport portfolio often switches departments altogether, a fact that does nothing to simplify the overall picture. The latter also signals the fluctuating importance of sport as a portfolio from time to time. Sport has never reached the status of a stand-alone portfolio. In this context, provinces and territories face two types of challenges with regard to intergovernmental relationships: vertical ones in terms of their relations with the federal and the local authorities, as well as horizontal ones in terms of the relationships with their fellow provinces and territories. One illustration of the latest type of constraints that may arise is the attempt by the Quebec provincial Minister to intervene in the case of the infamous assault by Québec Remparts goalie Jonathan Roy on a Chicoutimi goalie during an important junior hockey game in 2008. As a result of the incident, Minister Courchesne, then in charge of the sport portfolio, lobbied the Canadian Hockey League (CHL) and her provincial and territorial colleagues to ban fighting in junior hockey in Canada. As her colleagues would not and could not agree on the ban, because, as opposed to Quebec, they do not have the legislative power to intervene, the Province of Quebec was left with the option to push the Ligue de hockey junior majeur du Québec to adopt stronger rules against fighting within its league only.

So far, the factors listed above all refer to government machinery, but the very nature of sport, physical activity and recreation, as well as the presence of a myriad of organizations within civil society active in that field, also has a strong influence on intergovernmental relationships. First, because of the pyramidal structure of competitive sport, from the local club to international sport federations and the International Olympic Committee, sport calls for the attention of all levels of governments, as well as collaboration and co-ordination. Second, because the structure of sport is based mainly on non-profit or for-profit organizations, the members of these organizations try to influence the actions of governments in order to fulfill their own interest. Here the notion of multi-level governance reaches its full meaning.

Mechanisms of Intergovernmental Sport Policy

In the previous section, I reviewed the main factors that structure multi-level governance in sport. As mentioned before, tensions arise constantly between levels of government owing to the grey areas of our Constitution and our political system. In recent decades, several agreements have been put in place to manage these tensions and co-ordinate the actions of the different levels of government (see Table 2.2). These agreements can be divided in the following categories. The first category comprises general agreements passed in order to help clarify the grey areas of Canada's Constitution for the purpose of facilitating collaborative action towards shared objectives. For the purpose of this chapter, I call attention to the *High Performance Athlete Development in Canada* agreement of 1985 and the *National Recreation Statement* of 1987. A second category includes those agreements that have been put in place to guide the actions of governments in their respective jurisdictions. Two such instances would be the *Canadian Policy Against Doping in Sport* (initially developed in 1991, most recently renewed in 2011) and the *London Declaration on Expectations for Fairness in Sport* (2001). A third category includes all multi-party agreements relative to co-operation on issues that touch on all levels of government. In this category, I briefly discuss the *Clear Lake Resolution* of 1997 relative to the Canada Games, as well as the Multi-Party Agreement that created VANOC, the Vancouver Organizing Committee for the 2010 Olympic and Paralympic Winter Games. Not listed in Table 2.2, in a category of their own, are the formal mechanisms of intergovernmental sport policy development,

Table 2.2 Federal-Provincial/Territorial Agreements Relating to Sport and Physical Activity[10]

Year	Agreements
1985	*High Performance Athlete Development in Canada*
1987	*The National Recreation Statement*
1991	*The Canadian Policy Against Doping in Sport* (most recently renewed in 2011)
1995	*The Federal-Provincial/Territorial Planning Framework for Sport*
1996	*Physical Inactivity: A Framework for Action*
1997	*Governance of the Canada Games: 1997 Clear Lake Resolution*
2001	*London Declaration on "Expectations for Fairness in Sport"*
2002	*The Canadian Strategy for Ethical Conduct in Sport: Policy Framework*

the bilateral agreements between the federal government and territories with regard to sport participation in general and the new Implementation and Monitoring Group outlined in CSP 2012.

Agreements on Divisions of Jurisdiction

The first extensive agreement passed in order to draw a line between the federal government on the one side and the provincial and territorial governments on the other deals with the respective roles of these governments with regard to high performance sport. The *High Performance Athlete Development in Canada* agreement of 1985 stemmed from a perceived need by governments to "develop a comprehensive and co-ordinated plan of action for the development of high performance athletes in Canada" (Federal-Provincial/Territorial Ministers Responsible for Sport, Recreation and Fitness, 1985, p. 3). In this document, high performance sport "encompasses athletes who achieve, or, who aspire to achieve, or, who have been identified as having the potential to achieve excellence in World Class competition" (Federal-Provincial/Territorial Ministers Responsible for Sport, Recreation and Fitness, 1985, p. 3). In the preamble, governments acknowledged the limits of clarifying roles, recognizing first that any such exercise always involves some degree of overlap and second, that precise clarification is not possible in all instances. Finally, the governments underlined the fact that sport evolves with time and that delineations may eventually need to be revised accordingly. The core of the document was a discussion regarding a long list of areas in which some were identified as exclusive to the provincial and territorial governments, while others were exclusive to the federal government, and still others were shared between the two. Table 2.3 lists some of these areas of responsibility in each of the three categories (i.e., provincial/territorial, shared, and federal). The provincial and territorial mandate with regard to high performance sport consists of development up to the national level. As for the federal role, the agreement lists areas relevant to national and international sport. Despite this division of roles, "the shared responsibilities program areas outnumber those allocated to one level of government" as stated in the CSP (Sport Canada, 2002a, p. 12). Indeed, Table 2.3 clearly shows that, in many areas of high performance sport, responsibility is shared.

The second agreement I wish to discuss here is the *National Recreation Statement* of 1987. The 16-page document was approved at the Federal-Provincial/Territorial Conference of Ministers of Sport and Recreation in Quebec City in September 1987 (Interprovincial Sport and Recreation Council, 1987). It originated from earlier documents and declarations stating the 'primacy' of the provinces in recreation (defined as including sport) as well as recognition by the federal government of such primacy. In claiming this role, provincial and territorial governments were accepting broad responsibilities including the adoption of policies that put the emphasis on "the importance and value of recreation and leisure and the

Table 2.3 Areas of Responsibility on a Program-by-Program Basis[11]

Provincial/Territorial	Shared	Federal
Provincial/Territorial Team Program	High Performance Program Planning	National Team Programs
Provincial/Territorial Championships	High Performance Training Centres	Team Centralization
Provincial/Territorial Games	National Championships	National Coaching Programs
Participation Development	Identification of National Team Members	National Coaches
Coaches of Provincial/ Territorial Teams	Competitive Opportunities	Major Games—Related to Canadian Teams
Provincial/Territorial Facilities	Athlete Assistance and Support Services	World Championships— Related to Canadian Teams
	International Exchanges	Technical Information
	Supplies and Equipment	International Interface
	Sport Science	Sport Models
	Athlete Testing	
	Sport Medicine	
	Canada Games	
	Education of Coaches	
	Team Managers Development	
	Officials Development	
	Hosting International Events	
	Talent Identification	

importance of recreation and leisure as a social service," thus committing significant resources to support provincial organizations and municipalities—"the primary public supplier of direct recreation services"—as well as to meet regularly with other governments to co-ordinate public policies (Interprovincial Sport and Recreation Council, 1987, pp. 8–9). The statement also recognized a role for the federal government, but a complementary one, involving itself primarily in activities that are national and international in scope and by providing for the development of recreation programs "in facilities and institutions under the sole jurisdiction of the federal government" (Interprovincial Sport and Recreation Council, 1987, p. 12). The federal government was also expected to distribute information to encourage citizens to participate in recreation and physical activity, as well as to develop a central database for information on various forms of recreation and related programs. Interestingly enough for this chapter, the statement also included a complete section on mechanisms of intergovernmental co-operation and on the need thereof. It listed four main reasons why such co-operation is desirable: to enhance the quality of programs through the exchange of ideas, to avoid duplication, to define and maintain a clear delineation of roles, and to facilitate the resolution of issues. These motives are still relevant today.

Multi-Party Agreements

This category includes agreements that set the rules of co-operation as well as the respective roles of all parties involved in multi-level initiatives such as hosting sport events. These agreements are central to Canadian sport policy, since they provide the framework for the federal Hosting Program (see Chapter VIII on hosting). The *Clear Lake Resolution* was adopted in 1997 30 years after the first Canada Games. The Canada Games "represent a unity of purpose to celebrate the sporting character of Canada through a high quality multi-sport event, which includes opportunities for regional exchange and learning, making the Canada Games a national sport development asset" (Canada Games, 2010, paragraph 2). The Resolution also laid out rules reaffirming the Canada Games Council (incorporated in 1991) as the non-profit organization in charge of the Games. The Resolution included five appendices and two schedules. Appendix 1 described the strategic priorities of the ministers for the Games in terms such as athlete-centred, values-based, access, athletic excellence, and public interest. Appendix 2 provided the financial framework for the Games (i.e., what share of the funding each level of government must provide). For example, with regard to operating costs, the public sector funding is broken down as follows: 52% from the federal government, 16% from the hosting province or territory, and 32% from the hosting society.

With regard to 'base capital contribution,' the federal government, the provincial or territorial government, and the hosting municipality are expected to contribute CA$ 2M each. Also, Sport Canada is to provide funds to cover the travel costs for athletes, mission staff and officials. Appendix 3 provided a detailed list of the areas in which the Canada Games Council can make final decisions, relating mainly to the day-to-day operations of the Games. Any area that touches on the main provision of the Resolution and is political in nature remains the responsibility of the federal and provincial/territorial governments. Appendix 4 outlined the provincial/territorial rotation for hosting the Games from 1997 to 2009. The Resolution still constitutes the framework for the Canada Games under the current Canada Games component of the Federal Hosting Program. Interestingly enough, originally, although the Resolution involved municipalities, they were not partners in this agreement. In the development of the Resolution, provincial and territorial governments played the roles of mediation and regulation of federal-municipal relations with regard to the Games. However, as of 2009, multi-party hosting agreements have been introduced that include all three levels of government (Personal communication with a public official).

Interesting features of the Canada Games in terms of governance include the interplay between the Canada Games Council and the hosting societies. According to its stated mission, "the Canada Games Council delivers the Canada Games as a unique, premium, nation building, multi-sport event and works continuously to strengthen the Canada Games Movement, in partnership with government, the private sector and the sport community" (Canada Games, 2010, paragraph 5). The Canada Games Council is managed by a board of directors that includes ex-officio members from federal and provincial/territorial governments and national sport organizations as well as observers/members at large (i.e., members of current and future hosting societies). Several representatives of the private sector serve different functions on the Board, namely as chairs. The board of directors of hosting societies is similar to the Council in its composition. For example, the Board of Directors of the Halifax 2011 Host Society includes a chair originating from the private sector and representatives from both the provincial government and the community. Two additional members are from the Canada Games Council. Therefore, even if these structures are private organizations on paper, their governance structure presents complex inter-organizational linkages (Thibault & Harvey, 1997) wherein the two upper levels of government are ensured a significant presence, both centrally and locally, in decision-making processes related to the Games. They perceive themselves as partners with civil society, while ensuring oversight of these organizations, following a long-standing, neo-corporatist-like form of governance of sport (i.e., a model where the state plays an active role in the organization of interest groups) (Harvey, Thibault, & Rail, 1995).

The Multi-Party Agreement for the 2010 Olympic and Paralympic Winter Games had a similar structure to that of the Canada Games, but its scope with respect to the diversity of stakeholders involved is far greater. Signed on November 14, 2002, the agreement was set in motion before the Olympic and Paralympic Winter Games were to be awarded to Vancouver. The document was designed to accompany the Vancouver 2010 Bid Corporation and prepare the creation of the Organizing Committee of the Olympic Games (OCOG) in the event that the games were awarded to Vancouver. The Agreement was signed by the governments of Canada and British Columbia, the City of Vancouver, the Resort Municipality of Whistler, the Canadian Olympic Committee (COC), the Canadian Paralympic Committee (CPC) and the Vancouver 2010 Bid Corporation. The Agreement was 23 pages in length (with another 24 pages of appendices) and fulfilled the IOC's requirements with regard to the Organizing Committee of the Olympic Games and was consistent with all relevant Government of Canada policies and laws, such as the Hosting Policy and the *Official Languages Act* (see Chapter XII on official languages), among others. The Agreement also established the respective contributions of each level of government (which eventually ended up being higher). It also stipulated membership of 20 for the future OCOG, a non-profit agency. The members were to be appointed as follows: three by the Government of Canada, three by the Government of British Columbia, two by the City of Vancouver, two by the Resort Municipality of Whistler, seven by the COC, one by the CPC, one by the Lil'wat and

Squamish First Nations and one to be chosen by vote of the other members. The innovative feature of this board was undoubtedly the one seat allocated to the above mentioned First Nations' bands. As such, their role and status as hosting nations were recognized. Once again, in this example, there was a significant presence of government representatives on the board, 10 out of 22 when we include the First Nations. While it may be conceived as a way of ensuring seamless relationships between all levels of government and civil society—more precisely here the IOC through its local representatives in the COC—this feature also raised the question of the truly 'private corporation' nature of the OCOG.

Another interesting feature of the Agreement is section 43, which lists the provisions against conflicts of interest and where it is stated that no member of the House of Commons or Senate of Canada, no current or former federal public office holder or servant, no member of the Legislative Assembly of British Columbia and no member of the Vancouver City Council or Whistler City Council could be admitted to any share of the Agreement or to any benefits or profit that may arise.[12] While these provisions clearly protect the integrity of the OCOG, they do not mean that the representatives of the different levels of government were not actually representing the interest of their employer. Quite the contrary: for some, this kind of government representation in such multi-level agreements puts these representatives in a position of conflict of interest between the organizations of which they are members on the one hand and, on the other hand, the employer to which they report. Such was the opinion expressed by key stakeholders for the purpose of the evaluation of the 2005 FINA championships in Montreal (Parent, 2006).

The counterargument is that governments invested a great deal of financial resources and thus, should ensure that these funds were used appropriately and legislation and policy were complied with and followed. Moreover, the presence of the different stakeholders on the same board may facilitate the necessary flow of information between the stakeholders. The question that then arises relates to the transparency of these structures. They are presented as private but are they? It also raises the question of accountability of elected officials. Let us consider the example of the language scandal that erupted (mostly in Quebec) from the near-total absence of French during the opening ceremonies of the Vancouver Olympic and

Paralympic Winter Games. How could the Canadian Heritage minister not be held at least partially responsible for this oversight that became so divisive for the country, when he was so well represented on VANOC? The answers to these questions notwithstanding, for the purpose of this chapter, the multi-party agreement truly constitutes a mechanism of multi-level governance which, in the end, delivered successful Games. The Agreement also served as a template for the more recent multi-party agreement for the 2015 Toronto Pan Am Games, an agreement that has already resulted in controversy on the same language issue (Bourgault-Côté, 2010).

Mechanism for Federal-Provincial/Territorial Collaboration

Although presented somewhat late in this chapter, the mechanism for federal-provincial/territorial collaboration has been central to the multi-level governance of sport policy in Canada since the 1960s, although it only became an established mechanism in 1986 (see Figure 2.1). In the 1990s, its focus was primarily on initiatives relating to the Canada Games, the National Coaching Certification Program and Aboriginal issues.[13] Since 2000, the level of activity of that mechanism has increased significantly, as the CSP was developed, adopted and implemented. Today, as we shall see, it is active on a number of issues. Indeed, it is through this mechanism that the agreements discussed above have been negotiated and agreed upon; that the provincial and territorial governments have adopted the CSP; that the implementation and monitoring of the CSP have been carried out and common goals have been developed. In short, it is through this mechanism and its complex intricacies that collaboration between the two upper levels of government in sport and physical activity really takes place, or not. The current structure of the mechanism derives from, and follows, the *National Recreation Statement*, but its origin is earlier, as mentioned above. Before describing the mechanism, it is important to note that its structure is nevertheless informal in essence, meaning that it is not mandated through the Constitution, and therefore does not have any constitutional status. It is the result of evolving relationships between the two major levels of government. Reflecting the formal constitutional divide, municipalities are not part of the decision-making process, an exclusion that leaves the provincial and territorial governments free to exercise their prerogative over local governments.

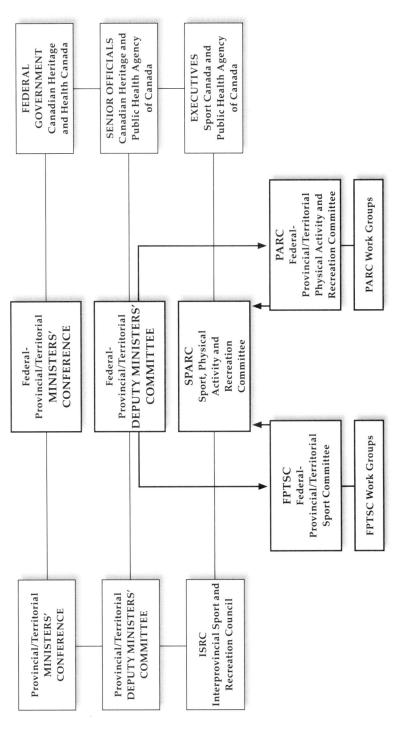

Figure 2.1 Mechanisms for Federal-Provincial/Territorial Government Collaboration[14]

At the top and centre of Figure 2.1 appears the Federal-Provincial/Territorial Ministers' Conference, the decisional body composed of all the provincial and territorial ministers in charge of sport, recreation, and physical activity. The two federal ministers present (i.e., Canadian Heritage (sport) and Health (physical activity)) are also both members and co-chairs of the Conference. As well, they preside over the agenda items that are relevant to their mandate. Finally, there is a third co-chair (who presides on all issues) who is the minister in charge of sport, recreation, and physical activity for the province or territory hosting the next Canada Games. As such, provincial/territorial co-chairing rotates from one province/territory to the next preceding the Canada Games. This represents a concrete illustration of how the separation of sport and physical activity in two distinct federal administrative units is a factor in the governance of federal-provincial/territorial government relationships. Not only does this separation lead to a complicated 'game of musical chairs' between the two federal ministers (in their role as co-chairs) when the time comes to discuss issues relevant to their respective mandates, it also results in a dual committee structure with, on the one hand, committees in charge of sport and, on the other hand, committees in charge of physical activity and recreation, as outlined below.

In the organization of meetings with federal-provincial/territorial ministers, it was agreed that ministers would meet three times over the span of four years, two of those meetings to occur just prior to the Canada Games. The conference is organized by the Canadian Intergovernmental Conference Secretariat (CICS), an agency created in 1973 by the first Ministers to manage the logistics of senior-level federal-provincial/territorial conferences in all areas of federal-provincial/territorial government collaboration. During these conferences, ministers make decisions that the deputy ministers have the responsibility of implementing. To achieve this, deputy Ministers created working groups to provide directions to the Federal-Provincial/Territorial Sport Committee (FPTSC) with regard to sport issues and to the Federal-Provincial/Territorial Physical Activity and Recreation Committee (PARC) with regard to issues related to physical activity and recreation and tasked their respective working groups with the ground work. It is really at the level of the FPTSC and PARC that detailed negotiations and recommendations are developed. These recommendations are then discussed, and issues are identified at a meeting of the Interprovincial Sport and Recreation Council (ISRC) (on which all provincial and territorial governments have representation) and federal officials (who are members of FPTSC and PARC). That meeting is chaired by the ISRC chair and is co-chaired by FPTSC and PARC chairs as issues of their respective mandates are discussed. The outcomes of these meetings are then reported to the Federal-Provincial/Territorial Deputy Ministers' Committee where decisions are drafted for submission and approbation at the Ministers' Conference. In short, it is through this movement back and forth from the ministers' conferences to the committees and working groups that federal-provincial/territorial collaboration occurs. As of December 2012, the FPTSC active working groups were: Canadian Sport for Life Management Team, Monitoring of CSP Implementation, High Performance Issues, and Sport and Recreation Infrastructure. Each year, working groups are formed or dismantled as a function of the needs emerging from discussions, meetings and conferences at the minister and deputy Minister levels.

The existence of this governance structure is a clear indication of the need for the two upper levels of government to collaborate on issues of sport and physical activity policy, given the nature of these two governing bodies and the intricacies of our Constitution. The collaborative nature of the structure was meant to uphold, among other duties, the intent of the *National Recreation Statement*, and to smooth out the jurisdictional grey areas of our Constitution where there is the potential for friction and divergence of opinion between governments about sport and physical activity policy in this country. While there is always impetus for the federal government to adopt national goals, policies and programs, there is also a constant preoccupation on the part the provincial and territorial governments to protect their jurisdictions while, at the same time, to influence the federal government to adopt those policies and programs that suit their own policy. I shall return to this later on, but at this point, it is important to understand what is being discussed at this level. One of the major functions of the mechanism that emerged from the process of developing and adopting the first version of the CSP (Sport Canada, 2002a) was the negotiation of multi-year federal-provincial/territorial priorities for collaborative action (Sport Canada, 2002b, 2007). These priorities set by both governments addressed each of the four CSP goals. The first priorities covered the years 2002–2005. For this period, in regard to the enhanced participation goal, priorities were to increase participation in sport and to increase the presence of sport and physical activity in school. For the enhanced excellence goals, enhancing athlete and sport system performance was the only priority identified. For the enhanced capacity goal, priorities were to implement the competence-based program for coaches, to develop a sport event hosting policy, to improve sport and recreation facilities, to implement the Canadian strategy on the ethical conduct in sport and to foster the diversification of resources for sport organizations and Aboriginal sport development. As for the enhanced interaction goal, priorities were to increase awareness of sport within government (i.e., other departments), to ensure regular communication with the sport community, to enhance collaboration between sport organizations and to negotiate bilateral government agreements to advance the CSP. A second set of priorities was developed for the years 2007–2012 and focused on continuing the initiatives established in the previous document and to work on new priorities in order to further implement the CSP. Among the list of 12 new priorities, the alignment of the overall sport system with the Sport for Life (Long-Term Athlete Development) model was the most pervasive theme. Three priorities were also adopted to pave the road for the evaluation of the CSP, in light of its eventual renewal when it expired in 2012.

On June 27, 2012, at the same time that the CSP 2012 was adopted, a new set of Priorities for Collaborative Action 2012 was made public, to be developed further for review and approval at the 2013 Ministers Conference (Federal and Provincial/Territorial Ministers Responsible for Sport, Physical Activity and Recreation, 2012). The 2012 priorities are as follows:

1. Support introduction to sport programming with a focus on traditionally under-represented and/or marginalized populations;
2. Develop a common data collection methodology with which to identify infrastructure priorities for the sport and recreation sectors;
3. Define and clarify the roles and responsibilities of governments and key stakeholder organizations in the high performance and competitive sport system;
4. Review progress and complete implementation of the Strategic Framework for Hosting International Sport Events in Canada;

5. Work with Aboriginal communities to identify priorities and undertake initiatives for Aboriginal sport development, and the use of sport for social and community development purposes;[15]
6. Introduce initiatives to improve safety and anti-harassment in all contexts of sport participation;
7. Promote implementation of Canadian Sport for Life (CS4L), or equivalent programming, in the sport and related sectors;[16]
8. Implement an engagement strategy to maximize the contribution of NGOs, in the sport and related sectors, to the implementation of CSP 2012. (Federal and Provincial/ Territorial Ministers Responsible for Sport, Physical Activity and Recreation, 2012, p. 1)

Bilateral Agreements

The last (but not the least) key feature of the multi-level governance of sport under the current CSP is formed by the bipartite agreements between the federal and the provincial/territorial governments. These bilateral agreements are yet another form of cost-sharing between the two upper levels of government. However, they were not only key in the adoption of the CSP by the provincial and territorial governments, but also play an important role for the federal government in that they provide a vehicle for this government to be active in sport participation where its jurisdiction is limited. The bilateral nature of these agreements gives the CSP the flexibility to adjust to the respective priorities of provinces and territories and, as such, is touted by the federal government as a Canadian policy (i.e., reflecting its decentralized nature) as opposed to Canada's policy.

Sport Canada has three types of bilateral agreements with the provincial and territorial governments: generic agreements aimed at increasing sport participation; Aboriginal agreements meant to increase the capacity of provincial/territorial sport organizations in charge of Aboriginal sport and physical activity; and agreements to support team travel for participation in the North American Indigenous Games. From one jurisdiction to another, the bilateral agreements take different forms, for example, some provincial or territorial governments have combined the generic and Aboriginal agreements while others have kept them separate and have targeted different priorities. The federal funding portion of every agreement is always based on the fact that the provincial and territorial governments will match the federal funds. Tables 2.4 and 2.5 provide detailed federal commitments for the generic and the Aboriginal bilateral agreements. The tables show a clear increase in the commitments between 2002 and 2011, which signals an increase in federal-provincial/territorial collaboration on issues of participation and Aboriginal sport. When compared with the overall budget of Sport Canada however, the bilateral agreements program remains a modest one.

In terms of the content of the bilateral agreements, as mentioned above, they vary significantly from one province/territory to another. For example, the 2009–2011 *Sport for More* bilateral agreement with Ontario supports the development of local sport programs in First Nations communities; projects designed to increase the sport participation level of underrepresented groups such as ethnic minorities and women; projects to reduce the number of drop-outs in provincial sport organizations; and funding for the Promoting Life-Skills in Aboriginal Groups (P.L.A.Y.) program. In Manitoba, the generic bilateral agreement is related to the community level. For example, the objectives include building community capacity and providing sustainable programming through the development of local partnerships, and developing low or no-cost sport programs for communities where youth are underserved. In Saskatchewan, among other objectives, the bilateral agreement is aimed at supporting the planning and implementation of the LTAD model in provincial sport organizations. All in all, bilateral agreements are becoming an important mechanism of federal-provincial/territorial collaboration in areas where the federal role is far from obvious.

An Implementation and Monitoring Group

Our last example of a mechanism for federal-provincial/territorial collaboration is the Implementation and Monitoring Group put in place in the context of the 2012 CSP. One of the innovative features of the policy is the inclusion of a logic model, which illustrates policy inputs and outputs, corresponding immediate outcomes, CSP 2012 objectives, CSP goals and ultimate outcomes. Actually, at the moment of the adoption of the policy, the complex two-page grid that constitutes the overall logic model was not complete, as the specific input/activities/outputs were still under development. The logic model is a

Table 2.4 Government of Canada Financial Contributions for Generic Bilateral Agreements (CA$) 2002–2011[17]

P/T	2002–03	2003–04	2004–05	2005–06	2006–07	2007–08	2008–09	2009–10	2010–11
AB		200,000	325,000	378,380	378,380	378,380	378,380	378,380	378,380
BC		100,000	434,360	434,360	434,360	434,360	434,360	434,360	434,360
MB		160,000	100,000	367,000	267,000	267,000	267,000	267,000	267,000
NB		180,000	180,000	240,000	240,000	240,000	240,000	240,000	240,000
NL		200,000	213,000	180,000	230,000	243,000	180,000	230,000	230,000
NS	150,000	150,000	254,540	254,540	254,540	254,540	254,540	254,540	254,540
NT	106,000	170,000	222,160	222,160	222,160	222,080	222,080	222,080	202,080
NU	72,000	140,000	191,620	191,620	191,620	178,620	204,620	191,620	201,620
ON			404,719	884,360	884,360	884,360	884,360	884,360	909,360
PE		200,000	200,000	200,000		208,100	208,100	208,100	208,100
QC			634,160	634,160	634,160	634,160	634,160	634,160	634,160
SK		140,000	258,680	258,680	258,680	258,680	258,680	258,680	258,680
YT		140,000	191,800	191,800	191,800	191,800	191,800	191,800	201,800
Total	328,000	1,780,000	3,610,039	4,437,060	4,187,060	4,395,080	4,358,080	4,395,080	4,420,080

classic feature of the new Public Management policy frameworks in which policies are evidence-based and evaluated through measurable outcomes and outputs. Indeed, the Implementation and Monitoring Group is ". . . responsible for collating and sharing the action plans of governments and NGOs, and for monitoring progress. This group will oversee the development of appropriate indicators and metrics and ensure that longer-term pan-Canadian impacts are tracked and evaluated" (Sport Canada, 2012, p. 19). How can this mechanism be seen as a multi-level governance mechanism? It is by virtue of Committee's make-up, which includes academics, representatives of federal-provincial/territorial governments and representatives of the sport system.

The Challenges of Multi-Level Governance

The purpose of this chapter was to focus on multi-level governance of sport in Canada. Several factors shaping this governance were described at length as well as current mechanisms of collaboration between different levels of government. Bilateral agreements foster

Table 2.5 Government of Canada Financial Contributions for Aboriginal Bilateral Agreements (CA\$) 2006–2011[18]

P/T	2006–07	2007–08	2008–09	2009–10	2010–11
AB	100,000	100,000	100,000	83,000	95,000
BC	100,000	0	85,000	85,000	95,000
MB	40,000	75,000	83,000	98,000	95,000
NB	0	60,000	50,000	55,000	0
NL	57,700	80,000	50,000	50,000	50,000
NS	60,000	60,000	50,000	55,000	50,000
NT	45,000	80,000	50,000	50,000	50,000
NU	60,000	60,000	50,000	55,000	50,000
ON	0	0	0	0	75,000
PE	29,250	0	50,000	50,000	50,000
QC	100,000	100,000	83,000	50,000	95,000
SK	100,000	115,000	83,000	83,000	95,000
YT	60,000	60,000	50,000	55,000	50,000
Total	751,950	790,000	784,000	769,000	850,000

better collaboration between the federal and provincial/territorial governments in areas of sport participation and Aboriginal sport. This does not mean that difficult issues will disappear. Tensions arising from the federal government's motivation to create a seamless sport system, which potentially translates into pan-Canadian plans and initiatives, may end up creating resistance from provincial and territorial governments. One possible example of just such an occasion for disagreement is the Canadian Sport for Life/Long-Term Athlete Development program that is percolating throughout the Canadian sport system as the federal government strives for its integration not only at the national level but also provincially and locally. Not all the provincial and territorial governments are open to change in their sport systems simply for the sake of adopting the federal plan.

One of the objectives of this chapter was to put some emphasis on the interaction of municipalities with the higher levels of government. The examination of existing forms of collaboration leaves us with the impression that multi-level governance only truly occurs with the hosting of games through multi-party agreements. In all other areas, relationships and collaborations occur at the federal-provincial/territorial levels. Where local authorities are concerned, provincial and territorial governments retain their decision-making prerogative over this level of government.

New challenges are foreseeable in the near future as sport for development within Canada is becoming a central preoccupation thanks to organizations like Sport Matters Group, which lobby the federal government to ensure that these challenges are at the forefront in the next iteration of the *Canadian Sport Policy*. In addition, new developments towards the use of sport as a strategy for larger social roles such as the integration of immigrants have the potential to partially redefine the role of Sport Canada. One such example is the Working Together Initiative where different federal government units, provincial/territorial governments as well as several multi-service organizations team up to find innovative forms of horizontal and vertical governance of sport programs.

In summary, this chapter has shown the sheer complexity of intergovernmental relationships in sport in Canada. The main factors structuring these relationships are not going to disappear, which means that mechanisms to manage these inter-relationships are a necessary feature of sport policy in this country. The decentralized nature of Canada may lead to greater complexity in the forms of multi-level governance of sport, but more centralized countries such as England, for example, do have similar issues of intergovernmental relationships, only at different levels according to the specificities of their political system. Moreover it can be argued that the decentralized nature of governance mechanisms in Canada are indeed a strength in the sense that they are more sensitive to the expression of regional differences in such a vast and diverse country.

Notes

1. The NFC was active from 1943 until the repeal of the *National Physical Fitness Act* in 1954.
2. As explained in Macintosh et al. (1987), Prime Minister Joe Clark granted responsibility for lotteries to the provinces in 1979.
3. For more on this, see Gruneau (1983), as well as Andrew, Harvey, and Dawson (1994).
4. For more elaborate discussions on constitutional and legislatives issues with regard to governments' roles in sport, see Barnes (1996, 2010).
5. The Children's Fitness Tax Credit is also discussed in Chapter VI.
6. This does not mean that this was the first instance of federal-provincial/ territorial, municipal cost-sharing in sport. With the Strathcona Trust, during the Depression of the 1930s, governments also entered into such programs, for example, the youth training programs of the National Employment Commission (1936–1938) put in place to increased youth employability. For more information, see Harvey (1988).
7. Studies on the involvement of the Canadian government in sport in Canada often overlook the fact that besides the two usual suspects, other parts of the government intervene in sport. For example, Canadian Forces has a vibrant competitive sport system. Moreover Immigration and Citizenship has programs that use sport as a means to integrate young new immigrants into Canadian society. For the purpose of this book, we limit our analysis to the two usual suspects.
8. With the notable exception of Quebec where physical activity is the mandate of the Kino-Québec program, attached to the Ministère de la Santé et Services sociaux.
9. Source: Provincial and territorial government websites, as of September 2013.
10. Source: Adapted from Sport Canada's website. Retrieved from http://www.pch.gc.ca/pgm/sc/pol/pcs-csp/2003/106-eng.cfm
11. Source: Adapted from Canada (1985).

12. Surprisingly no such provisions were aimed at the representatives of the COC and CPC, which does not mean such benefit or profit may have been derived by them.

13. This section of the chapter draws heavily from Canadian Heritage (2010), as well as from informal interviews with Canadian Heritage policy makers.

14. Source: Sport, Physical Activity and Recreation Committee (SPARC) Handbook (Federal-Provincial/Territorial Government draft document 2012).

15. "Quebec recognizes the positive impact of sport on economic and social development; however it does not subscribe to this goal as part of a Canadian sport policy" (Federal and Provincial/Territorial Ministers Responsible for Sport, Physical Activity and Recreation, 2012, p. 1).

16. Efforts with regard to "related sectors" will be made as judged appropriate by individual provincial/territorial governments. (Federal and Provincial/Territorial Ministers Responsible for Sport, Physical Activity and Recreation, 2012, p. 1).

17. Source: Canadian Heritage (2002–2011).

18. Source: Canadian Heritage (2006–2011).

References

Andrew, C., Harvey, J., & Dawson, D. (1994). Evolution of local state activity: Recreation policy in Toronto. *Leisure Studies, 13*, 1–16.

Barnes, J. (1996). *Sports and the law in Canada* (3rd ed.). Toronto, ON: Butterworths.

Barnes, J. (2010). *The law of hockey*. Markham, ON: LexisNexis Canada.

Bourgault-Côté, G. (2010, 20 novembre). Vers un autre fiasco linguistique? *Le Devoir*, p. A1.

Canada Games. (2010). *Canada Games Council—2009–2017 Strategic framework*. Retrieved from http://www.canadagames.ca/content/About-Us/strategic-plan.asp

Canadian Heritage. (2010). *Intergovernmental sport policy development*. Retrieved from http://www.pch.gc.ca/pgm/sc/pubs/FPTSC-eng.cfm

Federal-Provincial/Territorial Ministers Responsible for Sport, Recreation and Fitness. (1985). *High performance athlete development in Canada: A delineation of responsibilities of the federal and provincial/territorial governments*. Ottawa, ON: Authors.

Federal and Provincial/Territorial Ministers Responsible for Sport, Physical Activity and Recreation. (2012). *Federal-provincial/territorial priorities for collaborative action 2012*. Ottawa, ON: Authors. Retrieved from http://sirc.ca/csprenewal.cfm

Garcea, J., & Pontikes, K. (2006). Federal-provincial-municipal relations in Saskatchewan: Provincial roles, approaches and mechanisms. In

R. Young & C. Luprecht (Eds.), *Canada: The state of the federation, 2004: Municipal-federal-provincial relations in Canada* (pp. 333–370). Kingston, ON: Institute of Intergovernmental Relations.

Gruneau, R. (1983). *Class, sport and social development*. Amherst, MA: University of Massachusetts Press.

Guay, D. (1980). *L'histoire de l'éducation physique au Québec*. Chicoutimi, QC: Gaëtan Morin.

Harvey, J. (1988). Sport policy and the welfare state: An outline of the Canadian case. *Sociology of Sport Journal, 5*(4), 315–329.

Harvey, J., Thibault, L., & Rail, G. (1995). Neo-corporatism: the political management system in Canadian amateur sport and fitness. *Journal of Sport and Social Issues, 19*(3), 249–265.

Interprovincial Sport and Recreation Council. (1987). *National recreation statement*. Retrieved from http://lin.ca/Files/4467/statemen.htm

Kooiman, J. (Ed.). (1993). *Modern governance*. London: Sage.

Lenihan, D. (2012). *Rescuing policy: The case for public engagement*. Ottawa, ON: Public Policy Forum.

Luffman, J. (1999). Keeping score in sport spending. *Focus on Culture, 11*(1), 5–9. Statistics Canada, Catalogue no. 87-004-XPB.

Macintosh, D., Bedecki, T., & Franks, C.E.S. (1987). *Sport and politics in Canada. Federal government involvement since 1961*. Montreal, QC & Kingston, ON: McGill-Queen's University Press.

Marks, G. (1993). *Structural policy and multilevel governance in the EC*. In A.W. Cafruny & G.G. Rosenthal (Eds.), *The state of European Community* (pp. 391–410). Boulder, CO: Lynne Rienner Publishers.

Painter, M. (1991). Intergovernmental relations in Canada: An institutional analysis. *Canadian Journal of Political Science, 24*, 269–288.

Parent, M. (2006). *2005 FINA World Championships post analysis report*. Sport Consult MMP Inc.

Parliament of Canada. (2003). *Bill C-12. An Act to promote physical activity and sport* (S.C. 2003, c. 2). Retrieved from http://www.parl.gc.ca/Content/LOP/LegislativeSummaries/37/2/c12-e.pdf

Sport Canada. (2002a). *The Canadian sport policy*. Ottawa, ON: Department of Canadian Heritage. Retrieved from http://www.pch.gc.ca/pgm/sc/pol/pcs-csp/2003/polsport-eng.pdf

Sport Canada. (2002b). *The Canadian sport policy: Federal-provincial/territorial priorities for collaborative action 2002–2005*. Ottawa, ON: Department of Canadian Heritage. Retrieved from http://www.pch.gc.ca/pgm/sc/pol/actn/index-eng.cfm

Sport Canada. (2007). *The Canadian sport policy: Federal-provincial/territorial priorities for collaborative action 2007–2012*. Ottawa, ON: Department of Canadian Heritage. Retrieved from www.pch.gc.ca/pgm/sc/pol/actn07-12/booklet-eng.pdf

Sport Canada. (2012). *Canadian sport policy 2012*. Ottawa, ON: Canadian Heritage. Retrieved from http://sirc.ca/CSPRenewal/documents/CSP2012_EN.pdf

Thibault, L., & Harvey, J. (1997). Fostering intergovernmental linkages in the Canadian sport delivery system. *Journal of Sport Management, 11*(1), 45–68.

CHAPTER III

Canada and Sport for Development and Peace

Bruce Kidd, University of Toronto

Canadian policy makers, sport leaders and athletes eager to tackle the most pressing developmental challenges of our times have been at the forefront of the growing international effort to recruit sport and physical activity to the cause, the movement known as sport for development and peace (SDP). The idea is to use sport as an explicit strategy to help realize the United Nations' Millennium Development Goals with respect to basic education, gender equality, the treatment and prevention of human immuno-deficiency virus/acquired immunodeficiency syndrome (HIV/AIDS), infant and maternal health and the creation of sustainable global partnerships and similar ambitions such as the Commonwealth's goals of development and democracy and la Francophonie's goals of peace, democracy and human rights (Black, 2010; International Platform on Sport and Development, n.d.; Kidd, 2008; Levermore & Beacom 2009).[1] To this end, Canadians have helped apply the best Canadian technical knowledge, such as the coaching develop-ment curricula of the National Coaching Certification Program, to other countries and cultures, and created innovative new programs such as the Commonwealth Sport Development Program (CSDP) and the Canadian Sport Leadership Corps. They have success-fully lobbied diplomats and bureaucrats at the United Nations, in the Commonwealth and the Francophonie to insert SDP into their agendas, have contributed research, monitoring and evaluation and provided some of the resources to bring about implementation. They have created enabling legislative, policy and administrative support for these initiatives in the federal government in an effort to integrate SDP into the network of state and sport organizations known as the Canadian sport system.

SDP is not the only international Canadian initiative of recent years. As other chapters in this collection illustrate, Canadians continue to successfully bid for, and stage, major games and championships. Canadians have been in the forefront of the creation and leadership of the World Anti-Doping Agency, especially its testing protocols and educational programs. Sport Canada has negotiated bilateral agreements with nine other countries, primarily for the purpose of giving Canadian athletes and coaches privileged access to opportunities abroad. Canadians have also contributed significantly to the ongoing advocacy and policy development on women's issues, through their support of the International Working Group on Women and Sport and of other feminist organizations and women's causes. Not all of these interventions have been fruitful. Despite the opposition of Sport Canada and the Canadian Olympic Committee, the International Olympic Committee imposed a male-only ski jumping event and reinstituted the sexist gender verification test at the 2010 Olympic and Paralympic Winter Games in Vancouver (e.g., Vertinsky, Jette, & Hoffman, 2009).[2] It is unclear whether Canadian efforts to abolish the femininity protocols recently reinstituted by the International Olympic Committee and the International Association of Athletic Federations will be successful (Canadian Centre for Ethics in Sport, 2012; Dreger, 2011). Nevertheless, these efforts contribute to the portrait of Canada as a progressive, fair-minded sport nation.

While Canadian successes in, and contributions to, international sport have their greatest impact upon "the image Canadians have of themselves," as former prime minister Pierre Trudeau noted during the 1968 federal election, they also open doors for Canadian diplomacy, trade agreements, immigration, and tourism (Kidd, 2001, p. 4). Canadian efforts in international sport are continual and multifaceted (Kidd, 2001). For the purposes of this chapter, the focus will be upon SDP.

SDP contributes in much the same way to the image of Canada both at home and abroad. Canadian-based non-government organizations (NGOs) such as Commonwealth Games Canada's International Development through Sport (CGC IDS) and Right to Play (RTP) have inspired hundreds of athletes, physical educators and coaches to volunteer and work in the least developed countries and thousands in the general public to contribute money, sport equipment, books and technology. Canadian policy makers have kept Canada's name before decision makers at the United Nations, Commonwealth and Francophonie, while passionate athletes and sport leaders in Africa, Asia, the Caribbean and the Middle East show children and youth in impoverished and war-torn communities that 'Canada cares' on the ground. Arguably, SDP reaches further beyond the traditional sport communities than any international effort other than the staging of major games. Prior to the 1997 Commonwealth Heads of Government Meeting, 12 Commonwealth prime ministers wrote Prime Minister Chrétien extolling the CSDP and urging that it be renewed. After a series of panels and demonstrations brought SDP to the attention of economists, agriculturalists, epidemiologists, health workers and social workers at the 2006 World AIDS conference in Toronto, Stephen Lewis, the United Nations Special Envoy for HIV/AIDS in Africa, wrote that "sport is not instinctively seen as a vehicle for social development but used creatively, it can involve, educate, protect and mobilize the young people who participate" (as cited in Commonwealth Games Canada, 2002, p. 2). Anjali Gopalan, founder and director of the Naz Foundation, an NGO that combats HIV/AIDS in India, claimed much the same at a media conference directed at foreign aid professionals during the 2010 Commonwealth Games in Delhi. "I never thought sport would be appropriate to our work, but it can have a transformative effect upon marginalized people, especially young women in rural areas," she explained. "You can see it in the way that they carry themselves after they pick up a sport, the way that they want to go back to school, the way that they look beyond traditional expectations. It's very powerful" (CSDP, 1998, p. 12; Gopalan, 2010, personal communication[3]).

This chapter examines the origins, initiatives, achievements and shortcomings of Canadian contributions to SDP. In addition, policy lessons for Canadian involvement in SDP are also presented. I will argue that despite many innovative programs, the actual investment in SDP leaves much to be desired and the results uncertain. Like other areas of sport policy, SDP remains isolated within the sport sector, with few effective links to the major instruments of development in education, health and youth policy. Moreover, at the very time when international organizations like the International Olympic

Committee, the United Nations and the Commonwealth are stepping up their efforts to make SDP more effective, the Canadian government is pulling back. I write as a committed but critical insider. I have been a participant in many of the decisions affecting this movement in Canada from its origins in the early 1990s, served for a time as the volunteer chair of CGC IDS, and currently chair the Commonwealth Advisory Body on Sport. I am proud of what has been attempted and confident that good programs can contribute significantly. At the same time, I believe that many of the claims outdistance the evidence, and fear that some programs reinforce the unequal power relations they are intended to overcome. I will conclude with recommendations for effective interventions.

Origins

SDP is a renewed expression of the ambition of 'sport for good' that dates back to the nineteenth century. 'Sport for good' can be distinguished from 'sport for sport's sake' in that it employs sport explicitly as a means to a social end. It has been pursued by evangelists, educators, and 'moral entrepreneurs' of many different backgrounds and ideologies, including Christians in the YMCA and Catholic Youth Organizations, reforming Jews in the Young Hebrew Associations, secular urban reformers in the playground movement, socialists and trade unionists in the Worker Sport Associations, and immigrant sport associations in the burgeoning cities of Canada and the United States.[4] Probably the best known advocate was the Christian Socialist Thomas Hughes. His nineteenth-century runaway best-seller, *Tom Brown's Schooldays*, so successfully publicized the belief that sport has educational and civilizing power that 'sport for good' has remained an aspiration of school, college and university sport virtually around the globe ever since (MacAloon, 2010). His ideals had particular resonance with the early leaders of Canadian amateur and Olympic sport, who intended their activities to teach the values and habits of citizenship while inspiring Canadian nationalism[5] (Kidd, 1996, 2010). Many advocates of 'sport for good' took their programs to other countries and communities. Early in the twentieth century, for example, the YMCA and the amateur sport movement introduced sport into many parts of the then colonized world, and prominent Canadians contributed. John Howard Crocker, the manager of the 1908 Canadian Olympic Team and later the first director of physical education at

The University of Western Ontario, helped the YMCA introduce several Western sports into China, and served as the manager of the 1915 Chinese team that participated in the third Far Eastern Athletic Games, the precursor to today's Asian Games. In 1959, at a time when the British Caribbean colonies were in the final stages of their long struggles for independence, Olympic leader Jim Worrall took a team of track and field athletes to British Guyana and Trinidad for a series of coaching clinics and demonstrations (International Centre for Olympic Studies, n.d.; Torres, 2006; Worrall, 2000). There are strong parallels between these earlier efforts and those of today.

The first Canadian programs in what has become SDP were created by men and women imbued with these values. The context was the radically transformed international landscape opened up by the end of the Cold War (the worldwide political, economic, and military competition between capitalist and communist countries), the rise of neo-liberal globalization and the fall of apartheid (South Africa's system of compulsory racial classification that brutally subordinated the non-white majority) in the early 1990s, and the spirit of optimism and innovation that these changes inspired. The challenges and opportunities presented by the aftermath of apartheid were particularly significant. During the 40-year struggle to contain and eradicate such legalized racism, South Africans opposed to apartheid had asked their counterparts in other countries to 'say no,' to isolate the white apartheid establishment through sanctions and boycotts. In sport, this meant the systematic refusal to play against South African athletes, the suspension and expulsion of South African teams from the international federations in every sport and public protests against them whenever they managed (through complicit governments, dual passports, or forged identities) to appear in international competitions. The strategy was to show the supporters of apartheid the world's moral revulsion and to express solidarity with the oppressed majority through the symbolic denial of politics inherent in sport. Led by the South African exiles in the South African Non-Racial Olympic Committee and the Supreme Council of Sport in Africa, it became an internationally co-ordinated campaign (Ramsamy, 1982). With the release of Nelson Mandela from prison in 1990 and the clear end of apartheid in sight, the African leaders of the international campaign began to ask their allies to 'say yes,' to help them build a non-racial and democratic South Africa and rebuild the adjoining states of southern Africa that had suffered economic and social damage during the long struggle (Kidd, 1991).

The Commonwealth, the 54-government body that grew out of the British Empire, had long been an important site of the campaign against apartheid. South Africa was once a British colony, and its strongest economic and sport relations were with Commonwealth countries like the United Kingdom, New Zealand, Australia, and Canada. Moreover, the presence of a repressive, white supremacist government at the foot of the continent was a bitter affront to the newly independent Commonwealth nations of Africa. The Commonwealth became the first international body to expel South Africa, in 1961, and in 1977, in the Gleneagles Agreement, the Commonwealth prime ministers made opposition to apartheid sport a condition of participation in the Commonwealth Games. In 1991, the prime ministers committed themselves to bringing the fight against apartheid to a successful conclusion and establishing a free, democratic, non-racial, and prosperous South Africa. In their declaration, they stressed the unique role that sport could play in fostering development and established the Commonwealth Committee on Cooperation through Sport to oversee this work (Commonwealth Heads of Government Meeting, 1991). The Committee was to be chaired by Roy McMurtry, the distinguished Canadian politician and jurist who had served as High Commissioner to the United Kingdom during the last stormy years of apartheid, and staffed by Canadian foreign affairs sport officer Ann Hillmer. As a university student, McMurtry spent his summers as a volunteer for Frontier College, teaching English to immigrant workers in mining and lumber camps, using sports to give them a sense of community and life skills. The experience made him a lifelong advocate of 'sport for good.'

There were enabling forces at play within Canadian sport as well. The public hearings held by the *Commission of Inquiry into the Use of Drugs and Banned Practices Intended to Increase Athletic Performance* (i.e., Dubin inquiry), appointed to investigate the circumstances surrounding Canadian sprinter Ben Johnson's disqualification for steroids at the 1988 Olympic Games, unleashed an outpouring of 'sport for good' sentiment and proposals for reform. Justice Dubin (1990) reflected this spirit in his final report, arguing that while "the pursuit of excellence is worthwhile and should be encouraged" (p. 526), the ultimate purpose of sport should be "a means of unifying

Canadians, preserving our identity, redressing gender inequalities and discrimination against the disabled and minorities, and improving the health of our citizenry and the vitality of our society" (p. 524). He concluded that unless these "worthy social and national objectives" are realized, "then there is no justification for government support and funding of sport" (Dubin, 1990, pp. 524–525). Dubin's report led to a new regime of anti-doping education and testing, and reinvigorated campaigns for equity, fair play, and athletes' rights at every level of Canadian sport. Many provincial, municipal, and university gender equity policies stem from this period. Another important achievement of the period was the creation by national team athletes of a new organization, the Canadian Athletes Association (later renamed AthletesCAN), to collectively bargain for national team athletes with Sport Canada, the Canadian Olympic Association, and the Commonwealth Games Association, and to give them voice and vote on decision-making bodies. The leaders of the Canadian Athletes Association became influential supporters of sport for development. At the 1994 Commonwealth Games in Victoria, for example, Canadian Athletes Association president, Ann Peel, obtained signatures from athletes from all participating countries on a petition calling for member governments to invest in sport for development. The petition, known as 'the Victoria Declaration,' noted:

> Because of the extraordinary opportunity we have enjoyed to represent our countries and achieve personal goals, we believe that all citizens should enjoy the benefits of development through sport. But as we look around our societies, only a minority of young people has access to quality programs of sports and physical activity. In disadvantaged communities, opportunities are rare. Many social ills facing our brothers and sisters today—drug dependency, senseless violence, despondency and defeatism—stem from the lack of opportunities to develop themselves. Sport can help.
>
> We would like to give something back for what we have received. But there is little opportunity to do so. We therefore call upon the Commonwealth Heads of Government to enable us to make our contribution to education, social development and intercultural understanding. We ask you to improve opportunities for all citizens to participate in sports and physical activity.

> In particular, we ask you to create programs in which athletes,
> coaches, officials and teachers contribute to the urgent task of
> development through sport in the disadvantaged countries and
> communities of the Commonwealth.

Similar forces were at work in other countries. In Scandinavia, SDP
grew out of the region's longstanding commitment to international
development, and a history of youth volunteering. In the UK, it
was prompted by the ambition of the 'New Labour' government of
Tony Blair to forge 'active citizenship' and strengthen social capital.
In the European Union, as Donnelly, Atkinson, Boyle, and Szto (2011)
have written:

> as national sport policies in Europe during the 1990s began to
> revive this view of sport—claiming that participation in sport
> could assist in, for example, the reduction of delinquent behav-
> iour, improved health, and social inclusion/community building/
> immigrant integration—it became a straightforward proposition
> to apply these views to a new wave of international development
> initiatives. (p. 595)

During the spring and summer of 1992, McMurtry and Hillmer
convened a group of Canadian sport leaders to plan the creation of
a Canadian program. They included Ann Peel, Canadian Athletes
Association; Judy Kent, Commonwealth Games Association of
Canada; Geoff Gowan, Coaching Association of Canada; Richard
Pound, International Olympic Committee; and Lyle Makosky,
Ministry of State for Fitness and Amateur Sport. It was quickly
agreed that the program should focus on the Commonwealth countries, especially those in southern Africa, be undertaken in collaboration with partners in those countries employing the needs-based,
consultative approaches developed in Canadian adult education and
community development, and where appropriate, draw upon the
experience of well-established Canadian programs. While some of
us hoped that the new international program would be conducted
by government, Sport Canada did not see itself in this role, preferring instead to pursue its objectives through a subsidized arms-
length organization in the same way it pursues domestic objectives
through the subsidized national sport organizations (NSOs). After
considerable discussion, the Commonwealth Games Association of

Canada (now Commonwealth Games Canada) agreed to house what became the Commonwealth Sport Development Program, on the understanding that the costs would come entirely from government and other external sources.

At times, this relationship has caused distrust, with partners and participants wondering whether the program was in the right place. But what began as a 'location of convenience' has generally worked satisfactorily, and in the eyes of this contributor, has given Commonwealth Games Canada a new lease on life. The CSDP began as a five-year pilot in 1993, with CA\$ 3.375M in total funding from the Canadian International Development Agency and Sport Canada. It was renewed in 1998 (CA\$ 3.432M for five years), 2003 (CA\$ 3M for three years) and 2006 (CA\$ 4.523M for five years). The federal government also began to support sport development on a project-by-project basis in Francophone Africa; to provide multi-year block funding to the Toronto-based, international NGO Right to Play; and to support peace-building NGOs in the Middle East and the Americas. But the CSDP always held pride of place as the child of the Canadian sport system.

From Sport Development to Development through Sport

Initially the CSDP sought to enhance the capacity of the sport systems in African, Asian, and Caribbean Commonwealth countries by assisting with strategic planning and the training of coaches, referees, administrators, and athletes. For example, in Zimbabwe, it worked closely with the National Sport and Recreation Commission, the Zimbabwe Olympic Committee, and other donors such as UK Sport, the Australian Sports Commission, and the Norwegian Olympic and Paralympic Committee and Confederation of Sports to develop a comprehensive, multi-year strategic plan that could drive and co-ordinate investment and programming. It helped sport leaders in recipient countries adapt the National Coaching Certification Program to local conditions, in some cases translating materials into indigenous languages (e.g., Tamil and Sinhala in Sri Lanka), and to recruit and train coaches. In the Caribbean, it worked with the National Olympic Committees and other partners to create the Caribbean Coaching Certification Program, with theory and sport-specific components in cricket, netball, and soccer, a sport management module, and a workshop to combat the use of performance-enhancing and recreational drugs. The focus was 'train the trainers,' with the preparation of local course instructors in master classes and scholarships for outstanding leaders at the National Coaching Institute in Victoria, BC. The metrics were impressive. In 1997–1998, for example, 653 women and men (346 and 307, respectively) from nine Caribbean islands completed at least one of the modules (CSDP, 1998, p. 38). The CSDP also worked with regional governments to strengthen school-based physical education, and with colleges and universities to introduce courses in sport management. By 2000, it had regional offices in Barbados and Zimbabwe (a third in Sri Lanka was abandoned in 1999 when the civil war made activities too dangerous), and conducted programs in 13 African and Caribbean countries. By 2008, that number had increased to 23.

From the beginning, the CSDP sought to broaden the base of participation, focusing on girls and women, persons with disabilities, and children and youth 'at risk.' In Zimbabwe, for example, it helped establish Aerobics for Mothers, an intervention designed to address maternal and infant health in rural areas, preparing an instructor's manual, training instructors, and supplying audiotapes and portable radio/cassette players. The program became a runaway success. By 2002, 111,300 women had participated. The CSDP assisted the Zimbabwe Association of Sport for People with a Disability develop the sports of goalball, wheelchair basketball, and wheelchair track and field, sponsoring clinics and competitions. It financially supported African and Caribbean NGOs devoted to disadvantaged people, such as the Mathare Youth Sports Association, which has used soccer in imaginative ways to improve the education, environment, and safety of children in a Nairobi slum (Brady & Banu Khan, 2002; Mathare Youth Sports Association, n.d.; Willis, 2000), and Project Strong, a St. Kitts program that combines sport, life skills, and apprenticeships in an effort to help teenage school drop-outs become employable.

These relationships, and the changing landscape of international development, pushed the CSDP well beyond the sport sector and the familiar challenges of preparing facilities, coaches, and athletes for organized competition. It quickly became evident that the sport systems in the least developed countries and the 'small states' of the Caribbean and southern Africa could not be strengthened without simultaneously strengthening the education, health, economic well-being and human rights of these societies.

In Africa in particular, the terrifying epidemic of HIV/AIDS and the widespread scourge of poverty made organized sport difficult for all but a very few. Moreover, the message from the Canadian International Development Agency and other aid organizations was that simply strengthening the capacity for sport for sport's sake was not a priority, and that the CSDP needed to contribute in a more broadly based way to the priorities of social and economic development.

The consensus forged at the United Nations around the eight Millennium Development Goals (approved in 2000) heightened the urgency of this approach. So did the example of the remarkable athlete-led organization, Olympic Aid, created at the time of the 1994 Olympic Winter Games in Lillehammer by four-time gold medalist Johann Olav Koss and other Norwegian champions. Seeking to give something back, they began a program of sport-focused humanitarian assistance. At first, they donated their own prize money for vaccinations and emergency food and clothing to children in war-torn Sarajevo and Afghanistan. But slowly, they applied what they knew best—sport—and initiated a range of programs in refugee camps in some 23 countries around the world, raising money by auctioning other Olympic athletes' equipment and energetically pursuing public and private donors. In 2003, they broke away from the Olympic Movement and formed their own NGO, Right to Play (RTP). Although RTP has sometimes struggled to align its activities with locally-identified priorities, its programs have always been directed at those outside the established sport sector.

In this changing climate, the CSDP gradually broadened its focus to 'international development through sport.' This 'natural evolution' was first articulated in a 'framework paper' published in the fall of 2000:

> During its first three years, the CSDP focused on *development of sport*. It has strengthened sport systems and institutions, increased individual capacities, and established successful sport and physical activity programs. ... A major outcome of these efforts has been the realization that, in addition to *inherent value* (development of leaders, team building, perseverance, goal setting, self-esteem, and healthy lifestyles), sport has the *added value* of reaching further into the lives of individuals and

communities to address basic human and societal needs. This realization has led to the *development through sport* concept. Now sport is also used to

- Alleviate the negative effects of poverty;
- Help individuals achieve basic health and education;
- Reach out to youth, particularly youth at risk;
- Raise awareness of women's rights and issues;
- Reach out to people with a disability;
- Build communities and instill local pride and peace.

The *development through* sport concept enables sport and physical activity to have a broader reach and a more powerful impact upon the lives of individuals and communities. (CSDP, 2000, pp. 1–2, *emphasis in original*)

The shift was accompanied by a new program, the Commonwealth Sport Leadership Corps, which sent active and retired national team athletes and recent graduates from Canadian university programs of physical education and kinesiology to internships in Africa and the Caribbean, and eventually (in 2002) a new name, Commonwealth Games Canada International Development through Sport. CGC IDS strengthened the focus on needs- and asset-based strategic planning as a first step in intervention, and gradually shifted its partnering from the sport community to government departments and NGOs working in development. Aerobics for Mothers became the human face of this shift (until the Canadian government forced CGC IDS to withdraw from Mugabe's Zimbabwe in 2002). The trainers were public health nurses, not master coaches; none of the intended recipients were ever expected to participate in organized sport competition. Another major focus of CGC IDS in southern Africa became the battle against HIV/AIDS. It was felt that the popular messages of sport could be marshaled against stigmatization, and help children and youth navigate the difficult shoals of adolescent sexuality without becoming infected. In Zambia, for example, there was a desperate need for preventive education: while 29% of the adult population 15 years of age and older was considered to be infected with the virus in 2000, only 7% of those younger than 15 were infected. The challenge was to keep the 93% uninfected. In co-operation with other international and Zambian donors and NGOs, CGC IDS contributed to the Kicking AIDS Out Network, which developed and conducted a sport-based program about healthy lifestyles, including healthy sexuality. It also contributed to the lobbying that led the Government of Zambia to make physical education, with a focus on preventive education about HIV/AIDS, a compulsory and examinable subject in Zambian state schools. In Botswana, it brought the Kicking AIDS Out approach to a partnership designed to engage unemployed youth through soccer, in co-operation with the South East District, the City of Toronto, and the Mathare Youth Sports Association. In Namibia, it provided a steady stream of interns to Physically Active Youth, a sport-based after-school academic enrichment and health education program designed to reverse an alarmingly high school drop-out rate in the slum of Katatura, while combating the growth of HIV/AIDS (City of Toronto, n.d.; Kicking AIDS Out Network, n.d.; Njelesani, 2011; Physically Active Youth (P.A.Y.) Namibia, n.d.). The CGS IDS never completely abandoned sport development. Moreover, as Canadian cities bid for Olympic and Commonwealth Games, sport development programs were used with effect with voters from the African and Caribbean countries. But for the ensuing decade, the overarching focus became development through sport (e.g., Commonwealth Games Canada, 2004).

Establishing the Policy Framework

The early success of sport for development raised hopes that CGC IDS could be rapidly expanded. Yet it proved difficult to win significant additional financial support from either the Canadian sport community or the major national and international agencies that funded development. With the gutting of Sport Canada in the financial cuts of the Paul Martin budgets of the 1990s, there was little appetite for new ventures in other countries. When some funding was restored after 2000, the overarching focus was domestic sport. In 2002, Canadian Heritage Minister Sheila Copps proposed that the Canadian Sport Leadership Corps be grown to 100 interns but she was unable to win support from the Treasury Board. Among the development community, the elitist image presented by middle-class Olympic and highly paid professional athletes and the long history of 'white elephant' facilities from major games gave funders little confidence that sport could actually improve the lives of ordinary people, let alone those struggling with poverty, conflict and disease. Moreover, official development assistance was being cut back dramatically at the very time the first programs of sport for development were being tested. Between 1992 and 1997, the G7 countries reduced their contributions by US$ 13B or 20%, with devastating impacts upon the countries affected.[6] Few donor countries came close to attaining the target of 0.7% of Gross Domestic Product agreed upon by member-countries of the United Nations in 1970. Although the target had been championed by a former Canadian prime minister, Lester 'Mike' Pearson, Canada was no exception, contributing less than 0.4% of GDP. It meant fierce competition for funding for every dollar of aid (Fabre & Hillmer, 1998; Pound, 1992).

One strategic response has been to win endorsement in the pronouncements and policies of major international organizations. While there is always risk that such efforts will become bogged down in endless meetings and platitudinous communiqués, it was hoped that international legitimacy could be leveraged for domestic advantage. One avenue has been the Commonwealth. The Commonwealth Committee on Coordination through Sport and its successor, the Commonwealth Advisory Body on Sport, have taken the case for sport to the meetings of education, health, youth and prime ministers, arguing that sport can contribute to the highest priorities of governments and the Commonwealth as a whole (Commonwealth Advisory Body on Sport, 2008; Kidd, 2010). In 2010, the Commonwealth sports ministers agreed to accelerate this strategy, directing the Commonwealth Secretariat to 'mainstream' sport for development in education, health, gender affairs and human rights, and to work with member governments to establish "priorities, targets, strategies and mechanisms for Measurement and Evaluation" by 2012 in the manner of the Millennium Development Goals (Commonwealth Secretariat, 2011, paragraph 8). In 2011, the Commonwealth prime ministers endorsed it (Commonwealth Heads of Government Meeting, 2011), and as a result, in 2012 the Commonwealth Secretariat initiated four pilot projects designed to strengthen the capacity of member governments to integrate SDP into national policies.

Another avenue has been the United Nations. In 2001, the United Nations Secretary General Kofi Annan appointed former Swiss president Adolf Ogi Special Advisor on Sport for Development and Peace. The following year, Johann Olav Koss and Right to Play persuaded Annan to commission and publish a report on sport for development and peace, drawing upon the expertise of all United

Nations agencies (United Nations Interagency Task Force on Sport for Development and Peace, 2003). That report, which solidified the use of the term SDP, led the General Assembly to a series of resolutions endorsing sport as a tool of development and post-conflict reconciliation.[7] It declared 2005 as the International Year of Sport and Physical Education, and during that year, sponsored a series of conferences and other activities highlighting different aspects of this work (United Nations, 2006). An international working group was established to advise member governments on five areas of intervention—sport and gender, sport and child and youth development, sport and persons with a disabilities, sport and health, and sport and peace. Its massive report, *Harnessing the Power of Sport for Development and Peace: Recommendations for Governments*, endorsed at the time of the Beijing Olympic Games in 2008, led to the consolidation of the United Nations Office on Sport for Development and Peace (UNOSDP) in Geneva, and the decision to implement the recommendations with five target-specific working groups. The first of these, on sport and children and youth development, was established in May 2010. Working groups on sport and gender, sport and peace, sport for persons with disabilities, and sport and health were established in May 2011. The working groups are intended to raise the profile of SDP, to more effectively co-ordinate the work of the United Nations agencies and to help establish international standards (Sport for Development and Peace. International Working Group, 2008).[8]

Throughout the 'long march through the international organizations,' senior civil servants in sport have assisted these efforts with expertise and financial support. Canada was one of four governments to underwrite the initial costs of the international working group—the others were Austria, Norway, and Switzerland—and until 2012, it contributed to the upkeep of the UNOSDP in Geneva and the International Platform on Sport and Development administered by the Swiss Academy for Development, a comprehensive web resource. These contributions strengthened the reputation of Canada as a progressive, altruistic sport nation. In turn, the growing international profile of sport for development ensured the inclusion of legislative support for these efforts in the *Physical Activity and Sport Act* of 2003, and until 2011, the operation of the International Policy and Programs Directorate of the Department of Canadian Heritage.

Towards Confident Effectiveness

A key component of Canadian efforts in sport for development has been the commitment to rigorous monitoring and evaluation (M&E). What began as a necessity to convince skeptical decision makers that sport can actually make a difference has grown in step with the push towards results-based planning and accountability across all forms of development. In education, health, agricultural and rural development, poverty reduction, environmental sustainability and other areas of intervention, governments, NGOs and university research centres have sought to measure and report, in reliable ways, the means by which social objectives are pursued and what has been achieved. The extensive use of M&E is the result of the decades-long effort to strengthen public and business administration, major advances in the related social sciences, and the democratic expectation that governments, corporations and NGOs be transparent, accountable and effective in their expenditures (e.g., International Platform on Sport and Development, 2009; Sport England, 2005; World Bank, 2004).

The United Nations' Millennium Development Goals, the poverty reduction strategies employed by the World Bank, and the global fight against the pandemic of HIV/AIDS have all provided recent stimuli. To be sure, the requirements for M&E have engendered their own debates. Since they have been intertwined with the ascendency of globalizing neo-liberal capitalism, some fear that the focus (and in some cases, insistence) upon the end results diverts attention from the provision of education, health, sport and physical activity to all people as basic human rights and contributes to the downsizing and/or circumvention of the democratic state. Others fear that M&E reinforces the unequal status quo, privileging the outcomes sought by first-world donors and agencies while marginalizing the determinations of the people actually on the ground (e.g., Francovits, 1998; Giulianotti, 2004). Canadian policy makers and practitioners have maintained their commitment to M&E while wrestling with these concerns. From the outset, Commonwealth Games Canada carried out extensive reporting of inputs, activities and mid-term outcomes and struggled to develop an effective way to measure long-term impacts. At the conclusion of each multi-year grant, the Canadian International Development Agency commissioned independent evaluations. Between 2003 and 2006, CGC IDS conducted needs-

and asset-based strategic planning exercises in the five countries it targeted in southern Africa so that the goals and metrics of future programs could be significantly shaped by local leaders. At the same time, Canadian Heritage officials have encouraged critical research through the SDP International Working Group, the International Development Research Centre, the Sport Canada Research Initiative and Canadian universities. I am struck as I review the materials I have kept from my involvement in the program by how much time and effort has been invested in M&E.

Evaluation and research suggest cautious optimism, and much more sensitivity to complexity and nuance than impassioned and idealistic advocates have been prepared to accept. The scholarship confirms that sport can contribute to enhanced individual and community health, better intercultural understanding, the inclusion and affirmation of girls and women and many of the other beneficial outcomes claimed for SDP. But it also counsels that opportunities for sport and physical activity are not universal, nor are the benefits automatic. For example, while there is clear indication that participation is significantly linked to the reduction of non-communicable diseases such as cardio-vascular disease, diabetes, obesity, some cancers and osteoporosis and can slow the progress of communicable diseases such as HIV/AIDS, most of the evidence for these links has been drawn from studies of physical activity, not competitive sport. The health benefits—and risks—of sport is a contested topic (Zakus, Njelesani, & Darnell, 2007). The same can be argued about sport as a medium of conflict resolution and peace building. International Olympic Committee President, Jacques Rogge, has explained that "sport fosters understanding between individuals, facilitates dialogue between divergent communities and breeds tolerance between nations" and certainly that has been demonstrated (Rogge, 2007, paragraph 1). But the opposite has also been true: sport has been racist, sexist and homophobic, has contributed to intolerance and misunderstanding and has had to be cancelled in the presence of open conflict (Kidd & MacDonnell, 2007). In the case of girls and women, regular participation has been shown to enhance their physical health and decrease the likelihood of unhealthy practices, such as illegal drug use.

The research also suggests that sport and physical activity positively influences social integration and inclusion; it can affect self-esteem and self-worth and may offer a vehicle to empowerment, particularly during the vulnerable period of adolescence. However, the mechanism by which these outcomes occur is unclear, and researchers have questioned whether high self-esteem is beneficial. The participation of girls and women in sport and physical activity offers an opportunity for successful challenges to traditional and oppressive gender relations and important opportunities for leadership development, personal and professional growth. Yet many of the common theoretical assumptions regarding the use of sport to advance gender equity have not been tested empirically or consistently in low- and middle-income countries with different social systems. Moreover, many girls and women are active as a result of heavy, domestic labour and, lacking transport, they may spend several hours walking long distances each day. Unlike Western countries, where increased physical fitness and reduced obesity are the primary rationale for engaging in physical activity, the use of sport for these purposes in developing countries may have less relevance (Larkin, Moola, & Razak, 2007).

The literature reviews Peter Donnelly and I conducted for the international working group by a team at the University of Toronto led us to emphasize the limits and the contextual factors for sport as a social intervention:

> The physiological effects of participation in sport and physical activity are widely known, and one of the best established findings in the research literature. It is important to note that the effects are not a result of sport, as defined in this project, but of physical activity more generally—including both sport and manual labour. With regard to all of the other benefits of participation in sport identified in the research literature (i.e., psychological and social benefits and improved mental health), *the evident benefits appear to be an indirect outcome of the context and social interaction that is possible in sport rather than a direct outcome of participating in sport.* (Kidd & Donnelly, 2007, p. 4)

We drew several lessons from this review:

- Participants must feel that programs meet their needs (i.e., that it is 'their program,' and have genuine access, including equipment and transportation);

- Participants must feel physically safe, personally valued, socially connected, morally and economically supported, personally and politically empowered; and hopeful about the future;
- The nature and quality of the sport experience are crucial (i.e., it must be *good sport, with competent, ethical leadership*). There must be a research-based 'logic model' that is understood and agreed upon by programmers and participants;
- The benefits of sport participation and sport initiatives cannot be understood in isolation from other social and material conditions—sport is not sufficient. To be successful, sport programs should be part of multi-purpose intervention, linked to education, community affirmation, employment and other opportunities;
- Programs must be sustained to have a lasting impact.

These findings argue for much more sophisticated policy and funding frameworks, co-ordinated among funding partners and agencies in recipient countries. Yet despite calls for 'joined-up government,' 'common frameworks,' 'mainstreaming' and other co-ordination efforts, SDP has yet to be significantly embraced by the major development agencies, other federal ministries, or the sport NGOs, let alone linked to pan-Canadian sport for development. Moreover, it is plagued by a proliferation of volunteer organizations which compete with each other (and with the old 'sport for good' organizations) for donors, branding, and beneficiaries on the ground with uncritical claims for the 'power of sport,' circumvent and even compete with government agencies and generally eschew the co-ordinated regulation of youth sport that has been such an important advance in the Western world. "Do It Yourself Foreign Aid" (Kristof, 2010, paragraph 7) has often been extremely innovative and helpful, but at best it implements a patchwork quilt. It falls far short of the universal provision of sport and physical activity that Canada and the international community has proclaimed.

Recent research also argues for much more critical awareness of the unequal power dynamics inherent in SDP, and the role that aid workers, especially young volunteers, can unwittingly play in perpetuating the inequalities that necessitate development in the first place (Hayhurst, 2009; Darnell, 2011; Lindsey & Grattan, 2012; Darnell

& Hayhurst, 2012; Levermore & Beacom, 2012). Recent international conferences have also reported an alarming increase in gender-based violence in programs for girls and women where interventions failed to take the existing context of gender relations into account (e.g., Commonwealth Games Canada, 2011).

The Way Ahead

In the last two years, both CGC IDS and the international sport policy unit in the federal government have undergone significant changes. Commonwealth Games Canada has shifted its focus back to sport development, partnering with the Commonwealth Games Federation to help strengthen the administrative capacity of Commonwealth Games Associations in Africa and the Caribbean with a new internship program called Capacity Support. Seven interns assisted with the preparation of teams for the 2010 Commonwealth Games, and then with the electronic management and distribution of the results of all teams while at the Games in Delhi. At the same time, the Canadian Sport Leadership Corps, which placed interns in more broadly based development projects, has been refashioned as Sport Leaders Abroad to put experienced leaders (administrators, coaches and officials) on the ground to assist their counterparts in developing Commonwealth countries. As a result of this turn, the Canadian International Development Agency did not renew the CGC's funding when it came up for renewal in 2011.

In 2011, the federal government moved the International Policy and Programs Directorate from Canadian Heritage to Sport Canada. SDP is not a priority for Sport Canada. While domestic sport for development is a policy goal of the renewed Canadian Sport Policy, an effort to have international SDP inserted into the Policy was unsuccessful (Sport Canada, 2012). As a result, all financial support of SDP has been phased out, including the contributions Canada once made to the UNOSDP and the International Platform. When the Commonwealth requested contributions to the pilot projects that have been initiated to strengthen developing countries' capacity for SDP, Sport Minister Bal Gosal replied that Canada was not interested. Sport Canada does continue to support the CGC's efforts in sport development, albeit at a significantly reduced level, contributing CA$ 156,000 in 2012–2013. Regardless of the form these uniquely Canadian initiatives will take in the years ahead, the international movement they helped create will continue to grow and mature, as more international and national governments, NGOs, sport organizations and corporations take up the mantle of sport for development and peace, more young people are inspired to volunteer, and more universities offer courses and conferences on the methods. It is clear that both the United Nations and the Commonwealth will give greater priority to SDP in the years ahead. Popular NGOs like Right to Play will continue to thrive, in the latter case supported by a CA$ 17M, three-year grant from the Canadian International Development Agency in 2010. It is the obligation of those of us in the academy to continue to pursue the difficult research questions that this movement presents, to challenge our bright, idealistic students who want to become engaged to develop an informed, reflexive sense of humility about the possibilities and the contradictions and to ensure that future policy discussions are conducted in an open, evidence-based environment.

Notes

1. The best source for policies, programs, research, and resources is the International Platform on Sport for Development (see http://www.sportanddev.org).
2. In April 2010, the International Olympic Committee (IOC) added women's ski jumping to the Olympic winter program effective for the Sochi 2014 Olympic Winter Games (IOC, 2011).
3. Gopalan spoke at the media conference organized by the Australian Sport Outreach Program, Australian High Commission, Delhi, October 6, 2010.
4. The term 'sport for good' was coined by Donnelly (1993). For early examples, see Cavallo (1981), Krüger and Riordan (1996), and MacLeod (1983).
5. See Kidd (1996), Chapter II, "The making of men" pages 44–93.
6. G7 or Group of 7 countries consisting of a meeting of finance ministers from seven industrialized nations including France, Germany, Italy, Japan, United Kingdom, United States, and Canada.
7. The most recent General Assembly resolution (65/4) was passed on October 18, 2010; see http://www.un.org/ga/search/view_doc.asp?symbol=A/RES/65/4
8. The most recent update on the working groups is at http://www.un.org/wcm/content/site/sport/home/unplayers/memberstates/pid/18407

References

Black, D. (2010). The ambiguities of development: implications for 'sport for development.' *Sport in Society, 13*, 121–129.

Brady, M., & Banu Khan, A. (2002). *Letting girls play: The Mathare Youth Sports Association's football program for girls.* New York: Population Council.

Canadian Centre for Ethics in Sport. (2012). Sport in transition: Making sport in Canada more responsible for gender inclusivity. Retrieved from http://www.cces.ca/files/pdfs/CCES-PAPER-SportInTransition-E.pdf

Cavallo, D. (1981). *Muscles and morals: organized playgrounds and urban reform 1820–1920.* Philadelphia, PA: University of Pennsylvania Press.

City of Toronto. (n.d.). *Toronto-Botswana HIV/AIDS partnership.* Retrieved from http://www.toronto.ca/health/pdf/aids2006_toronto_botswana.pdf

Commonwealth Advisory Body on Sport. (2008). *Development through sport.* London: Commonwealth Secretariat.

Commonwealth Games Canada. (2002) *International development through sport: Using the power of sport to develop individuals, strengthen communities, build nations.* Brochure. Ottawa, ON: Author.

Commonwealth Games Canada. (2004). Sport beyond borders. *IDS Catalyst.*

Commonwealth Games Canada. (2011). Next Step 2011 promoting global sport for development partnerships. Press Release. Retrieved from http://www.commonwealthgames.ca/news/next-step-2011-promotes-global-sport-development-partnerships.html

Commonwealth Heads of Government Meeting. (1991, October 20). Harare Commonwealth declaration. Commonwealth functional cooperation. In Commonwealth secretariat (Ed.), *The Commonwealth at the summit: Communiqués of Commonwealth heads of government meetings* (pp. 86–110), (Volume 2: 1987–1995). London.

Commonwealth Heads of Government Meeting. (2011). Perth Outcome Documents 2011. Retrieved from http://www.thecommonwealth.org/files/249248/FileName/CHOGM2011OutcomeDocuments.pdf

Commonwealth Secretariat. (2011, October 4). *Sport for development and peace—its integration in the Commonwealth Youth Programme, the wider work of the Commonwealth Secretariat, and across the governments of the Commonwealth.* Concept Paper for the Commonwealth Sports Ministers' Meeting. Delhi, India.

Commonwealth Sport Development Program (CSDP). (1998). *Annual Report April 1997–March 1998.*

Commonwealth Sport Development Program (CSDP). (2000, October). Canadian progress in development through sport initiatives: A framework paper. Ottawa, ON: Commonwealth Games Association of Canada.

Darnell, S. (2011). Identity and learning in international volunteerism: 'Sport for Development and Peace' internships. *Development in Practice, 21*(7), 974–986.

Darnell, S., & Hayhurst, L. (2012). Hegemony, postcolonialism and sport-for-development: A response to Lindsey and Grattan. *International Journal of Sport Policy and Politics, 4*(1), 111–124.

Donnelly, P. (1993). Democratization revisited: Seven theses on the democratization of sport and active leisure. *Loisir et Société/Society and Leisure, 16*, 413–434.

Donnelly, P., Atkinson, M., Boyle, S., & Szto, C. (2011). Sport for development and peace: A public sociology perspective. *Third World Quarterly, 32*, 589–601.

Dreger, A. (2011, April 23). Redefining the sexes in unequal terms. *New York Times.* Retrieved from http://www.nytimes.com/2011/04/24/sports/24testosterone.html?_r=1

Dubin, C.L. (1990). *Commission of inquiry into the use of drugs and banned practices intended to increase athletic performance.* Ottawa, ON: Minister of Supply and Services Canada.

Fabre, J., & Hillmer, A. (1998, September 9–10). Common ground: The place of sport in development. International Olympic Forum for Development. Kuala Lumpur, Malaysia.

Francovits, A. (1998). *The rights way to development: A human rights approach to development assistance.* Sydney, AUS: Human Rights Council of Australia.

Giulianotti, R. (2004). Human rights, globalization and sentimental education. *Sport in Society, 7*, 355–369.

Hayhurst, L.M.C. (2009). The power to shape policy: charting sport for development and peace policy discourses. *International Journal of Sport Policy, 1*(2), 203–227.

International Centre for Olympic Studies. (n.d.). *John Howard Crocker.* Retrieved from http://www.uwo.ca/olympic/lectures/crocker_about.html

International Olympic Committee. (2011, November). *Skiing—ski jumping: Participation during the history of the Olympic Winter Games.* Research and Reference Service, Olympic Studies Centre. Retrieved from http://www.olympic.org/Assets/OSC%20Section/pdf/QR_sports_winter/Sports_Olympiques_ski_saut_%C3%A0_ski_eng.pdf

International Platform on Sport for Development. (n.d.). Retrieved from http://www.sportanddev.org

International Platform on Sport and Development. (2009). Monitoring and evaluation (M&E). Retrieved from http://www.sportanddev.org/toolkit/monitoring___evaluation/index.cfm

Kicking AIDS Out Network. (n.d.). Fight AIDS not people with AIDS. Retrieved from http://www.kickingaidsout.net/Pages/default.aspx

Kidd, B. (1991). Sports boycott crosses finish line. *Southern Africa Report, 7*, 30–31.

Kidd, B. (1996). *The struggle for Canadian sport*. Toronto, ON: University of Toronto Press.

Kidd, B. (2001). Essay. Canadians and the Olympics. Library and Archives Canada. Retrieved from http://www.collectionscanada.gc.ca/databases/olympians/001064-1000-e.html

Kidd, B. (2008). A new social movement: Sport for development and peace. *Sport in Society, 11*, 370–380.

Kidd, B. (2010). Muscular christianity and value-centred sport: The legacy of Tom Brown in Canada. In J. MacAloon (Ed.), *Muscular christianity in colonial and post-colonial worlds* (pp. 701–713). London: Routledge.

Kidd, B. (2010). Strengthening the Commonwealth through sport. In Commonwealth Secretariat (Ed.), *Commonwealth Yearbook 2010* (pp. 153–160). London: Nexus Strategic Partnerships.

Kidd, B., & Donnelly, P. (Eds.). (2007). *Literature reviews on sport for development and peace* (pp. 89–123). Toronto, ON: International Working Group on Sport for Development and Peace. Retrieved from http://www.righttoplay.com/International/news-and-media/Documents/Policy%20Reports%20docs/Literature%20Reviews%20SDP.pdf

Kidd, B., & MacDonnell, M. (2007). Peace, sport and development. In B. Kidd & P. Donnelly (Eds.), *Reviews on sport for development* (pp. 158–194). Toronto, ON: International Working Group on Sport for Development and Peace. Retrieved from http://www.righttoplay.com/International/news-and-media/Documents/Policy%20Reports%20docs/Literature%20Reviews%20SDP.pdf

Kristof, N.D. (2010, October 20). D.I.Y. foreign-aid revolution. *New York Times Magazine*. Retrieved from http://www.nytimes.com/2010/10/24/magazine/24volunteerism-t.html?pagewanted=all

Krüger, A., & Riordan, J. (1996). *The story of worker sport*. Champaign, IL: Human Kinetics.

Larkin, J., Moola, F., & Razak, S. (2007). Sport, gender and development. In B. Kidd & P. Donnelly (Eds.), *Literature reviews on sport for development and peace* (pp. 89–123). Toronto, ON: International Working Group on Sport for Development and Peace. Retrieved from http://www.righttoplay.com/International/news-and-media/Documents/Policy%20Reports%20docs/Literature%20Reviews%20SDP.pdf

Levermore, R., & Beacom, A. (2009). *Sport and international development*. New York: Palgrave Macmillan.

Levermore, R., & Beacom, A. (2012). Reassessing sport-for-development: moving beyond 'mapping the territory'. *International Journal of Sport Policy and Politics, 4*(1), 125–137.

Lindsey, I., & Grattan, A. (2012). An 'international movement'? Decentring sport-for-development within Zambian communities. *International Journal of Sport Policy and Politics, 4*(1), 91–110.

MacAloon, J. (2010). *Muscular Christianity in colonial and post-colonial worlds.* London: Routledge.

MacLeod, D. (1983). *Building character in the American boy: Boy Scouts, YMCA, and their forerunners, 1870–1920.* Madison, WI: University of Wisconsin Press.

Mathare Youth Sports Association (n.d.). Mathare Youth Sports Association. Retrieved from http://www.mysakenya.org.

Njelesani, D. (2011). 'Preventive HIV/AIDS education through physical education: reflections from Zambia. *Third World Quarterly, 32,* 435–452.

Physically Active Youth (P.A.Y.) Namibia. (n.d.). Physically Active Youth (P.A.Y.) Namibia. Retrieved from http://www.paynamibia.com/Home/index.aspx

Pound, R. (1992). Sport Development Assistance: A Challenge for the 1990s. *Olympic Review, 296,* 301–307.

Ramsamy, S. (1982). *Apartheid, the real hurdle: sports in South Africa and the international boycott.* London: International Defence in Aid Fund for Southern Africa.

Rogge, J. (2007, May 19). International Forum on Sport for Peace and the Olympic Truce. Olympia, Greece. Retrieved from http://www.olympicspirit.org/press_070521_peaceforum.php

Sport Canada. (2012). *Canadian sport policy 2012.* Ottawa, ON: Department of Canadian Heritage. Retrieved from http://sirc.ca/CSPRenewal/documents/CSP2012_EN.pdf

Sport England. (2005). *The Value of Sport—why we need to improve the evidence base for sport.* London: Author. Retrieved from http://www.sportengland.org/index/get_resources/vosm/about_vosm.htm

Sport for Development and Peace. International Working Group. (2008). *Harnessing the power of sport.* Retrieved from http://assets.sportanddev.org/downloads/rtp_sdp_iwg_harnessing_the_power_of_sport_for_development_and_peace.pdf

Torres, C. (2006). Latin American Olympic Explosion in the 1920s: Causes and Consequences. *The International Journal of the History of Sport (Special Issue), 23,* 1088–1094.

United Nations. (2006). *Final Report on the International Year of Sport and Physical Education.* New York: United Nations. Retrieved from http://www.un.org/sport2005/a_year/IYSPE_Report_FINAL.pdf

United Nations Interagency Task Force on Sport for Development and Peace. (2003). *Sport for Development and Peace: Towards Achieving the Millennium Development Goals.* New York: United Nations. Retrieved from http://www.un.org/themes/sport/reportE.pdf

Vertinsky, P., Jette, S., & Hoffman, A. (2009). Skierinas in the Olympics: Gender Justice and Gender Politics at the Local, National and International Level over the Challenge of Women's Ski Jumping. *Olympika, 18,* 25–56.

Willis, O. (2000). Sport and Development: the Significance of Mathare Youth Sports Association, Canadian *Journal of Development Studies, 21,* 825–849.

World Bank. (2004). *Monitoring and Evaluation: Some Tools, Methods and Approaches.* Washington, DC.

Worrall, J. (2000). *My Olympic Journey: Sixty Years With Canadian Sport and the Olympic Games.* Canadian Olympic Association.

Zakus, D., Njelesani, D., & Darnell, S. (2007). The use of sport and physical activity to achieve health objectives. In B. Kidd, & P. Donnelly (Eds.), *Reviews on Sport for Development* (pp. 48–88). Toronto: International Working Group on Sport for Development and Peace. Retrieved from http://www.righttoplay.com/International/news-and-media/Documents/Policy%20Reports%20docs/Literature%20Reviews%20SDP.pdf

THE *CANADIAN SPORT POLICY* AND ITS IMPACT ON THE SPORT SYSTEM

CHAPTER IV

Contemporary Policy Issues in High Performance Sport

Lisa M. Kikulis, Brock University

This chapter explores the contemporary high performance sport initiatives that are aimed at enhancing the performance of Canada's athletes at international competitions—increasing medals won and sustaining such performance levels in the future. In a paper commissioned by the Federal-Provincial/Territorial Ministers Responsible for Sport, Recreation and Fitness in 1985, the delineation of roles and responsibilities of the two levels of government relative to high performance sport were outlined and agreed upon. It is in this document where a definition of high performance sport was provided and has since guided policy, funding and program initiatives:

> High Performance Sport encompasses athletes who achieve, or, who aspire to achieve, or, who have been identified as having the potential *to achieve excellence* in World Class competition. The High Performance System is comprised of those activities, programs, agencies, institutions and personnel who have as one of their primary objectives the preparation of athletes who have achieved, or, who aspire to achieve, or who have been identified as having the potential *to achieve excellence* in World Class competition. (Federal-Provincial/Territorial Ministers Responsible for Sport, Recreation and Fitness, 1985, p. 3, *emphasis added*)

It is the understanding of '*to achieve excellence*' that, although debated, is defined as world championships and medals at international competitions, particularly at the Summer and Winter Olympic Games and Paralympic Games. Over two decades ago, Kidd (1988, p. 12) lamented this "philosophy of excellence—the view that top athletic performance, as measured by medals, rankings, and records set in international competition, should be the overriding goal for the Olympic Movement, and that all athletes, coaches and administrators should devote themselves to this goal," and that it has been used both to develop ranking thresholds that control who participates in efforts to improve chances for success and to justify how government and corporate financial investments are allocated. Justice Charles Dubin seemingly supported this critique when he stated, "the measure of success of government funding [should] be linked not to medal count, but to the degree to which it has met the social, educational, and national goals of government for sport" (Dubin, 1990, p. 531).

Nevertheless, the relevance of international sport to social, political and economic priorities on a global scale throughout the last two decades has meant that "the power struggle between nations to win medals in major international competitions has intensified. This has led to national sport organizations and governments throughout the world spending increasing sums of money on elite sport" (de Bosscher et al., 2008, p. 13). Oakley and Green coined the term 'global sporting arms race' to characterize the rapid increase in financial investment that governments have made in elite sport and in becoming the 'super power' of international sport. According to Donnelly (2010a, p. 44), "governments are apparently engaged in this 'race' in order to make symbolic statements about national identity, pride and virility." In Canada, such a rationale has historical roots in the early development of government intervention in sport under Pierre Trudeau's Liberal government of the 1970s when unity and identity defined a number of cultural policies including sport.

Fuelling Canada's place in this 'race' was the awarding of the 2010 Olympic and Paralympic Winter Games to Vancouver in 2003, where the goals became finishing first in the medal table for the Olympic Winter Games and in the top three in the gold medal count at the Paralympic Winter Games. These goals were supported by Own the Podium—a focused public and private investment in the development of high performance sport (discussed later in the chapter). The drive for medal success has continued with the goal for future Olympic Winter Games as being in contention for number one, for top 10 in the 2016 Olympic Games in Rio and top eight in 2020 and 2024. The medal goal for the London 2012 Paralympics was top eight based on gold medal count. Touted as a social investment in pride, inspiration and unity, international success as measured by medal tally has become the driving force of Canada's high performance system. Canada's total medal ranking in the Olympic and Paralympic Games (winter and summer) from 2000–2012 relative to the top three nation rankings is presented in Table 4.1.

De Bosscher et al. (2008, p. 122) stated that:

> More nations are adopting strategic approaches towards the development of elite athletes and as a result an increasing number of nations have developed genuine medal winning capability. As the supply of success, that is, the number of events and medals that can be contested is relatively fixed, and demand for success is increasing, the "market" adjusts by raising the price of success. The price of success is the investment in revenue and capital required to produce success.

Although in contention for 'global dominance' in the Olympic Winter Games, Canada has struggled to sustain a place of international dominance as the size, scope and enhanced investment, on a global scale, in the sports and the athletes involved in summer games and in paralympic sports has continued to grow. However, the backdrop to medal tables and tallies needs to be explored—in particular the policies and programs that provide the context for understanding Canada's place in this 'global sporting arms race' and the questions and conversations it raises.

The policy developments and legislative changes made in 2002 and 2003 (see Chapter I) provided the foundation for the current high performance sport system's emphasis on championships, medals and rankings. In particular, "the vision of the 2002 [*Canadian Sport Policy*] reflected governments' desire for the increased effectiveness of the sport system and for Canadian athletes to move to the forefront of international sport" (Sport Canada, 2012, p. 2). This vision was agreed upon by federal, provincial and territorial governments with each level of government working with agencies within its jurisdiction to implement actions that, over the last 10 years, have moved the system towards this goal. In an effort to achieve success in international

Table 4.1 Canada's Paralympic and Olympic Medal Standings 2000–2012

Paralympic Games

2000: Sydney

Rank	Country	Gold	Silver	Bronze	Total
1	Australia	63	39	47	149
2	Great Britain	41	43	47	131
3	Canada	38	33	25	96

2004: Athens

Rank	Country	Gold	Silver	Bronze	Total
1	China	63	46	32	141
2	Great Britain	35	30	29	94
3	Canada	28	19	25	72

2008: Beijing

Rank	Country	Gold	Silver	Bronze	Total
1	China	89	70	52	211
2	Great Britain	42	29	31	102
3	United States	36	35	28	99
7	Canada	19	10	21	50

Olympic Games

2000: Sydney

Rank	Country	Gold	Silver	Bronze	Total
1	United States	36	24	31	91
2	Russia	32	28	28	88
3	China	28	16	15	59
18	Canada	3	3	8	14

2004: Athens

Rank	Country	Gold	Silver	Bronze	Total
1	United States	36	39	27	102
2	Russia	27	27	38	92
3	China	32	17	14	63
19	Canada	3	6	3	12

2008: Beijing

Rank	Country	Gold	Silver	Bronze	Total
1	United States	36	38	36	110
2	China	51	21	28	100
3	Russia	23	21	28	72
14	Canada	3	9	6	18

Table 4.1 (Continued)

2012: London

Rank	Country	Gold	Silver	Bronze	Total
1	United States	46	29	29	104
2	China	38	27	23	88
3	Russia	24	26	32	82
13	Canada	1	5	12	18

Olympic Winter Games

2002: Salt Lake

Rank	Country	Gold	Silver	Bronze	Total
1	Germany	12	16	8	36
2	United States	10	13	11	34
3	Norway	12	5	7	25
4	Canada	7	3	7	17

2006: Turin

Rank	Country	Gold	Silver	Bronze	Total
1	Germany	11	12	6	29
2	United States	9	9	7	25
3	Canada	7	10	7	24

2010: Vancouver

Rank	Country	Gold	Silver	Bronze	Total
1	United States	9	15	13	37
2	Germany	10	13	7	30
3	Canada	14	7	5	26

2012: London

Rank	Country	Gold	Silver	Bronze	Total
1	China	95	71	65	231
2	Great Britain	34	43	43	120
3	Russia	36	38	28	102
13	Canada	7	15	9	31

Paralympic Winter Games

2002: Salt Lake

Rank	Country	Gold	Silver	Bronze	Total
1	Germany	17	1	15	33
2	United States	10	22	11	43
3	Norway	10	3	6	19
6	Canada	6	4	5	15

2006: Turin

Rank	Country	Gold	Silver	Bronze	Total
1	Russia	13	13	7	33
2	Germany	8	5	5	18
3	Ukraine	7	9	9	25
6	Canada	5	3	5	13

2010: Vancouver

Rank	Country	Gold	Silver	Bronze	Total
1	Germany	13	5	6	24
2	Russia	12	16	10	38
3	Canada	10	5	4	19

sport, two critical challenges were identified: developing "a systematic, analytical and collaborative approach to the development of high performance athletes" (Sport Canada, 2002a, p. 9); and improving international performances through systematic investment in sport and coaching science as well as "the collaborative setting of performance targets to guide the design, monitoring and evaluation of an effective athlete development system" (Sport Canada, 2002a, p. 10).

In 2005, Sport Canada confirmed its interest in high performance sport releasing their "Sport Excellence Strategy" where high performance sport success is linked to three specific activities: 1) collaborative leadership and establishing partnerships with agencies such as national/provincial/territorial sport organizations, Canadian sport institutes (CSIs) and Canadian sport centres (CSCs) to ensure a system of support for high performance athletes; 2) ensuring sustainable funding for high performance sport by monitoring existing funding requirements, co-ordinating funding decisions of funding partners to ensure efficient and effective allocation and exploring new funding opportunities; and 3) sport system performance, which is defined as support for the Long-Term Athlete Development (LTAD) model, coaching development, Own the Podium (OTP) strategy, and providing more international opportunities for competition in Canada by supporting the *Federal Policy for Hosting International Sport Events*. An important aspect of the strategy is the idea of accountability through performance objectives, both for athletes at the Olympic and Paralympic Games and other major international events but also for monitoring and evaluating collaborative leadership, sustainable funding and sport system performance objectives (Canadian Heritage, 2005).

It is this understanding of 'excellence' that will be used as the basis for framing a discussion of the current context of the high performance sport system in Canada. In particular, there are activities, programs, agencies, institutions and personnel that make up this system; this chapter will explore some of the current funding, training and development initiatives as well as the key stakeholders that have shaped and continue to shape current high performance sport in Canada. In the following section, the role of the Long-Term Athlete Development Model[1] and Own the Podium are discussed in relation to high performance sport. However, it is important to note that the renewal of the CSP in 2012 has confirmed and solidified high performance sport as a key policy priority for governments, stating that a desired outcome is that "Canadians are systematically achieving world-class results at the highest levels of international competition through fair and ethical means" (Sport Canada, 2012, p. 3). This policy priority has an important history and provides the backdrop for understanding the role that the policy priorities have played in providing opportunities for Canadian athletes to excel at international sport competitions.

In principle, the 2012 *Canadian Sport Policy* (Sport Canada, 2012) builds on its predecessor, the 2002 CSP (Sport Canada, 2002a), by continuing to promote a balanced approach between high performance sport and sport participation as policy goals; however, when the allocation of federal funding for specific programs is considered along with the manner in which various high performance sport initiatives have been supported, it is clear that although high performance sport and the production of medal performances have faced a number of crises, they are clearly entrenched as policy priorities.

The development of the high performance sport system over the past decade and in particular the development and implementation of more recent initiatives such as the Sport Funding and Accountability Framework, Own the Podium, and the Long-Term Athlete Development model point to an effort to strengthen in quality and quantity the key stakeholders that play an important role in the governance of high performance sport programs and policy and ensure their co-ordination with government policy priority. Table 4.2 provides a brief description of the key stakeholders discussed in this chapter and the role they play in the provision of high performance sport. Working collaboratively on a number of initiatives and also working independently on their various missions and programs, these organizations each play a significant role in providing services and funding for high performance sport in Canada. These initiatives are the focus of the remainder of this chapter.

The Sport Funding and Accountability Framework: Performance-Based Funding for Sport Organizations

Although the *Canadian Sport Policy* 2012 identifies a vision for sport that is broader than one focused exclusively on sport excellence, when we explore and expose current funding programs, which are important tools for achieving government goals, it is clear that federal government priorities favour the enhancement of sport excellence.

Table 4.2 Stakeholders and Descriptions

Stakeholder	Description
Canadian Olympic Committee (COC)	A national non-profit organization responsible for Canada's participation in the Olympic Games and the Pan American Games as well as for other initiatives that support the Olympic Movement and promote Olympic values at the community level. The COC's mission is "To lead the achievement of podium success at Olympic Games and to advance the Olympic Movement in Canada" (Canadian Olympic Committee, 2011, Mission, paragraph 9).
Canadian Paralympic Committee (CPC)	A non-profit organization that governs and supports high performance sport for Canadian Paralympic athletes. The CPC develops and provides programs to support the Paralympic Movement and Paralympic Games in Canada (this association is explored more fully in Chapter X) for athletes with physical disabilities. CPC's Mission is "to lead the development of a sustainable Paralympic sport system in Canada to enable athletes to reach the podium at the Paralympic Games (Canadian Paralympic Committee, 2011, About Us, paragraph 4).
Canadian Sport Centres/ (CSCs) Canadian Sport Institutes (CSIs)	Created through a partnership of Sport Canada, the COC, the CAC, and provincial level partners (e.g., government and non-profit organizations). Centres/institutes provide athletes and coaches with necessary support services such as athletic therapy, nutrition and access to advances in sport science. Currently, there is a network of seven centres/ institutes across the country (British Columbia, Alberta, Saskatchewan, Manitoba, Ontario, Quebec, and Atlantic Canada).
Coaching Association of Canada (CAC)	A multi-sport/service organization that oversees the training and certification of coaches in Canada through the National Coaching Certification Program. The CAC has also taken a leadership role in the development and implementation of the Long-Term Athlete Development initiative supported by Sport Canada.
Own the Podium (OTP)	A multi-service not-for-profit organization governed by an advisory board and administered by a management team and support staff who provide services and advice to athletes and national sport organizations (NSOs).

Table 4.2 (Continued)

Stakeholder	Description
Sport Canada	A branch in the Department of Canadian Heritage, it is the agency through which the Government of Canada is involved in high performance sport. Sport Canada is mandated to create policy, award grants, administer program initiatives and to support sport's contribution to Canadian identity and culture and advance the goals in the *Canadian Sport Policy*.
WinSport Canada	A non-profit organization that has developed from Canada's first high performance sport centre to become Canada's first comprehensive training institute providing facilities, technical and scientific expertise, educational support for athletes and administrative support and space for sport organizations.

In an effort to assist the government in achieving its policy objectives for sport excellence, Sport Canada has established several funding programs:

- Athlete Assistance Program (AAP)—which provides funding directly to athletes;
- Hosting Program—which supports national sport organizations and multi-sport/service organizations in their desire to host international multi-sport games (e.g., Pan Am Games, Olympic and Paralympic Games, North American Indigenous Games) or international single sport events (e.g., 2010 International Association of Athletics Federations World Junior Championships in Athletics; 2010 Union cycliste internationale Mountain Bike and Trials World Championships; 2010 World Wheelchair Rugby Championships);
- Sport Support Program (SSP)—which provides funding to national sport organizations, and multi-sport/service organizations;
- Project Stream—which provides funding to special initiatives to aid Sport Canada's strategic objectives in either sport excellence or sport participation by focusing on one or more the policy principles, namely, strengthening quality and capacity, promoting access and equity, promoting awareness and enhancing sport knowledge.

The focus of this section will be on the SSP, which is administered through the Sport Funding and Accountability Framework (SFAF), a multi-year federal government funding application for national sport and multi-sport/service organizations that is used to determine which organizations are eligible for federal funding. Following the application of an objective scoring of organizational programs and performances of eligible organizations, rankings are established that guide the level of funding for each funding cycle. In addition, each funded organization has an accountability agreement whereby standards must be achieved in certain federal policy objectives. The next section places the development of the SFAF in the broader policy context. This is followed by a section that explores the SFAF and its implications for high performance sport.

Policy Context

Social, economic and political forces converged in the late 1980s and early 1990s to interrupt and refocus Canada's approach to the funding of high performance sport, which was often characterized as the 'Eastern bloc' of the West—an implication that high performance sport was a state-controlled and directed machine. Ironically, the aftermath of Ben Johnson's positive doping test at the Summer Olympic Games in Seoul, Korea, in 1988 and the subsequent federal government *Commission of Inquiry into the Use of Drugs and Banned Practices Intended to Increase Athletic Performances* (i.e., Dubin inquiry) represent a critical moment in Canadian high performance sport, when the foundation upon which the high performance sport system was built in the 1970s and 1980s came 'crashing down' amid the testimony of athletes, coaches, and administrators at the Dubin inquiry. The inquiry subsequently exposed the practice of doping and the wilful blindness of both technical and administrative staff within the Canadian sport system, upsetting the preconceptions of the place of high performance sport and its importance to Canada (see also Chapter VII). This 'existential crisis' led not only to the adoption of a new anti-doping policy but also to a litany of policy discussions that focused on questions about the values that underpin high performance sport policy, what the role of government in high performance sport should be, and whether the government should support a narrower spectrum of core sports to allow sport organizations and the government to get a better return on its investment (Best, 1994;

Blackhurst, Schneider, & Strachan, 1991; Green & Houlihan, 2005; Minister's Task Force, 1992).

It is important to recognize that this crisis was occurring at a time of significant economic restraint where reducing the financial deficit became the primary political objective of the Progressive Conservative federal government of the day. As such, rolling back federal government spending became the deficit reduction strategy, and the recommendation for identifying 'core sports' aligned neatly with the federal government's interest in reducing public spending. The Core Sport Commission, established in June 1993 by the Progressive Conservative government, was mandated to provide recommendations to the federal government on the 'core sport concept' and on the identification of criteria for funding eligibility and accountability that would reduce the number of sport organizations receiving federal funding and instead focus resources on those sports determined to have the greatest value and significance to Canadians (Best, 1994). The Commission released the *Report of the Core Sport Commissioner* (known as the *Best Report*) in 1994, establishing a Sport Funding and Eligibility Framework that required organizations meet certain criteria, such as "value to Canadian society," to be eligible for funding. The 'core sport' approach was a fundamental shift from the way funding had been provided to national sport and multi-sport/ service organizations, wherein there was little transparency to the rationale for funding and funding levels. During the development of the core sport concept, a federal election took place in November 1993, and the Progressive Conservative Party, in power since 1984, was defeated by the Liberal Party. The new Liberal Government did not accept the recommendations regarding the core sports identified by the Core Sport Commission and charged Sport Canada's civil servants (the same civil servants involved in contributing to the 'shelved' *Best Report*) with the task of revisiting how best to manage funding contributions to sport. Although the political party in power changed in November 1993, concerns over the fiscal deficit did not.

With its commitment to a balanced budget, the Liberal Government embarked on a program review exercise requiring all departments to assess their programs to identify whether federal government involvement was essential to their implementation or could other levels of government or non-government organizations take over the delivery of the program (Savoie, 2000). For Sport Canada, programs that were to continue to receive funding, even at a reduced level, had to fit with their 'core business' objective, which was sport at the international, national and inter-provincial levels as well as the fulfilment of the government's social agenda policy priorities (Federal-Provincial Ministers Responsible for Sport, Recreation and Fitness, 1985). As such, in the reassessment of a funding strategy for national sport and multi-sport/service organizations, the Sport Funding and Accountability Framework (SFAF) was established in 1995 and fully implemented in 1996. For the first time, national sport and multi-sport/service organizations had to indicate their achievements and specific program objectives as well as how these aligned with larger social policy objectives established by government with respect to improving access and opportunity for underserved groups, an athlete-centred focus, harassment and abuse, athlete appeals, bilingual policies and anti-doping policies.

The SFAF was the Liberal Government's approach to the 'core sport' concept—maintaining the idea of establishing criteria for the objective evaluation and ranking of national sport and multi-sport/service organizations, while emphasizing the 'accountability' of organizations for achieving performance objectives—which involved altering the evaluation from 'are you eligible?' to 'are you accountable?'[2] While the Liberal government may have backtracked on supporting the *Best Report* submitted under the Progressive Conservative Government, the SFAF may in fact represent 'old wine in an old bottle' with a 'new label.' The SFAF, at least for the first cycle (1996–2001), achieved the same objective as the *Best Report*—reducing the number of organizations that received federal government funding and thus achieving the broader objective of developing a strategic approach to deficit reduction facing all governments at the time. Moreover, as a budget reduction exercise, the SFAF was successful; as demonstrated in Table 4.3 the introduction of the SFAF in 1995–1996 saw a dramatic decline in funding provided to NSOs and multi-sport/service organizations (MSOs). The SFAF is considered by government to be a comprehensive and objective policy tool designed to ensure

Table 4.3 Sport Funding and Accountability Framework (CA$)

	1994–1995 (pre-SFAF)	1995–1996 (SFAF Pilot)	1996–1997 (SFAF I)
NSO funding	$26,620,593	$21,343,218	$20,814,831
MSO funding	$16,539,852	$13,019,873	$ 7,204,968

that federal government funding is allocated to organizations that have demonstrated through specific program objectives that they are contributing to the federal government's policy priorities.

Through the SFAF, the federal government is able to determine which national sport and multi-sport/service organizations are eligible for funding, which areas are funded, and what level of funding each organization is to receive. It is through this policy tool that the federal government is able to steer these organizations towards achieving policy priorities. It remains to be seen whether the latest economic crisis and the current Conservative government's focus on deficit reduction for the next few years will result in similar budget reductions for national sport and multi-sport/service organizations. Moreover, despite promises to maintain funding commitments to Own the Podium (discussed later), there has been no such indication of support for the organizations responsible for the governance of their sport or for the co-ordination and development of sport services to support elite athletes.

SFAF and High Performance Sport

The SFAF has evolved since it was first introduced in 1995 in terms of eligibility criteria, area of funding, and how organizations are assessed to determine level of funding. However the fundamental process has remained the same. There are four stages to the SFAF process. The first stage, eligibility, requires organizations to apply to be recognized as eligible for federal government funding. The criteria at this stage require organizations to demonstrate sound governance practices and the proposed means of fulfilling federal sport and social policy objectives. In addition, NSOs must also meet criteria that indicate either an international scope (e.g., are affiliated with an international federation that complies with the World Anti-Doping Code, and have top-16 finishes in international events in the last decade) or a national scope (e.g., have a large membership base, have a national championship, and have the involvement of a minimum of eight provinces or territorial organizations). The eligibility criteria also require organizations to demonstrate a sound organizational structure—something that the federal government had prioritized in earlier funding programs in the 1970s and 1980s. In addition, the criteria require NSOs to implement specific federal government policies—ensuring government priorities for sport are implemented through NSOs, which fits with the broader government reforms identified in the Program Review.

Organizations that are assessed as eligible for funding move through to the assessment stage where evidence-based evaluations and performance indicators are used to assess performance in the areas of high performance and sport participation. Multi-sport/ service organizations are assessed with regard to performance in the areas of excellence, sport participation, and development. Table 4.4 shows the evaluation criteria for SFAF IV[3] for summer sports. With excellence weighted at 60%, this supports the federal government's policy interest on podium performances at the international level. As such, it is clear that the SFAF requires sport organizations to focus resources on achieving success at international events. However, the recent integration of the Long-Term Athlete Development model as part of eligibility requirements (i.e., investing in the development of future athletes) has become increasingly important in shaping the strategic deployment of NSO resources. It is important to note, however, that a focus on 'sport participation and development' weighted at 40% does not have a significant emphasis on enhancing sport participation through focusing on skill development and enhancing sport awareness and interest—rather the focus is on developing and sustaining a competitive sport structure through membership, championships, club development, coaching and official development. In essence, sport participation and development is being defined for national-level organizations as one that aims to develop sport participation initiatives that provide a broader and deeper pool of potential high performance athletes. The current SFAF ranking lists of summer and winter sports are shown in Tables 4.5 and 4.6.

Once organizations are ranked, the third phase requires the submission of a funding application following contribution guidelines identified by Sport Canada; funding is then allocated based on ranking and details provided in the funding application. In determining level of funding, Sport Canada considers not only ranking but also the unique aspects of the sport, for example, team sport versus individual sport and the global nature of the sport. In the first implementation of the SFAF in 1996–2001, only 53 NSOs met the eligibility criteria—and of those 53, only 38 qualified for funding. With significant budget reductions during this time, Sport Canada was able to use the SFAF to prioritize

Table 4.4 Sport Funding and Accountability Framework IV Summer NSO Assessment Weighting Grid

Area	Section	Component	Mainstream %	Athletes with a Disability %
EXCELLENCE (60%)	Athlete Results	Beijing Games	12	12
		Athens Games	6	6
		Sydney Games	2	2
		World Championships	20	20
		Note: Results from World Championships for the years 2000–2007 are evaluated with a consistently increasing value, which is dependent on the actual number of World Championships for each NSO		
	High Performance System	High Performance Management System	4	4
		National Team Coaches	8	8
		Athlete Annual Training and Competition Plans	3	3
		National Team Planning, Monitoring and Evaluation	3	3
		Integrated Support Teams	2	2
SPORT PARTICIPATION AND DEVELOPMENT (40%)	Sport Demographics	Membership	10	7
		National Championships	5	7
		Provincial/Territorial Championships	5	6
		Coaching Certification—NCCP Registrants	5	n/a
	Sport Participation	Skill Development and Awareness/First Contact	5	5
	Sport Development	NCCP Transition and Non NCCP Coach Development	5	7
		Officials Development	4	7
		Club/League Development	1	1

Table 4.5 Sport Funding and Accountability Framework Ranking and Sport Canada Funding for Summer Sport NSOs

Summer NSOs— Mainstream	Excellence Rank	Participation and Development Rank	2009–2010 Sport Canada Funding* CA$
Rowing	1	33	4,448,140
Swimming	2	6	5,008,000
Canoeing	3	12	3,561,152
Diving	4	24	2,501,540
Gymnastics	5	2	2,581,000
Synchro Swim	6	29	1,204,500
Athletics	7	11	4,177,100
Water Polo	8	34	1,522,750
Baseball	9	9	944,000
Softball	10	3	1,014,500
Cycling	11	14	2,598,010
Soccer	12	4	1,830,000
Wrestling	13	18	1,541,500
Triathlon	14	27	848,000
Judo	15	22	1,057,000
Basketball	16	10	2,625,750
Volleyball	17	7	1,080,500
Rugby	18	13	603,500
Taekwondo	19	26	659,000
Fencing	20	32	1,164,250
Sailing	21	8	1,330,250
Golf	22	1	715,000
Field Hockey	23	25	754,000
Water Ski	24	20	561,000
Equestrian	25	17	1,268,750
Racquetball	26	37	380,000
Boxing	27	38	405,500
Tennis	28	5	987,250
Squash	29	21	391,000
Table Tennis	30	23	540,900
Shooting	31	30	194,775
Karate	32	31	126,500

Table 4.5 (Continued)

Summer NSOs—Mainstream	Excellence Rank	Participation and Development Rank	2009–2010 Sport Canada Funding* CA$
Archery	33	36	236,200
Weightlifting	34	40	82,500
Badminton	35	28	357,500
Cricket	36	39	128,500
Lawn Bowls	37	35	168,000
Bowling	38	15	325,000
Sport Parachuting	39	41	98,500

*Sport Canada Funding—includes SFAF (evaluation of excellence and participation, in addition to any special project funding)

Table 4.6 Sport Funding and Accountability Framework Ranking and Sport Canada Funding for Winter Sport NSOs

Winter NSOs—Mainstream	2007 Excellence Rank	2007 Participation and Development Rank	2007–2008 Sport Canada Funding* CA$
Speedskating	1	7	3,706,428
Hockey	2	1	3,675,406
Bobsleigh, Luge and Skeleton	3	12	2,913,353
Freestyle Ski	4	11	2,875,794
Alpine Ski	5	6	4,481,521
Curling	6	3	2,055,438
Figure Skating	7	2	1,682,000
Cross Country Ski	8	5	2,702,525
Snowboard	9	10	1,920,391
Biathlon	10	9	602,500

*Sport Canada Funding—includes SFAF (evaluation of excellence and participation; in addition to any special project funding)

funding to organizations that met SFAF criteria. This contrasts with the current scenario, which is reflective of the pre-SFAF funding era in Canadian sport during which time over 60 NSOs received funding.

The final stage of the SFAF involves accountability agreements with each funded organizations. These agreements are tied to the social goals of the federal government identified earlier and are also linked to the goals of the Canadian Sport Policy. However, in their assessment of the SFAF over the 1995–2004 period, Havaris and Danylchuk (2007) found that there were no consequences for not meeting accountability standards for social policy objectives, suggesting "the SFAF has generated a tendency toward accountancy rather than accountability" (p. 49), which meant that organizations could satisfy the reporting requirements in terms of accountability agreements, but there were no consequences or penalties for non-compliance. As well, they found that, if standards were not met, Sport Canada would provide additional funding to assist them in achieving their goal.

With the SFAF solidly in place since 1996, it represents the shift in government to tie funding to specific public policy objectives enabling government to achieve these objectives through the work of external organizations (i.e., stakeholders). Such an approach makes it possible for government to adopt a co-ordinating or 'steering' role, shaping the direction of organizations that receive funds from this program. The SFAF serves as an economic policy tool as well, insofar as it achieves the broader public policy objectives of accountability and transparency. In addition, it serves specific sport objectives of the government and sport organizations. In its present form, achieving international success and programs aimed at supporting excellence are the clear funding priorities. The SFAF is really less about a division between excellence and participation than it is about national athlete/team performance and the development of national athletes/teams.

Own the Podium and the Pursuit of International Sport Success

Following the awarding of the 2010 Olympic and Paralympic Winter Games to Vancouver in July 2003, an immediate concern for much of the sport community was that Canada had the dubious distinction of being the only nation, as host of the Olympic Games (summer in

Montreal in 1976 and winter in Calgary in 1988), not to win a gold medal. With the aim of ensuring effective games, there was a collective effort to develop a comprehensive approach to ensure medal success in 2010. Specifically, key stakeholders (i.e., VANOC 2010, Sport Canada, Canadian Paralympic Committee, Canadian Olympic Committee and winter NSOs) collaborated to develop a national strategy to finish first in the medal table at the Olympic Winter Games and third at the Paralympic Winter Games—in other words, to 'own the podium.'

Own the Podium (OTP) is a strategic approach aimed at winning medals at the Olympic and Paralympic Games. The origins of this approach can be traced to the *Canadian Sport Policy* (2002) and the Work Group on Excellence that was established to explore how the priority for enhanced athlete and sport system performance identified in the Federal-Provincial/Territorial Plan for Collaborative Action 2002–2005 might be achieved (Sport Canada, 2002b). Key actions identified were to establish targets to assess athlete and sport system performance, enhance the use of sport science and establish the role of national sport centres. The work group submitted a report to the Interprovincial Sport and Recreation Council in January 2004 that recommended the adoption of specific performance targets for athletic performance:

- For Olympic winter sports, Canada consistently places in the top three nations in the medal count, with the goal being to finish first in the 2010 Vancouver Olympic Winter Games;
- For Olympic summer sports, Canada consistently places in the top eight nations in the medal count by 2012;
- For Paralympic winter sports, Canada consistently places in the top three nations in the gold medal count by 2010;
- For Paralympic summer sports, Canada consistently places in the top three nations in the gold medal count by 2012. (Brisson, 2004, p. v)

The report suggested performance targets would facilitate collaboration and greater co-ordination between key stakeholders in the sport system providing a unified focus for programs and funding. This suggested that funding would need to be focused on sports, athletes and teams with medal potential to ensure the most efficient approach to achieve desired performance targets.

In February 2004, winter NSOs, the Canadian Olympic Committee (COC), the Canadian Paralympic Committee (CPC), Sport Canada, the Calgary Olympic Development Association (CODA) (now WinSport Canada) and VANOC 2010 met to discuss the strategy for achieving the rank of first in the medal table at the 2010 Olympic Winter Games and top three at the 2010 Paralympic Winter Games. The COC formed a Task Force to develop the *"Own the Podium—2010"* plan and contracted Cathy Priestner Allinger[4] to co-ordinate a team of experts charged with reviewing winter sports and predicting the number of medals Canada should win at the 2010 Olympic and Paralympic Winter Games. They were also to provide direction on how to achieve the performance goal, determine funding priority for sports and establish a strategy for implementing OTP. The OTP Task Force released their report entitled *Own the Podium 2010* in September 2004, which set a goal of 35 medals in the 2010 Olympic Winter Games (Priestner Allinger & Allinger, 2004).

The report also recommended sports be tiered to identify level of funding. Tiers were determined based on assessments of each sport's importance to Canadian culture (i.e., sports that were considered popular and important to Canadians were assessed according to levels of pride and participation numbers), past Olympic success and medal potential. The recommended budget to "increase the number of potential medalists and the success rate of athletes in 2010" (Priestner Allinger & Allinger, 2004, p. 28) was estimated at CA$ 110M over five years. In February 2005, VANOC committed 50% of the budget through corporate-sector sponsorship, while the provincial and federal government budgets allocated CA$ 11M per year to winter sports and CA$ 12M per year to summer sports, covering the remaining 50%.

At the time of the review, Paralympic Alpine was the only sport involved in Own the Podium consultations (Priestner Allinger & Allinger, 2004). The report indicated that Paralympic sports did not have the capacity to identify performance targets:

> The priority for Paralympic Sport in Canada must be evaluated. It is the opinion of the review team that the CPC is under-resourced to truly provide technical support to their sports and therefore, the *Own the Podium* review was compromised. Paralympic winter sport is primarily organized by volunteers, coached by volunteers, and is successful primarily because of

the commitment these individuals have made to their respective sports. Canada must decide if Paralympic sport is important, and if so, what this means in terms of resources and attention. Canada, as a nation, does have the potential to be extremely successful internationally. Currently, it is disappointing to observe the lack of priority and resources provided to these sports if there is an expectation to be a leading nation in Paralympic sport. This, in addition to the challenge of full integration into able-bodied sport, has created the problematic situation that will impact Canada's potential to "*Own the Podium*" in 2010. (Priestner Allinger & Allinger, 2004, p. vi)

An important aspect of OTP was the strategy recommended for achieving the proposed OTP performance goals. In particular, the report recommended a consolidated approach to funding whereby a "Winter High Performance Sport Commission" would be charged with allocating funding. Centralizing OTP funding in this way was recommended to ensure an efficient, co-ordinated system of funding allocation and monitoring. In addition, the Task Force recommended that significant resources be allocated to research and development and sport sciences. The Top Secret program was created to concentrate research on developing training techniques, technology and equipment that would give Canadian athletes a performance edge. 'Dream team' groups of sport science researchers were recruited and funded to explore advances in the physiological, psychological, biomechanical and nutritional aspects of performance to give Canadian athletes an edge when competing at the 2010 Olympic and Paralympic Winter Games.

As OTP began to take shape, the 28 Olympic and Paralympic summer sport organizations, the COC, CPC and Sport Canada led by Dr. Roger Jackson (a former Canadian Olympic rower), CEO of Own the Podium, developed a business plan to guide athlete performance excellence for the 2008 Olympic Games in Beijing and the 2012 Olympic Games in London. *The Road to Excellence Business Plan for the Summer Olympic and Paralympic Sports* (RTE) was developed in April 2006. Alex Baumann, former double gold medalist in swimming at the 1984 Olympic Games was recruited from his leadership position with the Australian Institute of Sport to take the helm of RTE. Similar to the performance goals established for winter sports, the RTE established the following performance goals: Canada was expected to place among the top 16 nations in the total medal count (with 18 to 20 medals) by the 2008 Beijing Olympic Games (Canada finished in a tie for thirteenth place), and between top 10 and top 12 (with 24 to 30 medals) at the 2012 Olympic Games in London. In the 2008 and 2012 Paralympic Games, Canada was to place in the top five in the gold medal count (with 25 gold medals).

In November 2006 Roger Jackson was announced as CEO of a new organization, Podium Canada, a partnership between Sport Canada, VANOC 2010, the COC and the CPC. Podium Canada was established as a means of bringing OTP and RTE under one organization. A number of administrative and technical staff was hired to facilitate the implementation of OTP and RTE. Podium Canada's role was that of advising and making funding recommendations for the CA$ 110M in funding from government and commercial partners. OTP funding went directly to sport organizations for coaching, sport science and athlete training. In addition to corporate and public funding, 'grass roots' fundraising for OTP was initiated by the Canadian Olympic Foundation (COF), the fundraising arm of the COC. Communities and citizens were invited to join the fundraising challenge called the "OTP 2010 Municipalities Challenge." The Municipalities challenge was an initiative in which communities across Canada 'competed' to raise the most funds per capita for OTP to show their support and profile their community.

Following the 2010 Olympic Winter Games, the name "Podium Canada" was dropped in favour of Own the Podium. Both winter and summer Olympic and Paralympic sports operate under Own the Podium—a partnership of NSOs, federal and provincial governments, Canadian sport centres, the COC and corporate sponsors.

The development of OTP and the federal government's support of the initiative are in alignment with the CSP priority to "enhance athlete and sport system performance" (Sport Canada, 2007, p. 10). More specifically, the identification of performance targets was agreed upon as an important means of ensuring that this priority would be addressed. The development of OTP also builds on the historical precedent of policy and funding initiatives that have targeted athlete preparation for Olympic performances, that is, the Best Ever and Quadrennial Program Planning funding programs of the 1980s and the more recent Podium 2002 introduced in July 2001 to assist athletes in their preparation for the 2002 Salt Lake Olympic Winter Games. A public–private partnership between Sport Canada,

Petro-Canada, the COC and the Calgary Olympic Development Association, Podium 2002 provided approximately CA$ 1M to athletes with medal potential. Although OTP was developed outside of government and initiated by stakeholders in the sport community that were concerned about the status of high performance sport and the declining international performances, it fits neatly with broader public policy objectives.

Own the Podium—Beyond 2010

Although Canada did not attain the target of 35 medals or 'own the podium' at the 2010 Olympic Winter Games, the 14 gold medals (more than any other host-nation in Olympic Winter Games' history and four gold medals more than any other nation that participated in the 2010 Olympic Winter Games and the Canadian Paralympic Team's goal of top three in the gold medal standing, with 10 gold, was achieved, placing Canada third in the total medal standing behind Germany and Russia (see Table 4.1). The success at the 2010 Games assisted the lobbying efforts to secure ongoing federal government funding for OTP for future Olympic Games and Olympic Winter Games preparations. While the early days of the 2010 Games were rife with concern and mocking about failing to achieve the lofty goals, in the last week of the games the medal total climbed, and more Canadian athletes than ever before stood atop of the podium to hear their national anthem.

As the 2010 Games came to a close and lobby groups began trying to persuade the government to continue funding to OTP, politicians visible at the Games—Prime Minister Harper and Gary Lunn, Minister of State for Sport at the time—gave no indication that the government would continue its funding. As OTP and COC began to shore up support for the future, the COC argued that, following the Games, OTP should be brought under the COC. However, the CEO of OTP at that time, Roger Jackson, voiced a concern over the change in governance, claiming that the fact that the COC is a membership organization—its members being the Olympic sport federations that approve funding decisions—would make it difficult to ensure that funding be allocated based on objective criteria. Regardless of this internal strife and jockeying for control, there was a collective sigh from the high performance sport community a few days after the closing ceremonies of the

2010 Olympic Winter Games when the federal government released its budget and announced continued financial support for OTP. In the March 2010 federal budget, CA$ 44M were provided to support Canada's elite athletes—CA$ 10M over two years to renew funding for the identification and development of elite athletes and CA$ 34M over two years to renew and enhance programs that support training and preparation for competition for winter and summer elite athletes. In addition, the federal government provided CA$ 6M per year specifically for team sports and an effort to support the unique training and qualifying needs of Olympic program team sports.

In addition, CA$ 10M was provided to the CPC for the preparation of Paralympians. However, Priestner Allinger and Allinger's (2004) concern about the lack of priority, resources and attention given to Paralympic sport still holds true even after the successes of 2010 and the continued financial support. The OTP website, where news and information is provided and accessed, gives little attention to Paralympians beyond indications of the funding awarded. Unlike the celebratory stories presented about the success of Olympians at the 2010 Olympic Winter Games, the inclusion of similar stories about Paralympians and their successes at the 2010 Paralympic Winter Games is absent. Without this support and recognition one might question the commitment of OTP in sustaining long-term support for Canada's paralympic athletes.

In July 2009, the then Minister of State for Sport, Gary Lunn, announced the creation of a post-2010 review panel on high performance sport. The "2010 and Beyond" panel submitted their final report in December 2009; however the report was held back until after the 2010 Olympic Winter Games were completed at the end of February 2010 (Zussman, 2009). The panel scrutinized Own the Podium and the high performance sport system in general. A significant recommendation in the report was that a federally incorporated non-profit organization be created to take over the responsibility of high performance sport in Canada. This supports the recommendation for an independent entity made originally in the Brisson Report (2004). In April 2012, OTP moved from program status to legal entity by obtaining non-profit status as a multi-service sport organization. To what extent this new status ensures independence from its funding contributors, the federal government, the COC, the Canadian Paralympic Committee, the

Canadian Olympic Foundation and corporate Canada, remains to be seen.

New expertise was recruited to join OTP and consolidate it as the foundation to Canada's current high performance sport development—in May 2010 Alex Baumann became the new CEO of OTP. Starkman (2010a) reported that, under Baumann, the goals of OTP would become more long-term, as opposed to focused only on the most immediate Olympic Games and the pursuit of high performance sport institutes. With the next Olympic and Paralympic Winter Games in Sochi in 2014, the focus has shifted to development and sustainability. As reported in *The Toronto Star*, Baumann's agenda is the pursuit of developing high performance sport institutes—with his experience based in Australia's Sport Institutes—to "raise the bar and also help get more full-time coaches into the system" (Starkman, 2010a, paragraph 16). In addition, OTP hired Ken Read to direct the winter sports for OTP and Anne Merklinger as director of summer sports. With all three of these leaders having been high performance athletes in swimming, downhill skiing and curling respectively as well having experience in the sport setting—Read with Alpine Canada and Merklinger with CanoeKayak Canada—there was a clear signal that the leadership gap lamented in previous reviews of high performance sport was being addressed.

In addition, the federal government created the OTP board of directors. This advisory board is chaired by former VANOC 2010 CEO John Furlong. The 10-member advisory board is responsible for raising money and providing advice on the allocation of funds to support medal hopefuls and the preparation for Olympic and Paralympic Games.

Baumann's tenure at the helm of OTP, however, was short-lived—in September 2011 he resigned deciding that a move to New Zealand to take up a similar position was best for his family. In January 2012, Anne Merklinger, director of summer sports was promoted to CEO—the third leadership change in OTP's short history.

The organizational structure of OTP has developed to include full-time staff and sport advisors focused on technical and sport sciences in addition to administrative and strategic planning services. With the organizational structure of OTP in place, the evolution of OTP continued through 2011 and 2012 when a closer working relationship with the COC was forged through "a memorandum of understanding [which] represents a significant step to strengthen, co-ordinate and harmonize the high performance sport system focused on leading the creation and delivery of programs and services to increase podium results" (Canadian Newswire, 2011, paragraph 3). With the agreement to collaborate with technical expertise and sport science innovations that support "medal potential" athletes, sport teams and their coaches, the COC contributed CA$ 5M to OTP. The agreement also realigns the COC alongside Sport Canada as not only one of the founding partners of OTP but now a significant financial contributor. Bal Gosal, the Sport Minister stated, "The Government of Canada is proud to support Canadian athletes. We are very pleased to see the alignment of these two great organizations in supporting our athletes and coaches to continue Canada's great Olympic Games legacy" (Canadian Newswire, 2011, paragraph 11).

Own the Podium—Critique, Evaluation and Considerations

With the unveiling of OTP and the public announcement of a target of 35 medals and a first-place finish in the medal table at the 2010 Olympic Winter Games, the concern over an underfunded and unfocused approach to sport excellence was addressed; however, this new 'brash' and 'bold' approach did not go uncriticized. Professor Bruce Kidd, former Olympian and Canadian middle-distance record holder, educator and sport activist suggested in an interview with *The Globe and Mail* that OTP represents a reorientation in sport today—where the process of becoming and the experience of being an athlete are not the justifications for investment in high performance athletes, but rather the justification is medal results. Although Kidd, as a former elite athlete himself, recognized and supported the desire of athletes to be the best—like many who have lamented the 'un-Canadian' principles that underpinned the Own the Podium slogan—he stated quite emphatically, "I'm embarrassed by Own the Podium to this extent: we're saying 'World, come to Canada so we can beat the shit out of you.' ... Own the Podium would have made a great slogan for London 2012. But not when we're hosting the Games" (Brown, 2010, p. F6). Donnelly (2010b) goes further, suggesting a name change for any future funding related to the investment in Olympic medals:

The name Own the Podium made many uncomfortable from the start. Eventually it came to be used against the Canadian team (German sports officials used it to motivate their athletes to beat Canadians), and during the first week of the Olympics it became a joke. (p. 85)

Criticism notwithstanding, the OTP board of directors has declared that the name "Own the Podium" will remain. The key players are unapologetic for any offence it may have elicited and hold steadfast to their views that the name represents the aspiration of wanting to be the best and compete in the 'global sporting arms race.' In his recent book entitled *Becoming Canada*, Ken Dryden states:

During the Olympics, the phrase "Own the Podium" had been a source of national debate and division. Since the Olympics, it has become part of our daily language. "Own the Podium" is now part of how we think and part of who we are. Sometimes you have to believe to see. (2010, p. 238)

The critique, however, was not restricted to the slogan and definition of success. One of the outcomes of the 'top secret program' was that training partnerships between Canadian athletes and athletes from other nations were terminated; in addition, the funding approach meant that OTP created a tiered system where athletes with "medal potential" were deemed worthy enough to access special services and funding to assist their chances of podium success, thus leaving out other national athletes and creating what Donnelly (2010b) called "two classes of athletes." More importantly Donnelly pointed out that the strategy of OTP dismissed the lesson learned from Torino 2006 where there were many "unexpectedly won medals" (85) suggesting a bigger pool of athletes should be supported through OTP.

This approach was in place for the 2008 Beijing Olympic Games, where Road to Excellence funding was provided to selected athletes. This was clearly the problem experienced by David Ford, a kayaker who had his OTP funding cut off because of his age, poor results and the fact that the sport was not identified as a sport with potential medal status for the 2008 Olympic Games. Similarly, Canadian national team boxer, Adam Trupish who, after being eliminated in the first round at the 2008 Beijing Olympic Games, stated that a lack of funding, going into debt and having to work when he should have been training prevented him from accessing the best resources possible. Trupish, not funded through OTP, stated "we're saying 'give us funding and we can produce' and the government is saying 'produce and we'll give you funding'" (Christie, 2008, paragraph 8).

Investing 'with the odds' and singling out athletes has meant a shift in the cry heard from athletes when they failed to medal. At the 2000 Olympic Games in Sydney, the unified cry reported in the media from athletes in response to questions about their poor performance was the lack of funding support and the need for public and private investment in high performance sport. In 2008, at the Beijing Olympic Games and at the 2010 Olympic Winter Games in Vancouver, athletes who did not achieve their medal potential voiced various emotions that were linked to their understanding of OTP and what 'success' means. There were tearful apologies to the nation, for example, after failing to achieve desired results in Beijing in 2008, Canadian female fencer Sherraine Schalm, ranked fifth in the world, stated:

> I know no Canadian taxpayer wants to hear that I really did try my best and I really did give everything I have . . . But I swear to all of you that I really did and I'm very sorry that I didn't bring home a medal, but you train and you take your chances . . . Nobody made me sign a contract that I would guarantee to win, I just signed a contract that I would do my best and train my best and give it everything I can, but I'm sorry unfortunately it wasn't enough today. (Ewing, 2008, paragraphs 18–19)

Similarly, at the 2010 Olympic Winter Games in Vancouver, Melissa Hollingsworth stated, "I feel like I let my entire country down" after bumping the track and finishing fifth in the women's skeleton event and failing to succeed in her quest for a medal—a medal that was anticipated in OTP calculations. And although medaling on the first evening of competition, after her silver medal performance Jennifer Heil, the defending Olympic champion in the women's freestyle moguls event, and identified to repeat this feat in 2010, stated, "I won silver, I didn't lose gold . . . I know we're going for excellence, but I'm so proud to be Canadian" (Olsen, 2010, paragraph 3). These apologies to the nation were perhaps in recognition that the public was well aware of the heavy investment, declarations of medal performances and pressure to win gold on Canadian soil.

At the same Games, there was also anger and frustration voiced by Denny Morrison after finishing ninth in the men's 1,500 metre speed skating race and thirteenth in the men's 1,000 metre race. He claimed the OTP 'top secret' initiative prevented him from training with his friend, USA speed skater Shani Davis. Although this statement was later retracted as 'heat of the moment' frustrations, it does raise the question of whether the best interests of athletes were always considered in the implementation of the OTP initiative and to what extent athletes were involved in making decisions about their training.

More recent commentary about OTP has been positive, emphasizing gratitude for the much needed support that OTP has provided for training preparation including funding for sport science, medicine and nutrition. David Calder, coxless pairs rower, silver medalist in Beijing 2008 and sixth place finish in London 2012 stated:

> Own The Podium has been unbelievable for us . . . It makes sure we have the cutting-edge science and the access to top sports physiologists across the country . . . This sort of regimented, studied structure [of how to prepare and recover] didn't exist four years ago. (Mirtle, 2012, paragraphs 13–14)

However there is the recognition that how funding is allocated may need to change to ensure sustained success—critical examination of supporting developing athletes, not only 'medal hopefuls.' It remains to be seen then how or if OTP will be able to balance the focus on medals with the need to ensure investment in developmental athletes—something that has plagued other high performance funding programs.

Although the women's team pursuit won a bronze medal in London 2012, Gillian Carlton, a member of the squad reportedly went into debt to fund her training. Her observations are that "I think if we want to see more results like we are seeing at this Olympics from athletes, more gold medal performances, Canada needs to put more money into their athletes, for sure" (Parry, 2012, paragraph 25). In reflecting on Great Britain's success at the London 2012 Olympic Games, Sebastian Coe identified "high and predictable funding . . . You know, you do not get excellence on the cheap nor do you get all the other virtuous outcomes that come from that without long-term and predictable levels of funding, and that's what we've witnessed" (Cole, 2012, paragraphs 32–33).

Although the medal tally for London 2012 was seen to meet the goal of a top 12 placement, there was concern about the 'conversion rate' of world championships to Olympic Championships. Mark Tewksbury, Canadian chef de mission for London 2012 stated, "It is important that we have good conversion rates [of world rankings into Olympic medals], for sure, and we know that ... some of the more successful countries at these Olympics had high conversion rates. And that's a question that obviously is going to come under review" (Cole, 2012, paragraph 15). Whether in recognizing the absurdity of predicting the unpredictable or attempting to soften the critique on the OTP funded athletes that did not medal, he went on to explain:

> Of course we would have liked more gold medals, and no one wants a gold medal more than every athlete out there competing ... But every athlete at this Games has a story, and every medal has a story, and collectively that's what makes the narrative of this Canadian Olympic team—our athletes showed what excellence means to us. (Cole, 2012, paragraph 19)

These comments support Donnelly's (2010b, p. 44) critique that to date "Own the Podium [funding allocations] represents a particularly narrow strategy based on an extraordinarily narrow definition of success."

These critiques and comments align with an OTP evaluation conducted by the Sport Law and Strategy Group for OTP in 2011. This report presented the comments from individuals and organizations with respect to all aspects of OTP. There was overwhelming support for the focus and commitment towards medals however there was some concern about the sole focus on medal potential athletes and neglect of those athletes that require years of investment before potential is achieved, hindering long-term development and to creating a system of "have" and "have not" athletes (Lawrie & Corbett, 2011).

Although OTP ensured that athletes with medal potential had all the technical and scientific support they required in preparation for the 2008 and 2012 Olympic and Paralympic Games and the 2010 Olympic and Paralympic Winter Games respectively, it could not guarantee the desired outcome—it is sport, the outcome is uncertain. This understanding often gets lost in the medal predictions.

Despite the critiques of OTP in terms of the 'arrogance' of its slogan, the investment of resources in only select athletes, and the 'top secret' science and technology, this 'made in Canada' strategy for high performance sport has been adapted by other nations. For example, UK Sport has set medal targets for London 2012 and has adopted a 'no compromise' philosophy targeting sports and athletes with the best chance of medal success. In addition, key players in the development of OTP, such as Cathy Priestner Allinger and her husband Todd Allinger, who led the review of Canada's high performance system and authored the OTP report, have been hired by the Russian Olympic Committee to facilitate the development of a similar program for Russia in preparation for the 2014 Olympic Winter Games in Sochi (Starkman, 2010b, pp. A1–A2). Lawrie and Corbett (2011) also reported that OTP directors have been invited to present to International Olympic Committees. Indeed the globalization of high performance sport and the transfer of ideas and expertise (as well as athletes) to compete in the 'medals arms race' have clearly come of age.

Although Lawrie and Corbett (2011) highlight some concern from participants in their evaluation research suggesting that roles need to be clarified between Sport Canada, CSCs, the COC and OTP to avoid overlap and turf wars, OTP is unquestionably established as the 'agency' responsible for providing athletes, teams and national sport organizations with the assistance they need to achieve their medal performance objectives. Moreover, OTP has provided Canadian high performance sport with some stability, and while it may depend on government and corporate sponsors for the financial stability, OTP has demonstrated a commitment to providing athletes with the support they need to compete at the international level. OTP has developed the plans, monitoring devices, funding support and research and development expertise and has recruited top sport leaders to manage it. But as much as the success of OTP has been recognized both domestically, through continued support, and internationally, as witnessed by other nations mimicking or tapping into the resources that led the Canadian initiative—the Brisson Report (2004) called for an independent High Performance Sport Commission—its vision may be unattainable given that the backdrop to the 'co-operative' understanding between the COC and OTP is a competition for corporate sponsorship for funding elite athletes. And although athletes are probably less concerned about how they receive the money and who antes up, the duplication of roles regarding funding programs and initiatives is counter to an agreement that aims to "increase efficiency and . . . streamline the efficiency and expertise of each of the COC and OTP" (Canadian Newswire, 2011, paragraph 6).

Sustaining Podium Success—Long-Term Athlete Development Model

Although podium success is the focus of much of the high performance sport, the centrality of national team athletes has been accompanied by the adoption of a strategic approach to sustaining high performance sport through the Long-Term Athlete Development (LTAD) model (Canadian Heritage, 2005). LTAD is a development pathway within the broader Canadian Sport for Life movement. Specifically, LTAD refers to a seven-stage "made in Canada"[5] model that focuses on individual growth and development. The physiological needs of the athlete are aligned with each stage: "LTAD focuses on the general framework of athlete development with special reference to growth, maturation and development, trainability and sport system alignment and integration" (Canadian Sport Centres, 2005, p. 13). Although only three stages of the LTAD model focus on sport excellence (i.e., high performance sport), for Sport Canada, NSOs and MSOs it is those stages that have taken root and have been nurtured through various policy and funding initiatives that support investment in high performance sport and international success.

Although LTAD is framed as a Sport Canada initiative and fits with the broader public policy interests in social investment, it is an innovation developed outside of government. In particular, LTAD was developed in the mid-1990s by Dr. Istvan Balyi, with the National Coaching Institute in Victoria, British Columbia. Balyi presented the LTAD model as a systematic approach to support the successful development of high performance athletes based on scientific principles of growth and development (Balyi, 2001; Robertson & Way, 2005). "The need for the LTAD [arose] in part from the declining international performances of Canadian athletes in some sports and the difficulty other sports [were] having in identifying and developing the next generation of internationally successful athletes" (Canadian Sport Centres, 2005, p. 14). The idea is that the application of growth and development principles to fundamental

sport and movement skills in early life stages and throughout training and competitive programs at appropriate developmental ages
will result in a more effective athlete development system—where
athletes are prepared for international competition and where there
is a systematic approach to development ensuring the sustainability
of national-level teams—a feeder system based on scientific principles
of growth, training and competitive preparation.

For many within the sport system, the policy problem facing
high performance sport was a stagnating and underdeveloped athlete
development approach. The federal government's financial cuts to the
sport system in the 1990s, coupled with policy and program priorities
that adopted a short-sighted focus on national team needs and international performances, meant there was the lack of a comprehensive
and integrated approach to athlete training and development to ensure
athletes were prepared to compete at the international level and to
ensure a "pipeline" of athletes to support a "playground to podium"
movement (Canadian Sport Centres, 2005; Robertson & Way, 2005).

The CSP has enabled the federal government to focus and
co-ordinate stakeholders such as the provinces and territories
through the federal-provincial/territorial priorities, and multi-
sport/service organizations such as the Coaching Association of
Canada and Canada Games and all national sport organizations,
on matters of athlete development. Supported by Sport Canada, an
expert group developed a resource guide entitled *Canada Sport for
Life: Long-Term Athlete Development Resource Paper* and subsequently
developed a resource paper with adaptations for athletes with a disability in *No Accidental Champions*. In 2005, the LTAD initiative was
supported at the Federal Provincial/Territorial Meeting of Ministers
in Regina where ministers agreed to implement it as their athlete-
development model. Facilitating a system-wide approach, LTAD was
integrated into the *Canadian Sport Policy* through the renewed Federal-
Provincial/Territorial Priorities for Collaborative Action 2007–2012
(Sport Canada, 2007). LTAD was seen as:

> the potentially most significant advances in Canadian sport
> since the adoption of the *Canadian Sport Policy* [and its] imple-
> mentation . . . fundamental to the realization of the Vision and
> Goals of the *Canadian Sport Policy*. LTAD is the framework from
> which several priorities and actions will be developed and
> monitored over the next several years. (Sport Canada, 2007, p. 3)

To ensure NSOs and MSOs adopt LTAD as part of their athlete development strategy, in 2005 Sport Canada's LTAD initiative included its integration into their funding program (SFAF) as part of the funding eligibility requirements and has also established a part of the funding block of SFAF for the development of LTAD initiatives within these organizations. Funding may be allocated to develop sport-specific LTAD plans, collaborative projects with other organizations, or research on LTAD. In addition, Sport Canada has provided support directly to an LTAD expert group to assist with the development of communication and education tools to ensure system-wide adoption and integration of LTAD. Resources are made available for parents, schools, community recreation, coaches and athletes through the Canadian Sport for Life website (http://www.canadiansportforlife.ca) co-ordinated by the Canadian Sport Centres in collaboration with the Coaching Association of Canada. As such, an important aspect to the implementation of LTAD and its adoption across the sport system has less to do with the logic of the sport science of growth and development—the principles are well established in the coaching profession—and more to do with the development of a strategy for communicating these principles of training and coaching to levels of sport provision below the national team level, across the nation, and across all sports and agencies engaged in the delivery of sport.

Recognizing the diversity and lack of integration of sport delivery of the Canadian sport system and that there are many stakeholders involved in this system (Thibault & Harvey, 1997), LTAD has proposed a pathway for athlete development that is accessible and understandable to each stakeholder so they are able to understand where their organization and the role it plays fit into the development of Canada's future national athletes. The aim is to harmonize the Canadian sport system's approach to sport delivery at levels below the national level to ensure each individual (parent, coach, educator) and each association (community sport, school sport, province or territory) understands their role in the development of athletes and adopts the principles of training and coaching advocated in the teaching and coaching materials developed for LTAD (Norris, 2010).

Such a modernization agenda to make the 'science' of coaching and training more accessible throughout the sport system was based in part on a more strategic approach to talent identification and is intended to ensure the breadth and depth of the talent pool of potential future national team athletes. With its major focus on the sustainability of sport excellence at the international level, LTAD has been identified as the mechanism by which the sustainability of sport excellence at the international level can be achieved.

The LTAD model and the concepts used in support of it have come to play a significant role in the ideas about how sport organizations should be developing athletes and have been incorporated as part of federal funding criteria. However, the breadth and depth of LTAD across the system has not gone unquestioned. There has been some concern over the focus on physiological development at the expense of a more holistic approach that would include the social and psychological aspects. In addition, there has been critique over the 'universality' of its adoption without substantial supporting empirical evidence, and as such, concern has been voiced about the lack of an evaluation of the model and its impact on NSOs, MSOs, coaches, parents and athletes (Brackenridge, 2006; Collins & Bailey, 2013; Ford et al., 2011; Holt, 2010). Brackenridge (2006) has cautioned that "particularization of the young athlete is a trap that many sport scientists and coaches fall into: it suits their professional purposes yet it works against the child's development as a whole person" (p. 120). As a model that has a clear objective of ensuring sustained high performance sport success, the focus is on athlete development at the individual level—emphasizing the physiological and technical aspects of training and providing little discussion of a more holistic approach that places this training within a broader social and cultural context and recognizes the psychological and behavioural aspects to athlete development. The caution is in viewing development in narrowly prescribed stages.

LTAD is not presented as a panacea; however it is described as being helpful to package complex phases of development into a simple, but flexible model. The concern is whether these stages recognize the social and psychological complexity of development. Despite the athlete-centred principle of LTAD, the concern for some is that the stages objectify the athlete.[6] Brackenridge goes further in stating that LTAD fails to consider how to engage the athlete in making decisions about their training and development. Norris (2010) suggests that the LTAD model has provided a "universal language" across agencies and associations when discussing athlete development, facilitating communication and understanding of roles and responsibilities. He further suggests the critical reviews of LTAD provide the opportunity for constant improvement and continued research to facilitate athlete development. Collins and Bailey (2013) go further with their critique suggesting the widespread adoption of the LTAD model in the UK, Canada and other countries is a function of what they term "scienciness"—where the ". . . authority of science [has been attributed] . . . to methods and ideas [that] possess little or no underpinning evidence or theoretical base" (p. 184). The "pervasive and persuasive" (p. 186) LTAD model in a climate of evidence-based policy decisions, they suggest, is a result of so much investment that it becomes difficult to reverse or question the commitment. The concern here is twofold for both public policy and the sport system. First, the significant investment in policy tools that are not proven or evaluated; and second, if LTAD is part of the larger investment in high performance sport success—that is, the "sporting arms medal race"—"success is far more likely to follow science than non-science" (Collins & Bailey, 2013, p. 189). After all, the fear of the nuclear arms race is the fact that there is scientific evidence that success could be costly!

One aspect of the broader Canadian Sport for Life movement is the desire to have an integrated system, for high performance sport and for athlete development in particular, since connections with the educational system and the role of school sport is a new area of investment. In particular there has been recent support for "the establishment of sport academies and Sport-Étude programs..." (Canadian Sport Centres, 2005, p. 48). With provincial and territorial commitment to LTAD and with education being the responsibility of the provinces and territories, the development of sport academies in the school system will require inter-ministry as well as inter-governmental co-operation.

The report entitled, *Sport Schools in Canada: The Future is Here* published by the Canadian Sport Centre (Pacific), and written by LTAD experts, provides a comprehensive review of sport-specific academies and advocates for their role by providing recommendations for action. In particular the report states:

> while much is being done to own the podium on the international stage . . . up and coming athletes have not reaped the benefits of this increased focus on high performance sport and many student athletes may be "falling through the cracks" or dropping out of sport because they cannot manage the time demands of both sport and their educational endeavours. With

the expanded infrastructure and flexibility in high school education at our disposal many provinces are ready to become leaders
in the development of new Senior National team members for
Canada. (Way, Repp, & Brennan, 2010, p. 9)

The recommendation of the LTAD experts suggests that a "Canadian
Sport School model" would be co-ordinated through the Canadian
Sport Centre and become an established brand and presumably the
brand of choice to be licensed across the country (Way et al., 2010,
p. 27). The development of sport academies has been limited to
Quebec and British Columbia. In addition, the National Sport School
in association with the Calgary Board of Education is in the process
of establishing an on-site education location at WinSport Canada.
Developments include, a review by the Toronto District School Board
examining the potential for sport academies (Brown, 2009). The
school board in Hamilton, Ontario has adopted 'programs of choice'
in two schools allowing students to pursue their athletic interests in
the sports of basketball or soccer. Houlihan's (2000) investigation of
the development of sport schools in the UK uncovered the complexity
in such an approach and the competing interests that exist between
sport organizations and schools that hinders the implementation
of such innovations. In addition to co-ordination difficulties, an
investment in building the capacity of technical expertise would be
required by governments and other agencies. It remains to be seen
whether the schools may better serve LTAD through a focus on the
model's early stages and the development of movement and sport
skills rather than the development of sport excellence.

The importance given to LTAD is indicated by a commitment
by Sport Canada to ensure compliance by requiring all NSOs to
develop LTAD plans specific to their sport as a condition of funding
where funding to NSOs is assessed in terms of sport initiation and
development programs and not simply increasing and sustaining
membership participation in the sport. To what extent this centrality
given to LTAD was a result of advocates of the model lobbying for
support or a result of governments viewing LTAD as an ideal policy
tool to assist in ensuring greater accountability for funding remains
to be debated. The outcome, however, has been that LTAD has come to
represent a cornerstone in addressing the CSP goal of expanding "the
pool of athletes" to ensure sustained "world-class results at the highest levels of international competition" (Sport Canada, 2002a, p. 4).

LTAD's adoption of an 'athlete development' orientation to sport for children and youth together with the desire to connect more strongly with the education sector fits with the social investment policy perspective that is shaping current public policy. According to Jenson and Saint-Martin (2006) and Saint-Martin (2007), a social investment approach to policy has a foundation on three principles: an interest in investing in knowledge and human capital, a focus on children and a future orientation, and an interest in return on investment implying that social spending be focused in areas where returns will be profitable. The LTAD model, an initiative developed by coaching and training experts and integrated into public policy, has resulted in a broadening of programs that support sport excellence through not only a consideration of podium performances but also the sustainability of high performance programs through the capacity-building of junior development programs based on LTAD principles. At the national level then, LTAD has been adopted to ensure a strategic approach to sustained podium success.

Conclusion: Issues and Challenges for High Performance Sport

With the federal budget announcement in February 2012 of continued government support for high performance sport coupled with a high performance sport system that has grown both in terms of the quantity of stakeholder organizations and stakeholder quality or capacity to lead and manage high performance sport, there is much promise for the continued development of high performance sport in Canada.

Since the implementation of the *Canadian Sport Policy* in 2002, significant progress has been made towards achieving the goal of enhanced excellence. Like previous investments in high performance sport, a substantial impetus to its development over the past decade occurred because of the awarding of the 2010 Olympic and Paralympic Winter Games to Vancouver by the International Olympic Committee in July 2003. Like the 1976 Olympic Games in Montreal and the 1988 Olympic Winter Games in Calgary, the hosting status prompted public investments in high performance sport. However, unlike previous initiatives in the 1970s and 1980s, in the past decade we have witnessed a more comprehensive and more focused investment in ensuring medal results that has engaged both the private non-profit and commercial sectors as well as the public sector. Supporting athletes and ensuring best-ever performances

were not deemed sufficient goals; rather, medal targets were identified as the driving force for allocating resources. In addition, the
development and implementation of LTAD is intended to address
the issue of ensuring a sustained pool of athletes who will not be in
need of remedial training and coaching, and Own the Podium has
been identified as the foundation to ensuring Canadian athletes are
capable of competing for podium finishes at international competitions. However, greater podium success has been seen only in winter
sports to date.

In terms of the 2002 CSP goal of enhanced excellence, the
Summative Evaluation of the *Canadian Sport Policy* reported that the
commitment to performance targets has facilitated the achievement
of podium performances in international competitions particularly in winter sports. In addition, policy consultations during the
CSP renewal process in 2011 supported the direction that is being
navigated by the various stakeholders—one where excellence as
measured by medal success is emphasized—and fits with the federal
government's interest in "steering" the system through financial
contributions (Comeau, 2013). This is seen quite directly with the
commitment to support Canadian Sport Centres/Institutes in British
Columbia, Calgary, Saskatchewan, Manitoba, Ontario, Quebec and
the Atlantic. The recent transition of some centres to institutes (i.e.,
British Columbia, Calgary, Ontario and Quebec) signals not only
an investment in establishing training facilities but one that aligns
Canada on the global stage where institutes are seen as a sign of
leading sport nations. The development of Canadian Sport Institutes
was also championed by Alex Baumann, former CEO of Own the
Podium, who brought his experience from the Australian high performance sport system and their network of sport institutes.[7] The
challenge is ensuring the financial commitment to build and maintain expensive facilities. In September 2010, the federal government
announced a financial contribution of CA\$ 650,000 to the develop-
ment of a CSI in British Columbia. The province of British Columbia
has matched this contribution in an effort to develop the facilities
and expertise necessary to ensure sustained international sport success and announced the shift to institute status in December 2012.
The institute in Toronto gained momentum through preparation for
the Pan/Parapan American Games in 2015 hosted by Toronto. This
is also supported by the University of Toronto's recent investment in
the Centre for High Performance Sport at the new Varsity Centre in

downtown Toronto (Blackburn-Evans, 2007). The partnership with university facilities is an important element that has framed the successful relationship between the Canadian Sport Institute in Calgary and WinSport Canada.

Satisfied with the quality of the leadership and the direction of high performance sport, the system seems to be doing what the government (regardless of the party in power) in fact had intended or hoped—putting the required systems, structures and expertise in place to facilitate performance success and support public policy objectives.

The events that took place during the 2010 Olympic and Paralympic Winter Games in Vancouver—the visibility of the Own the Podium funding program, the performances of Canadian athletes, and the discussion of patriotism and Canadian identity in association with the performance of Canada's athletes—have fuelled the debate about the contribution that high performance sport makes to Canadian society. With similar interests and trends being observed in other nations, as part of the ongoing discussions about the connections to the public value of sport, the opportunity to explore the current context and future challenges is timely.

The importance of hosting major games (see Chapter VIII) as part of this debate about investment in high performance sport should not be ignored, as witnessed by Great Britain's success at London 2012 and Canada's success at the Vancouver 2010 Olympic Winter Games. Like many Canadians who have an interest in sport, I had an insatiable thirst for the 2010 Games and was an intense consumer of the media's portrayal and coverage. The Vancouver 2010 Olympic and Paralympic Winter Games and the events that characterized the games, from the torch relay to the protests, to the public assemblies in various locations to observe the games, to the athletic events themselves ignited my emotional ties to high performance sport.

Experiencing the highs and lows of performance of Canadians and athletes from other nations—from the unnerving death of Georgian luger Nodar Kumaritashvili, the joyous celebrations of the first Olympic gold medal won by a Canadian on Canadian soil by Alexandre Bilodeau in freestyle skiing (moguls), to the admiration for fair play displayed by Clara Hughes, as she not only skated to her own bronze medal in the 5,000 metre speed skating event, but celebrated the medals of her teammates and displayed the humanity of giving and sharing her success with underserved Canadian citizens[8]—I literally felt the stress hormones in my veins as I threw every rock with Cheryl Bernard in the tenth and extra end of the women's curling gold medal match, even though shamefully I had only ever thrown about 50 rocks in my entire life. I was equally motivated for my daily run after watching the exhaustion and exhilaration of Poland's Justyna Kawalczyk as she sprinted past Marit Bjørgen of Norway to win the women's 30K cross country ski race; and settled into reflective repose as the Canadian women's hockey team won gold again thinking of my own joyful childhood (too long ago in years, but like yesterday in my mind) on winter days and nights when I laced up my figure skates (with the toe pick filed down so I would not trip) and walked 500 metres to the outdoor rink at the local park to play pick up hockey, as the only girl amongst the neighbourhood children who owned a hockey stick and was ranked alongside the boys when teams were selected. To dream of being an Olympian hockey player was beyond my own imagination, not to mention my family's financial means, but today, young girls have their female hockey heroes who make those dreams possible and who symbolize achievements of excellence and actively support the growth of hockey for women and girls. The experience of all these events, and finally, jumping to high fives with family as Sidney Crosby's shot crossed the line to provide Canada with its final gold medal of the games and, if not *"the"* most important, the one that would have been lamented the most if not won. Was this the pride, unity, cohesion and participation intended as the outcome of investing in high performance sport?

Van Hilvoorde, Elling, and Stokvis (2010) argue that national pride is a stable characteristic and that sport-related national pride depends on an established sense of belonging. As such, we need to be cautious about the claims (largely reported in the media) that the euphoria that swept the nation during the 2010 Olympic Winter Games was experienced by all—even though such arguments are used to support increased investment in high performance sport.

Weaving through these emotions were threads of a more critical and perhaps sometimes cynical view of high performance sport policy and funding. Exploring high performance sport as part of this edited work on Canadian sport policy gave me an opportunity to reflect on these tensions that define and shape my view on sport policy in general and high performance sport policy in particular. I cringe when I hear the rationale for investing in high performance sport is because it 'trickles' down to the masses and results in increased participation—yes, the visibility and success of Canadian athletes at the 2010 Olympic and Paralympic Winter Games, of athletes who came before them, and of those who will compete in the future may result in some heightened interest and registration of memberships at local clubs (if they have the capacity to respond to this demand)—but there is little evidence that investing in high performance sport to ensure podium finishes is the optimum strategy to sustain participation. We need to explore this critical issue about the value of supporting high performance sport and what shapes a successful high performance sport system—where the outcomes, as agreed upon by all those affected, are achieved and shared by all.

The review in this chapter has identified the policy and programming initiatives that have been aimed at helping athletes achieve their goals of medal performances and personal bests. But the caution here is that these policy choices reinforced by the stories of success and failure at the Vancouver 2010 Olympic and Paralympic Winter Games and the London 2012 Olympic and Paralympic Games are the 'tip of the iceberg' or the 'top of the sport pyramid.' We need to establish a stronger policy link between this highly visible aspect of sport and what lies beneath. When asked about Canada's 'flag waving' euphoria—Donald Sutherland[9] quoted the Cherokee tale of the two wolves: An old Cherokee is teaching his grandson about life. "A fight is going on inside me," he said to the boy. "It is a terrible fight and it is between two wolves. One is evil—he is anger, envy, sorrow, regret, greed, arrogance, self-pity, guilt, resentment, inferiority, lies, false pride, superiority and ego." He continued, "The other is good—he is joy, peace, love, hope, serenity, humility, kindness, benevolence, empathy, generosity, truth, compassion and faith. The same fight is going on inside you—and inside every other person, too." The grandson then asked his grandfather, "Which wolf will win?" The grandfather replied "The one you feed." Sutherland's view of Canada is that as a nation we feed and therefore characterize the latter. I would add that when you have international competitions that pit nation against nation, and where national flags are symbolic of identity, claims of 'we win' or 'we are better than you' are inevitable but hopefully temporary. But the larger question is do medals matter; to whom do they matter; and in what way should they matter to contributing to a 'better' Canada. Still relevant today, the questions raised by Justice Charles Dubin (1990) are worthy of consideration:

> Have we, as Canadians, lost track of what athletic competition is all about? Is there too much emphasis by the public and by the media on the winning of a gold medal in Olympic Competition as the only achievement worthy of recognition? (p. 515)

Just as we know that sport is not a panacea for all the social ills in society and that sport participation or development initiatives do not eradicate HIV/AIDS, poverty, crime or childhood obesity, we also know that sport can make a positive contribution to the social, physical, and psychological health of individuals and communities. So, what contribution do we want high performance sport to make to Canada and Canadians? Which 'wolf' do we feed? The one that places medals above all else as the only performance indicator of success and where the accumulation of medals is seen as a symbolic representation of global superiority, or the one where success is translated into nation building and leveraging the achievements of excellence by all our national athletes so that the passion for excellence may be nurtured and celebrated in a way that contributes to strengthening the health and well-being of Canadian communities—the places, the spaces and the people. The public value, I would argue, is in the latter—a more tangible translation of nation building, unity, cohesion and sport participation for Canadians. Because like the nuclear arms race, where the stockpiling of nuclear weapons is deemed futile, so too I would argue is the stockpiling of international medals and championships. This is the challenge for future developments in high performance sport.

Notes

1. In Canada the Long-Term Athlete Development (LTAD) model has been adopted by Sport Canada and leaders of the Canadian sport system as part of a larger initiative called Canadian Sport for Life. The *Canadian Sport for Life* resource paper details LTAD and its relevance for the Canadian sport system. A supplemental paper, *No Accidental Champions* was developed to apply LTAD for athletes with a disability. National sport organizations, Multi-sport and service organizations and the federal, provincial and territorial governments are supporting Canadian Sport

for Life/No Accidental Champions through the implementation of LTAD. It should be noted that in high performance sport circles the focus is on the LTAD model, not on 'Sport for Life.'

2. The *Best Report* (Best, 1994) identified objective performance criteria to evaluate national and multi-sport/service organizations based on what they do, who participates, and how they perform on the international stage to determine the 'eligibility' of sports and their recognition as core to Canadian society as the foundation for federal funding. By contrast, the SFAF, in maintaining these objective criteria, emphasized 'accountability,' perhaps a 'kinder and gentler' approach to achieving the same objective—reducing the number of organizations that would receive funds.

3. SFAF IV represents the fourth cycle of the framework and thus covers the period from April 2009 until March 2013.

4. Cathy Priestner Allinger was a participant in the 1972 Olympic Winter Games, a silver medalist in long track speed skating in the 1976 Olympic Winter Games and a recipient of the Olympic order. Her continued involvement in sport through coaching, volunteering, and administration included Managing Director of Sport for the Salt Lake City 2002 Olympic Winter Games, and Managing Director of Games Operations for the Turin 2006 Olympic Winter Games.

5. The stages of LTAD are: Active Start, Fundamentals, Learning to Train, Training to Train, Training to Compete, and Training to Win. It is the last three stages that are focused on the identification, training and development of high performance athletes. The ideas that provide the foundation of LTAD are not new nor did they originate in Canada. However, it is the development of a pathway that has been translated into communication, teaching and training tools for coaches, parents, administrators and athletes that defines the 'made in Canada' approach. In addition, the UK, Australia, New Zealand and the USA have all adopted the principles of LTAD.

6. Many of the issues discussed here were highlighted during the Panel Discussion entitled "LTAD: Issues, challenges, and successes" at the 2009 North American Society for the Sociology of Sport Conference held in Ottawa, ON. The panel was chaired by David McCrindle, Manager, Sport Participation Policy, Sport Canada. Panel members were Richard Way, LTAD Expert with the National Coaching Institute, Dr. Jim Denison, Associate Professor, University of Alberta, Dr. Jean Côté, Queen's University, and Alain Lefebvre, Technical Director of the Fédération de Natation du Québec [Quebec Swimming Federation]. In addition, the recent reviews by Ford et al., (2011) and Holt (2010), review some of the concerns about a lack of empirical evidence and a more comprehensive and holistic approach to athlete development.

7. For further detail on the Australian sport system see Stewart, Nicholson, Smith, and Westerbeek's book entitled, *Australian Sport: Better by Design? The evolution of Australian sport policy* published in 2004.
8. Clara Hughes donated her CA$ 10,000 medal award bonus to the Take a Hike Foundation, an alternative education program that engages at-risk youth in Vancouver.
9. During the concluding day of the 2010 Games, Ben Mulroney, an entertainment TV broadcaster with the CTV network (the Canadian Olympic broadcaster for the 2010 Olympic and Paralympic Winter Games), interviewed Donald Sutherland (a Canadian actor and narrator of a CTV Olympic Winter Games advertisement) about his view on the Games.

References

Balyi, I. (2001). Sport system building and long-term athlete development in Canada. The situation and the solutions. *Coaches Report, 8*(1), 25–28.

Best, J.C. (1994). *Report of the core sport commissioner.* Hull, QC: Minister of Canadian Heritage.

Blackburn-Evans, A. (2007). Innovative centre will take research—and Canadian athletes to the next level. *Pursuit,* Spring. Retrieved from http://www.varsitycentre.ca/wp-content/uploads/File/Pursuit_Spring_2007_20-21.pdf

Blackhurst, M., Schneider, A., & Strachan, D. (1991). *Values and ethics in amateur sport: Morality, leadership, education.* London, ON: Fitness and Amateur Sport.

Brackenridge, C. (2006). Book review essay: Youth sport refocused. *European Physical Education Review, 12*(1), 119–125.

Brisson, T.A. (2004). *Targets for athlete performance and the sport system.* Draft report submitted to the Interprovincial Sport and Recreation Council in support of the Federal-Provincial/Territorial Enhanced Excellence Priorities for Collaborative Action 2002–2005.

Brown, I. (2010, February 13). Is Canada a spoilsport? *The Globe and Mail,* pp. F1 & F6.

Brown, R.S. (2009). *Research report: Research on sports activity and sports academies: An overview.* Toronto, ON: Toronto District School Board.

Canadian Heritage. (2005). *Sport excellence strategy.* Ottawa, ON: Canadian Heritage.

Canadian Newswire. (2011, November 17). Canadian Olympic Committee announces high performance funding for Canada's athletes. *Canadian Newswire.* Retrieved from http://www.newswire.ca/en/story/879905

Canadian Olympic Committee. (2011). *2012 London.* Retrieved from http://www.olympic.ca/en/newgames/summer-olympics/2012-london/

Canadian Olympic Committee. (2011). *The Canadian Olympic Committee.* Retrieved from http://www.olympic.ca/en/about/canadian-olympic-committee/role-coc

Canadian Paralympic Committee. (2011). *About Us.* Retrieved from http://www.paralympic.ca/en/About-Us/About-Us.html

Canadian Sport Centres. (2005) *Long-term athlete development. Resource paper v. 2. Canadian sport for life.* Vancouver, BC: Author. Retrieved from http://www.pacificsport.com/Images/PDFs/LTAD_ENG_66p_June5.pdf

Canadian Sport Centres. (2009–2011). *Canadian sport for life.* http://www.canadiansportforlife.ca/

Canadian Sport for Life. (2009–2011). *Canadian sport for life, Parents.* Retrieved from http://www.canadiansportforlife.ca/default.aspx?PageID=1001&LangID=en

Christie, J. (2008, August 10). Trupish casts a lonely shadow. *The Globe and Mail.* Retrieved from http://www.theglobeandmail.com/archives/article 703356.ece

Cole, C. (2012, August 12). Canada's Olympic medal hopes fall short in London. *National Post.* Retrieved from http://sports.nationalpost.com/2012/08/12/canadas-olympic-medal-hopes-come-up-short-in-london/

Collins, D., & Bailey, R. (2013). 'Scienciness' and the allure of second-hand strategy in talent identification and development. *International Journal of Sport Policy and Politics, 5*(2), 183–191.

Comeau, G.S. (2013). The evolution of Canadian sport policy. *International Journal of Sport Policy and Politics, 5*(1), 73–93.

de Bosscher, V., Bingham, J., Shibli, S., van Bottenburg, M., & de Knop, P. (2008). *The global sporting race: An international comparative study on sports policy factors leading to international sporting success.* Oxford, UK: Meyer & Meyer Sport.

de Bosscher, V., de Knop, P., van Bottenburg, M., & Shibli, S., & (2006). A conceptual framework for analysing sports policy factors leading to international sporting success. *European Sport Management Quarterly, 6*(2), 185–215.

Donnelly, P. (2010a). Own the podium or rent it? Canada's involvement in the global sporting arms race. *Policy Options, 31*(1), 41–44.

Donnelly, P. (2010b). Rent the podium revisited: Reflections on Vancouver 2010. *Policy Options, 31*(4), 84–86.

Dryden, K. (2010). *Becoming Canada: Our story, our politics, our future.* Toronto, ON: McClelland & Stewart.

Dubin, C.L. (1990). *Commission of inquiry into the use of drugs and banned practices intended to increase athletic performance.* Ottawa, ON: Minister of Supply and Services Canada.

Ewing, L. (2008, August 13). Veteran Canadian fencer devastated over loss. *The Toronto Star.* Retrieved from http://www.thestar.com/article/477597

Federal-Provincial/Territorial Ministers Responsible for Sport, Recreation and Fitness (1985). *High performance athlete development in Canada: A delineation of responsibilities of the federal and provincial/territorial governments.* Ottawa, ON: Authors.

Ford, P., De Ste Croix, M., Lloyd, R., Meyers, R., Moosavi, M., Oliver, J., Till, K., & Williams, C. (2011). The Long-Term Athlete Development model: Physiological evidence and application. *Journal of Sport Sciences, 29*(4), 389–402.

Green, M. & Houlihan, B. (2005). *Elite sport development: Policy learning and political priorities.* New York: Routledge.

Green, M. (2007). Policy transfer, lesson drawing and perspectives on elite sport development systems. *International Journal of Sport Management and Marketing, 2*(4), 426–441.

Havaris, E.P., & Danylchuk, K.E. (2007). An assessment of Sport Canada's Sport Funding and Accountability Framework, 1995–2004. *European Sport Management Quarterly, 7,* 31–53.

Holt, N.L. (2010). Interpreting and implementing the Long-Term Athlete Development model: English swimming coaches' views on the (swimming) LTAD in Practice A commentary. *International Journal of Sports Science and Coaching, 5*(3), 421–424.

Houlihan, B. (2000). Sporting excellence, schools and sports development: The politics of crowded policy spaces. *European Physical Education Review, 6*(2), 171–193.

Jenson, J., & Saint-Martin, D. (2006). Building blocks for a new social architecture: The LEGOTM paradigm of an active society. *Policy and Politics, 34*(3), 429–451.

Kidd, B. (1988). The philosophy of excellence: Olympic performances, class, power, and the Canadian state. In P.J. Galasso (Ed.), *Philosophy of sport and physical activity: Issues and concepts* (pp. 11–31). Toronto, ON: Canadian Scholars' Press.

Lawrie, K., & Corbett, R. (2011). *OTP Evaluation 2011. Full report.* Sport Law and Strategy Group. Retrieved from http://ownthepodium.org/getattachment/d3fb916c-b3a8-4222-be1f-804803967423/OTP-Evaluation-2011.aspx

Macintosh, D., Bedecki, T., & Franks, C.E.S. (1987). *Sport and politics in Canada. Federal government involvement since 1961.* Montreal, QC & Kingston, ON: McGill-Queen's University Press.

Minister's Task Force. (1992). *Sport: The way ahead. Minister's task force on Federal Sport policy.* Ottawa, ON: Minister of Supply and Services Canada.

Mirtle, J. (2012, August 2). How Own the Podium changed everything for Canada's Olympic athletes. *The Globe and Mail.* Retrieved from http://

www.theglobeandmail.com/sports/olympics/how-own-the-podium-changed-everything-for-canadas-olympic-athletes/article4459222/

Norris, S.R. (2010). Long-Term Athlete Development Canada: Attempting system change and multi-agency cooperation. *Current Sports Medicine Reports, 9*(6), 379–382.

Oakley, B., & Green, M. (2001). The production of Olympic champions: International perspectives on elite sport development systems. *European Journal for Sport Management, 8*(Special Issue), 83–105.

Olsen, L. (2010, February 14). Canada takes an early step down in climb to 'Own the Podium'. *AOL News*. Retrieved from http://www.aolnews.com/2010/02/14/canadas-goal-to-own-the-podium-takes-an-early-step-down/

Own the Podium. (2009). *Canadian Sport Institutes*. Retrieved from http://www.ownthepodium2010.com/Initiatives/institutes.aspx

Parry, T. (2012, August, 9). Olympic success? Canada's medal haul heavy on bronze. *CBC News*. Retrieved from http://www.cbc.ca/news/world/story/2012/08/08/f-vp-parry-olympics-canada-medals.html

Priestner Allinger, C., & Allinger, T. (2004). *Own the Podium—2010: Final report with recommendations of the independent task force for winter NSOs and funding partners*. Retrieved from http://www.sportmatters.ca/Groups/SMG%20Resources/Sport%20and%20PA%20Policy/otp_report_-_final_-_e.pdf

Robertson, S., & Way, R. (2005). Long-term athlete development. *Coaches Report, 11*(3), 6–12.

Saint-Martin, D. (2007). From the welfare state to the social investment state: A new paradigm for Canadian social policy? In M. Orsini & M. Smith (Eds.), *Critical policy studies* (pp. 279–299). Vancouver, BC: University of British Columbia Press.

Savoie, D.J., (2000). *Governing from the centre: The concentration of power in Canadian politics*. Toronto, ON: University of Toronto Press.

Simonson, M.G. (2009). *Heat stroke. Why Canada's summer Olympic program is failing and how we can fix it*. Toronto, ON: Bastian Publishing Services.

Sport Canada. (2002a). *The Canadian sport policy*. Ottawa, ON: Department of Canadian Heritage. Retrieved from http://www.pch.gc.ca/pgm/sc/pol/pcs-csp/2003/polsport-eng.pdf

Sport Canada. (2002b). *The Canadian sport policy: Federal-provincial/territorial priorities for collaborative action 2002–2005*. Ottawa, ON: Department of Canadian Heritage. Retrieved from http://www.pch.gc.ca/pgm/sc/pol/actn/index-eng.cfm

Sport Canada. (2007). *The Canadian sport policy: Federal-provincial/territorial priorities for collaborative action 2007–2012*. Ottawa, ON: Department of Canadian Heritage. Retrieved from www.pch.gc.ca/pgm/sc/pol/actn07-12/booklet-eng.pdf

Sport Canada. (2012). *Canadian sport policy 2012*. Ottawa, ON: Department of Canadian Heritage. Retrieved from http://sirc.ca/CSPRenewal/documents/CSP2012_EN.pdf

Starkman, R. (2010a, May 6). Baumann in deep end as new Own the Podium boss. *The Toronto Star*. Retrieved from http://www.thestar.com/article/805864

Starkman, R. (2010b, November 21). Top sports officials to work for Russia. *The Toronto Star*, pp. A1–A2.

Stewart, B., Nicholson, M., Smith, A., & Westerbeek, H. (2004). *Australian sport: Better by design? The evolution of Australian sport policy*. Abingdon, UK: Routledge.

Thibault, L., & Harvey, J. (1997). Fostering interorganizational linkages in the Canadian sport delivery system. *Journal of Sport Management*, *11*(1), 45–68.

van Hilvoorde, I., Elling, A., & Stokvis, R. (2010). How to influence national pride? The Olympic medal index as a unifying narrative. *International Review for the Sociology of Sport*, *45*(1), 87–102.

Way, R., Repp, C., & Brennan, T. (2010). *Sport schools in Canada: The future is here*. Victoria, BC: Canadian Sport Centre, Pacific. Retrieved from http://canadiansportforlife.ca/sites/default/files/resources/Sport%20Schools%20in%20Canada.pdf

WinSport Canada. (2008). *Our story*. Retrieved from http://www.winsportcanada.ca/aboutwinsportcanada/our_story.cfm

Zussman, D. (Chair). (2009). *The 2010 and beyond panel. Final report and recommendations*. Ottawa, ON: The 2010 and Beyond Panel.

CHAPTER V

Athlete Development and Support

Lucie Thibault, Brock University and
Katherine Babiak, University of Michigan

A thletes play an important role in any sport system. Athlete development and excellence in international competitions have been central to Canada's sport system for many years (cf. Macintosh, 1996; Macintosh, Bedecki, & Franks, 1987; Macintosh & Whitson, 1990). As so aptly noted by the leaders of AthletesCAN, an organization created for athletes by athletes, "athletes are the *raison d'être* of the sport system," and as such "it is critical that the sport experience be positive for athletes" (AthletesCAN, 1994, p. 3). In fact, the concept of an athlete-centred/participant-centred sport system has been raised as an important principle for Canadian sport. For example, the original *Canadian Sport Policy* (CSP) called for a system where "athletes/participants . . . are the primary focus in the development of policies, programs, and procedures. Athletes/participants [should be] involved throughout the system in decisions that directly relate to them" (Sport Canada, 2002, p. 13). In the 2012 CSP, athletes and sport participants are identified along with a number of other stakeholders involved in Canada's sport system. In addition to athletes and participants, stakeholders include "coaches, officials, administrators, leaders, educators, sponsors, organizers, spectators and parents" (Sport Canada, 2012b, p. 5). As well, the policy framework for the 2012 CSP (outlined in Figure 1.2), clearly identifies a number of key areas that need to be considered in all aspects of Canada's sport system.

Effective stakeholder management practices encourage parties to communicate, negotiate and engage in dialogue in managing the relationship (Freeman, 2004). The key stakeholders in the Canadian sport system have varied priorities, unique interests, values, needs and expectations. In this chapter, we discuss the key stakeholders involved in developing and supporting Canadian athletes throughout their sport careers. These stakeholders include provincial and national sport organizations (PSOs and NSOs), federal and provincial governments, the Canadian Olympic Committee and other national multi-sport and multi-service organizations (e.g., AthletesCAN, Canadian Centre for Ethics in Sport, Coaching Association of Canada), corporate partners, coaches, officials and the athletes themselves. We discuss the key role of athlete stakeholders in this system and the need for their representation in decision making on issues that affect them. As stakeholder theory suggests, it is prudent to engage, prioritize and understand the needs, interests, and power and influence of the constituents affecting and affected by the policies and operations of an organization or system (Buchholz & Rosenthal, 2004). This chapter tracks and traces the evolution of the interests, legitimacy and power of various entities involved in supporting and developing athletes involved in high performance sport in Canada. The emphasis on collaboration in the *Canadian Sport Policy* (Sport Canada, 2012b) encourages the consideration of the power, legitimacy and urgency (Mitchell, Agle, & Wood, 1997) of the key stakeholders upholding this system.

In the *Canadian Sport Policy*, the importance of strengthening "co-ordination and communication among governments and key stakeholders; athlete support, coaching and technical leadership; research and innovation in training methods and equipment design; the development of qualified and ethical officials; and athlete talent identification, recruitment and development" is emphasized (Sport Canada, 2012b, p. 12). The policy document calls for "partnerships between and among sport organizations, municipalities/local governments, and educational institutions [to] align and leverage athlete, coach, and officials' development (Sport Canada, 2012b, p. 13). The purpose of this chapter is to examine programs and services that have been developed for athletes in Canada's sport system over the past 15 years. Although the focus is predominantly on federal government and national initiatives, we also examine programs and services in various areas of the country aimed at assisting and supporting athletes and their development. For the purposes of this chapter, we cover three areas: 1) athlete development programs, 2) athlete funding programs, and 3) athlete advocacy and representation.

Athlete Development Programs

Several programs have been created to assist in the development of Canadian sport participants and athletes. In the following section, we examine programs and initiatives that are being implemented at the national level to contribute to participants and athletes' development. It is important to note that national, provincial and local sport organizations have programs and services available to participants and athletes to assist them in developing various sport-specific skills and to provide them with participation and competition opportunities. In addition to these sport-specific programs and services, there are generic sport programs developed by various organizations. These programs include Canadian Sport for Life, Canadian sport centres/institutes and Own the Podium, and are explained in the following paragraphs.

Canadian Sport for Life

The first such program is a relatively new initiative developed by members of the Canadian Sport Centres (Canadian Sport Centres, 2005). It is called Canadian Sport for Life and is also known as the Long-Term Athlete Development Model.[1] The Canadian Sport for Life initiative (including No Accidental Champions for athletes with a disability) is:

> a seven-stage Canadian model of Long-Term Athlete Development (LTAD), a training, competition and recovery program based on developmental age—the maturation level of an individual—rather than chronological age. It is athlete-centred, coach driven, and administration, sport science and sponsor supported. (Canadian Sport Centres, 2005, p. 7)

Canadian Sport for Life focuses on a progression from early initiation to sport skills and sport activities, to competitive opportunities and finally to high performance sport and/or to active for life initiatives. Initial stages of Canadian Sport for Life involve the development of physical literacy among youth and ensuring children are initiated to age-appropriate skills so they can enjoy their sport experience and achieve their potential in sport participation and competition. With more children and youth initiated to sport skills, instructors and coaches can draw a larger base from which to identify talent for better regional, national and international competition. As well, a healthier introduction to acquiring sport skills may decrease dropout rates, improve safety and encourage life-long participation in sport (Canadian Sport Centres, 2005).

Stages one through three focus on the fundamental skills required to participate in sport. These stages include: *Active Start*, *Fundamentals*, and *Learn to Train*. For up-and-coming high performance athletes and for new athletes, the Canadian Sport for Life's stages four, five, and six are particularly relevant. In stage four, *Train to Train*, athletes are "ready to consolidate their basic sport-specific skills and tactics" (Canadian Sport for Life, 2009b, paragraph 1). During this stage, athletes must focus on training in order to perfect skills and develop physically. In stage five, *Train to Compete*, athletes are now ready to specialize into one sport and be introduced to competition. It is at this stage that "high volume and high intensity training begins to occur year-round" (Canadian Sport for Life, 2009a, paragraph 1). By stage six, *Train to Win*, athletes have reached the elite level and are involved in intensive training "suitable for international winning performances" (Canadian Sport for Life, 2009c, paragraph 1). The final stage, *Active for Life*, targets the entire population and encourages all Canadians to be active in sport as participants, as coaches and/or as officials (Canadian Sport Centres, 2005).

Additional details of the role Canadian Sport for Life/LTAD plays in high performance sport are provided in the previous chapter (Chapter IV). As evident in the 2012 CSP, the stages of the Canadian Sport for Life model are infused throughout four of the five policy goals (i.e., Introduction to Sport, Recreational Sport, Competitive Sport and High Performance Sport) (Sport Canada, 2012b).

While Canadian Sport for Life prepares athletes for competition from the playground to the podium, there are other programs that focus exclusively on supporting and perfecting the skills and performance of our top Canadian athletes. Two such programs, Canadian sport centres/institutes (CSCs/CSIs) and Own the Podium (OTP), are discussed in the following paragraphs.

Canadian Sport Centres/Institutes[2]

CSCs are training centres for high performance athletes. The CSCs were founded as a partnership between three organizations: Sport Canada, Canadian Olympic Committee and the Coaching Association of Canada (Babiak, 2007; Canadian Heritage, 2010a). Collectively, these founding partners work together with provincial governments and other local partners to ensure that athletes train in an environment that is conducive to perfecting their skills. As part of their mandate, the CSCs "support the achievement of high performance athletes ... [through] an enriched training environment in key locations across the country" (Canadian Heritage, 2010a, paragraph 2). In total, there are three CSCs and four CSIs. Calgary was the first centre and was established in 1994. Others locations include Montreal, Ontario (Toronto), Manitoba (Winnipeg), Saskatchewan (Regina and Saskatoon), Atlantic Canada (based in Halifax with some support in Fredericton, New Brunswick, Charlottetown, Prince Edward Island, and St. John's, Newfoundland) and Pacific (Vancouver, Victoria, and Whistler) (Canadian Heritage, 2010a). Recently, four CSCs (Calgary, Ontario, Pacific, and Quebec) were reorganized as Canadian Sport Institutes. This change to Canadian sport institutes has led to "a shift from [an exclusive] service-based model . . . to establish[ing] or exploring plans for the building and construction of sport facilities" to better serve high performance athletes (CSI Pacific, 2012, paragraph 3). In order to have the 'Institute' designation, the organizations must meet a number of criteria, among them "dedicated sport and related training areas, world-leading performance staff and a critical mass of high performance athletes and coaches to develop an environment of excellence" (Own the Podium, 2009a, paragraph 2).

Within these centres/institutes, athletes can access a number of different services that support their quest towards success in international competitions. These include services related to living (i.e., life services) and services related to training and competition (i.c., performance services). Life services consist of assistance with everyday activities such as finding accommodations for athletes who are relocating to the 'Centres/Institutes' location for training purposes, seeking affordable travel to/from training facilities, providing academic support, finding part-time work or transitioning from being a full-time athlete to undertaking a career. Performance services include strength and conditioning and access to services from the following experts: dietitians, nutritionists, sport psychologists, physiotherapists, massage therapists, physicians specializing in sport medicine and exercise specialists (e.g., physiologists, biomechanists). Centres/institutes may have facilities where athletes can access most services in one central location and/or may operate in a decentralized fashion where leaders of the centres/institutes broker a wide-ranging gamut of programs and services for their athletes. As such, centres/institutes may provide a combination of centralized and decentralized service delivery options. During an announcement of increased funds invested in the Canadian Sport Institute—Pacific (i.e., British Columbia), a ski-cross national team member, Davey Barr, explained "just the access we have is amazing, to be able to come in here at any time and not have to fight for machines [for weight training] with the general public like I have been for a while … It just makes it a lot easier to really focus on what you need to get done" (as cited in Kingston, 2010, p. C4). The level of funding invested in Canadian sport centres/institutes by Sport Canada over a period of 12 years is shown in Table 5.1.

Own the Podium

As addressed in the previous chapter (Chapter IV), Own the Podium (OTP) was created in 2005 to provide targeted investments in winter athletes and sport organizations to enhance podium success at the Vancouver Olympic and Paralympic Winter Games. A parallel program targeting summer sports called Road to Excellence was subsequently initiated in 2006. Although Own the Podium and Road to Excellence have been operating jointly under the name Podium Canada since 2006, it was not until 2009 that a realignment of operations led to both initiatives being officially subsumed under the Own the Podium initiative (Own the Podium, 2009b). As stated in its mandate, OTP "is a national sport technical initiative" to enhance Canada's rank in Olympic and Paralympic Games (summer and winter) (Own the Podium, 2010a, paragraph 12). In other words, OTP is about devising strategies and investing in athletes and sports to maximize the number of medals at Olympic and Paralympic Games. The OTP program ties this objective to the goal of 'enhancing excellence' identified in the *Canadian Sport Policy*. Its funding originates from Sport Canada, from the Canadian Olympic Committee and from corporate partners.

For many athletes, Own the Podium represents an important source of training and competition support to assist them in reaching podium results in international competitions. In its structure, OTP does not provide this assistance to all national team athletes. The targeted athletes are specifically selected because of their potential to achieve medal results in high-profile international sport events (i.e., Olympic and Paralympic Games). In 2012–2013, for example, OTP supported athletes, teams and organizations dividing its pool of funds (i.e., CA\$ 21.7M) alotted to winter sports (Own the Podium, 2013b). The athletes, teams and organizations from summer sports shared a total of CA\$ 33.7M (Own the Podium, 2013a). As one of their 'pillars of excellence,' OTP has the following goal for athlete and team excellence:

> a sufficient number of highly-motivated athletes are training and competing without compromise, and are led by world-class coaches and support teams. Canadian athletes have the best equipment, information, competitive opportunities and innovative training practices of any country leading to the achievement of their performance goals. (Own the Podium, 2010b, paragraph 4)

OTP funding for the quadrennial period leading up to the 2010 Vancouver Olympic and Paralympic Winter Games consisted of CA\$ 97.5M (Own the Podium, 2009d). This funding was earmarked for NSO Olympic and Paralympic winter sports, for Canadian Sport Centres and for OTP operations (Own the Podium, 2009d). For summer sports, OTP funding for the quadrennial period leading up to the 2012 London Olympic and Paralympic Games consisted of CA\$ 59.2M (Own the Podium, 2009c).

Although OTP has helped a number of athletes achieve success in international sport events, it has been the object of several criticisms. For example, Donnelly (2010a, p. 44) argued that the program "represents a particularly narrow strategy based on an extraordinarily narrow definition of success"—medals. In an assessment of Own the Podium's success following the Vancouver Olympic Winter Games, Donnelly (2010b) explained that even though Canada collected 14 gold medals at the Games, they won only two medals more than the previous Games in Torino in 2006, and our position in the rankings behind Germany and the United

States did not change. Furthermore, Donnelly (2010b, p. 85) noted that:

> all of the athletes who won medals in Vancouver were expected to do so; so there were no surprises. Failing to spread the wealth, and creating two classes of athletes, may have discouraged some of the team from believing that they could win. A renewed funding program should support as many athletes as possible.

Along similar lines, Brean (2010) reported on the concerns of Roger Jackson, former Chief Executive Officer of Own the Podium—referring specifically to the program's timing relative to the Vancouver Olympic and Paralympic Winter Games. Jackson explained the program "did not have enough time to guide a solid amateur up to international level . . . and so the spending was focused on athletes who were already 'in the system', and especially in sports with an already deep talent pool, such as curling and hockey" (Brean, 2010, paragraph 21).

With renewed funding from Sport Canada announced in 2010 for OTP, the strategy of identifying athletes on the cusp of international success and providing them with the best technical and coaching support to achieve their goals may lead to an increase in the number of medals won in Olympic and Paralympic Games and other international events (Canadian Heritage, 2010b). We now turn our attention to another important element tied to the success of high performance athletes in international competitions—their financial support.

Athlete Funding Programs

In Canada, high performance athletes have been able to access a number of funding sources to assist in their training, competition and living expenses. Some of these sources have also helped them cover expenses beyond their sport (i.e., education, living). In the following section, we review a number of programs developed to financially support athletes' efforts in achieving international success. This financial support originates from traditional sources (e.g., federal and provincial governments, Canadian Olympic Committee, NSOs) and from non-traditional sources (e.g., charitable organizations, corporate sponsors).

In Canada, funding initiatives for athletes started in 1970–1971 with a student athlete Grants-in-Aid program. The program was devised for athletes at the national or international level who were also full-time students. At the time, national-calibre athletes received CA$ 1,000 per year while international-calibre athletes received CA$ 2,000 per year (Health and Welfare Canada, 1972; Macintosh et al., 1987). In 1971, another funding program called Intensive Care was initiated to help fund a few athletes with the greatest potential to win medals at the 1972 Summer and Winter Olympic Games (Beamish & Borowy, 1987, 1988; Macintosh et al., 1987; Macintosh, 1996). At the time, Sport Canada and provincial governments provided the funding for Intensive Care '72. In preparation for the upcoming Olympic Games in 1976 in Montreal, a more concerted effort took place to fund athletes. The Canadian Olympic Association,[3] with subsequent financial support from the federal government, NSOs and some provincial governments (i.e., Ontario and Quebec), provided the funds for a new athlete funding initiative called Game Plan '76 (Beamish & Borowy, 1987, 1988). This program funded international-calibre athletes. Game Plan '76 would eventually become the responsibility of Sport Canada following the 1976 Olympic Games (Macintosh et al., 1987). During this time, in addition to Game Plan '76, other programs were also developed to financially assist athletes—Lost Time Payments (compensation for lost income from training and competition) and Olympic Training Support. These two programs were developed by the Canadian Olympic Association and were based predominantly on the financial needs of athletes rather than on their athletic performances (Beamish & Borowy, 1987, 1988; Macintosh et al., 1987). In 1977, Sport Canada created the Athlete Assistance Program (Fitness and Amateur Sport, 1979). Then, both the Grants-in-Aid and Game Plan programs were eventually merged in 1979 and subsumed under the Athlete Assistance Program (AAP) where Sport Canada would focus on the financial support of top athletes in Olympic and non-Olympic sports (Fitness and Amateur Sport, 1979; Macintosh et al., 1987). In the following section, we review the AAP and other programs currently offered to support athletes financially.

Federal Government Funding—Athlete Assistance Program

The most common source of funding for high performance athletes in Canada originates from federal and provincial governments.

As discussed in the previous paragraph, the federal government funds high performance athletes through the Athlete Assistance Program (AAP). Athletes who are approved for funding and are financially supported through the AAP are referred to as 'carded' athletes. The Athlete Assistance Program:

> identifies and provides funding directly to athletes who have already placed, or demonstrate the potential to place in the top 16 in the world. The AAP recognizes the commitment that athletes make to the National Team training and competitive programs provided by their NSO and seeks to relieve some of the financial pressures associated with preparing for, and participating in international sport. (Sport Canada, 2012a, p. 1–1)

In the 2011–2012 budget, nearly CA$ 27M was allocated for the AAP (Sport Canada, 2012c). Table 5.1 outlines the level of funding invested in the AAP by Sport Canada. As well, the percentage allocated to

Table 5.1 Sport Canada Funding to Athletes and Canadian Sport Centres/Institutes from 2000–2012 (CA$)[4]

Year	Total Sport Canada Budget	Athlete Assistance Program (AAP) Funding	Portion to the AAProgram in %	Canadian Sport Centres Funding
1999–2000	$ 52,895,586	$ 9,010,000	17.03%	$ 1,903,000
2000–2001	$ 82,060,618	$14,750,000	17.97%	$ 3,003,000
2001–2002	$ 97,553,404	$15,117,854	15.50%	$ 3,200,000
2002–2003	$ 79,522,155	$15,108,514	19.00%	$ 3,200,000
2003–2004	$ 89,500,000	$15,200,000	17.00%	$ 3,400,000
2004–2005	$121,735,422	$19,845,324	16.30%	$ 7,448,000
2005–2006	$133,241,616	$24,800,000	18.61%	$10,409,357
2006–2007	$138,302,344	$25,300,000	18.29%	$ 7,033,722
2007–2008	$136,558,878	$25,345,868	18.56%	$ 7,677,295
2008–2009	$151,350,728	$26,518,955	17.52%	$ 8,173,022
2009–2010	$160,113,348	$26,426,161	16.50%	$ 8,718,805
2010–2011	$197,105,538	$25,820,645	13.10%	$15,217,803
2011–2012	$198,908,005	$26,913,932	13.53%	$14,676,333
2012–2013	$210,793,641	$27,366,946	12.98%	$15,614,796

high performance athletes relative to total Sport Canada contributions is presented.

More than 1,900 athletes participating in over 80 sport disciplines are funded through this program (Canadian Heritage, 2012; Sport Canada, 2012a). It is important to note that only athletes who participate in high performance sport programs that "are financially supported by Sport Canada following the successful completion of the Sport Funding and Accountability Framework (SFAF) process" receive funding (Sport Canada, 2012a). Since 2004, eligible high performance athletes receive CA\$ 1,500 per month (senior card) or CA\$ 900 per month (development card) based on their performance in international competition and the stage at which they are in their athletic career (Sport Canada, 2012a; Thibault & Babiak, 2005). The AAP also provides financial assistance for tuition support ("CA\$ 5,000 per carding cycle up to a lifetime maximum of CA\$ 25,000" (Sport Canada, 2012a, p. 8–1)) for athletes attending Canadian universities and/or colleges. In addition, special needs assistance is available (up to CA\$ 18,000 per carding cycle) (Canadian Heritage, 2012). Special needs include "excellence living and training allowance, excellence child dependent allowance, training and competition allowance for athletes with a disability, relocation assistance, child care assistance and retirement assistance" (Sport Canada, 2012a, p. 8–4). In a Government of Canada fact sheet, officials claim that since the inception of the program in 1977, over CA\$ 292M has benefited 10,556 athletes (Government of Canada, 2010).

On the topic of Sport Canada's AAP funding, Peel (2010), a former high performance athlete and an advocate for athletes for many years, argued:

> one of the greatest needs of athletes is access to adequate resources to support excellence. World-class Canadian athletes are eligible to benefit from the Athlete Assistance Program (AAP) . . . The AAP provides a tax-free monthly stipend as well as various financial and training supports, including post-secondary tuition. This allocation is of great benefit to athletes, but is rarely adequate. (p. 29)

As a condition of receiving AAP funding, athletes must sign an agreement with their NSOs. This agreement "sets down in writing the rights, responsibilities and obligations of the athlete and the

NSO" (Sport Canada, 2012a). It specifically addresses various elements, among them:

- Benefits available to the carded athlete through his or her NSO;
- The NSO's obligations;
- The athlete's obligations, including a commitment to follow an agreed-upon training and competitive program;
- Any other commitments to the NSO that the carded athlete is required to make (for instance, time, promotional activities or financial commitments);
- The agreement's duration (not to exceed one carding year). Specific Sport Canada and NSO policies the carded athlete must abide by, including the following:
  — The Canadian Policy Against Doping in Sport in effect;
  — The Canadian Anti-Doping Program;
  — The NSO's anti-doping policy;
  — AAP policies and procedures;
  — Federal government sport policy regarding competitions where participation is not permitted; and
  — Completion of the AAP anti-doping education module as requested and available on the Canadian Centre for Ethics in Sport website.
- The hearing and appeal procedure that will be used in any dispute between the carded athlete and the NSO;
- Details, if applicable, of the carded athlete's trust fund;
- The lead time for the publication of the NSO approved AAP compliant carding criteria. (Sport Canada, 2012a, p. 7–1)

According to Peel (2010, p. 29), these agreements "restrict athletes' abilities to determine their own paths by requiring athletes to attend predetermined competitions and training camps." As well, "the agreements usually include giving up the intellectual property in his or her image for the benefit of the NSO" (Peel, 2010, p. 29). On this topic of athlete/NSO agreements, Findlay and Ward (2006) noted:

> The main vehicle for establishing relations between athletes and their national sport organizations (NSOs) has been the athlete agreement. These agreements originated over two decades ago as a way to formalize the terms and conditions of the

government-funded athlete assistance program (AAP), which provided modest stipends to athletes to offset training costs. These agreements specified the respective obligations of the carded athlete and his or her sport organization and addressed details such as conduct, doping and training commitments, and largely followed a standard template. More recently . . . these standard agreements have begun to morph into full-fledged commercial contracts of 60 to 70 pages. Thus added to the basic athlete agreement is now a commercial transaction between the athlete and the sport organization over the athlete's image rights. In many cases, these agreements have called upon athletes to relinquish these rights to the sport organization, while in other cases the parties have achieved a delicate balancing act between the right of the athlete to exploit his or her image, and the right of the sport organization to derive its own commercial benefit to offset the costs it incurs providing programs for athletes. (paragraphs 4–5)

Setting aside the issue of athlete/NSO agreements, the AAP has received both praise and criticism from the athletes. As outlined in the *2009 Status of the High Performance Athlete* report, most athletes (80%) "agree that the AAP has made it possible to achieve higher levels of athletic performance" (Ekos Research Associates, 2010, p. 55). In fact, the largest proportion of athletes' annual income originated from the AAP at an average amount of CA\$ 12,136 (Ekos Research Associates, 2010). Several athletes surveyed (50%) however, felt that the funds received from the AAP were insufficient and 47% believed that AAP funding came too late in their athletic career (Ekos Research Associates, 2010). As outlined in this report, Sport Canada's AAP is one of many sources of direct funding to high performance athletes. In the following paragraphs, other sources of direct funding for athletes are presented.

Provincial Government Funding

The AAP has been replicated in most provincial and territorial governments. Several provincial and territorial governments developed funding programs for their own athletes. These provincial/territorial athlete assistance programs vary extensively in the level of funding and the selection criteria for athletes to receive funding. In some provinces, lottery funds are used to support athletes (e.g., British

Columbia Athlete Assistance Program; Nova Scotia Sport4Support program; Quest for Gold—Ontario Athlete Assistance Program; Saskatchewan Future Best; Northwest Territories High Performance Athlete Grant Program).

As an example, the Quest for Gold—Ontario Athlete Assistance Program provides financial assistance to Ontario athletes to encourage them to stay and train in the province. The program offers two different funding cards: the Canada Card and the Ontario Card. Canada Cards provide 'top up' for Ontario athletes who already receive funding from Sport Canada's AAP. Athletes in this category receive CA$ 6,000/year (Sport Canada's AAP Senior Card) or CA$ 3,600 per year (Sport Canada's AAP Development Card). The Ontario Cards target junior athletes who are identified as individuals likely to achieve national level competition. These junior athletes may receive full funding at CA$ 7,106 per year or half-funding, CA$ 3,553 per year. In the 2011–2012 fiscal year, a total of 1,229 athletes from 51 sports were funded through the Ontario funding program (Cooper, 2012, personal communication, October 22, 2012; Ontario Ministry of Health Promotion, 2009). In another example, New Brunswick's Athlete Assistance Program provides five different tiers of funding (ranging from CA$ 500 to CA$ 6,000) (Government of New Brunswick, 2012a, 2012b). In 2012, 88 athletes from New Brunswick received funding from this program (Government of New Brunswick, 2012b). For the Northwest Territories High Performance Athlete Grant Program, there are three levels of funding, gold, silver, and bronze. For the gold level, athletes may receive up to CA$ 15,000 per year in funding assistance. For the silver level, funding support is up to CA$ 10,000 per year and for the bronze level, athletes may receive up to CA$ 5,000 per year. In the 2011–2012 fiscal year, a total of 34 NWT athletes received funding (Government of Northwest Territories, 2009, 2011). In the 2009 Status of the High Performance Athlete report, average yearly funds received by athletes from provincial government sources were CA$ 3,490—an amount considerably inferior to Sport Canada's AAP at CA$ 12,136 (Ekos Research Associates, 2010).

Canadian Olympic Committee—Athlete Excellence Fund

In addition to Sport Canada's AAP and provincial government athlete assistance programs, athletes may also obtain funding from the Canadian Olympic Committee (COC). In 2007, the COC announced its Athlete Excellence Fund (Canwest News Service, 2007). The COC Athlete Excellence Fund is "an athlete support and reward program that . . . provide[s] Canadian athletes with performance awards of CA\$ 20,000, CA\$ 15,000 and CA\$ 10,000 for winning Olympic gold, silver or bronze medals. It . . . also provides funding of CA\$ 5,000 during non-Olympic years" to the top five Canadian athletes (Canadian Olympic Committee, 2010a, paragraph 1). For the first time, in 2008 the COC rewarded Canadian athletes who won medals at the Beijing Olympic Games. The COC allocated a total of CA\$ 515,000 to 34 medalists (Canadian Olympic Committee, 2010a). Following the 2010 Olympic Winter Games, the COC awarded CA\$ 1.7M to the athletes who collectively were responsible for Canada's 26 medals at these Games (Canadian Olympic Committee, 2010a). Just prior to the 2012 London Olympic Games, the COC extended the Athlete Excellence Fund to financially reward the coaches of Olympic medalists. The program is entitled the Coaches Reward Program and provides CA\$ 10,000 to the coach of a gold medalist, CA\$ 7,500 to the coach of a silver medalist, and CA\$ 5,000 to the coach of a bronze medalist (Canadian Olympic Committee, 2012).

It is important to note that the COC Athlete Excellence Fund and the Coaches Reward Program apply only to Olympic athletes and their coaches. Paralympians and their coaches do not have the same opportunities for earning financial rewards for medals obtained at the Paralympic Games. This situation led to some discussion following the Beijing Games about the unequal treatment of Paralympians (Handfield, 2008). The Canadian Paralympic Committee argued that it simply did not have the funds to undertake a similar reward program for its medalists.

In addition to the Athlete Excellence Fund, the COC through its charitable arm, the Canadian Olympic Foundation (COF), generates funds to support high performance athletes across winter and summer Olympic sports. Among the COF's most prominent fundraising initiatives, the Red Mitten campaign was launched in 2009 for the 2010 Vancouver Olympic Winter Games. In its first year, the Red Mitten campaign raised more than CA\$ 14M with sales exceeding 3.5 million pairs (Associated Press, 2011). Gold Medal Plates is another important fundraising event for the COF. Gold Medal Plates was created in 2003 as cross-Canada culinary competitions to celebrate "excellence in cuisine, wine, the arts and athletic achievement" (Gold Medal Plates, 2010, paragraph 1). These competitions include the participation of top Canadian chefs, members of the wine industry, food critics, Olympic and Paralympic athletes, sport officials and media.

In the following paragraphs, we address two other sources of funding for athletes: the Canadian Athletes Now Fund and B2ten, two charitable organizations that financially support high performance athletes.

Canadian Athletes Now Fund

The Canadian Athletes Now Fund (CAN Fund)[5] was created in 1997 by Jane Roos. The impetus for creating the CAN Fund was drawn largely from Roos's former role as heptathlete (Blatchford, 2010; Christie, 2009). When her athletic career ended, she decided to become a "fundraiser for financially struggling athletes on their Olympic [and Paralympic] journey" (Christie, 2009, p. S1). Since its inception, the CAN Fund has raised more than CA$ 11M to assist hundreds of athletes with grants of CA$ 6,000, which can be awarded up to twice a year (CAN Fund, 2012a, 2012b, 2012c). As explained in their mission statement, CAN Fund is:

> devoted solely to raising funds and awareness of our Canadian athletes . . . We provide our athletes with the opportunity to focus on success instead of focusing on unnecessary financial hurdles. Donations go directly to Canadian athletes so they can afford proper nutrition, better equipment, coaching, travel to competitions and training camps and basic living expenses. (CAN Fund, 2012b, paragraph 1)

On discussions of the CAN Fund, Peel (2010, p. 28) remarked that:

> athletes flock to support Jane Roos's Canadian Athletes NOW Fund. Jane gives funds to aspiring Olympians and Paralympians, no strings attached. One of her major sources of revenue is from athlete donations (athletes supporting athletes). Jane has no bureaucracy and no systems to support. She trusts athletes to know what they need to succeed.

B2ten

B2ten was created in 2005 by Olympic athletes, Dominick Gauthier, Jennifer Heil and business executive J. D. Miller, as "a privately funded, not for profit organization that supports Canadian elite athletes" (B2ten, 2010b, paragraph 1). The level of support includes financial resources, expertise, support services and technology to enhance athletes' chances to succeed in international competitions (B2ten, 2010b). In a newspaper article praising the efforts of the business community's involvement in supporting athletes, Starkman (2008, p. S1) wrote "the program provides services and goods to try to complement what already exists and generally recruits athletes who are on the cusp of an international breakthrough but might be short of resources." In early 2010, B2ten was supporting 24 athletes, 20 of which were expected to compete in the Vancouver Olympic Winter Games (B2ten, 2010b); a total of 14 of these athletes medaled at these Games (B2ten, 2010a). In 2012, B2ten was supporting 37 athletes (23 athletes from summer sports and 14 from winter sports) (B2ten, 2012). While CAN Fund raises donations from individuals and corporate sources, B2ten is funded by private donors who believe that they can play an important role in the success of Canadian athletes by providing them with the means to reach their goals in international sport.

Other Funds

Other sources of funding for athletes include NSOs or other national organizations. For example, some NSOs provide funding support to their athletes (e.g., Canadian Ski Coaches Federation—Alpine Canada Alpin Athlete Bursary Fund; Alpine Canada Alpin Win 2010. ca; Dressage Canada Levy Program; Skate Canada's Athlete Fund). The level of funding from NSOs is relatively low when compared to federal and provincial government sources. In fact, in the *2009 Status of the High Performance Athlete* report, athletes surveyed reported an average yearly income of CA\$ 843 from their NSOs (Ekos Research Associates, 2010).

In addition to NSOs' athlete funding programs, a number of initiatives have been undertaken by corporate Canada to financially assist athletes. For example, Petro-Canada's "FACE [Fuelling Athlete and Coaching Excellence][6] program provides 50 up-and-coming pre-carded athletes and coach pairings with an CA\$ 8,000 grant" to assist these athletes in their quest for success in high performance sport (Petro-Canada, 2013). Since 1988, FACE has provided over 2,300 athletes and coaches with financial support of over CA\$ 8M (Petro-Canada, 2013). Another example of funding support for athletes by corporate Canada is the Investors Group and their Amateur Athlete Bursary Fund. Created in 2000, Investors Group collaborates with AthletesCAN to award 20 bursaries of CA$ 5,000 each to top Canadian senior national team athletes. So far, Investors Group has provided more than CA$ 1.3M to athletes since the beginning of the program (AthletesCAN, 2010b). Other examples of corporate programs funding Canadian athletes include RBC (Royal Bank Canada) Olympians Program, Rona Growing with Our Athletes, and Team Visa.

As a novel and alternative source of funding and fundraising opportunity, crowdfunding has recently gained popularity for anything from small businesses, events, or individuals with an idea who want financial support in launching their initiative. Crowdfunding is the collective co-operation of individuals who pool their money/resources via the Internet to support innovations and ideas created by other people or organizations. Some of the top crowdfunding websites, such as *Kickstarter*, have seen tremendous success. In 2012, the *Kickstarter* platform supported "2,241,475 people who pledged a total of US$ 319,786,629.00 to successfully fund 18,109 projects" (Mott, 2013, paragraph 6).

In sport, an international crowdfunding website called *Sportfunder* helps amateur athletes and sport organizations around the world raise funds via 'the crowd' to help them pursue their goals. In Canada, a new crowdfunding vehicle called *Pursu.it* "enables Canadian athletes to set up their own funding campaign. Campaigns can raise money for everything from the purchase of a new track bicycle, travel to their next competition, or support for altitude training in a remote part of the world" (Springwise, 2012, paragraph 2). *Pursu.it*, launched in 2012 by five Canadian Olympic athletes, works by allowing an athlete to set up their own campaign with a video and description to inspire people to donate. They set a funding goal and time limit and spread the word to friends, family and members of the public. As of December 2012, *Pursu.it* athletes had raised more than CA$ 63,000 from 31,000 donors (Casey, 2013). This new innovation, while still in its infancy, has tremendous potential for providing financial support to Canadian athletes in the future.

Even though we have demonstrated a number of sources of funding for high performance athletes in Canada, for the most part, many of Canada's high performance athletes have expressed concerns about the level of funding they receive to serve unofficially as Canadian ambassadors in international competition. As outlined in the *2004* and *2009 Status of the High Performance Athlete* reports, athletes believe more financial support is needed. In the 2004 report, athletes called for greater levels of recognition and financial support (Ekos Research Associates, 2005, p. 92). In the most recent version of the report, athletes' yearly revenues were well below their expenses leading to a shortfall of approximately CA$ 10,000 (Ekos Research Associates, 2010). As noted by the executive director of AthletesCAN, "sport is expensive at the national team level . . . There has been great strides at the national team level by way of Own the Podium financing that came through for certain sports and for certain athletes. But certainly it doesn't speak to the broad spectrum of need and expenses within the national team athletic community" (The Canadian Press, 2010, paragraphs 6–7).

Although AAP funding has increased over the years (the last increase in monthly stipends to athletes occurred in 2004 after the Athens Olympic and Paralympic Games) and athletes have acknowledged the value of funding in assisting their training and competitive endeavours, there are still concerns that funding is not adequate (Thibault & Babiak, 2005). If athletes are to represent Canada on the international stage, then perhaps the level of financial support they receive from various sources (i.e., Sport Canada, COC, CPC, NSOs) should be increased.

Although financial support of athletes is an important element of the sport system, advocacy and representation are also important for the well-being of athletes. In the following section, athlete advocacy and representation are addressed.

Athlete Advocacy and Representation

Recent developments in Canada's sport system have resulted in better representation, fairness and advocacy for athletes. One of the organizations initiated by athletes for athletes was created in 1992. At the time, it was called Canadian Athletes Association and was renamed AthletesCAN in 1996 (Thibault & Babiak, 2005). The organization was created by a number of athletes under the leadership of Ann Peel, a race walker and an advocate for athletes' rights (Canadian Television Network, 1995; The Ottawa Citizen, 1999; Thibault & Babiak, 2005). As reported by Thibault and Babiak

(2005, p. 117), "as a lobby group representing high performance athletes' interests, leaders of AthletesCAN were able to exercise pressure on politicians and bureaucrats and on sport organizations." Peel (2010, p. 25) explained that the mandate of AthletesCAN "was to work with others in leadership, advocacy and education to ensure a fair, responsive and supportive sport system for athletes. In doing so, we were committed to accountability, equity, inclusiveness and mutual respect." Peel (2010, p. 25) also noted that AthletesCAN's strategy was to address athletes' major concerns such as "funding (the Athlete Assistance Program of Sport Canada), legal rights (fair selection, discipline and dispute resolution procedures), communication, leadership and self-marketing skills." AthletesCAN often argued for a more athlete-centred sport system calling for greater involvement of athletes in the governance of sport organizations.

In a 1994 report, leaders of AthletesCAN wrote "those responsible for leadership and decision-making in sport must include the athlete in both defining the needs and goals and in determining how to meet them; i.e., the athlete should be the *active subject* in, not the object of, sporting programs" (AthletesCAN, 1994, p. 3). In the report, elements of an athlete-centred system were identified. One of these elements is accountability, where "the sport system is accountable to its consumers—the athletes and to the membership of sport organizations" (AthletesCAN, 1994, p. 5). Other elements included as part of an athlete-centred system consist of respect, empowerment, equity/fairness, excellence and mutual support to name a few.

On the topic of representation, the report on the *Status of the High Performance Athlete in 2004* noted that athletes were aware of AthletesCAN, but their impression of AthletesCAN's impact on issues that affected them was moderate (Ekos Research Associates, 2005). In the subsequent research undertaken in 2009, 30% "were not able to rate their satisfaction with the representation of AthletesCAN" while 44% "rated their satisfaction as moderate" (Ekos Research Associates, 2010, p. 53). This suggests an apparent disconnect between AthletesCAN's perceptions of its own efforts and those formed by practicing athletes.

AthletesCAN's mandate to represent the interests of athletes has remained constant over the years and became an integral facet of the Canadian sport landscape as Peel (2010, p. 27) noted:

AthletesCAN is now over 15 years old. It is part of the sport system in Canada, and no longer fights for legitimacy. Perhaps because it is now so firmly entrenched in the system, it is no longer an activist organization.

Some current examples of AthletesCAN initiatives include an advocacy campaign to increase direct funding to athletes to match cost-of-living increases over the past six years, as well as efforts to enhance athletes' focus on social responsibility and giving back (AthletesCAN, 2010a).

In addition to AthletesCAN, some provincially focused organizations are now being created to provide a voice for their athletes, such as the British Columbia (BC) Athlete Voice. The BC Athlete Voice was established in 2005, and its mandate is "to ensure [athletes] have the opportunity to become leaders and advocates in sport and in the community" (BC Athlete Voice, 2009, paragraph 1).

Although athletes are increasingly gaining opportunities for advocacy, Peel (2010) expressed concerns that they are still not equal partners or stakeholders in the system. Simonson (2009) made similar claims in his work. Although there may have been some movement toward increasing athletes' involvement in the decision- and policy-making processes of their NSOs regarding issues that affect them, there is still evidence that athletes' issues are not fully addressed.

Some recently formed organizations have been established to assist athletes in other ways. Two such organizations are the Sport Dispute Resolution Centre of Canada and the Canadian Centre for Ethics in Sport. The focus of these organizations is discussed in the following paragraphs. The Sport Dispute Resolution Centre of Canada (SDRCC) was formally established in 2004 to assist in the area of disputes among stakeholders involved in sport. The "timely resolution of disputes in sport" was a founding policy principle in Bill C-12, *An Act to Promote Physical Activity and Sport*, which came into effect in March of 2003. To this end, the SDRCC has been working to prevent or reduce sport-related disputes and foster a culture of fairness in Canadian sport. The organization also provides tools to assist sport stakeholders to address disputes and to educate them about strategies to minimize the incidence of disputes in sport. In its 2011–2012 fiscal year, the SDRCC dealt with "a total of 47 new cases . . . including 6 carding [AAP] appeals, 8 team selection disputes and 27 asserted doping violations" (Sport Dispute Resolution Centre of Canada, 2012, p. 1). Based on a review of the SDRCC's Annual Reports, the organization has addressed a total number of 371 cases over years fiscal years (for the period covering 2003–04 to 2011–12) with an average of 41 cases per year. As Thibault and Babiak (2005, p. 113) noted, SDRCC contributed to a more athlete-centred sport system in Canada by providing athletes "with a new formal and legitimate channel to voice their concerns and have these concerns addressed outside of their national sport federations by an impartial group."

The Canadian Centre for Ethics in Sport is another organization that addresses important advocacy issues for athletes and coaches as well as the ethical dimensions of participation and governance of sport. For instance, the organization seeks to stimulate understanding and fairness in the areas of equal playing time, gender issues, multiculturalism in sport, athletes with disabilities, sport nutrition, bullying, and codes prohibiting certain conduct in sport—particularly in the area of doping and performance enhancing substances. In fact, in their 2011–2012 annual report (CCES, 2012), the CCES discusses the impact they have made regarding the education of over 25,000 Canadian athletes about making the right choices in sport (i.e., principles of True Sport, rules and procedures of anti-doping). As explained in CCES's annual report, the organization contributes "in three interconnected ways to fair, safe and open sport" (CCES, 2012, p. 3) in Canada's sport system. Central to their mission is "protecting the integrity of sport . . . work on preventing doping and other ethical issues by helping to activate a principle-driven sport system at all levels" and "advocating and facilitating an ethical orientation and approach to all issues in sport" (CCES, 2012, p. 3). CCES is also responsible for managing the Canadian Anti-Doping Program, and within this program the organization collected a total of 2,600 samples during the 2011–2012 fiscal year (CCES, 2012).

Conclusion

As central stakeholders in Canada's sport system, athletes have an important role to play in its governance. Although several changes have occurred in recent years to ensure an athlete-centred system, there are still improvements that could be made. Kihl, Kikulis, and Thibault (2007, p. 24) argued that Canada's sport system had "become more athlete-centred through the adoption of a more deliberative and democratic policy process"; however, they also noted that "deliberations involving athletes, or athlete representatives [were] often limited and/or expedited rather than judged as a critical component to enhancing the quality and value of decisions and policies."

This chapter has revealed the tensions and challenges in prioritizing objectives and engaging with stakeholders in a national sport system. Issues related to allocation and levels of funding, development, support and decision making require collaborative involvement in the Canadian sport system—with stakeholders (such as athletes) who have not traditionally been part of the discussions on issues affecting them. Balancing and prioritizing stakeholder interests is a difficult task, yet one which allows for a broader set of interests to be represented (Buchholz & Rosenthal, 2004). This approach will ultimately allow for a broader representation of constituents who have a voice in national sport strategies and policies. However, it must be noted that stakeholder salience in the Canadian sport system has shifted over time and may also be cyclical (e.g., in the months before an Olympic Games, athletes may receive more attention and focus with respect to their ability to perform as it relates to the resources allocated to them and thus they may have more legitimacy—and urgency—in the conversation as key stakeholders; similarly, federal government agencies such as Sport Canada who control the purse strings, may have more power prior to the hosting of an Olympic Games, as was the case when Canada hosted the 2010 Olympic and Paralympic Winter Games). Thus, a conversation on athlete support and development must necessarily consider the broad array of constituents and interests and will be useful in the development of guidelines on how to evaluate which groups of stakeholders deserve or require attention and priority over competing claims (Boesso & Kumar, 2009).

While there has been a considerable increase in funding commitments for sport by the federal government, non-profit sport organizations, and corporations leading up to and following the Vancouver 2010 Olympic and Paralympic Games, ongoing support for Canada's high performance athletes is still needed (Blatchford, 2010; Ekos Research Associates, 2010; Starkman, 2008). In their study of high performance athletes in Canada, researchers from Ekos Research Associates noted that athletes often leave their athletic careers because of insufficient support (financial and technical). Given the extent of resources invested in developing these athletes to reach international results and the important role they play in being ambassadors of Canada in high-profile sport events, their support is central to their success and longevity in the sport system.

Notes

1. Even though Canadian Sport for Life and Long-Term Athlete Development are officially the same initiative, when sport leaders refer to the Long-Term Athlete Development Model, they are usually focusing on high performance sport and the strategies needed to achieve it (e.g., skill acquisition, talent identification, training principles and access to competitions). When sport leaders discuss Canadian Sport for Life, they are usually referring to sport for all and lifelong participation in sport.
2. Some Canadian Sport Institutes (Calgary, Ontario, Pacific) were formerly called Canadian Sport Centres (cf. CSI Ontario, 2012; CSI Pacific, 2012). Quebec's high performance training centre was called *Centre national multisport Montréal* and is now called *Institut national du sport du Québec* (INS Québec) (cf. INS Québec, 2013).
3. In April 2002, the Canadian Olympic Association changed its name to the Canadian Olympic Committee.
4. Data for this table were obtained from Sport Canada's funding reports published online at http://www.pch.gc.ca/pgm/sc/cntrbtn/index-eng.cfm
5. The original name of the Canadian Athletes Now was 'See You In Sydney.' For subsequent Olympic and Paralympic Games, Sydney was replaced with the location of these Games (i.e., See You In ... Salt Lake, Athens, Turin, Beijing and Vancouver). In 2004, the Canadian Olympic Committee contested through the judicial system that Roos's organization's name was violating an official mark of the COC. In essence, the COC believed that Roos's charity's name was "creating an authorized commercial association with the Olympics" (Lee, 2007, paragraph 13). The courts ruled in favour of Roos's organization and ordered the COC to pay Roos's legal costs (Lee, 2007).
6. The FACE program was originally called the Olympic Torch Scholarship Fund (Canadian Olympic Committee, 2010b).

References

Associated Press. (2011, September 29). Canadian Olympic Committee revives red mitten campaign. CBC Sports. Retrieved from http://www.cbc.ca/sports/olympics/summersports/story/2011/09/29/sp-coc-mittens.html

AthletesCAN. (1994, September). Athlete-centred sport. Discussion paper. Retrieved from http://www.athletescan.com/Content/Publications.asp

AthletesCAN. (2010a). AthletesCAN calling on the government to increase the budget of the Athlete Assistance Program (AAP). Retrieved from http://www.athletescan.com/content/Calling-on-Government-to-increase-AAP/Info-for-Calling-on-the-Government-to-increase-APP.asp?langid=1

AthletesCAN. (2010b). Team Investors Group Amateur Athletes Fund. Retrieved from http://www.athletescan.com/Content/Programs%20and%20Services/00%20Investors%20Group.asp?langid=1

B2ten. (2010a). Athletes 2010 results. Retrieved from http://b2ten.ca/en/about-us/athletes-results.html

B2ten. (2010b). What is B2ten. Retrieved from http://b2ten.ca/about

B2ten. (2012). Athletes. Retrieved from http://b2ten.com/en/athletes/summer-athletes.html and http://b2ten.com/en/athletes/winter-athletes.html

Babiak, K. (2007). Determinants of interorganizational relationships: The case of a Canadian nonprofit sport organization. *Journal of Sport Management, 21*(3), 338–376.

Beamish, R., & Borowy, J. (1987). High performance athletes in Canada: From status to contract. In T. Slack & C.R. Hinings (Eds.), *The organization and administration of sport* (pp. 1–35). London, ON: Sport Dynamics.

Beamish, R., & Borowy, J. (1988). *Q. What do you do for a living? A. I'm an athlete.* Kingston, ON: The Sport Research Group, Queen's University.

Blatchford, C. (2010, February 23). Own the Podium's aims only half of the issue. *The Globe and Mail.* Retrieved from http://v1.theglobeandmail.com/servlet/story/LAC.20100223.OLYBLATCH23ART2314/TPStory/TPSports/

Boesso, G., & Kumar, K. (2009). An investigation of stakeholder prioritization and engagement: Who or what really counts. *Journal of Accounting and Organizational Change, 5*(1), 62–80.

Brean, J. (2010, February 26). Owning the podium comes with a steep price. *National Post.* Retrieved from http://www.cbc.ca/olympics/blogs/postblog/2010/02/owning-the-podium-comes-with-a-steep-price.html

British Columbia Athlete Voice. (2009). What is BC Athlete Voice? Retrieved from http://www.bcathletevoice.ca/Content/BCAV-Info/About-BCAV.asp

Buchholz, R.A., & Rosenthal, S.B. (2004). Stakeholder theory and public policy: How government matters. *Journal of Business Ethics, 51*(2), 143–153.

Canadian Athletes Now Fund (2012a). FAQ. Retrieved from http://www.canadianathletesnow.ca/about-us/faq.html

Canadian Athletes Now Fund. (2012b). Mission Statement. Retrieved from http://www.canadianathletesnow.ca/about-us/mission-statement.html

Canadian Athletes Now Fund. (2012c). Our History. Retrieved from http://www.canadianathletesnow.ca/about-us/our-history.html

Canadian Centre for Ethics in Sport (2012). *Celebrating 20 years. Annual report 2011–2012.* Retrieved from http://www.cces.ca/files/pdfs/CCES-AR-2011-2012-E.pdf

Canadian Heritage. (2010a). Canadian Sport Centres. Retrieved from http://www.pch.gc.ca/pgm/sc/csc-eng.cfm

Canadian Heritage. (2010b, May 18). News release: Government of Canada announces Own the Podium advisory board. Retrieved from http://www.pch.gc.ca/pc-ch/infoCntr/cdm-mc/index-eng.cfm?action=doc&DocIDCd=CGL100359

Canadian Heritage. (2012, October 5). Harper government announces improvements to Athlete Assistance Program. Newsroom. Retrieved from http://www.pch.gc.ca/eng/1349360990560

Canadian Olympic Committee. (2010a). Programs: Athlete Excellence Fund. Retrieved from http://www.olympic.ca/en/programs/athlete-excellence-fund/

Canadian Olympic Committee. (2010b). FACE program helps Canadian athletes and their coaches dream big for 2010. Retrieved from http://www.olympic.ca/en/news/petro-canada-fuels-olympic-size-dreams-50-developing-athletes/

Canadian Olympic Committee. (2012, November 8). Olympic medallist coaches rewarded. Media Release. Retrieved from http://olympic.ca/photo-releases/olympic-medallist-coaches-rewarded

Canadian Press, The. (2010, June 29). It's expensive being a high-performance amateur athlete. *The Globe and Mail.* Retrieved from http://www.theglobeandmail.com/sports/more-sports/its-expensive-being-a-high-performance-amateur-athlete/article1623461/

Canadian Sport Centres. (2005) *Long-term athlete development. Resource paper v. 2. Canadian sport for life.* Vancouver, BC: Author. Retrieved from http://canadiansportforlife.ca/sites/default/files/resources/CS4L%20Resource%20Paper.pdf

Canadian Sport for Life. (2009a). Athletes and coaches: Train to compete. Retrieved from http://www.canadiansportforlife.ca/default.aspx?PageID=1017&LangID=en

Canadian Sport for Life. (2009b). Athletes and coaches: Train to train. Retrieved from http://www.canadiansportforlife.ca/default.aspx? PageID=1016&LangID=en

Canadian Sport for Life. (2009c). Athletes and coaches: Train to win. Retrieved from http://www.canadiansportforlife.ca/default.aspx? PageID=1018&LangID=en

Canadian Sport Institute Ontario. (2012). Our history. Retrieved from http://csiontario.ca/web_page/who_we_are_b.php

Canadian Sport Institute Pacific. (2012). Canadian Sport Institute Network. Retrieved from http://www.cscpacific.ca/content/About/OurNetwork/ CSCNetwork.asp

Canadian Television Network. (1995, February 14). W-Five. Documentary on Canada's sport system and athlete funding. Toronto, ON: Canadian Television Network.

Canwest News Service. (2007, December 31). Olympic medals worth their weight in cash: Amateur sports year in review. Retrieved from http://www.canada.com/vancouversun/news/story.html?id=3637b3cb-ae16-49ce-8c6d-6189e3a763d8&k=36762

Casey, Q. (2013, January 2). It takes a crowd: Olympians use donation site to fund training. *Financial Post*. Retrieved from http://www.thestar phoenix.com/sports/takes+crowd/7763945/story.html#ixzz2Hpa9MSHV

Christie, J. (2009, January 14). Canadian sports: The power list 2009: 30. They're not all Canadians, but they wield enormous power and influence in much of what you see, hear or cheer for in Canadian sport. Keep your eyes on these individuals in the next 12 to 15 months—from the Winter Games to TV, these folks are making their mark. *The Globe and Mail*, p. S1.

Donnelly, P. (2010a). Own the Podium or rent it? Canada's involvement in the global sporting arms race. *Policy Options, 31*(1), 41–44.

Donnelly, P. (2010b). Rent the podium revisited: Reflections on Vancouver 2010. *Policy Options, 31*(4), 84–86.

Ekos Research Associates. (2005). *Status of the high performance athlete in 2004. Final report.* Ottawa, ON: Author. Retrieved from http://www.athletescan.com/Content/Publications.asp

Ekos Research Associates. (2010). *2009 Status of the high performance athlete. Final report.* Ottawa, ON: Author. Retrieved from http://www.pch.gc.ca/ pgm/sc/rpts/rpt-eng.pdf

Findlay, H., & Ward, B. (2006, October 13). Increased commercialization of athletics requires sophisticated athlete agreements. *Lawyers Weekly*. Retrieved from http://www.lawyersweekly.ca/index.php?section=ar ticle&articleid=363

Fitness and Amateur Sport. (1979). *Fitness and Amateur Sport Annual report 1977/1978.* Ottawa, ON: Minister of Supply and Services Canada

Freeman, R.E. (2004). The stakeholder approach revisited. *Zeitschrift für Wirtschafts und Unternehmentsethik, 5*(3), 228–241.

Gold Medal Plates. (2010). GMP Overview. Retrieved from http://www.goldmedalplates.com/overview.html

Government of Canada. (2010). Athlete Assistance Program: Supporting our athletes since 1977. Retrieved from http://canada2010.gc.ca/mmedia/kits/fch-10-eng.cfm

Government of New Brunswick. (2012a). New Brunswick Athlete Assistance Program Guidelines. Retrieved from https://www.pxw1.snb.ca/snb7001/e/1000/CSS-FOL-19-0022E.pdf

Government of New Brunswick. (2012b, July 16). News releases. Provincial government providing funding to high-performance athletes. Retrieved from http://www.pcnb.ca/en/news/news_releases/provincial_government_providing_funding_to_high-performance_athletes/

Government of Northwest Territories. (2009). Northwest Territories High Performance Athlete Grant Program. Municipal and Community Affairs. Retrieved from http://www.assembly.gov.nt.ca/_live/documents/documentManagerUpload/09-10-29%20NWT%20High%20Performance%20Athlete%20Grant%20Program.pdf

Government of Northwest Territories. (2011, December 9). High performance athlete grants awarded. News release. Retrieved from http://news.exec.gov.nt.ca/high-performance-athlete-grants-awarded/

Handfield, C. (2008, 18 septembre). Cinq médailles d'or, zéro bourse. *La Presse*. Retrieved from http://www.paraquad.eznetportals.com/web/site/nouvelles/2008/sept08/jeuxparal5or0bourse

Health and Welfare Canada. (1972). *Fitness and Amateur Sport Directorate Annual report 1971–1972*. Ottawa, ON: Minister of National Health and Welfare.

Institut national du sport du Québec. (2013). *Institut national du sport du Québec* (INS Québec). Retrieved from http://insquebec.org/fr/accueil

Kihl, L.A., Kikulis, L.M., & Thibault, L. (2007). A deliberative democratic approach to athlete-centred sport: The dynamics of administrative and communicative power. *European Sport Management Quarterly, 7*(1), 1–30.

Kingston, G. (2010, September 28). Whistler training centre earns $1.3m boost; Increased funding will ensure winter and summer athletes can access Canadian Sport Centre. *The Vancouver Sun*, p. C4.

Lee, J. (2007, April 21). See you in court: Charity wins trademark fight with Vanoc. *The Vancouver Sun*. Retrieved from http://www.canada.com/vancouversun/news/business/story.html?id=f1fc0d77-84c8-45d4-ad5b-8539a4c2ae93

Macintosh, D. (1996). Sport and government in Canada. In L. Chalip, A. Johnson, & L. Stachura (Eds.), *National sports policies. An international handbook* (pp. 39–66). Westport, CT: Greenwood Press.

Macintosh, D., Bedecki, T., & Franks, C.E.S. (1987). *Sport and politics in Canada. Federal government involvement since 1961.* Montreal, QC & Kingston, ON: McGill-Queen's University Press.

Macintosh, D., & Whitson, D. (1990). *The game planners. Transforming Canada's sport system.* Montreal, QC & Kingston, ON: McGill-Queen's University Press.

Mitchell, R.K., Agle, B.R., & Wood, D.J. (1997). Toward a theory of stakeholder identification and salience: Defining the principle of who and what really counts. *Academy of Management Review, 22*(4), 853–886.

Mott, E. (2013, January 12). Crowdfunding campaigns and sites are popping up everywhere. *Search Engine Watch.* Retrieved from http://searchenginewatch.com/article/2235916/Crowdfunding-Campaigns-and-Sites-are-Popping-Up-Everywhere

Ontario Ministry of Health Promotion. (2009, November 13). Quest for Gold—Ontario Athlete Assistance Program. Presentation made to the Petro-Canada Sport Leadership Conference. Retrieved from http://www.coach.ca/sportleadershipsportif/2009/e/presentations/documents/A5_Ozorio_HPSupport_OntarioE.pdf

Ottawa Citizen, The. (1999, December 15). Peel walked the walk, talked the talk: Citizen century countdown reaches no. 71 series: Year 2000. *The Ottawa Citizen,* p. B2.

Own the Podium. (2009a). Canadian Sport Institutes. Retrieved from http://www.ownthepodium2010.com/Initiatives/institutes.aspx

Own the Podium. (2009b, June 8). Press release: Canadian summer and winter sport excellence initiatives realign under Own the Podium. Retrieved from http://www.cscpacific.ca/content/MediaCentre/PressReleases.asp?ItemID=73979

Own the Podium. (2009c). Summer NSO excellence funding per quadrennial. Retrieved from http://www.ownthepodium2010.com/Documents/Summer%20NSO%20Historical%20Funding.pdf

Own the Podium. (2009d). Winter NSO excellence funding per quadrennial. Retrieved from http://www.ownthepodium2010.com/Documents/Winter%20NSO%20Historical%20Funding.pdf

Own the Podium. (2010a, August 24). News release: Own the Podium adds two key members to summer and winter high-performance teams. Retrieved from http://www.ownthepodium2010.com/News/

Own the Podium. (2010b). Pillars of excellence. Retrieved from http://www.ownthepodium2010.com/About/objectives.aspx

Own the Podium. (2013a). Summer sports 2012–2013. Retrieved from http://ownthepodium.org/Funding/Summer-Sports-2012-2013.aspx

Own the Podium. (2013b). 2012–2013 Winter sports 2012–2013. Retrieved from http://ownthepodium.org/Funding/Winter-Sports-2012-2013.aspx

Peel, A. (2010). The athletes as Sisyphus: Reflections of an athlete advocate. *Sport in Society, 13*(1), 20–31.

Petro-Canada. (2013). Fuelling Athlete and Coaching Excellence (FACE™). Retrieved from http://www.petro-canada.ca/en/olympics/1102.aspx

Simonson, M.G. (2009). *Heat stroke. Why Canada's summer Olympic program is failing and how we can fix it.* Toronto, ON: Bastian Publishing Services.

Sport Canada. (2002). *The Canadian sport policy.* Ottawa, ON: Department of Canadian Heritage. Retrieved from http://www.pch.gc.ca/pgm/sc/pol/pcs-csp/2003/polsport-eng.pdf

Sport Canada. (2012a). Athlete Assistance Program. Policies and procedures. Retrieved from http://www.pch.gc.ca/DAMAssetPub/DAM-sptCan-canSpt/STAGING/texte-text/aap-paa_1349455626133_eng.pdf?WT.contentAuthority=13.0

Sport Canada. (2012b). *Canadian sport policy 2012.* Ottawa, ON: Canadian Heritage. Retrieved from http://sirc.ca/CSPRenewal/documents/CSP2012_EN.pdf

Sport Canada. (2012c). Sport Canada contributions report 2011–2012. Retrieved from http://pch.gc.ca/pgm/sc/cntrbtn/2011-12/index-eng.cfm

Sport Dispute Resolution Centre of Canada. (2012). Overview of the report on operations for 2011–2012. Retrieved from http://www.crdsc-sdrcc.ca/eng/documents/SDRCC_2011-AR-Condensed-Eng_web.pdf

Springwise. (2012, October 23). Canada's future sports stars are offered funding help through site. Retrieved from http://www.springwise.com/lifestyle_leisure/site-enables-fans-fund-early-careers-canadas-sports-stars/

Starkman, R. (2008, November 28). B2ten could have the formula for Olympic medals; Program helps top-level Canadian athletes with equipment and support. *The Toronto Star,* p. S1.

Thibault, L., & Babiak, K. (2005). Organizational changes in Canada's sport system: Toward an athlete-centred approach. *European Sport Management Quarterly, 5*(2), 105–132.

CHAPTER VI

Sport Participation

Peter Donnelly, University of Toronto

[By 2012] A significantly higher percentage of Canadians from
all segments of society are involved in quality sport activities
at all levels and in all forms of participation.
Canadian Sport Policy (Sport Canada, 2002, p. 4)

In some ways, it is intriguing to write a chapter on 'sport participation' for a book on *Sport Policy in Canada* when Canada does not
have a specific policy on sport participation. In fact, the only policy
that is directly concerned with participation is Sport Canada's *Policy
on Aboriginal People's Participation in Sport* (2005). Of course, many
documents recognize the importance of participation, and in the
Canadian Sport Policy (Sport Canada, 2002) that was in effect from
2002–2012, 'participation' was given equal status to 'excellence.'
However, as outlined in the this chapter, the lack of formal policy
dealing specifically with participation provides an indication that the
federal government was more concerned with excellence than with
participation, and may help to account, in part, for the relatively low
levels of sport participation in Canada.

Participation in sport and recreational physical activity is still
often thought of as fun—the joy of movement and the pleasure of
sociality. However, starting some 150 years ago, participation also
began to be about something else. The middle class, Victorian,
rational recreation movement began to take a more functionalist or

instrumental view of participation—a view that quickly spread to British colonies such as Canada. Middle class values were imposed on sport and recreation in an attempt to accomplish two ends: (a) *social control*, to encourage respectable and 'civilized' behaviour when many of the activities of the working classes and the gentry involved drinking, gambling and rough pursuits; and (b) *self improvement*, in terms of health, fitness, education and character. Activities became productive, imbued with middle-class values such as rationality, purpose, respectability and, in the case of competitive sports, meritocracy.

Urban spaces for public participation began to be made available by local governments and philanthropists. These parks and playgrounds were regulated spaces, sometimes supervised and with many proscriptions on permissible forms of participation. Public provision of opportunities to participate has increased significantly since Victorian times, but the rationale for provision is still justified in terms of rational recreation—people should be involved because sport and recreational physical activity are good for them, and for society. The aims of *self improvement* and *social control* are still fundamental to the provision of opportunities to participate.

In Canada today, formal/organized opportunities to participate in sport and recreation have four main sources of provision—the educational system; clubs (with various levels of inclusion/exclusion in their membership policies); the commercial sector (including non-profit organizations such as the YMCA/YWCA); and various levels of government. This chapter considers the more recent strategies and trends to encourage involvement/participation in sport and recreational physical activity, examines the ongoing tension in terms of public funding for high performance sport *versus* grassroots participation, reviews the evolution and goals of the recent Sport Participation Strategy (including the development of the Sport Participation Research Initiative), discusses issues regarding the monitoring and measurement of participation among Canadians and the ongoing decline in rates of participation, and concludes by considering the potential effects of the new *Canadian Sport Policy* (Sport Canada, 2012) on sport participation in Canada.

From Recreation and Fitness to Active Living[1]

Local governments' Parks and Recreation departments (often in partnership with non-profit sport clubs and, more recently, non-profit providers such as the YMCA/YWCA) and public educational institutions are still the main providers of opportunities to participate in sport and recreational physical activity in Canada. Their involvement is governed by policies to determine access and provision and, in the case of education, by curricular and extra-curricular policies. However, all discussions of sport policy in Canada begin with the 1961 *Fitness and Amateur Sport Act* (Bill C-131, discussed in Chapter I). With this Act, Canada joined a worldwide, post-war trend of governments in high-income countries acknowledging that sport and recreation were now appropriate aspects of public policy and spending. In Canada, the Act was conceived to deal primarily with hockey and the international sport performances of Canadians, and to a lesser extent with the fitness of Canadians. Federal government involvement in mass sport and recreation was always considered to be problematic in two ways: first, mass sport, recreation and health/ fitness were considered to be matters of provincial jurisdiction; and second, there was little political gain from promoting mass sport and recreation participation.

Sport Canada, Fitness Canada, Recreation Canada, and Sport Participation Canada

The 1969 *Report of the Task Force on Sports for Canadians* recommended the establishment of Sport Canada as a non-profit organizational and administrative centre to develop high performance sport, leaving the Fitness and Amateur Sport Directorate (established by the *Fitness and Amateur Sport Act*) to deal with mass sport, fitness, and recreation (Rea, 1969). While numerous re-organizations occurred during the 1970s, Sport Canada continued to grow as a government unit under the Ministry of National Health and Welfare; Recreation Canada and Fitness Canada were finally established as separate branches in 1979, and in 1980 Recreation Canada was dissolved.

While many European countries were beginning to see sport and recreation participation as the right of all citizens and incorporated 'sport for all' into their national sport legislation, Canada continued to focus primarily on hockey and high performance sport. There were concerns about this narrow focus, and, to add to the limited and divided powers of the Fitness and Amateur Sport Directorate, Sport Participation Canada was established as an arm's length agency in 1971; the agency quickly became known by its motto, 'ParticipACTION'. ParticipACTION gave focus to the population health concerns, using publicity campaigns and public service announcements to educate Canadians about the benefits of participation in sport, exercise and recreational physical activity, and to motivate them to participate. MacNeill (1999) documented the problems with ParticipACTION, and it is not clear whether the campaign had any effect on increasing participation among Canadians. However, it was the closest Canada ever came to the now world-wide Sport for All movement.

The Canadian government was a signatory to the first international document declaring the right to participate in sport. The UNESCO International Charter of Physical Education and Sport (1978, paragraph 15) gave focus to the Sport for All movement; the first Article states: "The practice of physical education and sport is a fundamental right for all." However, while many European countries were enshrining that right for their citizens with policies, legislation and a widespread campaign of public facility-building (e.g., sport centres, pools, playing fields), Canadian governments (i.e., federal, provincial, local) never declared sport participation as a right for Canadians, and it is now widely acknowledged in Canada that there has not been a widespread campaign of sport facility-building since the Centennial (1967).

Despite these differences, the participation trend line in Canada shows a similar curve to those for a number of European countries in the second half of the twentieth century, and into the first decade of the twenty-first century. The S-shaped curves show steep increases in sport participation between the 1960s and the 1980s (accounted for in large part in Canada by the massive growth of sport programs for children and youth), followed in the 1990s by a flattening of growth and, in the case of Canada, a quite significant decline (as noted subsequently). Participation has been high in Scandinavia and northern Europe and relatively low in southern Europe—Canada falls between these extremes—but the S-shaped trend in participation is similar for a number of countries (van Bottenburg, Rijnen, & van Sterkenburg, 2005). These similarities suggest that government policies may have less influence on sport participation than other forces such as demographic change (e.g., aging population, immigration). Two major trends that have affected sport participation since the 1970s are *differentiation* and *commercialization*.

Differentiation

The growth of sport worldwide in the second half of the twentieth century led some German scholars to extend the figurational concept of sportization (Elias & Dunning, 1986) to refer to the "sportization of society" (*versportlichung der gesellschaft*; e.g., Cachay, 1990; Digel, 1990). This was accomplished with two quite distinct trends. In the first, traditional organized competitive sports shook off the old constraints of amateurism, combined the ideals of Olympism and professionalism, and emerged as a "global sport monoculture" (Donnelly, 1996) or, more precisely, a "global achievement sport monoculture" (Maguire, 1999). This occurred under the influence of processes such as commercialization, globalization, professionalization, scientization and specialization (Crum, 2001). Participation increased as a result of the emerging achievement-oriented (competitive and high performance) sport development systems, eventually slowing where selection and talent identification systems became more sophisticated.

The second trend has sometimes been referred to as the 'de-sportization of sport.' Influenced by the less formal and more permissive youth cultures that began to emerge in the 1960s, there has been a widespread growth of 'sports' and physical activities characterized by their lack of formal structure and competition:[2]

> In these sports—as diverse as jogging, surfing, rock climbing, mountain biking, snowboarding, rafting, skateboarding, paragliding, aerobics, and street dance—most people participate without the need of a formal club structure or competitive environment. They do not desire to move up to a higher level. They are motivated by having fun, experiencing nature, seeking adventure, socializing with friends, achieving body effects (improvements to one's physique) or health improvement. (van Bottenburg & de Bosscher, 2011, p. 602)

This trend democratized participation to population segments that were less likely to participate in achievement sports. It was crucial to the success of the Sport for All policies and, despite the absence of a formal Sport for All policy in Canada, the growth in participation during the 1970s and 1980s was, to a great extent, fuelled by the growth of these more informal and often non-competitive activities.

Commercialization

The growing interest in informal forms of participation, combined with the failure of all levels of government to provide enough opportunities to meet that growing interest, saw the growth of commercial-sector provision, beginning in the 1980s, in high-income countries worldwide. This was most evident in the areas of fitness and exercise, but it also encompassed the growth of ski resorts and golf courses, and significant increases in the production of specialized equipment and clothing for all sports and recreational physical activities.[3] The commercial sector also began to grow in achievement sports, with both specialized equipment and (in Canada, for example) a significant increase in the number of specialized private camps, schools and academies for the development of specific sport skills.

Involvement of the commercial sector provides a strong indication of the demographics of participation. Participants in sport, exercise and recreational physical activity include younger people rather than older people, men more than women, ethnocultural majorities rather than minorities and, above all, those in a higher social class (in terms of income, education and occupational status). The commercial sector became involved because those more likely to participate could afford their services. MacNeill's (1999) critical analysis of ParticipACTION pointed out that messages encouraging people to be more active were targeted precisely to those population segments that were already more likely to participate.

Active Living

While ParticipACTION provided positive messages about participation in sport and recreational physical activity, the emerging concept of 'active living' made a more direct connection between participation and population health, and represented a real attempt to overcome the evident failure of the medicalized/prescriptive model of exercise. Despite the fact that medical professionals, fitness specialists (including Fitness Canada), exercise scientists and public service announcements (e.g., ParticipACTION) had been advising Canadians that they had to exercise regularly, for a specific period of time at a specific intensity (e.g., between three and five times a week at 60 to 90% maximal heart rate for 15 to 60 minutes or longer) in order to experience any health benefits from exercise, the majority of the population was not achieving these targets. The message of 'active living' was more moderate and claimed to be more accessible and appealing by including the activities of everyday life (active transportation, housework and gardening, using stairs and so on) in an exercise regimen.

'Active living' was part of an overall shift during the 1980s from 'sport development' to 'development through sport.' In Europe, specific under-participating populations were targeted by new policies, and the values of *rational recreation*, which had never really disappeared, returned in force. Participation in sport and recreational physical activity became a policy tool for the achievement of health benefits and other non-sport objectives such as reducing juvenile delinquency, and achieving social inclusion and community building. Although there was awareness in Canada of the various potential non-sport benefits of participation, and small localized attempts to initiate such programs, the main policy focus was on health. *Active Living* is a Canadian construct that first emerged at the 1986 Canadian Summit on Fitness. Bercovitz (1998) argued that the Summit:

> marked (publicly) the beginning of Fitness Canada's shift away from program and service provision toward a strategic leadership, facilitating and facilitative role. Responsibility for direct program delivery was to fall within the jurisdiction of the provinces, municipalities, associations and the private sector. (p. 320)

The federal and provincial/territorial (F-P/T) governments affirmed the primacy of the provinces and territories with regard to recreation and sport participation in the *National Recreation Statement* developed in 1987 (Interprovincial Sport and Recreation Council, 1987); however, that agreement recognized that the federal government had "a clear and necessary [cooperative] role" in recreation and mass sport participation (Sport Canada, 2008), despite having dissolved Recreation Canada in 1980.

The 'active living' trademark was officially adopted in 1989, and after implementing a national infrastructure under the Administration Bureau for Active Living, Active Living Canada was officially inaugurated in 1992 as a non-profit organization run by a board of directors (that included representatives of Fitness Canada and ParticipACTION). As with the European campaigns, Active Living targeted specific populations and began to be incorporated into employee fitness programs.

Despite the good intentions associated with advocating a more accessible means of being active rather than the former prescriptive regime, and despite a clear raising of consciousness about the benefits of being active, Active Living also seems to have had only a short-lived effect on increasing participation. In many ways, Active Living and the other 'sport for development' policies were a clear representation of the neo-liberal era ushered in by Margaret Thatcher, Ronald Reagan and Brian Mulroney in the early 1980s. Responsibility for fitness was de-centralized, and the social responsibility for fitness and health was downloaded from government to the individual in a policy that fetishized terms such as 'lifestyle,' 'empowerment,' 'community,' and 'collaboration' (Bercovitz, 1998). As Ingham (1985) asked:

> what shall we say to the victims of the fiscal crisis of the Welfare State? What do we have to offer the currently ill and the about-to-be-ill segments of the population; those whose illnesses have more to do with the workplace rather than lifestyle, with the ravages of unemployment rather than defects of character, with the cumulative effects of impoverishment which is becoming increasingly feminized? Shall we say that they should aerobicize, jazzercise, and jog their problems away? (p. 54)

It is striking that the launch of Active Living was followed in 1993 by "the most significant downsizing and restructuring of government ever undertaken in Canada" (Office of the Prime Minister, 1993). Among others, the position of Minister of State for Fitness and Amateur Sport was abolished, Sport Canada was moved to Canadian Heritage, and Fitness Canada became a small part of the Health Programs and Services Branch of Health Canada.

As noted, Canada skipped the Sport for All phase of participation policy but still experienced increases in participation from the 1960s into the 1980s. The absence of Sport for All in some ways permitted Canada to be ahead of the trend in European countries in terms of 'sport for development,' with however an exclusive focus on health. According to the General Social Survey, participation in Canada peaked in 1992, with some 45% of the population over the age of 15 claiming that they participated in organized sport regularly during the previous year.[4] It is striking that, following the introduction of policies that limited Sport Canada's focus to high performance sport, marginalized Fitness Canada and downloaded federal government responsibility for all forms of non-elite participation, there has been a precipitous decline in participation since 1992. The subsequent General Social Surveys showed that participation declined to 34% in 1998 and 28% in 2005. This decline raised some clear concerns but, as noted subsequently, little in the way of government re-assuming responsibility for increasing participation.

The Great Divide

As suggested in the previous section, the federal government, Sport Canada, many national sport organizations (NSOs) and a number of provincial (e.g., Quebec, British Columbia) governments and sport organizations (PSOs) have focused their attention, and funding, on high performance sport. Just as the failure to implement Sport for All policies permitted Canada to be ahead of the trend in Europe in terms of 'sport for development' (specifically, ParticipACTION and Active Living), the absence of Sport for All policies also helped to give Canada a lead in the development of high performance sport policies. After failing to win any gold medals at the Montreal Olympic Games (1976), Sport Canada and a number of NSOs began to learn from the successful Eastern European systems of high performance development. The systems put in place in Canada were so similar to those in Eastern Europe that MacAloon (1990) referred to the Canadian sport system as "the Big Red Machine."[5] The system stalled in 1988, with the Ben Johnson doping scandal at the Seoul Olympic Games and the subsequent Dubin inquiry, and Canada winning a total of only 15 medals at the Winter (Calgary) and Summer Olympic Games that year. However, the high performance system quickly rebounded in the 1990s with a total of 25 medals in 1992, and 35 medals at the 1994 Winter (Lillehammer) and 1996 Summer (Atlanta) Olympic Games.[6]

During the Cold War, between the 1950s and 1990, many of the battles between the protagonists (the United States and the Soviet Union) and their satellites (mainly Canada and some Western European countries for the US; Eastern European countries for the USSR) were fought in terms of sport supremacy at the Olympic Games and world championships.[7] With the end of the Cold War, countries such as Australia and a number of Western European countries also shifted their focus to join more fully the 'global sporting arms race' (the struggle between countries to win Olympic and world championship medals) and began to outspend Canada in terms of high performance sport development. Canada fell back to 29 medals in the following two Olympiads (1998/2000 and 2002/2004) but rebounded sharply following substantially increased spending to win 42 medals in 2006/2008, and 44 in 2010/2012 (including a record number of gold medals in Vancouver 2010).

The key term here is 'spending.' As Donnelly (2010a) pointed out, Olympic medals cost a great deal of money.[8] Given that there is a finite amount of federal (and provincial) funding available for sport, investments in high performance sport and in hosting major events have certainly been made at the cost of grassroots participation. For example, Bercovitz (1998, p. 325) used Fitness and Amateur Sport annual reports from 1971 to 1993 to document the growing strength of Sport Canada in comparison to Fitness Canada. Funding allocations to Sport Canada during the 1970s exceeded those for Fitness Canada between 3:1 and 5:1; during the 1980s, the ratio was between 6:1 and 8:1; and by the early 1990s, the ratio ranged between 7:1 and 9:1. By 1992/1993, Sport Canada received a government allocation of CA\$ 72,162,084 while Fitness Canada received an allocation of CA\$ 9,823,289—a 7:1 ratio that was actually closer than the two preceding years (9:1 and 8:1 respectively).

Investing in high performance sport and the achievement of medal winning performances, and hosting major sport events are favoured by the federal government, and even provincial governments, because they command media attention in a way that mass participation never does, and because governments claim the positive effects of medal winning and hosting on national pride and international prestige. Government spending is also justified with the "convenient fictions" (Donnelly, 2010b) that medal winning performances *inspire* increased sport participation, and that the facilities built to host major sport events will be available for subsequent mass participation. Coalter (2004), Donnelly et al. (2008), Hogan and Norton (2000), Murphy and Bauman (2007) and others have all shown that there is very little substance to the widespread view that winning medals has a trickle-down effect that increases participation (finding, in some cases, that participation in a sport actually decreases after the success of national team athletes). Donnelly et al. (2008) have specifically argued that, while inspiration may occur, inspiration is not enough if a sport does not have the capacity, infrastructure and incentives to accommodate new 'inspired' recruits to the sport. McCloy (2006, see also Chapter VIII) has also shown that facilities constructed in Canada for major sport events are often turned over to professional teams after the event, reserved for high performance athletes or closed because of the costs of maintenance. Only in rare cases do they become available to the public for mass participation (e.g., the Calgary Olympic Oval) and then often at the cost of substantial user fees—the public pays to construct the facilities, and then pays to use them.

Some, such as Canadian Sport for Life, still claim that mass participation sport and high performance sport are inextricably linked *via* the 'pyramid'—the idea that a broad base of participation is necessary in order to discover, and develop through the ranks, talented athletes who will be recruited to the high performance sport system. However, the systems of talent identification and selection developed since the 1960s in Eastern Europe, and now widely used in countries involved in the 'global sporting arms race,' avoid the need and expense for a broad base of participation to feed the peak of the pyramid. Individuals who show talent in sports with well-established elite development systems are selected out from mass participation in order to train and participate in a separate system. If they continue to develop, this system leads to success in professional and/or international sport. In countries such as Cuba and China the system is relatively meritocratic, with children from all classes of society being identified and recruited on the basis of their talent. However, in neo-liberal societies such as Canada, the UK, and the US, with little public support for sport in schools and communities, parents are expected to fund the development of talented athletes (e.g., travel, equipment, instruction, and other costs) until they become eligible for other forms of government or National Olympic Committee support. Consequently, high performance athletes are drawn from a narrower and narrower segment of the population. In an extreme example, private school students in Britain constitute between 7 and 8% of the school population, but it is estimated that some 65% of the British Olympic team in 2012 will have gone to private school.

Other distortions appear in sport systems such as that in Canada where a significant public financial investment has been made into winning Olympic medals. For example, Canada and many other countries in the 'global sporting arms race' have begun to focus their efforts on individual sports—especially those such as swimming, track and field, cycling and boxing, where multiple medals are available. Only two gold medals (men's and women's) are available in team sports, and the rationalization of efforts to win medals results in team sports being starved of funding and other forms of support. Given the nature of individual sports, support actually goes to fewer and fewer athletes, with consequent limitations on participation. Focus on individual sports has the potential to become even more specialized—Christie (2010, p. S7) pointed out, with respect to track and field, "Kenyan dominance in distance events, Jamaican prowess in sprints, [and] Scandinavian and Eastern bloc power in throws." He went on to cite Canadian hurdler, Perdita Felicien: "Every country has picked what they're good at. In Canada we're not even remotely close to being a powerhouse. In hurdles, we're good but we need to have a supporting cast" (Christie, 2010, p. S7).

A further consequence of the distortions introduced by a single-minded focus on medals is high levels of funding for sports in which very few people are able to participate. A recent Australian report (*Crawford Report*, 2009) pointed out that more government funds were spent on archery (an Olympic sport with a relatively small number of Australian participants, but where a number of medals are awarded) than cricket (a national team sport, but not an Olympic sport). Joint public–private funding initiatives such as Own the Podium (OTP, in Canada) contribute to such extreme specialization, providing additional funding not just to sports where Canada is perceived to have a chance of winning a medal, but to specific athletes in those sports. According to OTP, the sliding sports (bobsled, skeleton, luge) received CA\$ 2.87M in OTP additional funding (over and above their usual levels of funding) in the year leading up to the Vancouver 2010 Olympic Winter Games. There are probably fewer participants in the sliding sports in Canada than there are in archery in Australia; but that level of funding needs to be compared with funding for a mass participation sport. For example, the annual budget for Basketball Canada is approximately CA\$ 3M.

Donnelly et al. (2008) have pointed out the need to support high performance athletes and, through strategic policy and planning, to also support mass participation sport. They proposed ways to achieve both, but current thinking tends to focus on high performance and the achievement of medals, despite the continuing decline in participation. As R. Gruneau (personal communication, April 29, 2010) and

Donnelly (2010b) pointed out, "the more medals we win, the fewer Canadians participate in sport" (Figure 6.1).

Evolution of the Sport Participation Strategy

Sport Canada's *Sport Participation Strategy 2008–2012* noted that: "The *National Recreation Statement*, the CSP [*Canadian Sport Policy*] and the *Act* [*Physical Activity and Sport Act*] provide the legislative and policy framework for Sport Canada's role in sport participation" (Sport Canada, 2008, p. 3). It is striking that, of these three documents, only the *National Recreation Statement* (1987) deals directly with mass sport and physical activity participation and recreation, identifying them as a 'social service,' conceding primacy in those areas to the provinces/territories ("Recreation in Canada, in common with other social services, lies within the jurisdiction of provinces") and reserving a supporting and co-ordinating role for the federal government (Interprovincial Sport and Recreation Council, 1987). The policy (Sport Canada 2002) in effect until 2012 and the legislation (Parliament of Canada, 2003) that governs Canadian sport at the time of writing both deal with the sport system as a whole, in particular attempting to resolve the struggles and disparities noted in the previous section. They give equal status to the two goals of

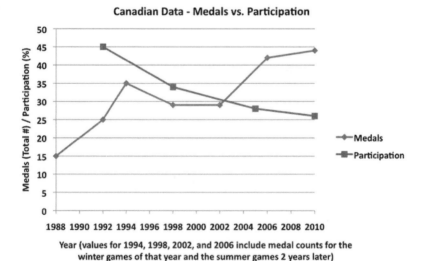

Figure 6.1 Canadian Sport Participation Levels and Medals Won in Olympic Games

Canadian sport—*participation* and *excellence*. The *Physical Activity and Sport Act* (Parliament of Canada, 2003, p. 3) is intended: "to increase *participation in sport* [and] support *excellence* in sport." The intent of the policy and legislation is clear: the two goals are to find a way to work together to create a seamless Canadian sport system. Unfortunately, for too long the relationship between the two goals has been at worst antagonistic, and at best one-way (with high performance sport often recruiting and taking fees from participation sport but providing little in return).

Van Bottenburg and de Bosscher (2011, p. 607) reminded us that sport policies do not develop independently of other social processes and policies, that there is a great deal of borrowing from other national sport policies,[9] but also that the policies and:

> processes have worked out differently in each country so that
> the sports development policy and its impact on sports participa-
> tion exhibit unique characteristics as well. The literature gives
> the impression that this (difference in) impact is particularly
> determined by the balance of power between the state, market
> and society in the sports sector, and—more specifically—the
> capability of national, provincial and local authorities, commer-
> cial agencies, schools and universities, and the voluntary sport
> organizations to influence the sports policy making process at
> the national level, and contribute to the provision and develop-
> ment of sport at the local level.

They also pointed out the importance of "critical junctures in the history of national sport policies." As noted, Canada's founding sport policy (*Fitness and Amateur Sport Act*) emerged during the Cold War, at a time when ongoing losses to the Soviet Union in Olympic and world championship ice hockey took on added significance. During the Trudeau years (1970s), pan-Canadian unification concerns were added to the need to achieve success in international sport, and the Canada Games became part of the high performance sport development system.

Given that Canadian sport policy was born and sustained in a policy climate that favoured high performance sport, the 1988 doping scandal became the first major 'critical juncture' for that policy. Analyses of the Dubin inquiry (1988–1989; Dubin, 1990), and the subsequent Sport Canada report, *Sport: The Way Ahead* (Minister's

Task Force, 1992), show that despite the fact Canada could have used the scandal to turn away from the strong emphasis on high performance sport in order to focus more on participation, that never happened.[10] The new emphases were to be on ethical, more equitable and athlete-centred high performance sport. As noted previously, Canada rebounded from the scandal to achieve its highest medal totals to that time in the 1992 Olympiad (25) and the 1994–96 Olympiad (35). "Choices made during these critical junctures . . . close off alternative options and lead to the establishment of institutions that generate self-reinforcing path-dependent processes" (Capoccia & Kelemen, 2007, p. 361).

With Fitness Canada marginalized to a relatively small branch in Health Canada, primacy for sport and recreational physical activity ceded to the provinces, and a relatively strong Sport Canada with staff, systems and procedures reinforced in their focus on high performance sport and working within a restrictive definition of sport that precluded exercise and most forms of recreational physical activity (including sports played recreationally),[11] it is not surprising that Canada reached the millennium without a policy on sport participation. However, two events occurred to change that situation: first, the 1998 General Social Survey showed that sport participation in Canada had declined to 34%, from 45% of the population in 1992; second, a series of cross-country consultations were held in preparation for the new *Canadian Sport Policy* (Sport Canada, 2002). During these consultations, the sport establishment in Canada heard clearly from a wide segment of the population that there were concerns about declining participation, that broad-based participation was important, that provinces/territories (and municipalities) were not living up to their part of the 1987 *National Recreation Statement* and that far more support was needed in order to increase sport participation across the country.

As noted, the resulting policy (*Canadian Sport Policy*) gave equal status to the two 'goals' of "enhanced participation" and "enhanced excellence," (along with "capacity building" and "interaction" as supporting goals) (Sport Canada, 2002), and the supporting legislation, Bill C-12 an *Act to Promote Physical Activity and Sport* (Parliament of Canada, 2003), affirmed the equality of "participation" and "excellence." However, Sport Canada's "self-reinforcing, path-dependent processes" were difficult to change. Three main responses were evident initially: first, a small administrative unit was established in Sport Canada to deal with sport participation. Of the other two responses, one is apparently cosmetic, and the other has the potential to assist in achieving enhanced participation. These are discussed in turn below.

Sport Funding and Accountability Framework

The Sport Funding and Accountability Framework (SFAF) was established in 1995 in order to establish a set of criteria for Sport Canada funding of NSOs. Only those sport organizations that meet the eligibility criteria and are in compliance with requirements for the SFAF (e.g., official languages, gender equity and so on) are supposed to receive funding. Following the introduction of the CSP (2002), the criteria changed to incorporate the four goals of the policy. However, the weighting of those criteria, and the assessment items for meeting those criteria, do not give equal weight to excellence and participation.

For both summer and winter sports, the current Assessment Weighting Grid allocates 60% to excellence and 40% to "sport participation and development"—the latter clearly incorporating capacity building. For example, of that 40% for summer sport NSOs, only 5% is actually for "sport participation"—explained as: "skill development and awareness/first contact" (NSOs are supposed to have a Long-Term Athlete Development (LTAD) model in place). With regard to the remaining 35%, 25% is allocated to "sport demographics" (including overall membership, and the number of individuals registered in coaching certification programs), and 10% to "sport development" (the development of coaches, officials and clubs/leagues). For the winter sport NSOs, the 40% for "sport participation and development" does not include a specific component for "sport participation." However, 6% is allocated to "sport initiation and growth," which includes the following criteria: skill development; awareness; targeted populations; delivery partners; non-member participants; and club/league development.

It is quite clear that the funding for NSOs does not depend on increasing the number of participants in the sport. Even for the item labeled "membership" (worth 10% for the summer sports and 7% for the winter sports), it is not clear whether additional points are given for increasing membership. The SFAF changes following the CSP appear to have been cosmetic, acknowledging that it is necessary to include participation and capacity building but not deflecting most NSOs from their main purpose of attempting to achieve excellence. Concerns have been expressed that even sport-specific LTAD programs have been used for talent identification and elite athlete development purposes. It is no surprise that, in a number of interviews with NSO staff carried out in 2009–2010 (Donnelly et al., forthcoming), it was not unusual for respondents to claim that the NSO was responsible only for developing high performance athletes, and not for "enhancing participation."

Sport Participation Research Initiative

The Sport Participation Research Initiative (SPRI), part of the Sport Canada Research Initiative (SCRI), was established in recognition of the fact that a great deal of scientific research had been carried out in the areas of exercise and fitness, and high performance sport, but very little research had been carried out in an attempt to understand sport participation. In an era of 'evidence-based policy,' Sport Canada had little evidence on which to base any new policies on sport participation. The SPRI grew out of the pan-Canadian consultations that led to the *Canadian Sport Policy* (Sport Canada, 2002) and the *Physical Activity and Sport Act* (Parliament of Canada, 2003). Consultations with the academic community made Sport Canada aware of the limitations of their former contract-based research program. The academic advisors argued that, if the research was to gain the respect of the academic community, it must be administered through the 'gold standard' granting councils (Canadian Institutes for Health Research (CIHR), Natural Sciences and Engineering Research Council (NSERC) and the Social Sciences and Humanities Research Council (SSHRC)), where research funds are allocated strictly on the basis of merit, as determined by peer review, and disseminated through peer-refereed conference presentations and publications.

The SPRI, the council-based research stream of the SCRI emerged from these considerations. Sport Canada pledged an initial sum of CA$ 1M per year for five years, to be administered through the granting councils. The criteria for the SPRI were established at a 2004 workshop of interested researchers to summarize 'what we know and what we do not know' about participation in sport, and to identify a research agenda for the first years of the program.

Representatives of the three granting councils were invited to attend the meeting, but only two (CIHR and SSHRC) attended and expressed a strong interest in co-operating. The workshop identified the following five priority areas for research:

- research concerned with identifying and overcoming barriers to participation in sport;
- research concerned with the training of participants, volunteers, coaches and administrators in sport;
- research concerned with the development, monitoring and evaluation of policies designed to enhance participation in sport;
- research concerned with the development of capacity and infrastructure for the purposes of enhancing participation in sport; and
- research concerned with determining the benefits and outcomes of participation in sport.

The SPRI was established in 2005, and made its first awards of grants through SSHRC in 2006. Academic research is a slow process, and no one expected to make startling discoveries that would immediately begin to increase sport participation. However, the SPRI has three important accomplishments. First, it has significantly enhanced the capacity of the Canadian research community to carry out sport participation-related research. Second, the annual conferences, where researchers report ongoing results of their work, are attended by staff from Sport Canada and the sport community, and they have become important sites for mutual understanding between the policy and research communities. The addition of a 'knowledge translation' requirement for those receiving grant funding was an outgrowth of discussions between the two communities. Third, the research funded by the SPRI is beginning to generate a substantial body of knowledge about sport participation, knowledge that is freely available because it is not the result of a private contract between Sport Canada and a researcher.

The Sport Participation Strategy

The 10-year CSP ended in 2012, and there is not, at the time of writing, any evidence of enhanced participation in sport. In fact, the 2005

General Social Survey reported a further decline in participation, to 28% (from 34% of Canadians over the age of 15 in 1998). This is clearly a problem for Canadian society and for governments at all levels when participation levels are measured against rising rates of obesity and the diseases of inactivity. Participation in sport, exercise and recreational physical activity could clearly help, but the majority of research funding related to obesity is channeled to the medical community rather than to consideration of the behavioural and social determinants of inactivity.

The Government of Canada has introduced two measures in an attempt to address declining rates of participation, both of which have little chance of success. First, the 2007 Children's Fitness Tax Credit (CFTC) provides tax credit on up to CA$ 500 of the expenses involved in children's participation in sport, fitness or activity programs. Parents eligible for the full amount receive a tax credit of less than CA$ 90. The CFTC was introduced despite available evidence that it would have no impact on increasing physical activity (Madore, 2007); and a recent expert panel (Faulkner et al., 2010) concluded that, not only would the CFTC provide no benefit for parents whose income was not taxable, but also that the only benefit was likely to be enjoyed by wealthier Canadians who would already have involved their children in programs of sport and physical activity—a view supported by the first study of the CFTC (Spence et al., 2010). Second, the government increased its allocation to ParticipACTION to support a new awareness campaign. There is no specific evidence that ParticipACTION was directly responsible for any increases in participation in its earlier incarnation; and it is not evident if there are many Canadians who are unaware that physical activity is good for them (or that smoking is bad for them)—what is missing is the possibility of realizing behavioural change.

A response by Sport Canada to declining rates of participation has been the *Sport Participation Strategy 2008–2012* (Sport Canada, 2008). The language is important here. Once more there was no specific *policy* to achieve enhanced participation; instead there was a *strategy*, developed for the last three years of the 2002 CSP[12] in an attempt to achieve the goal of enhanced participation. "Sport Canada's *strategic goal* in sport participation was *for more Canadians to participate in quality sport activities* as athletes/ participants, coaches, officials, administrators and volunteers" (Sport Canada, 2008, p. 9; *emphasis in original*). The *strategic objectives* included targeting specific populations (children and youth, and under-represented groups) and increasing participation in schools. However, the *Strategy* continually recognized that 'primacy' for participation has been downloaded to the provinces/territories; that any federal initiatives must occur in "consultation and cooperation" with the provinces/territories; and that the *Strategy* did not provide for any capital funding (for the construction or upgrading of facilities) (Sport Canada, 2008, p. 11). In the final analysis, the *Strategy* affirmed the targets and actions of the federal-provincial/territorial ministers responsible for sport, physical activity and recreation established at a 2006 meeting (Sport Canada, 2007). However, as noted in the following section, the *Strategy* included no reasonable means of achieving these targets, or of knowing if the targets had been achieved.

Current Issues, Problems and Resolutions in Sport Participation

The previous sections described the growth and decline of sport participation in Canada—a decline that is also evident in European data, although the top of the S-shaped curve actually turns down in Canada while just flattening out or showing slower increases in some other countries. In the 13 years between 1992 and 2005, the General Social Survey indicated a 17% decline in sport participation in Canada. This downturn is significant during a 'reported' crisis of obesity and increases in the diseases of inactivity. And yet, there is a policy void—no overall plan or direction to increase participation. This section considers the problems of measuring participation; the fragmentation of responsibility for attempting to increase participation and potential ways to resolve that fragmentation; and ends with a call for sport for all Canadians.

Measuring Participation

It is often assumed that we have accurate measures of sport participation and that announcements reporting, for example, 'the fastest growing sport in Canada,' or the previously noted decline in participation, have some validity. Nothing could be further from the truth. The data are quite crude, depend on a wide range of factors such as how sport is defined, the requested frequency of participation, the population sample surveyed and so on. In 2006, the federal-provincial/territorial ministers responsible for sport, physical activity and recreation used some available data to establish the following three participation targets for 2012 (Sport Canada, 2007; Sport Canada, 2008, p. 15):

- Girls, 5–9 years of age
  By 2012, increase sport participation rates of 5 to 9 year old girls by five percentage points, from 68% to 73%, while at least maintaining the current rate of participation of 5 to 9 year old boys (77%);
- Teens, 14–17 years of age
  By 2012, increase sport participation levels among teens (14–17 years old) by five percentage points (from 66% to 71%), while at least maintaining tweens' current participation rate of 78%;
- Women, 25–39 years of age
  By 2012, increase by six percentage points the sport participation levels of women aged 25 to 39 (from 27% to 33%), while at least maintaining the current rate of participation of men (53%).

These data are drawn from two quite different surveys (the General Social Survey, and the Physical Activity Monitor) and, given the stated concerns about the validity and accuracy of the surveys, it is quite reasonable to suggest that the surveys may not be able to accurately measure 5 or 6% targeted increases; and to ask, 'how will we know if the targets have been achieved?'

The General Social Survey (GSS; Statistics Canada) measurement of sport participation is carried out every six or seven years (1986, 1992, 1998, 2005); while the Physical Activity and Sport Monitor (PASM; Canadian Fitness and Lifestyle Research Institute) has been carried out annually since 1995 (except 1996). Both are telephone surveys, but the GSS has a far larger sample (25,000 in 2005, with a response rate of 80%) than the PASM (6,033 in 2005, with a response rate of 51%). The GSS has a somewhat more limited definition of 'sport' than PASM[13] and also stipulates a frequency of participation ("regularly," i.e., at least once a week during the season, in the past 12 months); thus, PASM could also include activities in which an individual only participated once in the past 12 months). It is therefore not surprising that PASM reports higher rates of participation than the GSS (36% in 2004 and 2006–07; compared with 28% for the 2005 GSS).

The *Sport Participation Strategy 2008–2012* (Sport Canada, 2008, p. 14) notes that PASM "can be used to collect data for children under 15 years of age (boys and girls)." Given that both surveys have the same target population (15 years of age and older), it is worth asking how the ministers, using these data, were able to report participation rates and establish targets for 5–9 year-olds, "tweens," and teens under the age of 15? The data are primarily drawn from PASM and GSS questions for parents in the sample, inquiring about the participation of their children. Thus, sampling and non-sampling errors are a problem for these surveys—for PASM even more than the GSS. Each person interviewed for the 2005 GSS represents approximately 1,300 Canadians. As the overall samples are divided to report on participation rates by gender, age, province, sport and so on, the samples become correspondingly smaller. Given all of the other potential sources of error in terms of recall, social desirability and interpretation of the questions, it is apparent that such surveys are useful, but particularly blunt instruments of measurement.[14] It is reasonable to assume that data from the GSS, a Statistics Canada time use survey, carried out periodically and using the same questions, may reliably show increasing or decreasing trends in participation. Whether it is possible to use such a survey to measure small increases in participation in relatively small population segments is much more open to question.

Even NSOs are concerned about the quality of their participation data. In recent interviews with staff at some 25 NSOs in Canada (Donnelly et al., forthcoming), only Bobsleigh Canada felt that they had reliable data on the number of participants. For a variety of reasons, including concerns about data reported by the PSOs, all of the other NSOs felt that they could not provide a reliable estimate of the number of participants in their sport. For example, although Hockey Canada maintains registration statistics for minor hockey, they do not have clear estimates of the number of players involved in high school, college and university hockey, intramural leagues, 'beer' leagues, industrial leagues, gay and lesbian leagues, church leagues, leagues associated with the Canadian Adult Recreational Hockey Association, outlaw leagues, regular pick-up games, and so on.

Further complicating the issue is the lack of reliable data on the frequency and intensity of participation; and data on the demographics of participants have the same sampling and non-sampling errors as participation data. Perhaps a starting point for setting any policy on sport participation should be the collection of a more reliable set of data. Without a good set of baseline data, it is impossible to determine if policies and measures intended to increase sport participation overall, or among specific targeted segments of the population, are effective. It is entirely possible that the GSS and PASM are under-reporting participation. Given the differentiation of sport participation noted above, and given the inclusive construct of active living (supported by recent studies suggesting that any activity is better than no activity in terms of health), it is important to attempt to achieve accurate and regular measures of all of the forms of sport, exercise and recreational physical activity in which Canadians are engaged, along with measures of the frequency and intensity of participation and accurate measures of participant demographics. Only with such data is it possible to more effectively identify target segments of the population for increasing levels of participation and to know if the measures taken in an attempt to increase participation actually worked.

Using the *Canadian Sport Policy* (2002) to Develop a More Integrated Sport System

Donnelly et al. (forthcoming) reviewed eight different surveys of sport and physical activity carried out recently in Canada (including the GSS and PASM). All have different questions, different samples, different definitions of sport and physical activity, and so on. They are symbolic of the fragmentation of the Canadian sport system and, for the purposes of this chapter, of the fragmentation of programs and initiatives intended to increase participation in sport, exercise and recreational physical activity. The programs and initiatives include those noted above undertaken by Sport Canada and the federal-provincial/territorial ministers in an attempt to follow the CSP, but they also include municipal initiatives, school-based initiatives, sport-specific initiatives, non-profit sector initiatives, commercial-sector initiatives, community initiatives, workplace initiatives, and so on. Such a diversity of programs and initiatives, usually sustained by anecdotes of success but carried out without any independent monitoring and evaluation, make it impossible to discover and determine best practices: What works, and what does not work, in what contexts?

While the development of a more 'seamless' sport system is unlikely, the CSP did provide an overall vision for Canadian sport. The four goals of the *Policy* provided a framework for action that has barely been realized. The goal of 'enhanced interaction' is evident in the regular meetings and co-ordination attempts of the federal-provincial/territorial ministers responsible for sport, physical activity and recreation—but has not really addressed the fragmentation of the system noted above. The goal of 'enhanced capacity' has increased awareness of the need to build facilities and develop programs and personnel, and a few steps have been taken in that direction *via* the recent 'infrastructure' program (federal spending in an attempt to alleviate the effects of the 2008–2009 worldwide economic crisis), facility construction for the Vancouver Olympic Winter Games and increased efforts to train coaches and officials. But capacity is expensive, and estimates of Canada's sport facilities deficit are huge. For example, in 2006, the Provincial/ Territorial Ministers Responsible for Sport, Physical Activity and Recreation estimated that the capital deficit was CA$ 15B for replacing and refurbishing sport facilities and adding facilities to accommodate the significant increase in Canada's population since the last major phase of facility building in the 1960s and 1970s (Christie, 2006).[15]

The goal of 'enhanced excellence' was the most politically popu-lar aspect of the CSP, and substantial federal-provincial/territorial government funds were provided to ensure both the success of hosting the Vancouver 2010 Olympic Winter Games and successful performances by Canadian athletes at those Olympic Winter Games. The goal of 'enhanced participation', while in many ways the most popular goal of the CSP, is also perhaps the goal on which the least progress has been achieved. The popularity of the goal is evident in public opinion surveys that routinely report, for example, that "91% of Canadians think that physical education should be manda-tory to Grade 12" (*Canadian Heritage*, reported by Christie, 2001), or that 90% of Canadians believe that sport has a positive influence on youth and is an effective vehicle for reinforcing societal values (True Sport, 2005). This chapter has emphasized the various ways in which little progress has been made towards the goal of enhanced participation.

If we consider participation and excellence as the two main goals of the Canadian sport system, two sides of the same coin (with capacity and interaction as the supporting goals), then the claims of the high performance system (excellence) about participation might be used to leverage a more mutually supportive relationship with participation. It is widely claimed that hosting major sport events and the successful performances of Canadian athletes in international sport events inspire increased participation in sport. In fact, such claims—repeated frequently by successful athletes and by sport leaders—are often used by sport leaders as a case for increased funding for high performance sport and as an example of the participation legacy of high performance sport. As noted previously in this chapter, these are "convenient fictions" (Donnelly, 2010b). Data from various studies show that inspiration is not enough unless policies and procedures are implemented to ensure that hosting major sport events and the success of athletes is directly tied to initiatives to increase sport participation. If young people are inspired and motivated by seeing 'excellence', then 'excellence' has a responsibility to ensure that such 'inspired' young people have the opportunity to become participants, and not to be turned away because they (their families) lack the resources to support participation and/or because the sport does not have the capacity or infrastructure to welcome 'inspired' young people. Donnelly et al. (2008) outlined one set of possibilities for suturing such a relationship between excellence and participation in anticipation of the Vancouver Olympic Winter Games. None of the proposals were implemented, and it is unlikely that Canada will experience 'enhanced participation' as a result of hosting those Games and winning a record number of gold medals.

Such missed opportunities are not exclusive to Canada—several studies showed a similar failure to 'inspire' participation in Australia following the Sydney 2000 Olympic Games (e.g., Bauman, Armstrong, & Davies 2003; Veal, 2003). In order to avoid such missed opportunities in the future and to realize the goals of the CSP in a more integrated manner, 'enhanced interaction' between high performance sport and participation sport, along with the 'enhanced capacity' to accommodate new participants, could assist in the achievement of 'enhanced excellence' and 'enhanced participation.' It would also help to resolve the imbalance and the tensions between participation and high performance addressed previously in this chapter.

Sport for All Canadians

One way to approach the development of sport policy intended to increase participation—a sport for all policy—is to attempt to understand the reasons why participation declines. A number of interpretations have been offered to account for the 17% decline in sport participation (as measured by the GSS) between 1992 and 2005 (Gruneau, 2010b; Ifedi, 2008). First, Canada's aging population helps to account for the decline since older Canadians are less likely to be involved in sport. Second, the growing number of immigrants helps to account for the decline since there is evidence that immigrants are less likely to be involved in sport than people born in Canada. However, it seems likely that socioeconomic factors are the most important in terms of accounting for the decline in participation. Data continually show that those with higher income and/or higher education (and their children) are significantly more likely to participate in sport than those with lower income and/or education; and a review of recent surveys indicates little or no decline in participation among higher income Canadians (cf. Gruneau, 2010b). A growing economic polarization of Canadian society since the introduction of neo-liberal policies in the 1980s (i.e., the rich are getting richer and the poor are getting poorer), combined with the increasing economic pressures of the last two decades that have people working longer hours, suggest that there are more people with less time and money to be involved, or to involve their children, in sport participation. The decline in participation appears to be accounted for mainly by this lower income population segment. In fact, lack of time is given as the main reason for non-participation by respondents to the GSS; and when the increasing costs of participation are also taken into account (for example, Slack (2003) found that, by the late 1990s, all municipal Parks and Recreation departments in Ontario were charging user fees), it helps to account for declining participation.

However, even before addressing the above concerns, an effective sport for all policy should start with good data on participation. As noted previously, the GSS employed Sport Canada's narrow definition of sport, leaving open the possibility that the decline in participation in a broader, more differentiated range of activities is not so significant. For example, the recent rapid increase in the number of people involved in running, especially women, would not for the most part be measured by a survey such as the GSS, since many would define it as a recreational or fitness activity. However, increases in obesity and diseases of inactivity, while not accounted for only by increasing inactivity, are indicators that large segments of the population are more inactive. A comprehensive measure of participation in a broad range of sports and recreational physical activities—a measure that may be repeated at regular intervals—is both a key starting point for a sport for all policy and a means to determine if the policy is working.

Another crucial aspect of a Canadian sport for all policy would be the targeting of older and immigrant populations, and any other population segments identified as having low levels of participation. Specific measures to increase participation among the targeted populations work best when they are a result of widespread consultations with those populations. Far too often, policies have failed because they did not take into account the wishes and life circumstances of those for whom the policies were developed. In the example of Women Organizing Activities for Women (WOAW), low-income single mothers in Vancouver (the targeted population) were at the table helping to negotiate the form of an activity program (Frisby & Millar, 2002). None of the 'experts' at the table had raised the crucial issue of child care, until the mothers pointed out that they would not be able to attend the program without the provision of care for their children. If the program had been developed without the involvement of the mothers, there would have been no child-care component, no one would have attended, and the experts could well have concluded that the target population was not interested in participation. The provision of child care ensured that the women were able to participate, and their presence at the negotiating table also meant that they had some control over the design of the program and which activities were included—thus making attendance even more attractive.

It seems likely that socioeconomic barriers are the most crucial to overcome, and the most expensive, when developing a sport for all policy. Evidence of the cost-sensitivity of participation is available in an example from Toronto. Following the 1998 amalgamation of Toronto into a mega-city, the former City of Toronto, which had no user fees for Parks and Recreation, joined with five other municipalities that all had different user fees. This was harmonized into a single fee-structure—introducing user fees into the former City of Toronto and reducing user fees in the five suburban municipalities. In the initial harmonization model, fees were introduced for all adult programs but removed for all children's and seniors' programs. The subsequent assessment of the effects showed a significant increase in the number of participants in the suburban municipalities where fees were reduced (e.g., an increase of 45% in Scarborough), and a significant reduction (33%) in participation in the former City of Toronto where fees were introduced for the first time (Clutterbuck & Howarth, 2002; Slack, 2003). These data suggest that user fees may have strong effects on participation. However, there is growing evidence that the cost of providing increased opportunities to participate may be offset and, in some cases, more than pay for itself in terms of reduced costs in other areas of public spending such as physical and mental health, crime, and education.

The shortage of sport facilities is Canada is significant (viz., the CA\$ 15B capital deficit for facilities noted previously). Anecdotal evidence lends support to the idea that, 'if you build it [a sport facility], they [participants] will come.' Many local governments have waiting lists for their Parks and Recreation programs and facilities, and some universities report waiting lists for their intramural sport programs. Whenever new facilities become available, they seem to quickly be filled with users. The Toronto example given above suggests that if those public opportunities are affordable and accessible, they fill up rapidly.

Well-designed financial subsidies to low-income populations can also be extremely effective in increasing participation. Poorly planned subsidies where, for example, tax returns have to be shown to Parks and Recreation or YMCA/YWCA staff in order to claim a means-tested subsidy, are considered to be demeaning and are often not claimed. 'Smart card' access to facilities, whereby no one knows who is receiving a subsidy, and appropriate and dignified means of applying for and granting subsidies, are far more effective. Subsidies may also be more program-specific. The following three examples show effective cases where subsidized programs of sport and/or recreational physical activity have been made available and, in two cases, where they have more than paid for themselves:

- Gina Browne and her colleagues at McMaster University carried out an extensive four-year study which, in part, provided recreation subsidies and transportation to children in low-income, sole-support families (Browne et al., 2000). The study, in the form of a field experiment, involved

765 households that included 1,300 children and youth. In a five group comparison, the study found that "the *child care/recreation alone* group was associated with the lowest per-child annual expenditures for use of health and social services four years after intake (CA\$ 908 ± CA\$ 2,041) even after including the cost of recreation" (Browne et al., 2000, p. vi). The report concluded that:

> Age-appropriate child care and recreation for children on social assistance results in a 10% greater exit of parents from social assistance in one year, maintains the academic, social and physical competence with baseline behaviour disorder at two and four years, and pays for itself within one year because of reduced use of professional and probationary services and after four years, not only continues to pay for itself but results in one-third the annual per child health and social expenditures when compared to children of parents [in the] *employment retraining* [group]. (p. vii)

Thus, recreation participation was sustained while cost subsidies and transportation were provided, and the children's health status improved.

- In research with a similar population, Dan Offord, a psychiatrist also at McMaster University, provided a one-year program of non-school skill development (including transportation) involving all children aged five to 15 living in a public housing complex in Ottawa. The apparent effect of recreation participation/skill development on improved school performance and home behaviour was marginal. However, overall levels of skill development and self-esteem were believed to have improved, and there was a clear effect on the reduction of anti-social behaviour. In fact, in terms of cost-effectiveness, the savings resulting from reduced vandalism and reduced police and fire costs were far more than the cost of the program (e.g., Jones & Offord, 1989; Offord & Jones, 1990; Offord, Hanna, & Hoult, 1992). Offord's work on this project led him to start the Christie Lake project for children and youth from low-income families in Ottawa.

In a later study, Offord, Lipman, and Duku (1998, p. 4) found that, "in the community domains, as would be expected, the presence of good parks, playgrounds and play spaces in the neighbourhood was strongly associated with increased rates of participation in supervised sports, and to a lesser extent, in unsupervised sports and the arts." As with Browne et al. (2000), Offord and his colleagues provide indirect evidence that participation increases and is sustained for the period of subsidization or when quality activity spaces are readily available.

- Wendy Frisby, at the University of British Columbia, started the WOAW project in several British Columbia communities, including Vancouver. The physical activity programs were provided for low-income single mothers and, as noted, with advice from the participants, the programs included child care. Although the main remaining barrier to participation was transport for those who lived some distance from the activity site, participation was sustained for the period of the subsidy.

Again, targeted subsidies to a specific population, when combined with additional funding to overcome other barriers to involvement (e.g., child care, transportation) suggest that this economic instrument is worthy of further exploration with regard to increasing participation. Unfortunately, many of these projects are based on short-term or grant funding, rather than being sustained in the base budget of the appropriate agency or department. When the funding ends, the program usually ends, sometimes leading to a reversion to the status quo. In fact, Offord suggest that there may be a relatively short 'halo' effect of the positive benefits of the programs, but noted that vandalism and false 911 calls were back to former levels within one year of the program ending.

Conclusion

This chapter ends as the former sport policy ends (CSP 2002–2012). In June, 2012, the federal, provincial and territorial ministers for sport, physical activity and recreation endorsed its replacement (Sport Canada, 2012) at their meeting in Inuvik, Northwest Territories. The new policy is intended to outline the direction for Canadian sport until 2022. It is far too early to determine any influences of the new policy, and it is only possible at this stage to suggest some possible outcomes. The policy vision of Canada as "a dynamic and innovative culture that promotes and celebrates participation and excellence in sport," and its values, principles and goals are all important ideals. As with the previous policy, the 2012 CSP outlines an integrated view of Canadian sport as a whole system while at the same time affirming the jurisdiction of the 14 governments involved. In addition, 'participation' and 'excellence' are given equal value as in the preceding policy (and current legislation), but no means are outlined for resolving the division and disparities between the two (Sport Canada, 2012).

The new policy outlines a direction for Canadian sport, and identifies desired outcomes, but—as with its predecessor—it fails to outline the means for staying on course and achieving the outcomes. With regard to participation, 'inclusive' sport is a key policy principle, and "[a] desired outcome of the Policy is that both the number and diversity of Canadians participating in sport will increase between 2012 and 2022" (Sport Canada, 2012, p. 3). This chapter suggests that we know quite a lot about what factors limit participation and how to overcome them in order to increase participation. The new policy still endorses the value of increased participation but does not provide any means for achieving increased participation and gives responsibility for achieving increased participation to federal and provincial sport systems that have "generate[d] self-reinforcing path dependent processes" (Capoccia & Kelemen, 2007, p. 361) to focus on (and receive funding for) achieving 'excellence.'

If sport participation is to increase in Canada, there is enough evidence to suggest an appropriate direction for policy—a direction that does not include tax credits and public service announcements. The European phase of 'sport for all' was accompanied by substantial provision of facilities for participation. Such facilities were designed to benefit both participation sport and high performance sport, and this would be an ideal place for Canada to start. The last major phase of facility provision occurred at the centennial (i.e., 1967); perhaps a new phase of facility construction would be an ideal goal for the sesquicentennial (i.e., 2017).

It will be key to develop a bridge between 'high performance' and 'participation'—a means to cooperate and share resources (e.g., facilities, expertise). To use an educational analogy, at this time all of the best teachers are contracted to teach only the best students in all of the very best facilities available. This is not an ideal situation in which to increase participation. For the not-so-skilled, participation is more difficult. The Long-Term Athlete Development model (now re-branded as Canadian Sport for Life) has influenced the new policy and envisages a track from 'physical literacy/introduction to sport' to 'high performance sport'—however, it too fails to incorporate any means to sustain 'recreational sport' i.e., participation among the vast majority of Canadians who enjoy sport but who are not continually improving their skills.

Effective measurements of participation, and the development of targeted programs resulting from inclusive consultations, are key to realizing the desired outcomes of the new policy. However, if we are unable to develop a way to involve that substantial proportion of the population who cannot find the time or the means to become (or for their children to become) participants, then the new policy will fail, just as the previous policy failed to realize increased participation.

Notes

1. The work of van Bottenburg and de Bosscher (2011) helped to provide focus and context for parts of this section.
2. Of course, there is some overlap between the two trends noted here, and some of the new activities that developed with little structure or competition eventually developed into new forms of achievement sport (e.g., snowboarding). The examples of activities in the following quotation could also include the revival/re-emergence of folk and traditional games.
3. As Donnelly (2007) pointed out, traditional Indian yogis would be astonished at how much clothing and equipment is now considered necessary in order to practice yoga, and at the growth of companies such as Lululemon to design and sell those items.
4. Questions relating to the definition and measurement of participation are addressed in a later section.
5. The double entendre is intentional, with 'Red' referring to both the Canadian team colour and to communism.
6. Before 1994, both Summer and Winter Olympic Games were held in the same year.

7. The famous 1972 hockey series between Canada and the USSR was characterized as a classic Cold War battle between capitalism and communism.
8. Or, as British Olympic champion rower, Steve Williams put it, "You can't buy gold medals, but you do have to pay for them" (as cited in Syed, 2008, paragraph. 1).
9. For example, Houlihan and Green (2008) and de Bosscher et al. (2008) point out the ways in which high performance sport programs in countries engaged in the "global sporting arms race" have grown to resemble each other.
10. In fact, Dubin's first recommendation (Dubin, 1990, p. 527) was to base sport funding on "broad participation in sport, not solely a focus on elite sport."
11. See footnote 13 for Sport Canada's particularly narrow definition of "sport."
12. The *Strategy* was published on December 5, 2008 (Sport Canada, 2008).
13. The GSS uses Sport Canada's (*Sport Participation in Canada—1998*) quite restrictive definition of sport ("...an activity that involves two or more participants engaging for the purpose of competition. Sport involves formal rules and procedures, requires tactics and strategies, specialized neuromuscular skills, a high degree of difficulty, risk and effort. Its competitive mode implies the development of trained coaching personnel and does not include activities in which the performance of a motorized vehicle is the primary determinant of the competitive outcome."). The GSS offers a list of "sports" provided by Sport Canada, and a list of exclusions ("...aerobics, dancercize, aquafit, bicycling for recreation or transportation, body building, car racing, fishing, hiking, jogging, lawn bowling, motorcycling, skate boarding, snowmobiling and walking.").
14. For example, the 1998 GSS found that 6.2% of Canadians claimed to play hockey regularly, while 2.7% claimed to play tennis regularly. Such claims call into question the accuracy of the data—it seems unlikely that there were almost half as many tennis players as hockey players (aged 15 and older) in Canada.
15. Ministers noted, for example, that 30 to 50% of the facilities in Ontario were nearing the end of their life. In a comparison that is often made between two similar-size cities, there are two Olympic-size swimming pools in Toronto (with a third now under construction for the 2015 PanAm/ParapanAm Game) and an estimated 30 in Sydney, Australia. The 2005 National Arena Census noted that 73% of arenas in Canada were built before 1973, and that the 'use by' date is imminent for many of them.

References

Bauman, A., Armstrong, T., & Davies, J. (2003). Trends in physical activity participation and the impact of integrated campaigns among Canadian adults, 1997–1999. *Australian and New Zealand Journal of Public Health, 27*, 76–79.

Bercovitz, K. (1998). Canada's Active Living policy: A critical analysis. *Health Promotion International, 13*(4), 319–328.

Browne, G., Byrne, C., Roberts, J., Gafni, A., & Whittaker, S. (2000). *Final report: When the bough breaks: Provider-initiated comprehensive care is more effective and less expensive for sole-support parents on social assistance— Four year follow-up.* Hamilton, ON: McMaster University's System Linked Research Unit on Health and Social Services Utilization.

Cachay, K. (1990). *Versportlichung der Gesellschaft und Ersportung des Sports: Systemtheoretische Anmerkungen zu einem gesellschaftlichen Phänomen.* In H. Gabler & U. Göhnher (eds.), *Für einen besseren Sport: Themen, Entwicklungen und Perspektiven aus Sport und Sportwissenschaft.* Schorndorf, DE: Verlag Karl Hoffman, pp. 97–113.

Capoccia, G., & Kelemen, D. (2007). The study of critical junctures: Theory, narrative, and counterfactuals in historical institutionalism. *World Politics, 59*(3), 341–369.

Christie, J. (2001, May 1). Turning sport vision into real action. *The Globe and Mail*, p. S2.

Christie, J. (2006, September 29). Sport ministers call for $10-billion. *The Globe and Mail*, p. S5.

Christie, J. (2010, July 31). High hopes in hurdles. *The Globe and Mail*, p. S7.

Clutterbuck, P., & Howarth, R. (2002). *Toronto's quiet crisis: The case for social and community infrastructural investment.* Research Paper 198. Toronto, ON: Centre for Urban and Community Studies.

Coalter, F. (2004). London 2012: A sustainable legacy? In, *After the Gold Rush: A Sustainable Olympics for London.* London: Institute for Public Policy Research/DEMOS.

Crawford Report. (2009). *The future of sport in Australia.* Australian Government: Independent Sport Panel.

Crum, B. (2001). *Over de versporting van de samenleving.* Harlem, NL: De Vrieseborch.

de Bosscher, V., Bingham, J., Shibli, S., van Bottenburg, M., & de Knop, P. (2008). *The global sporting arms race: An international comparative study on sports policy factors leading to international sporting success.* Oxford, UK: Meyer & Meyer Sport.

Digel, H. (1990). *Die Versportlichung unserer Kultur und deren Folgen für den Sport: Ein Beitrag zurUneigentlichkeit des Sports.* In H. Gabler & U. Göhnher (Eds.), *Für einen besseren Sport: Themen, Entwicklungen und*

Perspektiven aus Sport und Sportwissenschaft (pp. 73–96). Schorndorf, DE: Verlag Karl Hoffman.

Donnelly, P. (1996). 'Prolympism': Sport monoculture as crisis and opportunity. *Quest, 48*(1), 25–42.

Donnelly, P. (2007). *Sport, development and peace.* Presented at the World Congress of the World Association of Non-Government Organizations, Toronto, ON, 10 November.

Donnelly, P. (2010a). *Own the Podium* or rent it: Canada's involvement in the global sporting arms race. *Policy Options, 31*(1), 41–44.

Donnelly, P. (2010b). Rent the podium revisited: Reflections on Vancouver 2010. *Policy Options, 31*(4), 84–86.

Donnelly, P., with Kidd, B., Harvey, J., MacNeill, M., Houlihan, B., & Toohey, K. (2008). *Opportunity Knocks!: Increasing sport participation in Canada as a result of success at the 2010 Vancouver Olympics.* Position paper, presented to Sport Canada and the Canadian Olympic Committee. Toronto, ON: Centre for Sport Policy Studies. Retrieved from https://physical.utoronto.ca/Libraries/CSPS_PDFs/CSPS_Position_Paper_2_-_Increasing_Sport_Participation_in_Canada_as_a_Result_of_Success_at_the_Vancouver_Olympics.sflb.ashx

Donnelly, P., with Kidd, B., Harvey, J., MacNeill, M., Houlihan, B., & Toohey, K. (forthcoming). *Sport participation in Canada: Evaluating measurements, and testing determinants of increased participation: Final report.* Toronto, ON: Centre for Sport Policy Studies.

Dubin, C.L. (1990). *Commission of inquiry into the use of drugs and banned practices intended to increase athletic performance.* Ottawa, ON: Minister of Supply and Services Canada.

Elias, N., & Dunning, E. (1986). *Quest for excitement: Sport and leisure in the civilizing process.* Oxford, UK: Blackwell.

Faulkner, G., Nguyen, V., Ferrence, R., Mendelson, R., Donnelly, P., & Arbour-Nicitopoulos, K. (2010). *Economic policy, obesity and health.* Toronto, ON: Heart and Stroke Foundation of Canada.

Frisby, W., & Millar, S. (2002). The actualities of doing community development to promote the inclusion of low income populations in community sports and recreation. *European Sport Management Quarterly, 2*(3), 209–233.

Gruneau, R. (2010b). *Trends in community sport participation and community sport organizations since the 1990s.* Draft discussion paper prepared for the West Vancouver Department of Parks and Social Services.

Hogan, K., & Norton, K. (2000). The price of Olympic gold. *Journal of Science and Medicine in Sport, 3*(2), 203–218.

Houlihan, B., & Green, M. (2008). *Comparative elite sport development: Systems, structure and public policy.* Oxford, UK: Butterworth-Heinemann.

Ifedi, F. (2008). *Sport participation in Canada, 2005.* Ottawa, ON: Statistics Canada.

Ingham, A. (1985). From public issue to personal trouble: Well-being and the fiscal crisis of the state. *Sociology of Sport Journal, 2*(1), 43–55.

Interprovincial Sport and Recreation Council. (1987). *National recreation statement.* Retrieved from http://lin.ca/Files/4467/statemen.htm

Jones, M., & Offord, D. (1989). Reduction of anti-social behavior in poor children by nonschool skill development. *Journal of Child Psychology and Psychiatry, 30*(5): 737–750.

MacAloon, J. (1990). Steroids and the state: melodrama and the accomplishment of innocence. *Public Culture, 2*(2), 41–64.

MacNeill, M. (1999). Social marketing, gender and the science of fitness: A case study of ParticipACTION campaigns. In P. White & K. Young's (Eds.), *Sport and gender in Canada* (pp. 215–231). Toronto, ON: Oxford University Press.

Madore, O. (2007). *The impact of economic instruments that promote healthy eating, encourage physical activity and combat obesity: Literature review.* Ottawa, ON: Library of Parliament Publications.

Maguire, J. (1999). *Global sport: Identities, societies, civilizations.* Cambridge, UK: Polity Press.

McCloy, C. (2006). *The role and impact of Canadian federal sport policies in securing amateur sport legacies: Case studies of the past four decades.* Unpublished doctoral thesis, University of Toronto, Canada.

Minister's Task Force. (1992). *Sport: The way ahead. Minister's task force on Federal Sport policy.* Ottawa, ON: Minister of Supply and Services Canada.

Murphy, N., & Bauman, A. (2007). Mass sporting and physical activity events: Are they 'bread and circuses' or public health interventions to increase population levels of physical activity? *Journal of Physical Activity and Health, 4,* 193–202.

Office of the Prime Minister (1993). Unpublished news release. Ottawa, June 25.

Offord, D., & Jones, M. (1990). Skill development: A community intervention programme for the prevention of anti-social behaviour. In, S. B. Guze, F.J. Earls, & J.E. Barrett (Eds.), *Childhood psychopathology and development* (pp. 165–185). New York: Ravens Press.

Offord, D., Hanna, E., & Hoult, L. (1992). *Recreation and development of children and youth: A discussion paper.* Prepared for the Ontario Ministry of Tourism and Recreation.

Offord, D., Lipman, E., & Duku, E. (1998). *Sports, the arts and community programs: Rates and correlates of participation.* Ottawa, ON: Human Resources and Social Development Canada.

Parliament of Canada. (2003). *Bill C-12. An Act to promote physical activity and sport* (S.C. 2003, c. 2). Retrieved from http://www.parl.gc.ca/Content/LOP/LegislativeSummaries/37/2/c12-e.pdf

Rea, H. (Chair). (1969). *Report of the task force on sports for Canadians.* Ottawa, ON: Department of National Health and Welfare.

Slack, E. (2003). *Municipal funding for recreation.* Toronto, ON: Laidlaw Foundation. Retrieved from http://www.laidlawfdn.org/sites/default/files/resources/Municipal_Funding_for_Recreation_final_draft.pdf

Spence, J., Holt, N., Dutove, J., & Carson, V. (2010). Uptake and effectiveness of the Children's Fitness Tax Credit in Canada: The rich get richer. *BioMed Central Public Health, 10,* 356.

Sport Canada. (2002). *The Canadian sport policy.* Ottawa, ON: Department of Canadian Heritage. Retrieved from http://www.pch.gc.ca/pgm/sc/pol/pcs-csp/2003/polsport-eng.pdf

Sport Canada. (2007). *The Canadian sport policy: Federal-provincial/territorial priorities for collaborative action 2007–2012.* Ottawa, ON: Department of Canadian Heritage. Retrieved from www.pch.gc.ca/pgm/sc/pol/actn07-12/booklet-eng.pdf

Sport Canada. (2008, December 5). *Sport Participation Strategy 2008–2012.* Ottawa, ON: Canadian Heritage. Retrieved from http://www.pch.gc.ca/pgm/sc/pubs/part/part-eng.pdf

Sport Canada. (2012). *Canadian sport policy 2012.* Ottawa, ON: Canadian Heritage. Retrieved from http://sirc.ca/CSPRenewal/documents/CSP2012_EN.pdf

Syed, M. (2008, October 16). Unacceptable cost of heroes' Olympic success. *The Times of London Online.* Retrieved from http://www.thetimes.co.uk/tto/sport/olympics/article1744525.ece

True Sport. (2005). *Survey of Canadian True Sport Values.* http://www.truesportpur.ca/en/page-9-resources

van Bottenburg, M., & de Bosscher, V. (2011). An assessment of the impact of sports development on sports participation. In B. Houlihan & M. Green (Eds.), *Routledge Handbook of Sports Development* (pp. 599–613). Abingdon, UK: Routledge.

van Bottenburg, M., Rijnen, B., & van Sterkenburg, J. (2005). *Sports participation in the European Union.* Nieuwegen, NL: ARKO Sports Media.

Veal, A. (2003). Tracking change: Leisure participation and policy in Australia, 1985–2002. *Annals of Leisure Research, 6*(3), 245–277.

SECTION III

POLICY ISSUES

Olympic Ideals versus the Performance Imperative: The History of Canada's Anti-Doping Policies

Rob Beamish, Queen's University

The Modern Olympic Games have always been plagued by the fundamental tension that exists between Baron Pierre de Coubertin's original, lofty vision for the Games and the realities of modern, competitive sport. Throughout the twentieth century, this opposition has grown as the forces of modernity have increasingly permeated more and more aspects of the Olympic Games, but nowhere is the tension between de Coubertin's original aspirations and the cold, calculated pursuit of victory more evident than in the use of performance-enhancing substances.

After a brief overview of some of the central aspects related to de Coubertin's vision of the Modern Games and the forces that led to the introduction of performance-enhancing substances into the Olympics, this chapter focuses on the development of Canada's policies regarding banned, performance-enhancing substances.

Steroids and the Cold War Games

De Coubertin launched the Modern Olympic Games to change the course of European cultural history as the nineteenth century was giving way to the twentieth. Sharing with other cultural conservatives like Samuel Coleridge (1849), Thomas Carlyle (1896), J. H. Newman (1915) and Matthew Arnold (1932) the same deep concerns about the impact capitalist industrialization and the forces of modernity were having on traditional European culture and values, de Coubertin (2000, p. 559) sought to save European youth from a world in which they were being "trained into the mentality of the anthill." Subscribing to the Classical Greek notion that character is not created solely by the mind—it "is formed above all by the body"—de Coubertin (2000, p. 532) believed that sport could play a major role in reviving the spirit and drive of European youth while reaffirming and instilling Europe's traditional, aristocratically based value system in a new elite.

Grounded in the proper philosophical foundation, the Modern Olympic Games would foster "a delicate balance of mind and body, the joy of a fresher and more intense life, the harmony of the faculties, [and] a calm and happy strength" (de Coubertin, 2000, p. 534). In complete contrast to commercial sport, the Olympic Games would be "a lofty, uplifting experience that built character, spirit, and vision."

"The athlete enjoys his effort" de Coubertin (2000, p. 552) maintained. "He likes the constraint that he imposes on his muscles and nerves, through which he comes close to victory even if he does not manage to achieve it." "Imagine" he continued, "if it were to expand outward, becoming intertwined with the joy of nature and the flights of art. Picture it radiant with sunlight, exalted by music, framed in the architecture of porticoes." It was this vision of honourable men becoming brothers-in-arms as they engaged in fair and chivalrous competition that served as the foundation to de Coubertin's Olympic project.

From the inaugural Games of 1896 through to the 1932 Summer Games at Los Angeles and Winter Games in Lake Placid, de Coubertin and the International Olympic Committee (IOC) were moderately successful in containing the tension between the Games' lofty ideals and the realities of competitive sport in the modern, industrialized world. The 1936 Games in Nazi Germany, however, changed the nature of the Olympic Games irrevocably. The Berlin Games clearly demonstrated the symbolic and political potential of the Games, laying the groundwork for the increasing politicization of the Olympics in the post-World War II period. At the same time, from the 1936 Games onward, the Olympics were faced with the growing impact of modernity and the increasing influence of commercial forces on de Coubertin's project.[1]

As much as the 1936 Games stand as a key point of transition and transformation, it was the 1952 Games in Helsinki that served as one of the most significant watershed points in the history and nature of the Modern Olympic Games—especially with respect to performance-enhancing substances. The 1952 Games were more than the first Cold War confrontation between the United States of America (USA) and the Union of Soviet Socialist Republics (USSR)— important as that was. The Games were the first in which athletes, selected, trained and developed within a national athlete development system, competed with the overall goal of pursuing victory for national aggrandizement. The Helsinki Games served as a powerful impetus for the creation of national, athlete development systems on both sides of the iron curtain and accelerated the professionalization of Olympic athletes over the course of the next half century. At the same time, the 1952 Games took the overt politicization of the Games which began in 1936 to a new level of significance—the Olympic Games became the symbolic struggle between not just two super-powers, but two vastly different economic, political and social systems.

As important as all those factors were, it was the introduction of steroids in athlete preparation programs that are among the most dramatic developments in Olympic sport during the 1952 Games. Although the stories vary—John Ziegler (1984), the American weightlifting team's physician argues that it was in response to Soviet use of steroids that he developed methandieone (Dianabol) to give to American weightlifters to level the playing field, while Paul Dimeo (2007) indicates that Ziegler's story is too convenient and self-serving, placing the onus on the Soviets for the introduction of steroids into the Games—there is no doubt that steroid use among high performance athletes increased dramatically in the 1950s and 1960s (cf. Dimeo, 2007; Dubin, 1990; Franke & Berendonk, 1997; Todd & Todd, 2001; Yesalis & Bahrke, 2002).

While steroids were, in retrospect, a significant issue in the early East/West confrontations, at the time, they really were a low-profile issue. The IOC's major concern was the very real threat that a win-at-all-costs approach to high performance sport was destroying the Games. The drama of a no-holds-barred athletic confrontation between the two superpowers was the direct antithesis of de Coubertin's lofty aspirations for the revived Games. As a result, IOC President Avery Brundage defended the Movement's central principles and emphasized their particular relevance for the Cold War era. The Olympic Games kept "the flag of idealism flying,"

Brundage maintained, and if the spirit of fair play and respect for the adversary could ever prevail in international affairs then "the cat force, which rules there now, will slink away, and human life will emerge for the first time from the jungle" (as cited in Guttmann, 1984, pp. 115–116).

Although steroids would eventually become the performance-enhancing substance of most concern, Danish cyclist Knud Jensen's death, allegedly from a nicotinyl titrate and amphetamine cocktail at the 1960 Summer Games, was the pivotal event that brought the use of performance-enhancing substances to centre stage. And even though Jensen's death was due to extreme dehydration resulting from his and his time trial teammates' unwavering commitment to the pursuit of victory in a race held in 40+ Celsius temperatures—and not an amphetamine overdose—the strength of the rumour and the rush to judgement demonstrated how much concern there was over the use of performance-enhancing substances in international sport (Møller, 2006).

Faced with growing concerns over the use of performance-enhancing substances at the Games, Brundage appointed Arthur Porritt, the Chair of the British Association of Sports Medicine (BASM), as the first head of the IOC's anti-doping commission in 1962 (Dimeo, 2007). Porritt shared Brundage's views on performance-enhancing substances. "Doping is an evil—it is morally wrong, physically dangerous, socially degenerate and legally indefensible" Porritt had argued (as cited in Dimeo, 2007, p. 108). Drug use, he continued, reflects a "weakness of character" and is a "temptation in this fast-moving dynamic and somewhat amoral world" which had to be controlled.

Porritt and the BASM hosted the first major, international conference on drugs in sport—an issue that had added urgency with the death of British cyclist Tommy Simpson in the 1967 Tour de France (Dimeo, 2007). The conference provided an international stage for Porritt and others to emphasize the moral grounds for strictly controlling pharmaceuticals in sport (Dimeo, 2007). By the end of the year, the IOC had defined "doping," drafted the first list of banned substances—ranging from cocaine, pep pills and vasodilators, to alcohol, opiates and hashish—adopted the principle of testing athletes for banned drugs and enshrined it all in Rule 28 of the *Charter*. Despite the inclusion of steroids on the list, there was no test for them until 1973, and the IOC did not conduct tests until 1976. For more than two decades world-class, high performance sport was an open competition in which athletes used steroids without fear of detection (Todd & Todd, 2001). The all-out pursuit of world record, athletic performances at the outer limits of technologically-enhanced human potential was constrained by mere moral authority.

The Scandal in Caracas: Canada Confronts Steroids

Although testing began in 1973, it was the sophisticated techniques employed at the 1983 Pan American Games in Caracas that demonstrated the scope of steroid use in international sport. Nineteen competitors, including two Canadians—weightlifters Guy Greavette and Michel Viau—tested positive, were ejected from the Games and suspended for two years. More important, dozens of athletes either left the Games for "personal reasons" or performed well below their normal standards to avoid testing. The Caracas Games showed that testing was improving—driving drug use further underground.

In Canada, the Caracas suspensions showed the dividing tension between the founding principles of international competition and the now prevalent modernist forces. Canadian Chef de Mission Barry Nye maintained that anabolic steroid use "can't be condoned on a moral or ethical basis" while Jack Lynch, the Canadian Olympic Association's (COA) technical director, noted that although the COA encouraged athletes to perform on the basis of their natural abilities, "Let's face it, this is competition. You play to win. This isn't recreation" (Fraser, 1983, p. 1). The events in Caracas initiated a debate that occurred partly through public media but largely within the policy-making bodies of the IOC and the different NOCs and sport organizations throughout the sport system (Johnson, 1983).

The response in Canada was quick and decisive. Sport Canada (1984b) left no room for debate: Canada's policies would stem from de Coubertin's founding principles irrespective of how much the Games had fundamentally changed. Each NSO had to develop a plan that would eliminate drug use by Canadian athletes. There were 11 points the NSOs had to cover, including a detailed policy statement, an operational plan for regular testing, educational activities, international lobbying strategies for "the eradication of drugs in sport," stipulated penalties for positive tests, due process guarantees for any appeal, and commitments to not use, possess and to discourage the use of banned substances.

That same year, the COA (1984) issued its own formalized policy on banned performance-enhancing substances. The COA emphasized that its policy stemmed from the desires to ensure that competition among athletes was fair and equal as well as the need to protect athletes' health. The COA indicated that its policy did not represent the development of an independent, COA drug testing program; the COA policy stemmed from, and complemented, Sport Canada's (1984b) national policy on drug use and doping control. The COA policy was written to make it clear that the national sport policy would be applied to any athletes eligible for nomination to, or performing as a member of, any team participating in sport competitions that fell under the COA's jurisdiction (e.g., the Summer and Winter Olympic Games, the Pan American Games). The policy clearly indicated that the COA policy did not extend to other sport events.

Like the Sport Canada policy, the COA indicated that the use of substances or procedures prohibited by the Olympic Charter and all substances prohibited by the IOC Medical Commission was strictly forbidden. Like Sport Canada, the COA would respect all sanctions imposed by the IOC and other appropriate IFs while reserving the right to impose greater sanctions for competitions falling under the COA's jurisdiction. Both policies ensured athletes' rights to due process, athletes' obligations to follow all doping control procedures, and required all personnel comprising a COA sponsored team to sign a declaration that they were aware of the COA policy on doping and that they were not in violation of that policy.

Finally, the IOC's (1984) Medical Commission published a *Medical Guide* which purported to outline structural changes in the Medical Commission that would allow it to do more than issue longer and longer lists of banned substances and sanctions. While it would continue to condemn drug use, the Medical Commission would point out natural methods to improve performance (IOC, 1984, p. 19). The Biomechanics and Sports Physiology Subcommission would take on the role of proving "that there are scientific training methods which make it possible to improve performance quality without danger and without cheating" (IOC, 1984, p. 19, see also pp. 21–23). But aside from three pages devoted to coverage of biomechanics and sport physiology, the remaining 31 pages deal with drugs and drug testing.

In 1985, Sport Canada issued a revised, stronger policy. Despite Canada's more aggressive stance on banned performance-enhancing substances, just before the weightlifting competition began at the 1984

Los Angeles Games, two Canadian lifters—Terry Hadlow and Luc Chagnon—were suspended when pre-Games tests revealed traces of methyltestosterone (Christie & Fisher 1984). These suspensions, which embarrassed Sport Canada and the COA, along with a change in government as the Progressive Conservatives won the 1984 election leading to Prime Minister Brian Mulroney's appointment of Otto Jelinek to the post of Minister of State (Fitness and Amateur Sport), led to a revised national policy. Jelinek, a former pairs figure skater, Olympian, and, with his sister Maria, 1962 World Champion, was heavily invested in the predominant neo-liberal ideology of the Progressive Conservative Party, holding the individual responsible for his or her successes and failures; he was also a strident anti-communist. Because of his background—athletic and political—Jelinek was a very 'hands-on' Minister of State (Fitness and Amateur Sport) who wanted to return the Olympic Games to their founding principles, eliminate drug use from sport, and remove, as much as possible, any perceived advantages that the Communist Bloc athletes enjoyed—especially in the use of banned substances. As a result, Jelinek wanted Canada to be a leader in the war against drugs in sport. In view of the above, Sport Canada issued a revised and stronger policy in 1985.

In the preamble to the policy, Jelinek indicated that from the 1983 policy onwards, Canada was "not only doing its duty to ensure that standards of fair play and the protection of the health of participants are upheld," it was also providing "significant international leadership in this important area" (Sport Canada, 1985, p. 1). The revised policy made the Canadian government's position clear:

> On the premise that the use of drugs which artificially enhance performance in training and competition is harmful to health, ethically wrong and ultimately a threat to high performance sport as we know it today, Sport Canada has developed this policy to lay the groundwork for measures which have as their objective the eradication of the use of performance enhancing substances, not only by Canadian athletes but also by their international counterparts. (Sport Canada, 1985, p. 4)

No matter what other countries' athletes were doing, Sport Canada would impose the highest standards possible. To make its position crystal clear, the new policy had a lifetime ban from all federal government sport programs and benefits for any athlete who violated "antidoping rules involving anabolic steroids and related compounds" (Sport Canada, 1985, p. 6). In cases involving other banned substances, the suspension was for a minimum of one year. The new policy also stipulated that "the only relief from life suspension is through direct appeal to the Minister of State, Fitness and Amateur Sport" (Sport Canada, 1985, p. 7).

A week before the 1986 Commonwealth Games, Jelinek banned six athletes—Rob Gray (discus), Mike Spiritoso and Peter Dajia (shot put) along with weightlifters Jacques Demers, Glenn Dodds and Mario Parente for positive tests for steroids (Christie, 1986). With the new policy only allowing an appeal through the Minister, Jelinek told reporters that although he was "always prepared to listen, I can't see how I could change my mind" (Christie, 1986, p. S1). Assured there was no chance of error, Jelinek was categorical: "Their amateur careers have come to an end. There's no use pussyfooting around on this issue . . . they didn't think I was serious . . . they were warned. I have to stick to my guns" (McAuley, 1986, p. A1).

In 1987, the COA approved a policy that reflected Sport Canada and Jelinek's stance on positive steroid tests. The COA (1987, p. 2) could now impose a lifetime ban from all COA-sanctioned events on any athlete "found guilty of a doping offence within the scope of this policy." A hearing would be held "to determine the circumstances relating to the offence, and the sanction to be imposed" but the athlete could not challenge the results of any test conducted by an IOC-accredited laboratory.

While Sport Canada and the COA were implementing stringent policies to try and legislate fair play and a humanist approach to sport, Canadian sport leaders continued to deal with the modernist reality of world-class, high performance sport. The recommendations from a task force commissioned by the next Minister of State (Fitness and Amateur Sport), Jean Charest, to guide national sport policy into the next millennium appeared in *Toward 2000: Building Canada's Sport System* (Government of Canada, 1988). Until *Own the Podium—2010* (Priestner Allinger & Allinger, 2004), it was the most modernist, achievement-oriented document in Canadian high performance sport history. "A commitment to excellence has been developed within the Canadian sport community" the report (Government of Canada, 1988, p. 28) emphasized, "a commitment which has produced results, which has given young athletes a sense of confidence that Canada can achieve, and which has changed the attitude of Canadians to high performance

sport and sport generally." Despite progress, Canada's high performance sport system "is still in its infancy" . . . "There is a need to build
on the accomplishments of this last quadrennial [1984–1988] and to take
advantage of the momentum which currently exists."

The task force (Government of Canada, 1988, p. 35) noted that
"a mature high performance sport system" required professionalized
coaching, improved performances by Canadian athletes, better facilities and a stronger financial commitment from the private and public
sectors. The report recommended prioritizing sports, a fully integrated system of athlete development, and promoting "the concept
of sport excellence such that achievement in high performance sport
will be recognized and valued by the Canadian public" (Government
of Canada, 1988, pp. 36–37).

Two specific recommendations are particularly noteworthy.
Recommendation 2.3.2.3 proposed the creation of national, multi-sport,
high performance centres employing professional administrators,
coaches, sport scientists, and sport medicine practitioners to serve high
performance athletes, coaches and clubs across Canada (Government
of Canada, 1988). Recommendation 2.2 established specific goals for
the next quadrennial: Canada would rank "among the top three leading Western sporting nations" and among the top six nations overall
at the Albertville Games with medals in six of the 10 winter sports;
Canada would rank sixth to eighth overall at the Barcelona Games with
medals in 18 of the 28 summer sports (Government of Canada, 1988,
p. 36). The report presented an unabashed commitment to medals in
world-class, high performance sport.

Much of the enthusiasm in *Toward 2000* stemmed from the
federal government's 1982 approval of the "Best Ever '88" Winter
Olympic Team Project which would ensure the "best performance
ever in Winter Olympic competition" at the Calgary Games (Sport
Canada, 1984a, p. 1). Best Ever injected CA$ 25M into the winter
sports, doubling the existing commitment. In August 1984, the government extended Best Ever and committed an additional CA$ 38M to
the summer sports. Canadian policy seemed to have fully embraced
the modernist forces that dominated the Olympic Movement.

The Steroid Debacle in Seoul

Despite the pervasive, modernist rationalism in professional and
high performance sport, the humanist principles of sport still had

powerful defenders. Thus, before the 1988 Seoul Games, *Sports Illustrated* initiated a concerted attack on the use of steroids and articulated the framework within which ensuing discussion of steroids in sport would take place (Johnson, 1985; Todd, 1983). After Ben Johnson's positive test following his dramatic victory in the 100 metre final—the premier event of the Games—the magazine printed, with renewed zeal, another series of agenda-setting pieces that criticized steroids and their use (Chaikin & Telander, 1988; Johnson, 1988; Johnson & Moore, 1988; Telander, 1988, 1989).

In concert with *Sports Illustrated's* intervention, Senator Joe Biden presided over the Senate Committee on the Judiciary's 1989 deliberations *Steroids in Amateur and Professional Sports: The Medical and Social Costs of Steroid Abuse.* Biden had been instrumental in establishing the USA's first major steroid legislation—the *Anti-Drug Abuse Act of 1988*—by successfully linking steroids to America's war on drugs (United States Sentencing Commission, 2006, pp. 3–4).

At the 1989 hearing, Biden wanted to classify steroids with heroin, crack, and cocaine as controlled substances (Assael, 2007). To succeed, Biden needed to demonstrate that steroids were a genuine threat to the public so he focused on steroids in sport—paying particular attention to the National Football League (NFL). "The NFL's words and actions, together with those of successful college and pro athletes and coaches around the country, can demonstrate that taking steroids is dangerous [and] wrong," Biden told the Committee (as cited in Assael, 2007, p. 51). Tens of millions of Americans, he maintained, look to the "stars on the athletic field as the role models in our schools, in our colleges, and in our lives" (as cited in Assael, 2007, pp. 51–52). If athletes are able to benefit from steroid use without penalty, Biden emphasized, "then it seems to me the message is overwhelmingly clear to the rest of America that drug abuse in any form is not that big a deal" (as cited in Assael, 2007, p. 52). A seasoned politician, Biden burned into the public psyche his main themes—steroids are dangerous, their use is wrong, knowing star athletes use them will corrupt young people and ignoring steroid use is tantamount to giving heroin junkies a free pass. In a parallel House of Representatives' inquiry, the same themes prevailed— steroids pose potential health risks for athletes, they contravene the rules and spirit of sport and their use sends the wrong message to American youth (Assael, 2007; House of Representatives, 1989, 1990).

The American events are important for Canadian policy because even though Johnson's positive test triggered the federal *Commission of Inquiry into the Use of Drugs and Banned Practices Intended to Increase Athletic Performance*, the inquiry did not take place in a vacuum. Dubin (1990) drew upon the American developments even as the same process of contextualizing steroid use was developing in Canada through the media, among politicians and within the legal system.

Three things made the Canadian inquiry such a landmark in Canadian policies on banned substances. First, and most obvious, the inquiry's recommendations shaped the legal and policy structure for banned performance-enhancing substances. Second, it concentrated so much information into one, highly respected report. Finally, a point rarely recognized, Dubin's report is fraught with the same divisive forces that tear the Olympic Movement in two directions—de Coubertin's original humanist, philosophical principles versus the real, embodied forces of modernity. It is this dimension of Dubin's report that merits attention here.

By the end of the inquiry, Dubin (1990, p. xv) recognized that Olympic athletes were not amateurs "who competed only for the thrill of competition and the chance of victory." World-class, high performance sport involved athletes who "engage in sport on a full-time basis and for monetary reward" (Dubin, 1990, p. xv). But as much as Dubin recognized all of the modernist features of world-class, high performance sport, his overall frame of reference stemmed from the same principles that de Coubertin had tried to establish in and through the Games. "A commission of inquiry should not dwell solely on the past" Dubin (1990, p. xxii) wrote. One must understand the past to determine what went wrong and to define the issues but one must then "seek to correct the errors of the past." Dubin (1990) articulated the fundamental premises upon which he assessed the state of high performance sport:

> The use of banned performance-enhancing drugs is cheating, which is the antithesis of sport. The widespread use of such drugs has threatened the essential integrity of sport and is destructive of its very objectives. It also erodes the ethical and moral values of athletes who use them, endangering their mental and physical welfare while demoralizing the entire sport community.

> I have endeavoured to define the true values of sport and restore its integrity so that it can continue to be an important part of our culture, unifying and giving pleasure to Canadians while promoting their health and vitality.
>
> I have also sought to protect and advance the interests of Canadian athletes and have endeavoured to obtain for them a healthy athletic climate in which they can compete honourably in the future, both nationally and internationally, in accordance with the true objectives of sport. (pp. xxii–xxiii)

For Dubin, it was the "true values of sport," "its integrity," and the honour of "the true objectives of sport" that guided his overall assessment of the evidence presented to him and the recommendations he made. At the same time, he could not ignore the realities of late twentieth century, high performance sport. The result was a set of recommendations that tried to pull back the forces of modernity, the professionalization of high performance athletes and the realities of the Games as an athletic spectacle in which the pursuit of athletic accomplishment, at the outer limits of human performance capacities, drew world audiences and generated political rewards and enormous revenues for specific constituencies in international sport.

To demonstrate the extent to which his guiding philosophy was deeply influenced by de Coubertin's image of what the Games should accomplish, Dubin (1990, p. 516) placed his recommendations within the context of the Olympic Movement's fundamental principles as they are enshrined in the *Olympic Charter*: the promotion of physical and moral qualities through sport; educating young people through sport to build understanding, friendship and "a better and more peaceful world"; and "to spread the Olympic principles throughout the world, thereby creating international goodwill." According to the *Charter*, Dubin (1990, p. 516) emphasized, the Games *"unite Olympic competitors of all countries in fair and equal competition* [italics in original quotation]." "Unfortunately," Dubin wrote, "the noble sentiments and lofty ideals proclaimed in the Olympic Charter are a far cry from the reality of international competition."

Dubin (1990, p. 525) captured the contradictory tensions within the Canadian context as he continued to emphasize the spirit of Olympic competition and how that could justify government involvement in sport as "worthy social and national objectives." "However," he continued, "as the degree of involvement in and funding of sport has increased, there has been a shift of emphasis in the nature and focus of that involvement."

> While task force reports and government white papers acknowledge the broad objectives set forth above and the benefit of widely based participation in sport, in fact government support of sport, particularly since the mid-1970s, has more and more been channelled towards the narrow objective of winning medals in international competition. Notwithstanding presentations to the contrary, the primary objective has become the gold medal. This is evidenced by the most recent task force report—*Toward 2000: Building Canada's Sport System*—in which the proposed long-term goal of government funding and the measure of its success are clearly related to the winning of medals. (Dubin, 1990, p. 525)

Dubin (1990, p. 526) maintained that the "changed emphasis from the broad-based support of sport for the general community of ordinary Canadians to high-level competitive sport demands a re-examination." He went a full step further in his first recommendation which stated that "the mandate for those responsible for administering funds provided by the Government of Canada for sport reflect a commitment to those principles on which government funding of sport was originally based" (Dubin, 1990, p. 527). Dubin's next three recommendations sought to return government involvement in sport to de Coubertin's founding principles.

The recommendations that had the most immediate impact concerned drug testing in Canada and projecting a strong anti-drug image internationally. "Canada's leadership in the fight against doping in sport," Dubin (1990, p. 535) emphasized, "is a matter of record, not merely of national pride." He reiterated points made earlier concerning the First Permanent World Conference on Anti-doping in Sport that Canada hosted, its strict domestic policies beginning in 1983 and strengthened in 1985 as well as Sport Canada's leadership in pressing for more stringent controls on athletes.

At the same time, Dubin (1990) was openly critical of resistance in some NSOs to the policies and the overall failure of Sport Canada and the NSOs to properly implement them. As a result, Dubin (1990, p. 538) recommended that the Sport Medicine Council of Canada should "expand its present role to become the central independent agency responsible for doping control of Canadian athletes and coordination of Canada's anti-doping activities." This recommendation put added force behind the policing of performance-enhancing substances among Canadian athletes even though it did not address the reality of high performance sport at all. Aware of the contradictory tensions between world-class, international sport and de Coubertin's original principles, Dubin was advocating prohibition and testing, hoping that sanctions would keep athletes more in line with the by-gone ethos of amateurism rather than following the modernizing forces that controlled the overall nature of international sport.

The World Anti-Doping Agency Takes Control

At the end of 1990, Bob Porter and John Cole, the Chairs of the Sub-Committee on Fitness and Amateur Sport, prepared a status report on high performance sport in Canada that centred on *Toward 2000* and the Dubin inquiry (Porter & Cole, 1990). The committee's deliberations and recommendations established the framework and institutional structures that continue to govern Canadian policy in the use of performance-enhancing substances up to the current point in time.

Within the sub-committee's report two points are particularly important. First, the sub-committee noted the tension between the approaches found in *Toward 2000* and Dubin (Porter & Cole, 1990). While *Toward 2000* had targeted medal counts and objective performance expectations, Dubin (1990) had argued for a system that allowed athletes to perform as best they could without the pressures of taking performance-enhancing substances to reach the top of the podium. The sub-committee preferred Dubin's position.

Second, the sub-committee supported Dubin's (1990) position on the Sport Medicine Council of Canada and recommended that its mandate expand "so that the Council can become the central agency in policing and enforcing anti-doping policy" (Porter & Cole, 1990, p. 19).

In 1991, the federal Minister of State (Fitness and Amateur Sport), Pierre Cadieux, established the Canadian Centre for Drug-Free Sport, providing it with a 13-member staff and a CA$ 3.1M budget (Corelli, 1996). With this step, the government formally backed its claim that Canada was at the forefront of the war against drugs in high performance sport. Following federal government cutbacks to sport in the early 1990s, the Centre was merged with Fair Play Canada to form the Canadian Centre for Ethics in Sport (CCES). Based on the foundational principles of its predecessors—fair play and drug-free sport—the CCES stands as an independent, non-profit organization that implements, manages, and oversees Canada's Anti-Doping Program (Canadian Centre for Ethics in Sport, 2011).

The final major policy document that continues to shape Canada's stance on performance-enhancing substances was *Sport in Canada: Everybody's Business* (Mills, 1998).[2] In "Part V, Recommendations," "Section 1: High-performance Athletes and National Sport Organizations," "B. Problems and Solutions," the first recommendation of the Mills (1998) report reinforced Dubin's first recommendation in his Commission of Inquiry—the government should "maintain a substantial commitment to and support for sport in Canada over the long-term due to its overall benefit to Canada." The report maintained that funding must be tied to specified ethical standards "including provisions for drug-free sport" (Mills, 1998). It also recommended that the CCES continue to receive federal funding, remain an independent agency responsible for the promotion, monitoring and evaluation of ethics in sport and that it continue to promote drug-free sport in Canada.

Although steroids were not involved in the 1998 Tour de France drug seizure, that event became the catalyst for several far-reaching decisions concerning the use of performance-enhancing substances in sport. The events began with a rather unprecedented seizure of 24 vials of human growth hormone and testosterone, 234 doses of erythropoietin (EPO) and 60 capsules of the blood thinner Asaflow from the Festina cycling team's van by customs officials at Reims. Two weeks later, TVM team director Cees Priem and team doctor Andrei Mikhailov were arrested for transporting poisonous substances and the possession of dangerous merchandise (Beamish & Ritchie, 2006).

Those events took on a much higher profile when, in an interview published by the Spanish daily newspaper *El Mundo*, IOC President Juan Antonio Samaranch stated that if a performance-enhancing substance could damage an athlete's health then that was a problem but if it simply improved performance, he did not think it was doping (cf. Beamish & Ritchie, 2006, p. 1; Assael, 2007, pp. 161–162). Samaranch's remarks virtually forced the IOC to support a proposal it had long resisted—the creation of an independent body to oversee the testing of all Olympic and world-class athletes. Created in 1999, the World Anti-Doping Agency (WADA) quickly dominated all discussions and policies related to banned, performance-enhancing substances in sport. Houlihan (2004) has emphasized the power and influence that WADA would exert. Prior to the formation of WADA, the movement opposing the use of banned performance-enhancing substances was "characterized by fragmentation of effort, mutual suspicion among key actors, a general lack of momentum and a severe lack of resources. While there was much activity, there was little effective action" (Houlihan, 2004, p. 19).

WADA came into existence following the first World Conference on Doping held in Lausanne, Switzerland in February 1999. The Conference involved participants from various government, inter-governmental and non-governmental organizations, the IOC, IFs and NOCs. Those delegates passed the "Lausanne Declaration on Doping in Sport" (1999). Clause four stated:

> An independent International Anti-Doping Agency shall be established so as to be fully operational for the Games of the XXVII Olympiad in Sidney in 2000. This institution will have as its mandate, notably, to coordinate the various programs necessary to realize the objectives that shall be defined jointly by all the parties concerned. Among these programs, consideration should be given in particular to expanding out-of-competition testing, coordinating research, promoting preventive and educational actions and harmonizing scientific and technical standards and procedures for analyses and equipment. A working group representing the Olympic Movement, including athletes, as well as the governments and inter-governmental organizations concerned, will meet, on the initiative of the IOC, within three months, to define the structure, mission and financing of the Agency. The Olympic Movement commits to allocate a capital of US $25 million to the Agency. (Lausanne Declaration, 1999, pp. 17–18)

When it was constituted in Switzerland, WADA had an explicit mandate. Its first objective was "to promote and coordinate at the international level the fight against doping in sport in all its forms" (WADA, 2009, p. 1). "[T]o this end," the mandate continued:

the Foundation will cooperate with intergovernmental organizations, governments, public authorities and other public and private bodies fighting against doping in sport, inter alia the International Olympic Committee (IOC), International Sports Federations (IF), National Olympic Committees (NOC) and the athletes; it will seek and obtain from all of the above the moral and political commitment to follow its recommendations. (WADA, 2009, p. 1)

WADA's first order of business was the creation of a set of universally applicable regulations concerning the use and detection of banned substances. Over its first 18 months in existence, the World Anti-Doping Code team consulted with a number of relevant groups, organizations, and individuals. The list included several national anti-doping organizations, several IFs, internationally recognized experts in drug testing and detection, athlete groups, various national governments, the Council of Europe and the International Intergovernmental Consultative Group on Anti-Doping in Sport (IICGADS).

By April 2002, a draft code had been completed which was then vetted by many of the same individuals, groups, and organizations consulted originally. On the basis of that feedback, a second draft was prepared by October, followed by further consultations. The third draft was completed in February 2003 and presented at the second World Conference on Doping in Sport which was held from May 3–5, 2003 in Copenhagen. The conference was attended by members of the IOC, representatives from 80 governments, 60 NOCs, 70 IFs, 30 national anti-doping organizations, as well as some athletes. At the end of the conference, the delegates agreed to the "Copenhagen Declaration on Anti-Doping in Sport" (Copenhagen Declaration, 2003). The declaration positioned WADA as the primary, international actor in the anti-doping movement and established the WADA Code as the basis for establishing the list of banned performance-enhancing substances and the procedures by which they would be controlled. The purpose of the Declaration was "to articulate a political and moral understanding among Participants" to four key points:

> 1.1. Recognise the role of, and support, the World-Anti-Doping Agency (WADA);

1.2. Support the World Anti-Doping Code (the "Code") adopted by the WADA Foundation Board at the World Conference on Doping in Sport (Copenhagen, 3–5 March 2003);

1.3. Sustain international intergovernmental cooperation in advancing harmonisation in anti-doping policies and practices in sport; and

1.4. Support a timely process leading to a convention or other obligation on points 3–8 below, to be implemented through instruments appropriate to the constitutional and administrative contexts of each government on or before the first day of the Turin Winter Olympic Games. This process should draw upon the expertise of representatives of governments from all the regions of the world and international organisations. (Copenhagen Declaration, 2003, p. 3)

Because WADA was constituted as a private organization it could not force any jurisdiction to formally comply with the code. As a result, WADA sought to bind governments, as much as possible, to the Copenhagen Declaration through a UNESCO Convention.

At the Third International Conference of Ministers and Senior Officials Responsible for Physical Education and Sportheld in Uruguay in December 1999, ministers had "expressed concern over unethical behaviour, in particular doping in sport" and urged the international community to take action (UNESCO, 2010). While finalizing its Code, WADA also worked with UNESCO to gain its support and involvement. In January 2003, during the 32nd session of the UNESCO General Conference, UNESCO (2010) agreed to "to tackle the question of doping in sport through an international convention." The Convention provided the legal framework that would permit governments to act in domains that are outside of the domain of various sport organizations. The Convention was drafted, revised and finally adopted in October 2005 at which time it was ratified by almost 100 countries (cf. UNESCO, 2005a, 2005b).

While many have applauded the creation of both WADA and the WADA Code—and there is a strong argument that can be made for the existence of a single code administered by one body—there are some important, negative consequences that have emerged from WADA's creation. The most important implication, by far, is the loss of national autonomy in the deliberations over, philosophy behind, implementation and control over policies related to

performance-enhancing substances. The interpretation and direction of all such policies are now directly and indirectly controlled
by an international body that is heavily resourced and can act with
considerable freedom and independence. Regional, national, and/or
local variations in culture, values, sport history and sport objectives
are all lost under the powerful forces of WADA.

For Canada, the adoption of the WADA Code in 2003 meant
a complete overhaul of the Canadian system. The resulting policy,
The Canadian Policy Against Doping in Sport (Sport Canada 2004), which
came into effect on June 1, 2004, replaced the 2000 *Canadian Policy on
Doping in Sport* and the 1991 *Canadian Policy Against Doping in Sport*.
Indicating Canada's complete surrender of autonomy in the policies
governing performance-enhancing substances in sport, under the
heading "International Harmonization," the 2004 policy stated:

> The *Canadian Policy Against Doping in Sport* commits to the
> implementation of the mandatory and other portions of the
> World Anti-Doping Program, including the World Anti-Doping
> Code, the mandatory International Standards and the Models
> of Best Practice. The POLICY further recognizes the role of
> the World Anti-Doping Agency in setting global standards
> and co-ordinating anti-doping world-wide. The mandatory
> International Standards and Models of Best Practice address,
> among other things, the Prohibited List, Doping Control, doping
> violations and consequences, and appeals, and are situated in
> the Rules and Standards of the Canadian Anti-Doping Program.
> (Sport Canada, 2004, paragraph 8)

The 2004 policy was revised in 2008 and again in 2011 (Sport Canada,
2008, 2011). The *Canadian Policy Against Doping in Sport* serves as the
basis for the Canadian Anti-Doping Program, which is administered
by the CCES. The Canadian Anti-Doping Program has gone through
two versions, a 2004 version and the recent 2009 program,[3] both of
which recognized "the role of WADA in setting global standards
and coordinating anti-doping worldwide" and "adopts and applies
the anti-doping rule violations set forth in the [WADA] *Code*" (CCES,
2011, p. 2).

Among the more controversial aspects of WADA's regulations,
imposed on Canadian athletes through the Anti-Doping Program, are
the requirements for athletes to be subject to testing at any time and

in any place, necessitating them to submit a "Whereabouts Filing" to the CCES (CCES, 2011, p. 25). That filing must provide "accurate and complete information about the Athlete's whereabouts during the forthcoming quarter, including identifying where he/she will be living, training and competing during that quarter, so that he/she can be located for Testing at any time during that quarter" (CCES, 2011, p. 27). The failure to submit the filing is considered a "Whereabouts Failure" which can be constituted as an "anti-doping violation" (CCES, 2011, p. 65).

Another controversial feature of the WADA Code and the Canadian Anti-Doping Program is the issue of strict liability. Clause 7.24 states that: "It is each *Athlete's* personal duty to ensure that no *Prohibited Substance* enters his or her body. *Athletes* are responsible for any *Prohibited Substance* or its *Metabolites* or *Markers* found to be present in their *Samples*." As a result, "it is not necessary that intent, fault, negligence or knowing *Use* on the *Athlete's* part be demonstrated in order to establish this anti-doping violation" (CCES, 2011, p. 64). Because some of the banned substances may be found in over-the-counter medications—pseudoephedrine, an ingredient in many cold medicines has caused the most controversy through inadvertent use, including costing Canadian rower Silken Laumann a gold medal at the 1995 Pan-American Games, its removal from the banned list in 2004 and subsequent return in 2010—there is an inordinate amount of pressure on athletes to monitor every aspect of their lives.

Finally, in any anti-doping violation—termed an "adverse analytical finding" (CCES, 2011, p. 71)—the standard of proof is simply "greater than a mere balance of probability but less than proof beyond a reasonable doubt" (CCES, 2011, pp. 74–75) which, given the possible outcome of suspension, has grave consequences for the athlete on the basis of information that leaves room for reasonable doubt.

Modernity versus Humanism: Harm Reduction in High Performance Sport

Even though the humanist premises and the transcendental image of the spirit of sport that de Coubertin wanted to instill as the foundation for the Modern Olympic Games remain moving and inspiring principles, the realities of contemporary, high performance sport are impossible to deny. World class sport today requires athletic performances at the outer limits of human potential. As a result, unless one is prepared (and able) to dismantle the entire socio-political foundation and edifice of international sport and the national systems of athlete development as they have evolved over the last half century; to disband the armies of applied sport scientists, chemists, technology experts, medical and paramedical personnel who support the quest for increasingly high-risk, athletic performances at the outer limits of human capacity; to replace a well-entrenched spectator thirst for athletic mega-spectacles, and the media and corporate appetite for the financial rewards that accrue for covering and sponsoring athletic performances of an increasingly incredible magnitude with some other entertainment forms then one must accept the reality that performance-enhancing substance use in high performance sport will continue. The most well thought through policies of prohibition and repression have failed.

While an invigorated appeal to the ethics of fair play and the spirit of sport might temper substance use, this approach has not had much impact either. A fundamental change is required with respect to the ethical questions and actual practices that shape policies regarding performance-enhancement in high performance sport— and that change is required with increasing urgency although WADA has well entrenched interests in maintaining the current regimes of repression and prohibition.

The key ethical shift that must occur is one that focuses directly on the real, human athlete at the centre of high performance sport. The major concern in high performance sport must be the safety of a fully informed, knowledgeable independent athlete who is free to make choices. Canadian policies on high performance sport need to adopt the harm-reduction strategies that are becoming increasingly widespread in the field of public health (cf. Kayser & Smith, 2008). A harm reduction approach would have several significant outcomes. First, it would allow sport scientists to systematically gather robust data on the long-term health effects that various performance-enhancing substances have on people. This vital information simply does not exist at present.

Second, it would not eliminate athlete testing. Under harm reduction policies, however, one would test for health impacts rather than the presence of drugs. How a particular substance, at specific dosages, affects an athlete's short and long-term health could be closely monitored.

Third, the open use and monitoring of substances would allow sport scientists to determine the extent to which different training regimes and practices—those with and without substances—actually affect athletes' performance capacities. Do certain substances really enhance performance significantly? If so, in what sports and how? What are the alternatives?

These three steps would allow athletes, coaches, scientists and medical professionals to replace the existing truncated, scientific knowledge and locker room 'ethnopharmacology' with reliable data on training, performance and health so that athletes could make genuinely informed decisions about how they would develop their athletic talents and capacities. In a world so thoroughly informed and guided by scientific knowledge, it is concerning that high performance athletes are denied vital elements to the knowledge systems upon which their lives are so dependent.

Fourth, a harm reduction strategy that opens sport to the use of all potential performance-enhancing substances would bring world-class sport in line with the existing, broader social attitudes to a number of personal and performance enhancement practices. At present, despite the widely growing use of drugs, surgery and technology to improve personal appearance, performance and quality of life, high performance sport prevents athletes from using the most up-to-date and effective drugs to overcome injuries, recover from increasingly demanding training regimes, or simply enhance particular elements in the execution of athletic skill and prowess. Within the current context of world-class sport, not allowing the use of all the most advanced technology and knowledge puts athletes' health at risk in far too many ways—and that is avoidable.

In 1967, to protect the fundamental humanist principles and spirit upon which de Coubertin launched the Modern Games from the encroaching forces of modernity, the IOC chose to ban certain performance-enhancing substances, technologies and practices. When the IOC eliminated the amateurism clause from the *Olympic Charter* and revised the eligibility code in 1974 to formally permit professionalized athletes to participate in the Games, it abandoned de Coubertin's cardinal principle and brought the Games more in line with the reality of the modern, twentieth century world (Beamish & Ritchie, 2006). In 1990, Dubin detailed the tension between de Coubertin's original, fundamental principles and the forces of modernity and he advocated forcefully for the former. In the two decades since his report, the forces of modernity have made high performance sport more spectacular as athletes perform at levels previously thought humanly impossible in contests that are increasingly high-risk and competitors are separated by mere thousandths of a second. In view of the fundamental change to the *Olympic Charter* in 1974 concerning athlete eligibility and the realities of contemporary sport entertainment, it is time to ask—how does one best manage high performance sport under modernity's full impact? Most important, what policies best ensure the health and safety of the athletes at the centre of modern, high performance sport?

Notes

1. For a detailed account of the impact of modernity and the politics of the Cold War upon the Olympic Games, see Beamish (2011).
2. This document is also referred to as the Mills Report since Dennis Mills, a member of parliament, was chair of the committee that produced the report.
3. The 2009 Canadian Anti-Doping Program was revised in October 2010 and March 2011 (CCES, 2011).

References

Arnold, M. (1932) (1875). *Culture and anarchy: An essay in political and social criticism.* Cambridge, UK: Cambridge University Press.

Assael, S. 2007. *Steroid nation.* New York: ESPN Books.

Beamish, R. (2011). *Steroids: A new look at performance enhancing drugs.* Santa Barbara, CA: Praeger.

Beamish, R., & Ritchie, I. (2006). *Highest, fastest, strongest: A critique of high-performance sport.* New York: Routledge.

Canadian Centre for Ethics in Sport. (2011). Canadian Anti-Doping Program. Ottawa, ON: Author. Retrieved from http://cces.ca/files/pdfs/CCES-POLICY-CADP-E.pdf

Canadian Olympic Association. (1984). *Policy on Doping and Drug Usage.* Montreal, QC: Canadian Olympic Association.

Canadian Olympic Association. (1987, July). Policy on the use of banned substances and procedures in sport. *Olympinfo, 35,* 1–2.

Carlyle, T. (1896). *Works of Thomas Carlyle* vol. 2. London: Chapman and Hall.

Chaikin, T., & Telander, R. (1988, October 24). The nightmare of steroids. *Sports Illustrated, 69*(18), 84–102.

Christie, J. (1986, July 17). Jelinek bans six athletes. *The Globe and Mail,* p. S1.

Christie, J., & Fisher, M. (1984, July 30). Steroid use in weightlifting Another setback for sport. *The Globe and Mail*, p. S1 & S5.

Coleridge, S. (1849). *Confessions of an inquiring spirit and some miscellaneous pieces.* London: William Pickering.

Copenhagen Declaration on Anti-Doping in Sport. (2003). Retrieved from http://www.wada-ama.org/Documents/World_Anti-Doping_Program/Governments/WADA_Copenhagen_Declaration_EN.pdf

Corelli, R. (1996, July 22). The drug detectives: Technological wizardry will try to keep the Olympics clean—But is it enough? *Maclean's, 109*(3), 28–29.

de Coubertin, P. (2000). *Olympism: Selected writing* [edited by N. Müller]. Lausanne, CH: International Olympic Committee.

Dimeo, P. (2007). *A history of drug use in sport 1876–1976: Beyond good and evil.* New York: Routledge.

Dubin, C.L. (1990). *Commission of inquiry into the use of drugs and banned practices intended to increase athletic performance.* Ottawa, ON: Minister of Supply and Services Canada.

Franke, W., & B. Berendonk. (1997). Hormonal doping and androgenization of athletes: A secret program of the German Democratic Republic government. *Clinical Chemistry, 43*(7), 1262–1279.

Fraser, G. (1983, August 23). Steroid use strips Canadians of five Pan-Am Games medals. *The Kingston Whig Standard*, pp. 1–2.

Government of Canada. (1988). *Toward 2000: Building Canada's sport system: The report of the Task force on national sport policy.* Ottawa, ON: Minister of Supply and Services Canada

Guttmann, A. (1984). *The Games must go on: Avery Brundage and the Olympic Movement.* New York: Columbia University Press.

Houlihan, B. (2004). Harmonising anti-doping policy in sport: The role of the World Anti-Doping Agency. In J. Hoberman & V. Møllen (Eds.), *Doping and public policy* (pp. 19–30). Odense, DK: University Press of Southern Denmark.

House of Representatives. (1989). *The Anabolic Steroid Restriction Act of 1989: Hearings before the Subcommittee on Crime of the Committee of the Judiciary of the House of Representatives* 101st Congress, 1st Session.

House of Representatives. (1990). *The Anabolic Steroid Restriction Act of 1990: Hearings before the Subcommittee on Crime of the Committee of the Judiciary of the House of Representatives* 101st Congress, 2nd Session.

International Olympic Committee. (1984). *Medical Guide.* Lausanne, CH: IOC Press.

Johnson, B. (1983, September 17). Is cheating the name of the game?" *The Globe and Mail*, p. 10.

Johnson, W.O. (1985, May 13). Steroids: A problem of huge dimensions. *Sports Illustrated, 62*(19), 38–61.

Johnson, W.O. (1988, September 19). Hit for a loss. *Sports Illustrated, 69*(13), 50–57.

Johnson, W.O., & K. Moore. (1988, October 3). The loser. *Sports Illustrated, 69*(15), 22–26.

Kayser, B., & Smith, A.C.T. (2008). Globalization of anti-doping: The reverse side of the medal. *British Medical Journal, 337*(7661), 85–87.

Lausanne Declaration on Doping in Sport. (1999, February-March). *Olympic Review, XXVI*(25), 17–18.

McAuley, L. (1986, July 17). Drug use ends 6 athletes' amateur careers. *The Ottawa Citizen*, p. A1 & A16.

Mills, D. (1998). *Sport in Canada: Everybody's business. Leadership, partnership and accountability.* Standing Committee on Canadian Heritage, Sub-Committee on the Study of Sport in Canada. Ottawa, ON: Government of Canada. Retrieved from http://www.parl.gc.ca/HousePublications/Publication.aspx?DocId=1031530&Mode=1&Parl=36&Ses=&Language=E

Møller, V. (2006). "Knud Enemark Jensen's death during the 1960 Rome Olympics: A search for truth?" In P. Dimeo (Ed.) *Drugs, alcohol and sport* (pp. 99–118). New York: Routledge.

Newman, J.H. (1915). *On the scope and nature of university education.* New York: E.P. Dutton & Company.

Porter, B., & Cole, J. (1990). Amateur sport: Future challenges. Second Report of the Standing Committee on Health and Welfare, Social Affairs, Seniors and the Status of Women. Ottawa, ON: Queen's Printer.

Priestner Allinger, C., & Allinger, T. (2004). *Own the Podium—2010: Final report with recommendations of the independent task force for winter NSOs and funding partners.* Retrieved from http://www.sportmatters.ca/Groups/SMG%20Resources/Sport%20and%20PA%20Policy/otp_report_-_final_-_e.pdf

Sport Canada. 1984a). *Scorecard.* Ottawa, ON: Minister of State, Fitness and Amateur Sport.

Sport Canada. (1984b). *Drug Use and Doping Control in Sport: A Sport Canada Policy.* Ottawa, ON: Minister of State, Fitness and Amateur Sport.

Sport Canada. (1985). *Drug Use and Doping Control in Sport: A Sport Canada Policy UPDATE.* Ottawa, ON: Minister of State, Fitness and Amateur Sport.

Sport Canada. (2004). The Canadian Policy Against Doping in Sport. Ottawa, ON: Department of Canadian Heritage. Retrieved from http://www.waterpolo.ca/admin/docs/clientuploads/About_Us/DopingControlJune04_ENG.pdf

Sport Canada. (2008). *The Canadian Policy Against Doping in Sport.* Retrieved from http://www.pch.gc.ca/pgm/sc/pol/dop/index-eng.cfm

Sport Canada. (2011). The Canadian policy against doping in sport—2011. Retrieved from http://www.pch.gc.ca/DAMAssetPub/DAM-comn-comn/STAGING/texte-text/dop-2011_1307556248723_eng.pdf

Telander, R. (1988, October 24). A peril for athletes. *Sports Illustrated, 69*(18), 114.

Telander, R. (1989, February 20). The death of an athlete. *Sports Illustrated, 70*(8), 68–78.

Todd, J., & Todd, T. (2001). Significant events in the history of drug testing and the Olympic Movement: 1960–1999. In W. Wilson & E. Derse (Eds.), *Doping in elite sport: The politics of drugs in the Olympic Movement* (pp. 65–128). Champaign, IL: Human Kinetics.

Todd, T. (1983, August 1). The steroid predicament. *Sports Illustrated, 59*(5), 62–77.

UNESCO. (2005a, January 10–14). Oral report of the rapporteur of the 3rd session of the intergovernmental meeting of experts on the draft international convention against doping in sport. Retrieved from [http://unesdoc.unesco.org/images/0013/001388/138867e.pdf

UNESCO. (2005b, October 19). International convention against doping in sport 2005. Retrieved from http://portal.unesco.org/en/ev.php-URL_ID=31037&URL_DO=DO_TOPIC&URL_SECTION=201.html

UNESCO. (2010). Towards a better sport. Retrieved from http://www.unesco.org/new/en/social-and-human-sciences/themes/sport/anti-doping/international-convention-against-doping-in-sport/background/

United States Sentencing Commission. (2006). *2006 Steroids Report.* Retrieved from http://www.ussc.gov/USSCsteroidsreport-0306.pdf

Yesalis, C., & Bahrke, M. (2002). History of doping in sport. *International Sports Studies, 24*(1), 42–76.

World Anti-Doping Agency. (2009). Constitutive instrument of foundation of the Agence Mondiale Antidopage—World Anti-Doping Agency. Lausanne, CH: Author. Retrieved from http://www.wada-ama.org/Documents/About_WADA/Statutes/WADA_Statutes_2009_EN.pdf

Ziegler, J. (1984). Forward (pp. 1–2). In B. Goldman, *Death in the locker room: Steroids and sports.* South Bend, IN: Icarus Press.

CHAPTER VIII

Hosting Policies of Sport Events

Cora McCloy, University of Toronto and
Lucie Thibault, Brock University

Hallmark or "mega-events" are large-scale, planned occurrences of limited duration which can have a substantial social, economic, political, environmental and/or cultural impact on the host region (Emery, 2002; Essex & Chalkley, 1998; Hall & Hodges, 1998; Kavestos & Szymanski, 2010; McCloy, 2002; Roche, 2000; Whitson, 2004). Mega-events also involve significant mass media coverage usually on a global scale (Hiller, 2000; Roche, 2000). Multi-sport events such as the Olympic Games, Commonwealth Games, and Pan American Games, as well as specialist world-level international sport competitions such as the Fédération internationale de football association (FIFA) World Cup and the International Association of Athletics Federations (IAAF) World Championships fall under the rubric of mega-events. Hiller (2000) further clarified the mega-event description in suggesting that, from an urban analyst perspective:

> any large-scale special event can be considered a mega-event
> if it has a significant and/or permanent urban effect—that is,
> if it is considered so significant that it reprioritizes the urban
> agenda in some way and leads to some modification or alteration
> of urban space which becomes its urban legacy ... [and] when
> it intervenes in the normal functioning of the city to mobilize
> resources for event preparation and event hosting. (p. 183)

Canada has frequently held such mega-events in sport. Since the hosting of the 1930 British Empire Games in Hamilton, the number, cost and impact of such events have steadily increased. Other high-profile and increasingly larger-run multi-sport events include the 1967 Pan American Games in Winnipeg, the 1976 Montreal Olympic Games, the 1978 Commonwealth Games in Edmonton, the 1988 Calgary Olympic Winter Games, and the 2010 Vancouver Olympic and Paralympic Winter Games. A complete list of major multi-sport events hosted in Canada is outlined in Table 8.1. As well, several communities across Canada have hosted many large-scale and mid-scale single sport events, for example, the IAAF World Championships in Edmonton in 2001, the 2003 Union cycliste internationale (UCI) Road World Championships in Hamilton, the 2005 Fédération internationale de natation (FINA) World Aquatics Championships in Montreal,

Table 8.1 Major International Multi-Sport Games Hosted by Canada

Year	Games	Location
1930	British Empire Games	Hamilton
1954	British Empire and Commonwealth Games	Vancouver
1967	Pan American Games	Winnipeg
1976	Olympic Games	Montreal
1978	Commonwealth Games	Edmonton
1983	Summer Universiade Games	Edmonton
1988	Olympic Winter Games	Calgary
1990	North American Indigenous Games	Edmonton
1993	North American Indigenous Games	Prince Albert
1994	Commonwealth Games	Victoria
1997	Winter Special Olympics World Games	Collingwood and Toronto
1997	North American Indigenous Games	Victoria
1999	Pan American Games	Winnipeg
2001	Jeux de la Francophonie	Ottawa-Hull
2002	North American Indigenous Games	Winnipeg
2008	North American Indigenous Games	Cowichan
2010	Olympic and Paralympic Winter Games	Vancouver
2014	North American Indigenous Games	Regina
2015	Pan and Parapan American Games	Toronto

the 2009 International Ice Hockey Federation (IIHF) World Under 20 Championships in Ottawa, the 2012 World Women's Curling Championship in Lethbridge, and the 2012 Fédération internationale de volleyball (FIVB) Junior World Championships in Halifax. The federal government has made significant financial contributions to the hosting of these large-scale events, in some cases, far in excess of the program and operational funding for sport provided through its Sport Canada unit.

The codification of the federal government's role in the hosting of international sport events began in 1967 during Canada's centennial year celebrations. The purpose of this chapter is to provide an overview of the federal sport hosting policies that have been a part of the policy landscape since 1967. This chapter briefly touches upon the evolution and goals of the 1978 and 1983 hosting policies and more recent variations (1996, 2000) of the policy. Particular attention is devoted to the most recent policy (2008) guiding the federal government's strategy for hosting multi-sport games and international single sport events.

Research clearly demonstrates that federal hosting policies have rarely been implemented in a manner that engaged federal officials from the earliest bid stages (Blais, 2003; Macintosh et al., 1987; McCloy, 2002, 2009). The benefits for Canadian amateur sport have not always been fully realized in such a climate (Blais, 2003; McCloy, 2002, 2009). This chapter captures some of the key stages and milestones within policy development and situates the rationale for bidding alongside the achievement of longer term sport and community legacies. The complexities and issues of the hosting sport policy process are also highlighted within this context.

Historical Overview of Canada's Hosting Policy

Early in the development of Canada's sport system, leaders in the federal government felt it was important to have a public policy to guide their involvement in the numerous multi-sport games and single sport events as proposals were submitted by interested Canadian communities and agencies. In addition, the increasing desire on the part of the federal government to achieve greater and longer lasting benefits for the amateur sport community became a vital element of their hosting policy. In the following pages, we review the main features of Canada's hosting policies since 1967.

The 1967 Hosting Policy

The 1961 Fitness and Amateur Sport Act (Bill C-131) served as a central element in the development of the first federal sport hosting policy. This first hosting policy was more specifically a Memorandum to Cabinet dated November 23, 1967 by Allan MacEachen, Minister of National Health and Welfare at the time, entitled, *Report on Federal Policy in Support of Fitness and Amateur Sport, With Special Reference to the Sponsorship of International Events.* During the 1960s, a major concern for the federal government was the commitment of increasingly larger sums of public money to events that some federal Cabinet members felt could not always justify such expenditures. The 1967 Report was commissioned to examine this important issue. This first hosting policy effectively set the stage for subsequent policies in this area (cf. McCloy (2009) for more details on the 1967 hosting policy). The first hosting policy by the Government of Canada (i.e., Sport Canada) was based on similar rationales identified in subsequent reiterations of this policy, which we will discuss in this chapter.

As noted by McCloy (2009, p. 1167), the 1967 hosting policy was founded on "providing opportunities for Canadian athletes to compete on home soil; another motivation for hosting was a means of strengthening the amateur sport system and showcasing Canadian athletes to the nation." However, as McCloy argued:

> the government's wish list did not end there, and the past four decades of hosting can affirm that amateur sport would struggle to gain benefits amidst other broad governmental goals combined with influential business leaders vying for a space in the bidding competition. It appears that the centennial celebrations [1967] were clearly an event to celebrate national unity through sport, but hosting the world was an additional goal, one that could further achieve wider governmental goals such as nation-building, showcasing its strength to the outside world, a place to visit (tourism objectives emerged in the 1967 Report) and supporting business and economic opportunities in local hosting communities. (2009, p. 1168)

It is important to note that similar rhetoric has been evident in many of the motives provided in all subsequent versions of the Canadian government's hosting policies for international sport events.

The 1978 Hosting Policy

The creation of *Canada's Hosting Policy: Guidelines for Federal Involvement in Major International and National Amateur Sport Events in Canada* (November, 1978) was the next federal policy statement to bring some consistency and rationality to the manner in which bid groups requested federal financial support. The author of the 1978 hosting policy was Iona Campagnolo, the first federal Minister of State for Fitness and Amateur Sport. The 1978 hosting policy applied to both national and international sport events hosted in Canada. There were few, if any, references to the reasons why the policy was created beyond what is included in the text of the document. Campagnolo's preface to the policy lends key insights into the role of the federal government in hosting and sets the stage for the need for a policy in this area. Specifically, the Minister stated:

> in recent years, the federal government has had the opportunity to provide direct and indirect assistance for several major international and national amateur sport events. This assistance has often been provided on an ad hoc basis dependent on the specific circumstances surrounding each event. (Campagnolo, 1978, n.p.)

Referring to the "considerable" experience Canada had gained in hosting, the Minister contended that the nation's role as host to amateur sport events would increase. Hosting was also perceived as beneficial for Canadian athlete performances. However, while the policy document acknowledged Canada's past success as a "desirable" host, the focus was directed to the need for federal procedures to ensure "proper bidding can take place" (Campagnolo, 1978, n.p.). Guidelines for determining federal support were deemed important and would "assist organizing authorities, the federal government, and indeed other levels of government, in working together to determine support for future events" (Campagnolo, 1978, n.p.). This rationale addressed the recurring one-off manner in which bids proceeded and the limited involvement of federal officials in this process and, as such, solidified the role of the federal government in each bidding case.

The 1978 policy was divided into three major parts: the event approval process, factors affecting level of financial support, and the data to be included in submissions for federal support. Of note, the policy requested that bid applicants address the question of who would benefit from the newly constructed sport facilities in the post-event period. Interestingly, following the approval of this 1978 hosting policy, Campagnolo appeared to bypass this aspect of her own hosting policy by offering Calgary's bid/organizing committee for the 1988 Olympic Winter Games an informal promise of CA\$ 200M in federal government support (Cushing, 1996; McCloy, 2006). According to Cushing (1996), "there was no formal assessment through the government's hosting policy of the financial request by the Calgary bid/organizing committee" (p. 120).

The 1983 Hosting Policy

Following the 1978 hosting policy, Sport Canada released a new iteration in June 1983. The rationale for this new policy was borne out of discontent by federal officials with the manner in which events such as the 1983 Summer Universiade Games (a multi-sport event organized by the Fédération internationale du sport universitaire (FISU)), held in Edmonton, proceeded without prior federal approval. The absence of this approval step had immersed the federal officials in a mire of difficult negotiations as government officials struggled to meet the Fitness and Amateur Sport objectives for the period leading up the 1984 Olympic Games (McCloy, 2006).

In 1981 Gerald Regan, the then Minister of State for Fitness and Amateur Sport, pursued updates to the hosting policy. With the release of the federal government policy paper, *A Challenge to the Nation—Fitness and Amateur Sport in the 80s*, Regan (1981) sought to continue its commitment to the pursuit of excellence during the decade of the 1980s. In identifying the importance of hosting and redefining the process of taking on the responsibility of staging large games, some of the rationale for an updated policy emerged. According to McCloy's (2006) findings, some Sport Canada officials characterized the overall climate in amateur sport in Canada following the Montreal Olympic Games and heading into the 1980s as "a rudderless ship." Concerns were expressed about the dearth of leadership in sport combined with a weak organizational base for national sport. Although Sport Canada officials acknowledged some positive steps with the appointment of the first Minister of State for Fitness and Amateur Sport, Iona Campagnolo, in 1976 and the creation of programs such as Game Plan 76, which provided aid to Canadian athletes leading up to the Montreal Games, an overall lack of financial resources limited the development of sport policies and programs. In addition, with ongoing changes in ministers at the helm, the leadership within Fitness and Amateur Sport suffered from some instability (see Table 1.2 for a list of ministers of state for Fitness and Amateur Sport since 1976).

The amateur sport scene, however, soon experienced a major injection of focus and energy into the system as measures to enhance its effectiveness, such as the development of a quadrennial planning program for national sport organizations, the creation of national training centres for high performance athletes and the development of coaching training programs, were implemented (Macintosh et al., 1987; Macintosh, 1996). Through both a central leadership change within Sport Canada (with the appointment of Abby Hoffman as Director in 1981) and the selection of Calgary as host city of the 1988 Olympic Winter Games, greater emphasis was placed on developing strong national leadership, and Canadian sport began the slow journey towards a stronger sport system.

The 1996 and 2000 Hosting Policies

The 1996 and 2000 hosting policies are addressed collectively because both of these versions originated from the 1983 policy. As noted in the summative evaluation of Sport Canada's hosting program, the 1983 hosting policy "was substantially revised in 1996" (Prairie Research Associates Inc., 2004, p. 10) and then updated in 2000 (Prairie Research Associates Inc., 2004; Scrimger, 2005). The impetus for the 1996 revisions to the *Federal Policy for Hosting International Sport Events* was attributed to the increasing number of events being held in Canada as well as the rising costs associated with bidding for and hosting these events (Cushing, 1996). In addition, the context for federal support of sport was changing. From the mid-1980s until the mid-1990s, the Government of Canada was in a period of retrenchment. During this period, the federal government reconsidered Sport Canada's financial contributions to sport organizations, programs and services. For example, in a 1988 Task Force Report, Jean Charest (the then Minister of State for Fitness and Amateur Sport) wrote, "in our future plans for sport we should not assume that the federal government alone will maintain its current very high proportionate share of funding" (Government of Canada, 1988, p. 14). Charest believed that Canada's corporate sector needed to invest in amateur sport. A few years later, in 1993, Prime Minister Kim Campbell undertook some "drastic measures in an effort to cut spending within her government" (Harvey, Thibault, & Rail, 1995, p. 261), and sport was not spared from these cuts. In light of budget cuts, sport leaders within the federal government wanted to ensure that the events in which they invested had "significant sport, economic, social, and cultural benefits" (Cushing, 1996, p. 125).

In addition to the increased opportunities to host sport events and the Canadian government's financial cuts, the 1996 hosting policy emerged from a realization that the federal government needed to work in closer partnerships with other levels of government and other government agencies, as well as with the private sector (including non-profit and commercial organizations). It is important to note that the 1996 hosting policy differs from previous versions of the policy (i.e., 1967, 1978 and 1983), in that the 1996 version required that federal government support be obtained *prior to* a bid being submitted to an international sport federation. It also contained a new provision stipulating that bid/organizing committees had to follow environmental laws and conduct environmental screenings (if facilities needed to be built for the events). As well, this policy included more detailed criteria about the Government of Canada's financial obligations with respect to sport events hosting and legacies (Cushing, 1996).

Consistent with criticism directed toward previous hosting policies, the 1996 and 2000 hosting policies also contained provisions that were not followed or enforced. Specifically, as explained by Blais (2003, p. 8), since 1996 a key component of the hosting policy requirement has in many cases been bypassed, namely, that of obtaining prior federal support for the event bid before submission to an international franchise holder. As well, sometimes the requirement to conduct an economic impact assessment was not implemented due to the cost of conducting such assessments.

The most important change from the 1996 Hosting Policy to the 2000 policy was an "increase, from 25% to 35%, in the cap on Government of Canada's contributions to international sport events held in Canada" (Prairie Research Associates Inc., 2004, p. 10). As noted in the summative evaluation of Sport Canada's hosting program, not only must supported events "have the potential to accrue net benefits to Canada" but these events must also "be financed within the fiscal capacity of the federal government" (Prairie Research Associates Inc., 2004, p. 11). Features of the 1996 and 2000 policies included the following: proactive partnerships between bid committees and the federal government; provision of legacies directly related to sport programming in addition to economic, social and cultural legacies within the community; compliance with federal standards; no-deficit guarantees; equitable financing; community support; and sound management.

The 2008 Hosting Policy

The most recent iteration of the hosting policy draws on two federal reports borne out of the recent federal legislation that replaced the 1961 *Fitness and Amateur Sport Act* in Canada. Passed in 2003, the *Act to Promote Physical Activity and Sport* (Parliament of Canada, 2003) was closely linked to both the *Canadian Sport Policy* (Sport Canada, 2002a) and a strategy document entitled *Federal-Provincial-Territorial Priorities for Collaborative Action 2002–2005* (Sport Canada, 2002b) with regard to goals and targets for Canadian sport including targets for hosting international events. The *Canadian Sport Policy*, in particular, draws attention to the "fragmented approach" that has plagued Canadian hosting efforts (Sport Canada, 2002a, p. 11). According to the CSP, this unplanned approach has put pressure on public and private funding sources and resulted in the reproduction of regional disparities (i.e., where western provinces have received a disproportionate amount of funding for hosting international events in relation to the Atlantic region) (Sport Canada, 2002a).

The *Canadian Sport Policy*'s recommendation to develop a strategic hosting framework initially resulted in the *Report to the Secretary of State (Physical Activity and Sport) on Hosting International Sport Events in Canada—A proposal for a strategic framework* (Blais, 2003). In particular, this report identified a wide range of issues that surround the hosting of international sport events. These issues included the increasing financial pressures on all levels of government (i.e., federal, provincial, and local), concerns over the limited financial, sport programming and facility legacies, the imbalance in the distribution of international events across Canada, the best interests of sport being overlooked by community leaders motivated by gains in tourism and local economies, and inconsistent measures of the economic impact of the events. Blais (2003) addressed how the repeated delays in financial negotiations between the federal and provincial/territorial governments over the size of their contributions to the event have often occurred after the event has been awarded to a community. In turn, these delays have had an impact on the "careful planning and consideration of such issues as legacy—fiscal, sport programming and facility-based" (Blais, 2003, p. 15).

More importantly, Blais's (2003) report emphasized that the sport community is rarely central to these governmental decisions, and thus legacy planning falters without the involvement of knowledgeable sport leaders. The report concluded that events have been pursued:

> by enthusiastic communities who have recognized the benefits of hosting international sport events and have led the drive to attract these events to their communities mainly for economic as opposed to sport development, social or cultural development reasons . . . The sport community is not involved, or involved at the level they [sic] should be, in these discussions to ensure the best interests of sport are being considered. (Blais, 2003, p. 14)

Another issue raised by Blais (2003) included the increasing financial expectations on the part of leaders of international sport federations (IFs) regarding the expenses to be covered by host communities. These expectations often put additional pressures on the host community. As Blais (2003, p. 14) noted, "IFs are requesting that international delegate travel and athlete accommodation be covered [by the host], while retaining the rights for marketing and broadcasting the event." As a result, host communities are restricted in the strategies they can use to market and fundraise for the event and thus, turn to governments to request more funds.

Given the complexity of hosting international events and the "shared jurisdiction" of sport in Canada, Blais (2003) provided a strategic hosting framework to assist government leaders and sport stakeholders in making fiscally responsible decisions regarding hosting international sport events. The framework outlined objectives, principles and conditions to support sport events. As well, the framework provided communication and co-ordination mechanisms to ensure collaboration among all levels of government and the sport community. Blais's (2003) report also provided detailed timelines of major multi-sport events for which Canada should consider bidding over the next 20 to 30 years. In these timelines, the following events are identified: Summer and Winter Olympic and Paralympic Games, Commonwealth Games, Pan American Games, Summer and Winter World University Games, and Summer and Winter Special Olympics World Games. In addition to these multi-sport events, bidding and hosting single sport international events are also encouraged. Blais (2003) also developed 29 recommendations geared toward "fiscally responsible decisions; regional balance to distribute capacity building across the country; a sport development focus with community leadership; and coordination and collaboration among municipalities" (Blais, 2003, p. 4).

Shortly after the publication of Blais's (2003) document, a second key report was released entitled *Summative Evaluation of the Department of Canadian Heritage's Sport Hosting Program* (Prairie Research Associates Inc., 2004). This report was conducted to "assess the Program's relevance, effectiveness, adequacy of its design and delivery and its performance measurement practices" (Prairie Research Associates Inc., 2004, p. 3). Only events between 2000 and 2003 were examined in this review, although a broad sweep of facility and financial legacies associated with eight major events between 1988 and 2003 were also included. One of the key findings of the report challenged the widely held belief that hosting events is equated with positive sport development initiatives. This chapter also examines and challenges this predominantly positive hosting view. The federal report underscores this problematic area of hosting:

> the relationship between hosting events and sport development is asserted as self evident . . . while it is reasonable to expect that hosting an event may contribute to the development of athletes, coaches, etc., for example through the creation of financial and facility legacies, this expectation is, of itself, not sufficient proof of a link. The [hosting] program needs to more clearly demonstrate that this rationale is sound and that supporting sports events leads to sport development. (Prairie Research Associates Inc., 2004, p. iii)

Thus, both reports (Blais, 2003; Prairie Research Associates Inc., 2004) raise crucial points regarding sport legacy issues stemming from hosting of international sport events. As well, they underline the need to ensure that a strategy is in place to maintain a strong voice from the sport community during the bidding and hosting periods. The following statement speaks to the heart of the hosting issues but it does not account for the lengthy list of federal policy initiatives that have preceded it:

> Unless a coordinated, collaborative approach by both orders of government along with the sport community is taken, the current unplanned approach will continue and there will be no assurance that the events attracted will be the ones meeting sport development, community development and economic development objectives. Along with that, continued risk of exposure to unplanned government expenditures and the lack of balance across the country will be the inescapable consequences. The proposed Strategic Hosting Framework is intended to bring order to the haphazard approach that has characterized the hosting of international sport events in recent years, through a collaborative process involving all stakeholders interested in bidding for and hosting international sport events. (Blais, 2003, p. 35)

The 2008 *Federal Policy for Hosting International Sport Events* emerged from these reports and included the following objectives: a proactive and strategic approach to bidding for and hosting international events, transparent decision making, targeted investment to projects that advance the Strategic Framework and ensure "sound program and fiscal management" in selecting and managing hosting projects (Canadian Heritage, 2008, p. 2). This policy differs from previous versions in that sport plans and bidding and hosting opportunities are to be prioritized over a 10- to 25-year horizon. As a rationale for this approach, the policy makers argued that the 2003 *Physical Activity and Sport Act* (Parliament of Canada, 2003) and the 2002 *Canadian Sport Policy* (Sport Canada, 2002a) reinforce "the benefits of hosting international sport events, but noted that Canada's fragmented approach in determining which events to fund had created pressure on public and private funding sources, and resulted in disparities with respect to the benefits from hosting such events" (Canadian Heritage, 2008, p. 1). In line with Blais's (2003) recommendations, the 2008 policy calls for federal government support for the hosting of:

- Two (2) International Major Multisport Games every ten (10) years;
- One (1) Large International Single Sport Event every two (2) years;
- Thirty (30) or more Small International Single Sport events each year; and
- International Multisport Games for Aboriginal Peoples and Persons with a Disability. (p. 3)

Furthermore, the policy document acknowledges that the number of bids supported for sport events "may vary, as it may be necessary to bid multiple times in order to win the rights to host" these international events (Canadian Heritage, 2008, p. 3). This federal government effort to quantify the number of events demonstrates their willingness to support a planned approach to hosting and to eliminate unplanned investment of resources in events they did not endorse a priori.

It is evident that historically, many backroom negotiations occurred during the bidding and hosting processes, and the end result has often been that the federal government (and its hosting policies) has been left in a position of *reacting to* rather than leading the negotiations. The 2008 hosting policy signals a more proactive federal role in the bidding and hosting process of sport events.

Overall, the federal hosting policies have not been fully implemented due in large part to resilient and "enthusiastic communities" (Blais, 2003, p. 2) that pursue large-scale sport events with well-connected and powerful coalitions including business leaders, political supporters, and to a lesser extent, sport administrators. The increasing drive by members of bid groups has been interwoven with those of strong and influential political leaders, many of whom actively promoted the event in anticipation of the positive economic returns. In addition, the ability to secure government funding for the event has been predicated on bids conducting economic assessments. Seldom have the assessments been done by arms-length groups, and the assumptions of positive economic return were rarely questioned. This pattern has been evident since the 1960s. The political and economic forces surrounding many sport events, some coalescing with greater strength than others, would suggest that in the face of such powerful interests, amateur sport has often struggled to find a space to meet some of its core objectives related to sport and athlete development.

Federal Government Motivations Across Hosting Policies

The 1967 hosting policy provided a snapshot of federal government hosting experiences in the 1960s. By the late 1960s a movement was clearly afoot to provide opportunities for Canadian athletes to compete on home soil. Yet another motivation for hosting was to have the event serve as a means to strengthen the amateur sport system and showcase Canadian athletes to the nation. This was intended purpose of the 1967 Centennial celebrations—to host a series of events celebrating national unity through sport—but the events would also serve to provide further opportunity to pursue wider governmental goals such as nation-building, showcasing its strength to the outside world, touting Canada as a place to visit (tourism objectives emerged in the 1967 Report), and supporting business and economic opportunities in local hosting communities. What emerges in the 1967 Report is a striking range of concerns that continue to dominate current hosting discussions, most notably, how local community groups pursue large-scale international sport events despite being ignorant or wary of the federal bureaucratic levels of involvement.

In a similar vein, all other federal hosting policies sought to include a wide range of objectives that extended beyond amateur sport. For example, in the 1978 hosting policy bidding groups were requested to achieve a range of sport benefits, with the added stipulation that the event must also strive to generate revenue through additional means such as tourism and job creation. The 1996 hosting policy document articulates an even stronger shift in federal government motivations to host sport events, citing the contributions to be made to Canada: "[hosting has] the potential to bring direct and significant benefits across a broad range of government priorities and can act as a catalyst for the achievement of other federal objectives" (Government of Canada, 1996, p. 1). Thus, from the outset this policy acknowledges the role of sport hosting as something unique for a range of government sectors, not just amateur sport (McCloy, 2006, p. 239).

The federal government's wish list to gain benefits beyond amateur sport thus began in the 1967 hosting policy but did not end there, and the past three decades of hosting can affirm that amateur sport would struggle to gain benefits amidst other broad governmental goals, which had influential business leaders vying for a space in the bidding competition. Indeed, the 2012 CSP includes a range of hosting outcomes such as "increased civic pride, engagement and cohesion" as well as "increased economic development and prosperity" (Sport Canada, 2012, p. 4). Other motivations include "community-building objectives" (Sport Canada, 2012, p. 21).

Legacies and Sport Canada's Hosting Policies

For this chapter sport legacy can be broadly defined as both planned and unintended long- and short-term usage of sport facilities and the development of sport programs and services in the post-event period. Included here are contributions to both grass roots and elite sport. The assumption is that 'sport legacy' can only be positive, that is contribute beneficially to the development of communities and to a strong Canadian sport system if it provides for the health and well-being of citizens in the mega-event host region and beyond (McCloy, 2006). This next section addresses the role of federal hosting policies in garnering amateur sport legacies across a range of participant groups and addresses serious gaps in achieving such legacies.

Although the federal hosting policies have incorporated provisions to ensure that sport legacy items were met, they have been only partially successful. As previously noted, specific legacy stipulations whereby bid groups were requested to address these issues in their quest for federal funding only made it into the 1996 hosting policy document. In this respect, the 1988 Calgary Olympic Winter Games had a significant impact on the codification of legacy items as outlined in the multi-party agreements signed between the major funding parties. Of note is that the 1978 hosting policy—in effect when Calgary organizers were bidding for the 1988 Olympic Winter Games—did not stipulate such plans and details for the post-event period. Calgary Olympic event organizers, however, laid the groundwork for conducting long-term amateur sport legacy planning: Calgary's Olympic Oval (speed skating) serves as one of the more obvious examples. The combination of revenues from the American Broadcasting Company (ABC), combined with strong planning and foresight (beginning in large part with Frank King's visionary plan) in agreements between many government partners and the Calgary Olympic Development Association (CODA, now renamed WinSport Canada), ensured that capital and endowment funds were spent on the needs of amateur sport. Other facilities such as the Canadian Sport Centre in Calgary and others set up across Canada have further highlighted the positive benefits to be accrued through hosting large-scale amateur sport events.

The sport legacies achieved as a result of the 1999 Winnipeg Pan American Games are a second notable example. Despite difficult negotiations between federal officials and the 1999 Pan Am Games Society (PAGS), a positive outcome was the resultant endowment fund for the Canadian Sport Centre—Manitoba. This endowment fund was a result of federal sport officials insisting that certain key sport legacy elements of the 1996 hosting policy be implemented.

Although both the 1988 Calgary Olympic Winter Games and 1999 Winnipeg Pan American Games offer some illustrations of positive amateur sport legacies, overall, it appears that throughout Canada's lengthy history of sport event hosting, Canadian professional sport franchises have received a disproportionate amount of financial support directly linked to these amateur events (via new facilities or substantial upgrades to existing structures) (Whitson, 2004; Whitson & Macintosh, 1996). For example, the Edmonton Commonwealth Stadium, the Calgary Saddledome, the Edmonton Coliseum (now Rexall Place), Shaw Park in Winnipeg, and the Montreal Olympic Stadium are obvious examples of professional sport venues that have received large infusions of federal (and other levels of government) financial support to bolster the sport teams that use them for training. Important upgrades to BC Place and the Pacific Coliseum for the Vancouver 2010 Olympic and Paralympic Winter Games have also benefited Canadian professional sport franchises. Even though some of these sport facilities were built with substantial public funds, community-wide access to these facilities has been lacking. In fact, community participation in such facilities is often associated with spectatorship, rather than individual use.

With respect to community-level sport legacies, the 1996 and 2000 hosting policies and their subsequent iterations have had some positive impact in this area, and the legacies and benefits from hosting international events for community level sport have improved dramatically in recent years. For example, the Pan Am Pool in Winnipeg (1999 Pan Am Games), Commonwealth Place in Victoria (1994 Commonwealth Games) and a number of facilities at Canada Olympic Park in Calgary (1988 Olympic Winter Games) support this claim. As well, several of the sport facilities used during the 2010 Vancouver Olympic and Paralympic Winter Games were promptly re-configured into community spaces for the public's use, for example the Richmond Olympic Oval and the Doug Mitchell Thunderbird Sports Centre.

Other beneficiaries of the legacies from hosting sport events have been university communities, for example, the 1983 Edmonton World University Games (FISU) and the 1978 Commonwealth Games left valuable sport facilities for the University of Alberta, the 1988 Calgary Olympic Winter Games for the University of Calgary, and the 2010 Vancouver Olympic and Paralympic Winter Games for the University of British Columbia.

Other important legacies of hosting sport events include infrastructure development (e.g., improvements to public transit, transportation, airports and public meeting spaces). As examples, the 2010 Vancouver Olympic and Paralympic Winter Games developed and upgraded a number of infrastructures (e.g., light rapid transit to/from the Vancouver International Airport; highway upgrade between Vancouver and Whistler), and non-sport facilities (e.g., Vancouver Convention Centre, community centres).

It is also important to note other legacies that have occurred in the development of programs and key initiatives in Canada's sport system. For example, the 1988 Calgary Olympic Winter Games led to the introduction of long-term planning programs within national sport organizations (i.e., Quadrennial Planning Program/Best Ever '88). As another example, the 2010 Vancouver Olympic and Paralympic Winter Games served as a catalyst for the development of Own the Podium, an initiative to target efforts and funding to enhance our performances at these Games (Donnelly, 2010a, 2010b; Government of Canada, n.d., 2010; Priestner Allinger & Allinger, 2004).

In addition, it is important to highlight the development of legacy strategies ahead of the event, which was the case for the 2010 Olympic and Paralympic Winter Games. With funds from governments (federal and provincial) and from corporate sources, 2010 Legacies Now was created in 2000 to ensure important legacies for the community and the province, prior to the Games, during the Games, and after the Games. The non-profit organization identified various social and community-based legacies for Aboriginal initiatives, for the arts, for people with disabilities, for literacy and learning, volunteerism, and sport and healthy living (2010 Legacies Now 2012). The organization is unique in that it was created 10 years prior to the event and ensures that the legacy of the Vancouver Games lasts well beyond the event and benefits as many individuals as possible.

While legacies are at the forefront for event organizers—largely because of the hosting policy and the guidelines provided by the international sport federations (i.e., International Olympic Committee bid requirements)—it is interesting to note that budget cuts have occurred to sport and recreation programs in the communities where these large-scale events have been held. For example, during the immediate post-1999 Pan Am Games period, the City of Winnipeg witnessed service cuts to recreation programs; such cutbacks are hardly consistent with the position that recreation and community sport will benefit directly from legacy endowments following the Games, as highly touted as these may be (McCloy, 2006). Similar sport and recreation cuts were announced by the Government of British Columbia during and after the 2010 Olympic and Paralympic Winter Games (cf. CBC, 2009; Hunter, 2010; O'Neill, 2010). These examples illustrate that legacies are not always congruent with the economic reality of local, provincial and federal governments. The initial optimism in the sport community with respect to the building of new facilities and facility improvements for large-scale sport events can quickly diminish when legacy endowments may not include support for ongoing programs and services for residents.

Conclusion

This chapter traced the evolution of a series of federal hosting policies from their first formulation in 1967 through to 2008. As discussed in the chapter, international sport events have been held for myriad reasons: some have secured civic improvement projects, while others have provided some benefits, albeit limited, for the long-term development of amateur sport in Canada. The hosting policies were borne out of the federal government's attempts to exert control over the long list of Canadian bid groups seeking federal financial support for their international event. The following comments and insights address some of the issues that have emerged in hosting sport events in Canada. In particular, attention is drawn to the impact the federal hosting policies have had on the development of Canadian 'amateur' sport. While we acknowledge that host communities have experienced immense civic pride, the point of contention here is the extent to which municipal, provincial and federal interests have sidestepped important citizen goals in pursuit of their own political and economic goals and objectives. The increasing pressure for cities to succumb to a global ideology, in which place marketing and city enhancement become the primary goals for success in today's marketplace, makes it difficult for amateur sport organizations to find a place at the negotiating table.

The federal hosting policy stipulations have, over the course of policy iterations, extended beyond sport benefits and have required bid groups to demonstrate the social, cultural and economic benefits to be accrued to the community through hosting the international event. Such wide-ranging federal goals and objectives have made it difficult for Sport Canada officials to ensure benefits are sought and achieved for Canadian sport communities. While Canadian hosting experiences have been deemed successful from the standpoint of the actual staging of the two-week event itself, the same cannot be said for the development of coherent and well-thought-out plans for the sport community at both the recreational level and the elite levels. Strategizing for amateur sport became one of the vital reasons for the federal government to pursue the various iterations of its hosting policies. It is hoped that the policy's most recent iteration (2008) will lead to solid, well-planned and strategic options for sport development in Canada.

Concerns over the social impact of large-scale sport events have driven the debate over the types of community benefits that should be achieved (Kidd, 1992; Lenskyj, 2000; McCloy, 2003). Thus, for example, the Vancouver 2010 Olympic and Paralympic Winter Games ensured that legacies for the community extended far beyond sport and recreation. In addressing the moments or places in which change has occurred, the final section discusses key ways in which current federal policies and practices can work in tandem with other organizations and associations that have a role in the hosting of international sport events. First, each hosting community group should conduct long-term evaluations and commit sufficient resources to ensure that federal expenditures have met federal hosting policy guidelines, thus ensuring a measure of accountability to the amateur sport system. Such assessments by Sport Canada or independent researchers can provide much-needed information on how legacies are created and managed when, for example, hosting policy guidelines are implemented.

Second, amateur sport legacies tend to become more evident in the long-term. Assessments of long-term outcomes should be considered and the appropriate baseline data obtained prior to the event being held. Follow-up assessments on the effect of the event on sport participation rates, youth involvement, volunteer legacies, athlete services, and so forth can provide invaluable data for future organizing communities. It is necessary for future bid groups to clearly ascertain the needs of the broader community and, where possible, conduct social impact assessments well in advance of hosting the event, ideally as part of the bid process. Moreover, a broader concern with quality of life issues must be an integral component of early bid efforts, otherwise bid groups will inevitably face opposition. In addition, issues of access, equity and inclusion with respect to communities are important considerations to ensure that everyone is included in each stage of the event.

Third, one of the primary concerns associated with hosting large-scale events has been the ability of local civic boosters to achieve their objectives, and the subsequent negative impact it has had on amateur sport community goals. Whether it is professional sport franchises benefiting (e.g., with access to new or refurbished facilities) or the skewing of the civic agenda towards tourism and economic development concerns, it is necessary for federal officials to uphold Sport Canada's hosting policies, which were created in large part to be accountable for public spending. Bid groups need to be aware of the federal policy from the outset and develop concrete legacy plans for their events.

Finally, amateur sport legacies are beginning to be planned out in a much more coherent manner, as witnessed by the Vancouver 2010 efforts; however all bid communities should be mandated to create Legacy Committees from the outset of bid plans: benefits for both elite and recreational participants must be carefully incorporated at every stage in the development of all facilities and programs. Part of this planning should include the strong, central presence of national sport organizations to ensure that their specific needs and requirements are met from the earliest stages, including solid efforts to support athlete preparation for participation in the event. As Canadian athletes performed strongly on home soil important support was garnered from the Canadian public during the 2010 Vancouver Olympic Winter Games. Such sustained national sport organization and public support for these athletes may ensure a healthier future for all athletes from the grassroots level through to Olympic medallists.

References

2010 Legacies Now. (2012). *2010 Legacies Now—About us.* Retrieved from http://www.2010legaciesnow.com/about-us/

Blais, J.P. (2003). *Report to the Secretary of State (Physical Activity and Sport) on hosting international sport events in Canada—A proposal for a strategic framework.* Ottawa, ON: Government of Canada. Retrieved from http://www.sportalliance.com/Images/Resource%20Documents/Sport%20Tourism%20Articles/Report%20on%20Hosting%20International%20Sporting%20Events.pdf

Campagnolo, I. (1978). *Canada's hosting policy: Sport event guidelines.* Ottawa, ON: Health and Welfare Canada, Fitness and Amateur Sport.

Canadian Broadcasting Corporation. (2009, September 14). Critics slam B.C. government sports cuts. *CBC News.* Retrieved from http://www.cbc.ca/news/canada/british-columbia/story/2009/09/14/bc-sports-funding-cuts.html

Canadian Heritage. (2008). *Federal policy for hosting international sport events.* Ottawa, ON: Her Majesty the Queen in Right of Canada. Retrieved from http://www.pch.gc.ca/pgm/sc/pol/acc/2008/accueil-host_2008-eng.pdf

Cushing, J. (1996). *Planning national sport facilities for high performance athletes.* Unpublished master's thesis, University of Alberta, Canada.

Donnelly, P. (2010a). Own the podium or rent it? Canada's involvement in the global sporting arms race. *Policy Options, 31*(1), 41–44.

Donnelly, P. (2010b). Rent the podium revisited: Reflections on Vancouver 2010. *Policy Options, 31*(4), 84–86.

Emery, P.R. (2002). Bidding to host a major sports event: The local organising committee perspective. *International Journal of Public Sector Management, 15,* 316–335.

Essex, S., & Chalkley, B. (1998). Olympic Games: Catalyst of urban change. *Leisure Studies, 17,* 187–206.

Government of Canada. (n.d.). *Together in 2010: 2010 Legacy initiatives.* Ottawa, ON: Canada 2010. Retrieved from http://www.canada2010.gc.ca/mmedia/kits/fch-5-eng.pdf

Government of Canada. (1988). *Toward 2000: Building Canada's sport system. Report of the task force on national sport policy.* Ottawa, ON: Minister of Supply and Services Canada.

Government of Canada. (1996). *Federal policy for hosting international sport events: Policy tenets and assessment guide.* Ottawa, ON: Minister of Supply and Services Canada.

Government of Canada. (2010). *Canada's Games. The Government of Canada and the 2010 Vancouver Olympic and Paralympic Winter Games.* Catalogue

No. CH20-40/2010E-PDF. Ottawa, ON: Canadian Heritage. Retrieved from http://www.canada2010.gc.ca/fin-rep2010/rep-eng.pdf

Hall, C., & Hodges, J. (1998). The politics of place and identity in the Sydney 2000 Olympics: Sharing the spirit of corporatism. In M. Roche (Ed.), *Sport, popular culture and identity* (pp. 95–111). Aachen, DE: Meyer and Meyer Verlag.

Harvey, J., Thibault, L., & Rail, G. (1995). Neo-corporatism: The political management system in Canadian amateur sport and fitness. *Journal of Sport and Social Issues, 19*(3), 249–265.

Hiller, H. (2000). Mega-events, urban boosterism and growth strategies: An analysis of the objectives and legitimations of the Cape Town 2004 Olympic bid. *International Journal of Urban and Regional Research, 24,* 439–458.

Hunter, J. (2010, March 9). Province draws fire over cuts to sports programs. *The Globe and Mail*, p. S2.

Kavestos, G., & Szymanski, S. (2010). National well-being and international sports events. *Journal of Economic Psychology, 31,* 158–171.

Kidd, B. (1992). The Toronto Olympic Commitment: Towards a social contract for the Olympic Games. *Olympika, 1,* 154–167.

Lenskyj, H. (2000). *Inside the Olympic industry.* Albany, NY: State University of New York Press.

Macintosh, D. (1996). Sport and government in Canada. In L. Chalip, A. Johnson, & L. Stachura (Eds.), *National sports policies. An international handbook* (pp. 39–66). Westport, CT: Greenwood Press.

Macintosh, D., Bedecki, T., & Franks, C.E.S. (1987). *Sport and politics in Canada. Federal government involvement since 1961.* Montreal, QC & Kingston, ON: McGill-Queen's University Press.

McCloy, C. (2002). Hosting international sport events in Canada. Planning for facility legacies. In K.B. Wamsley, R.K. Barney, & S.G. Martyn (Eds.), *The global nexus engaged: Past, present, future interdisciplinary Olympic studies.* Proceedings of the Sixth International Symposium for Olympic Research (pp. 135–142). London, ON: International Centre for Olympic Studies.

McCloy, C. (2003, October). *Community legacies or liabilities? The 2010 Vancouver-Whistler Olympic bid.* Paper presented at the North American Society of Sport Sociology Conference, Montreal.

McCloy, C. (2006). *The role and impact of Canadian federal sport policies in securing amateur sport legacies: Case studies of the past four decades.* Unpublished doctoral dissertation, University of Toronto, Canada.

McCloy, C. (2009). Canada hosts the world: An examination of the first federal sport hosting policy (1967). *International Journal of the History of Sport, 26,* 1155–1170.

O'Neill, E. (2010). *B.C. budget cuts since March 2, 2010.* Vancouver, BC: BC Teachers' Federation Information Services.

Parliament of Canada. (2003). *Bill C-12. An Act to promote physical activity and sport* (S.C. 2003, c. 2). Retrieved from http://www.parl.gc.ca/Content/LOP/LegislativeSummaries/37/2/c12-e.pdf

Prairie Research Associates Inc. (2004). *Summative evaluation of the Department of Canadian Heritage's sport hosting program.* Ottawa, ON: Canadian Heritage.

Priestner Allinger, C., & Allinger, T. (2004). *Own the Podium—2010: Final report with recommendations of the independent task force for winter NSOs and funding partners.* Retrieved from http://www.sportmatters.ca/Groups/SMG%20Resources/Sport%20and%20PA%20Policy/otp_report_-_final_-_e.pdf

Regan, G. (1981). *A challenge to the nation: Fitness and amateur sport in the 80s.* Ottawa, ON: Minister of State, Fitness and Amateur Sport.

Roche, M. (2000). *Mega-events and modernity: Olympics and Expos in the growth of global culture.* London: Routledge.

Scrimger, T. (2005, November 11). *Sport Canada's Hosting Program.* Presentation made to the Sport Leadership Sportif Conference held in Quebec City.

Sport Canada. (2002a). *The Canadian sport policy.* Ottawa, ON: Department of Canadian Heritage. Retrieved from http://www.pch.gc.ca/pgm/sc/pol/pcs-csp/2003/polsport-eng.pdf

Sport Canada. (2002b). *The Canadian sport policy: Federal-provincial/territorial priorities for collaborative action 2002–2005.* Ottawa, ON: Department of Canadian Heritage. Retrieved from http://www.pch.gc.ca/pgm/sc/pol/actn/index-eng.cfm

Sport Canada. (2012). *Canadian sport policy 2012.* Ottawa, ON: Canadian Heritage. Retrieved from http://sirc.ca/CSPRenewal/documents/CSP2012_EN.pdf

Whitson, D. (2004). Bringing the world to Canada: 'The periphery of the centre.' *Third World Quarterly, 25,* 1215–1232.

Whitson, D., & Macintosh, D. (1996). The global circus: International sport, tourism, and the marketing of cities. *Journal of Sport and Social Issues, 20*(3), 278–295.

CHAPTER IX

The Double Helix: Aboriginal People and Sport Policy in Canada

Janice Forsyth, Western University and
Victoria Paraschak, University of Windsor

In 2005, the federal government, through Canadian Heritage, released *Sport Canada's Policy on Aboriginal Peoples' Participation in Sport* (Canadian Heritage, 2005).[1] It was a prolonged process, set in motion by a formal declaration of support from the federal-provincial/territorial ministers responsible for sport, recreation and fitness in 2002 and concluded with the public release of the document three years later. During that time, a number of representatives from relevant sectors including Canadian Heritage, Sport Canada, Indian and Northern Affairs, Aboriginal Affairs, Justice Canada, Health Canada, the Aboriginal Sport Circle (ASC, the national organization for Aboriginal sport development in Canada) and academe (including both authors) shared in its construction.

It was a remarkable time to be involved in Aboriginal sport. The initiation of the policy process signalled a major milestone in government support for Aboriginal sport in Canada, while the output of that process—the policy—remains, at the time of writing this chapter, the only strategy of its kind in the world. Even in Australia, where substantial human and financial resources have been allocated for Aboriginal sport development, no such policy exists.[2] In this regard, the Canadian government can reasonably state that it is making a genuine effort to create a "dynamic and leading-edge sport environment" (Sport Canada, 2002a, p. 4) that meets the needs and interests of its constituent groups, in this case Aboriginal people.

As one of three policies dealing with access and equity issues for underrepresented groups in sport (the other two being persons with disabilities, and women and girls), the Aboriginal sport policy is significant: it is the primary instrument guiding Sport Canada's efforts as it works with other governments and sport organizations to tackle the inequities that limit Aboriginal people from gaining access to and maintaining their involvement in sport. As a direction-setting agenda for government, the policy deserves attention if "we are to reach our destination" by "pulling together in the same direction," as cited by an elder at an Aboriginal Sport Circle presentation at the 2005 Ministers' Conference in Regina, Saskatchewan (Daniels, 2005). To do so, important questions about the background, creation and implementation of this policy need to be addressed. For instance, what broader social, political and economic factors contributed to its development? Why did it take three years to construct? What priority areas have received the most attention? What areas are missing from the strategy? Seeing as the policy was to be reviewed in 2010, and an action plan to guide its implementation was never publicly released, how would the federal government measure its success?

In this chapter, we examine the key issues surrounding the development and implementation of the Aboriginal sport policy, and through that process respond to the questions raised above. The chapter is divided into four parts. In the first section, we outline our approach to understanding Aboriginal sport and policy development in Canada. Here, we use the concept of the 'double helix' to examine the relationship between the mainstream and the Aboriginal sport system. We then link that concept to Gidden's (1984) theory of structuration to explain how individuals make decisions that enable and constrain their ability to achieve their desired goals for sport. The second section focuses on the background and objectives of the policy, and includes an overview of the key social, political, and economic factors that played a role in its development. The third section provides an analysis of the current issues and limitations of the policy while calling attention to the opportunities and challenges it presents. In the fourth and final section, we summarize our thoughts about the Aboriginal sport policy and offer some recommendations about how to improve its implementation.

Examples and reflections based on our own experiences with the development and implementation of the policy are interspersed throughout the text. The first author was a member of the working group that negotiated the overall objectives and scope of the policy, was the primary person responsible for consulting with Aboriginal sport leaders in Ontario on its parameters, and along with the second author, edited various sections of the document. We believe that our personal insights are important to share with students and scholars because they provide a deeper understanding of the context in which policies take shape, as well as the boundaries in which historically marginalized groups, like Aboriginal people, seek to achieve their desired goals for sport.

Theoretical Framework

The Double Helix

Our starting point for examining *Sport Canada's Policy on Aboriginal Peoples' Participation in Sport* (Canadian Heritage, 2005) is derived from a universal model in the biological sciences, the double helix. The anatomy of a double helix consists of parallel strands stabilized by cross-links. The parallel strands represent the mainstream and the Aboriginal sport system, each operating independently of the other. The cross-links represent the sites where the two systems connect. Our inspiration for beginning here comes from Alex Nelson, a leading figure in the Aboriginal sport movement in Canada, who used the model to explain the relationship between the mainstream and the Aboriginal sport system to federal representatives throughout the policy-making process. Though the double helix is not the only way to portray the relationship, it was nevertheless a central unifying concept throughout discussions related to the development of the policy.[3] Thus, the model served as a discursive element structuring the way people imagined the two sport systems in relation to one another, while at the same time providing an effective way of communicating the existence of an alternative sport system, characterized by specific sites where Aboriginal sport connects to, and remains distinct from, the mainstream sport model.

There are at least three key benefits to using the double helix model when discussing the relationship between the Aboriginal and mainstream sport system. First, as a familiar and easy image to grasp, it is useful for facilitating complicated dialogues about the philosophical underpinnings and political objectives that differentiate the two systems. A case in point is the way in which Aboriginal people use sport to assist their broader goals for self-determination.

For many Aboriginal people, self-determination is fundamentally about having the right to make decisions on how to live and govern themselves as a people, and having those efforts supported by government through equitable resource allocation (Royal Commission on Aboriginal Peoples, 1996). In his statement to the Royal Commission on Aboriginal Peoples, René Tenasco, Councillor for Kitigan Zibi Anishnabeg Council, said, "Self-determination is looking at our desires and our aspirations of where we want to go and being given the chance to attain that . . . for life itself, for existence itself, for nationhood itself . . ." (Royal Commission on Aboriginal Peoples, 1996, p. 108). Although not applied directly to sport, Tenasco's understanding of self-determination captures the essence of the way we wish to frame that concept. Our point about the relationship between the double helix model and self-determination is illustrated by the history of the Northern Games, an annual competition comprised mostly of traditional Inuvialuit activities. The Northern Games were established in July 1970 in part as a response to the rejection, by organizers, of a request that they incorporate Inuvialuit games into the inaugural Arctic Winter Games in March 1970 (Paraschak, 1991). The Arctic Winter Games are similar to the Canada Games in that they are a government-controlled spectacle featuring mainstream sport events, albeit limited to circumpolar teams only. As a counter-hegemonic initiative, the Northern Games were developed to provide opportunities for indigenous northerners to participate in their traditional games and dances, and thus pass on their cultural values and skills to the youth—an objective that is apparent in the following statement from the organizers: "Through the Northern Games youth discover the rich history they have inherited from their ancestors, and take pride in their cultural heritage" (Gordon, 2009). These Games, created and administered by indigenous northerners, are thus an example of Aboriginal self-determination in sport.

Second, the model of the double helix is useful for the way it positions Aboriginal sport practices and the Aboriginal sport system as a separate and equally legitimate sport system that is worthy of government funding—a position that authorities in the mainstream system have repeatedly challenged and rejected. Tensions surrounding competing visions for 'sport' during the life of the Native Sport and Recreation Program (herein NSRP) are instructive. Established in 1972 by Fitness and Amateur Sport, a unit of the federal government's Ministry of National Health and Welfare, the NSRP was designed to increase sport and recreation opportunities for Aboriginal people on and between reserves throughout the country (Paraschak, 1995). For almost 10 years the program flourished as Aboriginal organizers co-ordinated local, regional and national-level activities in a wide range of events from popular mainstream activities like basketball, hockey, and rodeo, to sport and cultural events like Métis Days and Indian Summer Games. However, friction over the legitimate vision for sport between Aboriginal and federal sport leaders continued throughout the lifetime of this program. In keeping with this ongoing debate, in 1978, Fitness and Amateur Sport sent the Northern Games Association a letter that stated funding would be reduced and then stopped by 1981 because the mainstream activities in the Arctic Winter Games fit better with the department's mandate for sport development than did the traditional activities performed in the Northern Games (Paraschak, 2004). Then, in 1981, the federal government terminated the NSRP when it shifted its priorities towards high performance sport and away from recreation, which federal officials saw as the mandate of the provincial/territorial level of government. Similar to the rationalization provided to the Northern Games Association several years earlier, federal officials had determined that the range of activities fostered through the NSRP fell outside the scope of sport activities supported by Fitness and Amateur Sport, and, furthermore, that those activities would not produce the high performance results desired by government (Paraschak, 1995).

Third, the double helix model conveys movement between the two systems, showing how the Aboriginal sport system connects and contributes to the Canadian mainstream system—just as the Canadian mainstream system connects and contributes to the Aboriginal sport system, albeit in an unequal system of power relations. This movement is evident in dialogues around a parallel system in official reports and policies leading up to and including the Aboriginal sport policy. One of the first reports to do so was *Sport in Canada—Everybody's Business, Leadership, Partnership and Accountability*[4] (Mills, 1998). This report included a recommendation to enhance coaching development for Aboriginal people, thereby supporting the ASC's perspective that coaching was a "cornerstone of the emerging Aboriginal sport delivery system" (Mills, 1998, p. 87). In so doing, members of the committee responsible for writing the report were supporting the right of Aboriginal people to create a separate sport delivery system aligned with their vision of sport.

It was thus surprising to read in the eighth draft of the Aboriginal sport policy that:

> Aboriginal Peoples in Canada have worked diligently for several years to bring the major barriers concerning Aboriginal Peoples' participation in sport to the attention of both government and the Canadian sport system. Although this movement has made an impact on the healthy, active lifestyles of Aboriginal youth, the ultimate vision of broad-based participation of Aboriginal Peoples in the Canadian sport system will need to be achieved through the committed, cooperative effort of Aboriginal Peoples, the Canadian sport community and all levels of government. *There is no desire to create a distinct sport system for Aboriginal Peoples.* (Canadian Heritage, 2003, p. 3, *emphasis added*)

We assume that this statement means the "emerging Aboriginal sport system" identified and supported in the 1998 report is not considered legitimate by the federal, provincial and territorial sport administrators. Certainly, the fact that Aboriginal people have actively created a distinct sport system over the last 40 years—as outlined in the section on background and objectives—is evidence of *their* desire to do so.

Duality of Structure

While the double helix provides a clear and common visual for representing the relationship between the two systems, it does not explain how or why the two systems came into contact, how the links were strengthened or destabilized over time, or how decisions about which aspects of each system should be enhanced or ignored were made. In light of this, we turn to Giddens (1984) to examine the relationship between individual and collective agency and the seemingly organized, enduring patterns of social life. We are particularly interested in his concept of 'duality of structure' to help explain the way agents, whether as individuals or groups, are able to gain access to, take advantage of, and shape the rules and resources to secure better positions for themselves in sport. It is worth noting that within this framework agents do not have to be aware of their actions or even be able to verbalize how they know what they know, for a great deal of their competence is based on their lived experience, or what Giddens (1984) referred to as their "practical consciousness."

In this chapter, we use duality of structure to examine the ways that Aboriginal people, through their ongoing actions, have responded to and shaped the sport system around them, and how they did this within the boundaries of what they believed (through lived experience) was possible. Viewing the double helix model from the point of view of duality of structure thus calls attention to the ways that Aboriginal and non-Aboriginal people are impacted by each other's ideas and actions.

Sport as a Socially-Constructed Practice

Our theoretical positioning of the double helix is further linked to our understanding of sport as a cultural practice. If culture, simply defined, is the "way of life" of a people (Williams, 1983), then Aboriginal people in Canada have their own cultural practices that in part align with, but also differ from, other Canadians. Essential to, though not explicit in, this definition is the assumption that people have the right to shape their own cultural practices in ways that provide meaning for them. For example, in *The Constitution Act*, 1982, existing Aboriginal rights are identified as a legitimate part of the Canadian political framework. In other words, Aboriginal people in Canada did not give up their status as separate nations when Canada was formed. This truth has been reinforced through various court decisions where Aboriginal rights and treaty rights have been upheld or created anew, as with the Nisga'a Treaty in British Columbia.[5] Aboriginal people thus have a unique status in Canada, a justification that underlies their differential treatment from other identifiable groups in the country.

Furthermore, we understand sport to be a "socially-constructed" practice, which is to say that sport practices are constantly being produced, reproduced, and reshaped by individuals and groups acting within the boundaries of what they think are possible. These boundaries, including the rules for how things work and the distribution of resources needed to achieve the desired objectives thus continuously shape, and are shaped by, Aboriginal and non-Aboriginal people. Those who make the rules have more power because they can decide what the rules will be and how the resources will be distributed. These individuals get to legitimize their preferred forms of sport, their preferred sport traditions and the meanings and practices associated with dominant sport forms (Gruneau, 1988). Over time, the ways that sport is constructed as a cultural practice become part of most peoples' practical consciousness as they naturalize that this is 'the proper' way to organize and participate in sport. Unequal power relations thus lie at the base of this process because those who get to shape the rules ultimately have a better chance of naturalizing their way of doing sport as *the* way that sport will be reproduced and understood. These unequal relations exist within Aboriginal sport, but they also exist between different groups within the mainstream system, including Aboriginal sport leaders and government. This latter group currently has greater access to desired resources and is more able to shape and implement its desired goals for sport. Policies, such as the Aboriginal sport policy, accelerate and crystallize this naturalizing process based on unequal power relations, further institutionalizing sport practices in a manner that best fits with those defining and benefiting most from the development and implementation of policies.

Background and Objectives

Background

Policies are constructed at every level of government, from the local to the federal. As decision-making instruments, they help to define a particular course of action for a specific issue, such as racism in competitive sport, or for a bundle of related issues, as with problems concerning equity and access for Aboriginal people and sport. Equally important, policies also render visible, by way of exclusion, areas that will not receive systematic attention, thus institutionalizing a legitimized direction for how human, financial, and infrastructural resources will be deployed (Pal, 2010).

The level of authority given to a policy determines how government can respond to any given situation. Similar to the policy for women and girls in sport, and sport for persons with a disability, the Aboriginal sport policy is a departmental policy, situated in Sport Canada, the administrative authority responsible for sport development throughout the country. As a departmental policy it enables vertical relationships *within* the department where it is located; that is, Canadian Heritage. More specifically, Sport Canada is a branch of the International and Intergovernmental Affairs sector, one of five divisions in the Department of Canadian Heritage. Established in 1993, Canadian Heritage is responsible for "national policies and programs that promote Canadian content, foster cultural participation, active citizenship and participation in Canada's civic life, and strengthen connections among Canadians" (Canadian Heritage, 2009d). Within the context of Canadian Heritage, sport is viewed as a means to enhance national identity, social inclusion, and citizenship.

Herein lies a significant problem we see with the Aboriginal sport policy: as a departmental strategy, the Aboriginal sport policy can refer to—but not directly address—an array of important issues tied to Aboriginal sport development, including weight loss and obesity prevention, diabetes, suicide, substance abuse, justice and education. These issues are vitally connected to Aboriginal sport development but are beyond the scope of what Sport Canada and Canadian Heritage have been empowered to tackle, and thus would play no role in the implementation or evaluation of this policy. Only select policies, such as the *Federal Policy for Hosting International Sport Events* (Canadian Heritage, 2008), incorporate accountability *across* federal departments. Had the Aboriginal sport policy been structured as a federal rather than a departmental policy, it could have permitted horizontal relationships among relevant federal government units such as Health Canada, Indian and Northern Affairs, and Justice, *as well as* vertical relationships within Canadian Heritage thereby allowing the issues to be addressed in a more holistic fashion.

To be sure, several federal departments were involved to a limited extent in policy discussions. Their presence thus held promise for enhanced structural relations. However, these relationships were never institutionalized through the policy framework. Instead, federal sport officials 'hoped' the policy would facilitate horizontal relations across departments by allowing their representatives to partially engage in meetings about the policy. We will return to the limitations of a departmental policy in the following section. For now, it is enough to say that the greater the number of partnerships, the greater the range and amount of resources that can be made available for programs and activities thereby helping to create a more effective policy situation. In other words, with multiple federal stakeholders addressing a variety of issues connected to sport, a policy is given more force in terms of being able to achieve its goals.[6]

As with all policies, the Aboriginal sport policy must be understood as the result of a long period of focused attention and promotion by interest groups whose concerns are tied to patterns they see in the broader social, political and economic environment. Related social concerns, for example, arose from statistics outlining the poor quality of life faced by many Aboriginal people in Canada (e.g., Mills, 1998), combined with recognition that Aboriginal people perceived sport as a way to counteract negative behaviours in their communities, especially for the youth. Political concerns were strengthened by the desire of the federal government to improve its relationship with Aboriginal people more generally, as could be seen in their establishment of the Royal Commission on Aboriginal Peoples. The final lengthy report, published in 1996, included a number of recommendations specific to sport. As well, the two Speeches from the Throne prior to the release of the Aboriginal sport policy also stressed the federal priority "to work with Aboriginal Peoples so that they can participate fully in national life as well as share in Canada's prosperity" (Canadian Heritage, 2006, p. 1). Broader economic concerns, tied to increasing levels of physical inactivity and the costs to health care this created, made addressing the health of Canadians through increased sport participation more attractive. A commitment by all governments to reduce inactivity among Canadians by 10% by 1993 (Canadian Heritage, 2005, p. 10) necessitated action across the country and amongst its many constituents, including Aboriginal people.

Sport-specific concerns provided an additional impetus for the creation of this policy. In his detailed report on the use of banned substances in sport, prompted by the scandal surrounding Canadian sprinter Ben Johnson at the 1988 Olympic Games in Seoul, Korea, Charles Dubin (1990) identified a moral crisis in Canadian sport that required a re-examination of its values. He recommended that government funding should be based not on medal counts but rather on ethical principles, such as the extent to which programs are available to the broader community, and the encouragement of women, minorities, the disadvantaged, and the disabled in sport (Jennings, 1990). Also in 1990, the inaugural North American Indigenous Games (NAIG) were held in Edmonton: these Games became a cornerstone of the emerging Aboriginal sport system. In the federal report, *Sport: The Way Ahead* (Minister's Task Force, 1992), a national body for Aboriginal sport was recommended. In 1995, that recommendation became a reality with the creation and federal funding of the ASC. Provincial and territorial Aboriginal sport bodies (PTASBs) soon followed, at times receiving funding from their mainstream government counterparts. Aboriginal requests for funding to prepare and send provincial and territorial teams to the NAIG became an issue all levels of government needed to address. As pointed out in the Mills

Report (1998), governments were having to respond to an emerging Aboriginal sport system, which in and of itself was an outcome of both Aboriginal and non-Aboriginal actions.

In 1995, the federal and provincial/territorial ministers responsible for sport, recreation and fitness recommended a focus be placed on the physical activity needs in Aboriginal communities (Canadian Heritage, 2005). Two years later, the ASC reported to the ministers about the barriers affecting Aboriginal sport participation, and they agreed to tackle the issues. Contributing to this heightened concern for addressing Aboriginal sport, two roundtables were held as part of the process leading to the creation of the *Canadian Sport Policy* (CSP) (Sport Canada, 2002a), the overarching policy for sport development in Canada. The February 2000 National Recreation Roundtable on Aboriginal/Indigenous Peoples produced the *Maskwachees Declaration* (Federal-Provincial/Territorial Advisory Committee, 2000). This document outlined strengths and challenges facing Aboriginal involvement in physical activity, physical education, sport and recreation, and called on governments and the non-profit sector to endorse the Declaration. A roundtable later that year focused on elite athletics and Aboriginal people.

In terms of federal support, the 2002 CSP outlined all 13 governments' commitment to a values-based approach to sport, including equity and access for underserved groups. This federal commitment was repeated in Bill C-12, *An Act to Promote Physical Activity and Sport*, released in 2003 (Parliament of Canada, 2003). One of the underserved groups was Aboriginal people. Federal funding was attached to the CSP, and bilateral agreements created a structure for distributing new resources across the country in keeping with the priorities identified in the policy. These factors all provided an impetus for the creation of Sport Canada policies promoting access and equity for underserved groups, the first of which became the Aboriginal sport policy.

A three-year process followed to craft the eventual policy, and involved multiple partners, including provincial and territorial government representatives who did not wish to see the legitimation of a distinct Aboriginal sport system in the policy, as this could lead to a parallel Aboriginal sport system that would compete with the mainstream sport system for limited resources. It was, for many supporters of the double-helix model, a frustrating process. One participant explained:

> We tried to get that [acceptance of a parallel system] into the policy; we tried to put that explanation into the policy. They [the government officials] appreciated the values of those models in understanding why we are different; [but] they absolutely refused to include that in the document. It was actually in the initial draft but as it worked its way up through the food chain people became very uncomfortable about that. (Te Hiwi, 2009, p. 124)

Eventually, after prolonged debates with government officials, as well as many edits to the policy, an Aboriginal sport system was formally recognized in the document in the guiding principles that stated, "An Aboriginal sport delivery system exists and it is important to work with the ASC, its national body, to identify and address the areas of priority to advance Aboriginal Peoples' participation in sport" (Canadian Heritage, 2005, p. 6). Then, consultation with Aboriginal groups on the eighth draft of the policy resulted in concerns being raised over the scope of 'sport' in the policy. Aboriginal respondents voiced their commitment to a holistic approach to sport (and life more generally); however, this contradicted mainstream notions of Sport Canada's mandate. In the end, the policy makers acknowledged the unique holistic approach taken by Aboriginal people to sport in the policy, but they did not incorporate that understanding, using the model of the double helix, into the structures created through the policy.

Objectives

By now it should be clear that policies are not neutral instruments (Pal, 2010). Rather, they are developed and implemented to address specific issues that have been identified as needing attention. How those issues are addressed within the context of each policy varies according to its design. For example, some policies have objectives (or goals) while others do not. The approach can vary for a number of reasons. A case in point is *Actively Engaged: A Policy on Sport for Women and Girls* (Canadian Heritage, 2009a). As discussed in Chapter XI, several policy objectives are identified to address federal priorities in this area. The objectives for *Actively Engaged* are explained in more detail in the *Action Plan, 2009–2012* (Canadian Heritage, 2009b) that accompanies the policy.

In comparison, *Sport Canada's Policy on Aboriginal Peoples' Participation in Sport* (Canadian Heritage, 2005) does not identify any objectives specific to Aboriginal people. Instead, it offers broad statements about the need for more and more equitable opportunities for Aboriginal people in sport and outlines four key areas tied to CSP where development is needed:

- 'Enhanced excellence' focuses on creating a more welcoming environment for Aboriginal athletes, coaches and officials in high performance sport;
- 'Enhanced participation' deals with significantly increasing the number of Aboriginal people at all levels and in all manners of participation;
- 'Enhanced capacity' involves building human resource capacity; and
- 'Enhanced interaction' is about fostering collaboration between governments, organizations and Aboriginal people in Aboriginal sport development.

These broad-based statements should not be viewed wholly as a weakness in the policy. Rather, they are a starting point for determining measurable objectives that can indicate the success (or not) of government actions tied to the policy. The guiding principles for the Aboriginal sport policy aligned with the 2002 CSP, as evidenced through the listing of the four goals of the 2002 CSP as the framework for the Aboriginal sport policy. Eventual details were to be worked out through an action plan for the Aboriginal sport policy, which would further identify key intentions and associated resources, providing the foundation for evaluating the effectiveness of the policy. However, the action plan was never publicly released.

The possibility of sport being used for broader social development among Aboriginal people is mentioned in the Aboriginal sport policy, but was undeveloped in its details. To the contrary, their linkage to the four goals of the CSP suggests that the Aboriginal sport policy is *only* about sport development. Broadening the Aboriginal sport policy to a federal focus would have allowed other federal government units, such as Health Canada and Justice, to link with the policy, connecting and contributing to sport by addressing the issues that fit within their mandate but extend beyond the reach of Sport Canada and Canadian Heritage. Since the policy did not institutionalize relationships across different federal units, the possibility that such relationships—which are essential to broader social development—would, in fact, be formed were unlikely.

Aboriginal sport leaders were rightly concerned about the way in which the objectives for the policy were being construed. Throughout the policy-making process, we acknowledged that they had the potential to foster relations between different government units while countering that it was equally probable the emphasis on sport could reinforce silos between them. In other words, Health Canada is not in the business of doing sport, just as Canadian Heritage does not concern itself with physical health. Our primary concern was that a departmental policy emphasizing sport would undermine the broader community and health objectives long hoped for by Aboriginal sport leaders. On these broader social issues, Sport Canada states clearly in the Aboriginal sport policy that its role is limited to sport development: "Sport Canada is committed to *contributing*, through sport, to the health, wellness, cultural identity and quality of life of Aboriginal Peoples" (Canadian Heritage, 2005, p. 3, *emphasis in original*). We were reminded several times throughout the process that the policy was intended merely to "open doors" to other federal departments, not establish formal connections with them. This approach would thus require each department to construct its own policy in relation to the one that Canadian Heritage would ultimately endorse. Our concerns were reinforced with the new CSP, released in June 2012, which clearly states Sport Canada will "encourage the development of new partnerships (*while respecting government roles and responsibilities*) with local and national, domestic and international, sport and non-sport partners" (Sport Canada, 2012, p. 22, *emphasis added*). In other words, Sport Canada will do its best to encourage relationships between federal departments but will stop short of building those relationships by breaking down the administrative boundaries to address matters of broad social importance. We knew this departmentalized process could take years and (still) wonder whether it will ever be successful at all.

Current Issues and Limitations

In this final section, we identify and discuss the key issues and limitations of the Aboriginal sport policy. We begin with an analysis of the outcomes that are ostensibly linked to its implementation, specifically a CA$ 12M commitment by the federal government to support programs to increase Aboriginal participation in sport. This money, provided over five years, from 2005 to 2010, was the most strategic investment ever made by government to foster Aboriginal sport development in Canada. With a policy in place, Sport Canada had a general outline to help guide its decision making about how to enhance this area of public administration.

How was the CA$ 12M allocated? In view of the fact that the Aboriginal sport policy was designed to build on the 2002 CSP, the overarching policy for Canadian sport, funding was given to activities that would augment that framework. Four areas were targeted for support: (1) funding for hosting the NAIG in Canada; (2) financial support for athletes travelling to the NAIG; (3) grants for provincial and territorial sport development programs and capacity building; and (4) increased funding for the ASC.

First, up to CA$ 3.5M was provided to assist with hosting the NAIG, a major sport and cultural festival held approximately every three years in either Canada or the United States. Following this cycle would mean that the Games should be hosted in Canada every six years. However, the NAIG hosting dollars had been made available in the past. In 2003, two years before the Aboriginal sport policy was released, the federal and provincial/territorial ministers responsible for sport, recreation and fitness agreed to support the hosting component of the NAIG when they are held in Canada, with the federal and host provincial governments contributing up to 35% of the Games' total budget to a maximum of CA$ 3.5M each (Sport Canada, 2003a): these were the exact same terms that were agreed to after the policy was released in 2005. Furthermore, in 2004, the ministers endorsed a multi-party funding agreement for the NAIG, which included a formal support mechanism for the hosting of the NAIG when in Canada (Canadian Heritage, 2009c). Bearing this information in mind, it is debatable whether or not the provision of NAIG hosting dollars can be seen as an outcome of this policy. What is certain, and likely more accurate, is that the policy further institutionalized government support for this area of the NAIG, ensuring the hosting component would receive a reasonable level of funding on an ongoing basis thereafter. Practically, it meant that Canadian host societies would not have to scramble for dollars with every NAIG, as they had done in the past (Forsyth, 2000), since permanent funding for this culturally significant event was now in place.

A second area targeted for support was athlete travel to the NAIG. In 2009, the Ministers agreed to provide up to CA$ 1M for athlete travel to the Games whether in Canada or the United States (Canadian Intergovernmental Conference Secretariat, 2009). Funding for this aspect of NAIG was a noteworthy victory. Many Aboriginal people occupy the lower rungs of the socio-economic ladder with the implication being that involvement in competitive sport is more a luxury than a normal part of everyday life. Federal support for travel to and from the NAIG was thus intended to provide athletes, many of whom otherwise would not have the means to participate in sport, with an opportunity to experience the Games. This is particularly true for athletes who live in rural and remote areas, where the costs associated with sport development often make sport participation unaffordable. According to a report compiled by the ASC (1998), approximately 25% of all Aboriginal people in Canada live in census metropolitan areas, meaning the vast majority of Aboriginal people live in smaller towns and cities or in rural or remote areas. Furthermore, statistics on Aboriginal community population size and remoteness show that 58% of Aboriginal communities have populations between 100 and 499 residents. Of those communities, 166 are located between 50 to 350 kilometers from service centres (which have access to government services, banks, suppliers) and 22 are located more than 350 kilometers from the nearest service centre (ASC, 1998, p. 12). Much of the Aboriginal population is thus located far from urban areas where the structure of sport is usually best supported.

The issue of costs was raised several times in the report on the regional consultations (Sport Canada, 2003b) for the development of the Aboriginal sport policy. As noted in the report from Ontario:

> Aboriginal people who live in isolated communities must factor in the cost of an airplane ticket in order to get to a store that sells equipment. They do not have the luxury of traveling by car to the nearest supplier to buy the gear they need to play or compete. These are some of the everyday realities for Aboriginal people living in small or isolated communities. (Sport Canada, 2003b, p. 11)

Yukon respondents went further in their analysis of the socio-economic landscape. They linked historical oppression through

More than a decade later, in 2009, while each region has a represen-
tative body, several affiliates still do not have a consistent funding
base, a limitation that has had a significant bearing on their ability to
influence sport development in their region. Among other things, it
means the PTASBs cannot hire personnel for programming, let alone
deal with the intricacies of policy development. With little or no staff,
some areas such as Quebec and most of the Maritimes have operated
almost wholly on volunteer help from Aboriginal and non-Aboriginal
people highly dedicated to Aboriginal sport. Predictably, this results
in uneven development throughout the country, as some regions are
more able than others to create and sustain initiatives.

The bilateral funding is reminiscent of the Native Sport and
Recreation Program in the 1970s (discussed in the *Background* section) in that it has led to the creation of a number of Aboriginal sport
participation initiatives throughout the country. For example, in
Alberta in the 2004–2005 fiscal year, 40 trained youth workers ran
36 sport camps, with 14,589 Aboriginal youth participating (Treasury
Board of Canada, 2005). There is, however, a conspicuous difference between the two programs. In the 1970s, Native sport leaders
were provided with decision-making authority about the types of
programs that should be developed and how they should be implemented. In the current bilateral agreements, however, the regional
governments—not the PTASBs—are given programming autonomy,
and very few provincial and territorial governments consult with
the regional Aboriginal sport bodies about program development
and implementation.

In so doing, the bilateral agreements reinforce historically
oppressive relations between Aboriginal people and government. To
be sure, the PTASBs and the ASC consider this process unacceptable
and have registered their displeasure at the highest level of government, as indicated by the following comment from Lyle Daniels,
Chair of the ASC, in addressing the 2005 Ministers' Conference in
Regina, Saskatchewan:

> We have advocated for years about all of the very practical
> things we would like to do to support community-based pro-
> gramming, and to some extent we have accepted the reality that
> funds are limited. As we have examined the bilateral process
> and compared notes among our Provincial/Territorial Aboriginal
> Sport Bodies, the discrepancies have become apparent. While I

want to commend those governments that have made Aboriginal
sport development a major priority within the bilateral agreements, it is clear that others have chosen a very different focus.
(Daniels, 2005)

His remark about some governments having chosen "a very different route" than was hoped for by the PTASBs is a sharp reminder
that the Government of Canada is still resistant to the notion of the
model of the double helix. In some regions, funding went to well-
established mainstream sport and recreation organizations rather
than to Aboriginal community groups or to the PTASB, the principal
agent for developing and delivering Aboriginal programming in the
Aboriginal sport system. So while this funding further reinforces the
mainstream sport system and its involvement in Aboriginal sport, it
does not help to stabilize and support the Aboriginal sport system's
delivery system.

Lastly, the bilateral funding provided the ASC with CA$ 535,000
per year for three years beginning in 2003. Organizational support
is critical but it is only provided at the national level, a top-heavy
approach that further widens the asymmetry between the Aboriginal
and mainstream sport system. A second round of bilateral funding
was made available for the ASC for another three years beginning
in 2006. Until the provinces and territories commit serious dollars
for administration and staffing of the PTASBs, the ASC as a collective will continue to struggle to address barriers at the *community*
level. While the PTASBs are contributing to the development of elite
athletes through initiatives such as the NAIG and coaching and
athlete development camps, community development remains an
area that has fallen very short. The ministers, along with relevant
federal departments need to address this gap by training community
leaders and developing sustainable grassroots programs. This issue
is exemplified by the lack of attention paid to the highly anticipated
report, *Best Practices—Physical Activity Programs for Aboriginal Youth*
(The Sutcliffe Group Inc. and Sluth Management Consulting, 2007)—a
compilation of information generated from data collected by people
working in Aboriginal sport and recreation development throughout
the country. The insights provided in this document could be enhancing community capacity for Aboriginal sport but the government
has shelved it: the federal-provincial/territorial ministers responsible
for sport, recreation and fitness abandoned the report shortly after

it was concluded. Why? We argue that the data collected through this report, which shows a real need and interest in sport as a tool for broader social development (not simply elite participation), runs counter to the institutionalized and naturalized views of 'sport' held by federal officials, so that 'best practices' at the Aboriginal community level are definitely not the same 'best practices' imagined by the power bloc in government.

In terms of key weaknesses not being addressed, there is only one—but it is significant: there remains no action plan for *Sport Canada's Policy on Aboriginal Peoples' Participation in Sport* (Canadian Heritage, 2005), even though it states that an action plan will be developed (p. 8). Without an action plan, transparency and accountability tied to the policy becomes impossible to achieve. Action plans have been released for subsequent Sport Canada policies created to enhance access and equity for other historically marginalized groups in sport. The *Policy on Sport for Persons with a Disability* (Canadian Heritage, 2006) has an action plan with clear resource commitments, as does *Actively Engaged: A Policy on Sport for Women and Girls* (Canadian Heritage, 2009a) (see Chapters X and XI for more details). The same needs to be done—and has been promised in the policy—for Aboriginal people and sport.

Why no action plan? We believe that this omission is tied to challenges embedded in the development of the Aboriginal sport policy. The Reference Group, comprised of selected members from the Aboriginal Sport Circle and government involved in the development of the Aboriginal sport policy, stated their belief that most provincial and territorial governments felt that Aboriginal sport and recreation could be addressed through a generic policy that encompassed all citizens; that is, the CSP (Sport Canada, 2003c, pp. 4–5). The absence of an action plan reinforces this approach, assuming that the provincial and territorial governments can (and should) adequately address the needs and interests of Aboriginal people in sport. No action plan also means no clear measures for evaluation. What is more, the 2012 CSP does not offer any indication that an action plan for Aboriginal sport will be developed. Indeed, Section 7, "Policy Implementation and Action Plans," suggests the government's preferred course of action will be the status quo:

> Consistent with the first CSP, this approach to implementation
> will *respect the existing roles and responsibilities* of the federal and

> provincial/territorial governments that are described in the
> National Recreation Statement (1987) and other existing gov-
> ernmental agreements addressing *specific jurisdictional realities*.
> The renewed policy direction is supported by governments and
> non-governments to the extent of their *desired* commitment.
> (Sport Canada, 2012, p. 15, *emphasis added*)

In this kind of policy environment, how can Sport Canada and the
ASC really assess what they have accomplished as a result of the CSP
or the Aboriginal sport policy to determine where the gaps are and
how best to move forward?

Conclusion

Policy, by its nature, sets boundaries for how activities within
its purview are structured. Our examination of the creation and
implementation of the Aboriginal sport policy highlights several
strengths arising from this policy, tied to further issues that need to
be addressed. Sport Canada has become a leader worldwide through
its formal recognition and legitimation of government support for
Aboriginal sport, including the Aboriginal sport system. The policy
pays some attention to the particular, holistic approach taken by
Aboriginal people to sport, broadly understood. Likewise, the possibilities for social development through sport are noted. And financial resources have been directed to Aboriginal organizations and
athletes. All these elements hold promise for enhancing the access
and equity of Aboriginal people in sport, and for their contribution,
therefore, to a values-based approach to sport in Canada.

However, the promised action plan has not emerged, which
could have clarified objectives tied to these strengths, generating a uniquely Aboriginal vision of sport participation. How can
Aboriginal organizers demonstrate, and thus further legitimate their
preferred approach towards sport participation, and/or revise it as
necessary, when there is no formal set of objectives and accompa-
nying evaluation plan in place? Without this action plan, resources
are instead being directed to provincial and territorial governments rather than to PTASBs, reinforcing the mainstream portion
of the double helix instead of those organizations that facilitate the
operation of the Aboriginal sport system. This pattern of resource
distribution does not allow for the further legitimizing of the

Aboriginal sport system; instead, its legitimacy is undercut along with its perceived suitability for government resources. Funding to NAIG and to the ASC reinforce a focus on elite sport more so than the community-based development necessary for social goals to be reached. And the departmental focus of the Aboriginal sport policy lends itself to an emphasis on sport development, rather than social development *through* sport. Creating structural links between federal departments is one way that Aboriginal aspirations linking sport and social development can be pursued more concretely. Generating an action plan with Aboriginal people that gets resources into the communities and generates capacity within Aboriginal sport bodies, thus enhancing Aboriginal self-determination is a second way that sport development can combine with social development. This process would ensure that Aboriginal people are involved in their own visioning and provision of sport, broadly understood and holistically framed.

The evaluation that follows from that action plan would help assess their success in that endeavour. It would also serve as a values-based approach that the mainstream sport system could draw upon as it works to enhance access and equity across Canada. This outcome is the strength of the double helix model of Aboriginal sport—both Aboriginal and non-Aboriginal people have much to learn as we share our separate and intertwined approaches towards the provision of sport in a manner that enhances the lives of all Canadians. However, the Aboriginal sport system must be further legitimized before its many contributions to the mainstream sport system can be seen and adopted. Once these steps are taken, we will be closer to developing novel ways in which disadvantaged groups in Canada can receive enhanced access and equity in the Canadian sport system, which is surely the goal of a truly values-based sport system.

Notes

1. In this chapter, *Sport Canada's Policy on Aboriginal Peoples' Participation in Sport* (Canadian Heritage, 2005) will also be referred to as the "Aboriginal sport policy" and "the policy." This policy can be found online at: http://www.pch.gc.ca/pgm/sc/pol/aboriginal/2005/aboriginal-eng.pdf
2. The Australian Sports Commission (2010) currently has a National Indigenous Sport Development program, which directs human and financial resources to Aboriginal communities and mainstream sport

organizations that work with Indigenous communities. A national network of indigenous sport development officers work in partnership with indigenous communities, mainstream sport organizations and state/territory departments of sport and recreation to assess community sport needs and priorities and to deliver programs, resources and services in order to build the sport capacity of Indigenous Australians. Funding is also available for travel and accommodation for indigenous sportspeople (athletes, coaches, officials, managers, trainers) involved in mainstream official national championships and international sport competitions. However, no overarching Indigenous sport policy directs these efforts to enhance Indigenous sport opportunities in Australia. Retrieved from: http://www.ausport.gov.au/participating/indigenous

3. In response to a question about the usefulness of the double helix as a model for discussing Aboriginal sport in Canada, one interviewee in Braden Te Hiwi's (2009) thesis noted her preference for the image of two canoes in the two-row wampum as a way for moving indigenous peoples and the government forward, rather than the more "heavily scientific grounding" of the double helix (p. 130). The Mohawk concept of the two-row wampum belt is a model of how people should govern themselves in Mohawk society, as well as how Mohawks see themselves relating to other groups around them.

4. This document is also referred to as the Mills Report since Dennis Mills, a member of parliament, was chair of the committee that produced the report.

5. Here, we make a distinction between Aboriginal rights and treaty rights. Aboriginal rights are not clearly defined, and must be established through the courts on a case-by-case basis. Treaty rights are negotiated and can be exhaustively set out and described in detail. With respect to the Nisga'a in British Columbia, as a modern treaty, the Nisga'a Treaty describes in detail how the rights of Nisga'a citizens will be exercised. Any Aboriginal rights of the Nisga'a are modified to become rights set out in the Treaty. In this way, the negotiating parties have agreed to rights—rather than extinguishing them. Retrieved from http://www.ainc-inac.gc.ca/ai/mr/is/nit-eng.asp

6. This can be seen, for example, with the Indigenous Sport Program in Australia. Funding for Indigenous Sport Development Officers (ISDOs), as well as for the Travel and Accommodation Assistance Program grant, are both shared with the Department of Health and Ageing. "In addition ISDOs work with Indigenous Coordination Centres and the Department of Health and Ageing to ensure programs are delivered to Indigenous Australians and their communities with an integrated whole of government approach." Retrieved from: http://www.ausport.gov.au/participating/indigenous

7. A bilateral agreement is a formal contract between two parties, outlining what each will contribute to the relationship. Usually, bilateral agreements are constructed for special projects that do not normally receive ongoing (baseline) funding. Chapter II addresses bilateral agreements between the federal and provincial/territorial governments.

References

Aboriginal Sport Circle. (1998). *The role of coaching development, The North American Indigenous Games and Provincial/Territorial Aboriginal Sport Bodies.* Report presented to the Federal-Provincial/Territorial Sport Committee on Aboriginal Sport Development, October.

Australian Sports Commission. (2010). *Indigenous sport.* Retrieved from http://www.ausport.gov.au/participating/indigenous

Canadian Heritage. (2003). *Sport Canada's Policy on Aboriginal Peoples' Participation in Sport, Draft 8.* Ottawa, ON: Minister of Public Works and Government Services Canada.

Canadian Heritage. (2005). *Sport Canada's Policy on Aboriginal Peoples' Participation in Sport.* Ottawa, ON: Minister of Public Works and Government Services Canada. Retrieved from http://www.pch.gc.ca/pgm/sc/pol/aboriginal/2005/aboriginal-eng.pdf

Canadian Heritage. (2006). *Policy on Sport for Persons with a Disability.* Ottawa, ON: Her Majesty the Queen in Right of Canada. Retrieved from http://www.pch.gc.ca/pgm/sc/pol/spt/pwad-eng.pdf

Canadian Heritage. (2008). *Federal policy for hosting international sport events.* Ottawa, ON: Her Majesty the Queen in Right of Canada. Retrieved from http://www.pch.gc.ca/pgm/sc/pol/acc/2008/accueil-host_2008-eng.pdf

Canadian Heritage. (2009a). *Actively engaged: A policy on sport for women and girls.* Ottawa, ON: Her Majesty the Queen in Right of Canada. Retrieved from http://www.pch.gc.ca/pgm/sc/pol/fewom/ws-b-eng.pdf

Canadian Heritage. (2009b). *Actively engaged: A policy on sport for women and girls. Action plan, 2009–2012.* Ottawa, ON: Her Majesty the Queen in Right of Canada. Retrieved from http://www.pch.gc.ca/pgm/sc/pol/fewom/ws-a-eng.pdf

Canadian Heritage. (2009c). *C—Highlights of progress to date.* Retrieved from http://canadianheritage.gc.ca/pgm/sc/pol/actn07-12/105-eng.cfm

Canadian Heritage. (2009d). *Welcome.* Retrieved from http://www.pch.gc.ca/index-eng.cfm

Canadian Intergovernmental Conference Secretariat. (2009). *Conference of Federal-Provincial Territorial Ministers responsible for Sport, Physical Activity and Recreation.* Federal-Provincial-Territorial Ministers Take Action to Increase Physical Activity for Children and Youth.

Daniels, L. (2005). Untitled presentation made on behalf of the Aboriginal Sport Circle to the Ministers Conference, Regina, SK, 4–5 August.

Dubin, C.L. (1990). *Commission of inquiry into the use of drugs and banned practices intended to increase athletic performance.* Ottawa, ON: Minister of Supply and Services Canada.

Federal-Provincial/Territorial Advisory Committee. (2000). *National Recreation Roundtable on Aboriginal/Indigenous Peoples, Final Report.* Ottawa: Federal-Provincial/Territorial Advisory Committee on Fitness and Recreation. Retrieved from http://www.lin.ca/resource/html/sp0087.pdf

Forsyth, J. (2000). *From assimilation to self-determination: The emergence of J. Wilton Littlechild's North American Indigenous Games, 1763–1997.* Unpublished master's thesis, The University of Western Ontario, Canada.

Giddens, A. (1984). *The Constitution of Society: Outline of the Theory of Structuration.* Los Angeles, CA: University of California Press.

Gordon, J.D. (2009). *Northern Games Society. History and philosophy.* Retrieved from http://www.northerngames.org/history/

Green, M. (2004). Power, policy, and political priorities: Elite sport development in Canada and the United Kingdom. *Sociology of Sport Journal, 21*(4), 376–396.

Green, M. (2007). Olympic glory or grassroots development?: Sport policy priorities in Australia, Canada and the United Kingdom, 1960–2006. *The International Journal of the History of Sport, 24*(7), 921–953.

Gruneau, R. (1988). Modernization or hegemony: Two views on sport and social development. In J Harvey & H. Cantelon (Eds.), *Not just a game: Essays in Canadian sport sociology* (pp. 9–32). Ottawa, ON: University of Ottawa Press.

Jennings, P. (1990, June 26). Dubin inquiry report released. CBC Broadcast. Retrieved from http://archives.cbc.ca/sports/drugs_sports/clips/9013/

Mills, D. (1998). *Sport in Canada: Everybody's business. Leadership, partnership and accountability.* Standing Committee on Canadian Heritage, Sub-Committee on the Study of Sport in Canada. Ottawa, ON: Government of Canada. Retrieved from http://www.parl.gc.ca/HousePublications/Publication.aspx?DocId=1031530&Mode=1&Parl=36&Ses=&Language=E

Minister's Task Force. (1992). *Sport: The way ahead. Minister's task force on Federal Sport policy.* Ottawa, ON: Minister of Supply and Services Canada.

Pal, L.A. (2010). *Beyond policy analysis: Public issue management in turbulent times* (4th ed.). Toronto, ON: Nelson Education.

Paraschak, V. (1991). Sport festivals and race relations in the Northwest Territories of Canada. In G. Jarvie (Ed.), *Sport, racism, and ethnicity* (pp. 74–93). Philadelphia, PA: Falmer Press.

Paraschak, V. (1995). The native sport and recreation program 1972–1981: Patterns of resistance, patterns of reproduction. *Canadian Journal of History of Sport, 26*(2), 1–18.

Paraschak, V. (2004). Histories in the (un)making: Aboriginal sport histories and federal sport policy in Canada. Paper presented at the *Annual Convention for the North American Society for Sport History*, Pacific Grove, CA, 31 May.

Royal Commission on Aboriginal Peoples. (1996). *Report of the Royal Commission on Aboriginal Peoples.* Volume 2, Part 1: Restructuring the Relationship. Ottawa, ON: Minister of Supply and Services Canada

Sport Canada. (2002a). *The Canadian sport policy.* Ottawa, ON: Department of Canadian Heritage. Retrieved from http://www.pch.gc.ca/pgm/sc/pol/pcs-csp/2003/polsport-eng.pdf

Sport Canada. (2002b). *The Canadian sport policy: Federal-provincial/territorial priorities for collaborative action 2002–2005.* Ottawa, ON: Department of Canadian Heritage. Retrieved from http://www.pch.gc.ca/pgm/sc/pol/actn/index-eng.cfm

Sport Canada. (2003a). *North American Indigenous Games (NAIG) Funding Framework for 2008 and Onwards, Hosting Component.* Ottawa.

Sport Canada. (2003b). *Sport Canada Aboriginal Sport Policy. Report on Consultations with Provincial/Territorial Aboriginal Sport Bodies on the Draft Policy Framework.* Ottawa.

Sport Canada. (2003c). *Sport Canada Aboriginal Sport Policy. Report of Feedback Received from Reference Group on the Draft Policy Framework.* Ottawa: Sport Canada.

Sport Canada. (2012). *Canadian sport policy 2012.* Ottawa, ON: Department of Canadian Heritage. Retrieved from http://sirc.ca/CSPRenewal/documents/CSP2012_EN.pdf

Sutcliffe Group Inc. and Sluth Management Consulting, The. (2007). *Best practices—Physical activity programs for Aboriginal youth.* Report prepared for the Federal-Provincial/Territorial Sport Committee, Federal-Provincial/Territorial Physical Activity and Recreation Committee, and Aboriginal Sport & Physical Activity Workgroup.

Te Hiwi, B.P. (2009). *What is the spirit of our gathering? Self-determination and indigenous sport policy in Canada.* Unpublished master's thesis, University of Windsor, Canada.

Treasury Board of Canada. (2005). *DPR 2004–2005, Canadian Heritage, Detailed performance story, strategic objective 2: Cultural participation and engagement.* Retrieved from www.tbs-sct.gc.ca/rma/dpr1/04-05/PCH/PCHd4503_e.asp

Williams, R. (1983). *Culture and society, 1780–1950.* New York: Columbia University Press.

CHAPTER X

Policy on Sport for the Disabled

P. David Howe, Loughborough University

It is rather disappointing that a book on sport policy in Canada should require a chapter on issues related to persons with a disability. This is not a reflection on any research that has been carried out on sport policies, but rather it highlights that legislation and policy positions established by the government that deal with 'sport for all' have failed. Over a quarter of a century ago the *Canadian Charter of Rights and Freedoms* of 1982 established equality rights for individuals who were considered marginal to mainstream society. Section 15(1) of the Charter states:

> every individual is equal before and under the law and has the right to the equal protection and equal benefit of the law without discrimination and, in particular, without discrimination based on race, national or ethnic origin, colour, religion, sex, age or mental or physical disability. (1982, p. 3)

If this legislation were enforceable then there would be no need to highlight the policies that relate to persons with a disability because it would be an act of discrimination to have separate policies. Unfortunately the *Canadian Charter of Rights and Freedoms* has an additional section (15(2)) which states that:

> Subsection (1) does not preclude any law, program or activity that has as its object the amelioration of conditions of

> disadvantaged individuals or groups including those that
> [sic] are disadvantaged because of race, national or ethnic ori-
> gin, colour, religion, sex, age or mental or physical disability.
> (1982, p. 4)

This subsection 15(2), I believe, is at the root of many of the problems that have faced marginal individuals in Canadian society. If the *Canadian Charter for Rights and Freedoms* had been a strong, enforceable document, then subsection 15(2) would not be needed. The fact that this subsection is present isolates and marginalizes individuals and communities of difference as a 'problem' that needs special measures. In other words, if the charter were robust, subsection 15(1) would be all that needed to be stated.

It is my intent in this chapter to briefly explore the evolution and continual development of policies related to sport for people with a disability. The chapter begins by focusing upon early devel-opments in sport for the disabled.[1] Following this, the integration process and sport is critically examined in order to make sense of why elite sport has been the focus of attention, rather than sport participation. Positioning integration at the high performance end of the sport spectrum has begun to spark debates surrounding whether participation or high performance sport was most advantageous for athletes with impairments and is an issue that this chapter addresses when focusing on the culture of Canadian Paralympic sport. This provides a backdrop in which to highlight the integration of the Para-Athletics program in Athletics Canada.[2] Athletics Canada has been chosen as the focus of the case study for two reasons. Firstly, track and field athletics is arguably the flagship sport of both the Olympic and Paralympic Games and was one of the first sports, along with swimming to be integrated within the Canadian sport system. Secondly, it is the sport in which I have intimate, insider knowledge (cf. Howe 2008). Following the case study, the chapter concludes by exploring issues, controversies, and limitations of current sport poli-cies in Canada as they relate to sport for the disabled.

Early Developments in Sport for the Disabled

On a very basic level, there appears to have been three stages in the development of the sport provision for the disabled. The first stage of development was designed to aid in the rehabilitation of individuals who were seriously injured during World War II. It was felt that sport along with arts and crafts were important vehicles into a productive life (Anderson, 2003; Scruton, 1998). In the second stage, sport for the disabled was about participation, and as a result a number of international federations were established. Each of these federations had a responsibility to a constituent body of member nations and structured a sport calendar for impairment-specific groups, from grassroots to international level (Howe, 2008). These federations, namely the Cerebral Palsy International Sport and Recreation Association (CP-ISRA), the International Blind Sport Association (IBSA), the International Sports Federation for Persons with Intellectual Disability (Inas) and the International Wheelchair and Amputee Sport Association (IWAS),[3] were established with the explicit intention of creating opportunities for people with disabilities and using sport as a vehicle for their empowerment. This group of impairment-specific federations is known collectively as the International Organizations of Sports for the Disabled (IOSD). It was these federations and their predecessors that helped to organize the Paralympic Games from 1960 through to 1988. These early Games, where participation was the primary mantra, were organized and run on a much smaller scale than those under the influence of the International Paralympic Committee (IPC).

The establishment of the IPC in Dusseldorf on September 21, 1989, officially began what has commonly been referred to as the Paralympic Movement and was the dawn of the third stage of development of sport for the disabled. Since 1989, there has been rapid growth in the IPC that has seen it establish an extensive network of 164 national affiliates that, in some cases, replicate or replace the national governing bodies of the federations. The IOSD were still instrumental to the success of the IPC, as they introduced distinctive classification systems that were designed to create a level playing field for each impairment group. Classification in sport for the disabled continually evolves to allow for equitable and fair competition. As Sherrill suggests:

> a basic goal of classification is to ensure that winning or losing an event depends on talent, training, skill, fitness, and motivation rather than unevenness among competitors on disability-related variables (e.g., spasticity, paralysis, absence of limb segments). (1999, p. 210)

These sport organizations were on the front line offering expertise, in 1989, when the IPC was established. Since many of the first officials of the IPC had previously held posts within these founding federations in the early days of the IPC, there was initially carte blanche acceptance of the IOSD classification systems. One of the legacies of this heritage is a complex classification system that many in the IPC regard as cumbersome, logistically problematic, and a potential threat to the marketability of the Paralympic Games (Steadward, 1996).

Since the establishment of the IPC, those involved with this institution have worked tirelessly to heighten the public profile of elite sports for the disabled. A year prior to the establishment of the IPC, the Paralympic Games began a pattern of following directly after the Olympic Games, adopting the same sport calendar and making use of the same venues and state-of-the-art facilities. In many respects, this helped to legitimize elite sport for the disabled. The IPC first became the international partner to the local Paralympic Games Organizing Committee in 1992 and as such has been able to strongly influence the direction and organization of all subsequent Paralympic Games. As a result, under the supervision of the IPC, there has been a move toward the normalization of sport for the disabled that has been managed in partnership with increased media coverage of flagship events (Howe, 2008).

Canada first competed in international sport for the disabled in the early 1950s in wheelchair basketball, and the nation was first represented at the third Paralympic Games in 1968 in Tel Aviv (Canadian Paralympic Committee, 2012). While the first Canadian Paralympic team was small, comprising 22 wheelchair athletes, the act of representing the nation internationally in disability sport is important insofar as this was one of the intentions of Bill C-131 *An Act to Encourage Fitness and Amateur Sport* (Macintosh, Bedecki, & Franks, 1987; Houlihan & Green, 2005).

There had been a degree of tension in Canada surrounding the use of sport as a leisure pursuit after World War II in spite of the establishment of the *National Physical Fitness Act* of 1943 (Harvey, 1988). The overriding feeling at the time was that "[s]port was something that one outgrew when adulthood was reached. It was time to move on to the more important matter of making one's way in life" (Macintosh et al., 1987, p. 17). These attitudes towards sport would have clearly influenced the development of sport for the disabled, which was an extension of rehabilitative medicine (Howe, 2008), and may go some way in explaining Canada's relatively late involvement within the Paralympic Games. In spite of there being no explicit mention of provision for the disabled in Bill C-131, following Harvey:

> one can surmise that even for the political party in power, given the hegemony of the social democratic role of the state to equalize opportunities, the bill had to at least give the image of equality of opportunity in order to gain legitimacy. (1988, p. 324)

This statement highlights nicely the intentionality of those in power and of all policies regarding the issues of rights for the marginal within society. From the image of equality identified by Harvey (1988), it is clear to see, in the *Canadian Sport Policy* of 2002, (p. 8) where "Barriers to Access" are mentioned should have been where sport policy development ended for a time. Yet, in June 2006, the government marginalized the disabled community by releasing the *Policy on Sport for People with Disabilities* (Canadian Heritage, 2006). The development of this policy document following the publication of the *Canadian Sport Policy*, which explicitly states, in the vision for sport, "Canadians of all ages and *abilities*" (Sport Canada, 2002, p. 13, *emphasis added*); so the question that, perhaps, should be asked is: Why is there a need for a separate policy for the disabled? Some will argue that the current *Canadian Sport Policy* highlights inclusivity as one of its key policy principles. "Sport delivery is accessible and equitable and reflects the full breadth of interests, motivations, objectives, abilities, and the diversity of Canadian society" (Sport Canada, 2012, p. 6). This of course is welcome, and the whole tone of this important document is inclusive; however, nowhere in this document is it stated that the *Canadian Sport Policy* supersedes the *Policy on Sport for People with Disabilities*. What is clear is that if this policy is ineffective in policing the right of impaired individuals to access sport in the not too distant future there will be a 'new and improved' *Policy on Sport for People with Disabilities*.

In recent years, Sport Canada has provided core funding for the Canadian Paralympic Committee (CPC), the organization that has governance over athletes who represent Canada in Paralympic competitions. Funding of the CPC by Sport Canada may be seen as the first step toward a fully inclusive sport system and a precursor to the integration of sport for the disabled throughout Sport Canada's provision (Green & Houlihan, 2005; Sport Canada, 2002). Publication in 2006 of *No Accidental Champions*[4] (Canadian Sport Centres, 2006) highlights the importance the government is placing upon the integration of high performance sport for the disabled within the Canadian sport system. Canada is not alone in developing policy that will lead to the integration of sport for the disabled into the mainstream sport as the International Paralympic Committee (IPC) has been openly expressing this desire for some time (Labanowich, 1988; Steadward, 1996; Vanlandewijck & Chappel, 1996). In fact, a policy shift away from a disability-centred model of sport provision at the elite level within Canada aims to enhance the competitive opportunities as well as educate the public about [dis]ability as it relates to high performance sport (Steadward, 1996).

The adoption of *No Accidental Champions* highlights the degree to which Sport Canada considers disabled athletes a special population. In the introduction of *No Accidental Champions* the following statement attests to this:

> athletes with a disability (AWADs) are first and foremost athletes, and for that reason, virtually everything in the able-bodied Long-Term Athlete Development (LTAD) model is applicable. The able-bodied LTAD and its resource paper, Canadian Sport for Life, should be the starting point for all athletes. *No Accidental Champions* is therefore, only concerned with additional factors that need to be considered when working with AWADs. (Canadian Sport Centres, 2006, p. 4)

This statement to the critically unaware may seem liberal and forward thinking but it still acts to segregate particular elements of the Canadian sport population. Segregation is solidified by the heading 'Not Different, But in Addition' which is absurd for the simple fact that all of human kind is different in one way or another and it is something we need to be upfront about and celebrate (cf. Silva & Howe, 2012). The fact that athletes with disabilities still need to be separated from 'able' athletes on the Canadian Sport for Life virtual platform demonstrates that acceptance of difference is far from being achieved (cf. Canadian Sport for Life, 2011).

In the following sections, I highlight issues of integration at the high performance end of the sport spectrum. The reason for this is rather simple. While mainstream sport provision can be graphically represented in the shape of a pyramid, which is familiar to those interested in sport development and in which the LTAD is the current Sport Canada rubric, in sport for the disabled participation numbers are so low the graphic representation that is more appropriate is an obelisk. In other words, there are very few participants from which to draw high performance athletes. As such, exploring integration in the high performance is felt to be appropriate.

The Integration Process and Sport

The integration process that is being undertaken by Sport Canada is seen as important if an inclusive society is to be achieved. Broadly speaking, integration is the equal access and acceptance of all in the community. Some scholars have distanced themselves from the discussion of integration since the concept implies that the disabled population is required to change or normalize in order to join the mainstream (Oliver, 1996; Ravaud & Stiker, 2001). In other words, the concept of integration requires members of the disabled community to adopt an 'able' disposition in order to become members of the mainstream. Because of its shortcomings, Oliver dismisses integration as being heavily laden with policy rhetoric and sees the term inclusion, because of its association with politics, as more appropriate (Northway, 1997; Oliver, 1996). Inclusion means that members of the disability community have a choice in whether to fully embrace the mainstream:

> Equality (defined as "the participation and inclusion of all groups") may sometimes be best achieved by differential treatment. This does mean that if oppressed groups so choose they can opt for groups-specific recognition in policy and provision, since within an inclusive approach difference would be accepted or included as a natural part of the whole. (Northway, 1997, p. 166)

Following these debates, there has been a shift within the literature on disability from the dichotomy of integration/segregation to another where inclusion/exclusion are seen as a more politically appropriate way to advocate the acceptance of the disabled. It is possible, however, to see integration as a literal intermixing that entails the culture of both groups adapting to a new cultural environment.

To this end, scholars working within sport studies have adopted a continuum of integration that is useful in the current exploration of Athletics Canada. Sørensen and Kahrs (2006), in their study of integration of sport for the disabled within the Norwegian sport system, have adopted a continuum of compliance with the aim of exploring the success of their nations inclusive sport system. Within this study, integration wherein both the athletes with disabilities and those from the mainstream adapt their cultural systems is referred to as *true* integration. Where athletes with a disability are forced to adopt the mainstream culture without any attempt at reciprocal action is seen as assimilation. Finally the least integrated model is seen as segregation where neither group is willing to transform its core cultural values in spite of being jointly managed within the sport system.

For the purpose of this chapter it is the process of successful integration which allows an inclusive society to be established that is most relevant. If society is going to become more inclusive "it is necessary for existing economic, social and political institutions to be challenged and modified. This means that disabled people [sic] are not simply brought into society as it currently exists but rather that society is, in some ways, required to change" (Northway, 1997, p. 165). True integration therefore has to be undertaken in order to establish an inclusive NSO.

Bearing this in mind, scholars more recently have shown that integration can be effectively understood as an outcome (van de Ven, Post, de Witte, & van den Heuvel, 2005) of an inclusive society. More specifically it is argued that "[i]ntegration occurs through a process of interaction between a person with a disability and others in society" (van de Ven et al., 2005, p. 319). In other words, it is the process of interaction between an individual with a disability who possesses his/her own attitude toward integration, strategies, and social roles and others in society who adopt certain attitudes and perceptions of people with disabilities. As a result, factors that influence the success of the integration process are both personal as well as social but also include an element of support provision that will be distinct depending on the severity of the individual's disability (van de Ven et al., 2005; see also Kelly, 2001).

It is possible, for example, to see true integration as a literal intermixing that entails the culture of both groups adapting to a new cultural environment. Dijker uses the term community integration to articulate a similar conceptualization to true integration. Community integration:

> is the acquiring of age, gender, and culture-appropriate roles,
> statuses and activities, including in(ter)dependence in decision
> making, and productive behaviours performed as part of multi-
> variate relationships with family, friends, and others in natural
> community settings. (Dijker, 1999, p. 41)

True integration therefore is "a multifaceted and difficult process, which although it could be defined at a policy level rhetoric, [is] much less easy to define in reality" (Cole, 2005, p. 341). The difficulty when exploring the success of integration policies is that the balance between the philosophical position and the reality (in this case a cultural sport environment) is not always clear. Simply exploring the policy landscape means that any interpretation is devoid of explicit cultural influences though all policy is a cultural artefact. This being said, the aim of integration is to allow the disabled to take a full and active role within society. The ideal would be:

> [a] world in which all human beings, regardless of impairment,
> age, gender, social class or minority ethnic status, can co-exist as
> equal members of the community, secure in the knowledge that
> their needs will be met and that their views will be recognised,
> respected and valued. It will be a very different world from the
> one in which we now live. (Oliver & Barnes, 1998, p. 102)

Within the context of high performance sport, this aim is hard to achieve. By its very nature elite sport is selective and it is based on how well individual bodies perform against one another (DePauw, 1997) and this can lead to individuals with or without disabilities being excluded (Bowen, 2002). As Bowen suggested, "within profes-sional sport, though, all but the super-able 'suffer' from 'exclusion or segregation'" (2002, p. 71). How then, if "sport isolates indi-viduals, but only those who are *super*-able. The rest *are* left to the realm of the minor leagues, masters leagues, local tournaments, or backyard pick-up games" (Bowen, 2002, p. 71), can we establish whether integration has actually been a success within an institu-tion such as Athletics Canada? This understanding of sport makes it problematic to address the issue of integration without realizing that elite sport can never be completely integrated in spite of recent attempts by the Canadian government to develop policy where integration is seen as vitally important (Canadian Heritage, 2000; Green, 2004; Green & Houlihan, 2005; Sport Canada, 2002, 2012). It is important, however, that Sport Canada achieves integration at the high performance end of the spectrum in order to send a clear message regarding the positioning of people with disabilities within Canadian society. The development in 2006 of the *Policy on Sport for Persons with a Disability* may be designed to promote inclusion but as we will see it may have a more marginalizing impact. In order to fully understand the success or failure of integration within Athletics Canada, it important to explore certain elements of the culture of sport for the disabled, and it is to this issue that the discussion now turns.

Canadian Paralympic Sport Culture

To high performance athletes with a disability, the act of including the Paralympic Athletics Program within Athletics Canada has solidified their identity as elite athletes. Acceptance within the mainstream, able-bodied organization is seen as justifying the hard work and energy put into their training by rewarding them with funding from Sport Canada. However, this integration process has not occurred entirely smoothly, or completely, as the cultural environment of mainstream athletics and that of sport for the disabled are distinctive.

Within the field of sport for the disabled, key elements of this particular culture are the charitable mandate for the IOSD and the systems adopted for the organization of the sport practice, commonly referred to as classification.

A distinctive element of the disability sport culture of the Canadian affiliates of the IOSDs is their charitable foundation. These organizations were founded to 'look after' socially marginal individuals. The IOSDs were established with the explicit intention of creating opportunities for disabled people to be involved in the practice of sport using it as a vehicle for their attempted empowerment. It was the IOSDs and their predecessors that helped to organize the Paralympic Games from 1960 through to 1988 and, as a result, these games were different because there was less emphasis on high performance. This is not to say that elite athletes were not involved but that participation was the main imperative. These early Games were organized and run on a much smaller scale than those under the influence of the IPC.

Canada has played an important role in the transformation of the Paralympics from a movement focused on opportunity and participation to one where excellence through high performance training is the sole aim. The first president of the IPC was Canadian Dr. Robert Steadward. Steadward's tenure in office (1989–2001) saw the IPC, among other initiatives, forge closer links with the Olympic Movement. Benefits include long-term financial support, access to the high quality facilities in which to hold the Paralympics, and countless other commercial benefits. An agreement between the IOC and the IPC was signed in 2001 to formalize these closer ties. In 2003, this agreement was amended to transfer "broadcasting and marketing responsibilities of the 2008, 2010, and 2012 Paralympic Games to the Organizing Committee of these Olympic and Paralympic Games" (IPC, 2003, p. 1). Agreements such as this will ease financial concerns for the IPC and allow the Olympic and Paralympic Games to be marketed as a single, high performance sport spectacle.

Closer links with the IOC highlight the serious intent of the IPC and its networks of national affiliates to transform sport for the disabled from a pastime to a high performance sport event (Howe, 2004). Athletics Canada has been relatively quick to notice the transformation in sport ethos that has occurred within sport for the disabled but integration is not an altogether simple process. The charitable foundation of the IOSDs is a stumbling block that is in the process of being overcome. However, the categorization or classification of athletes with a disability provides other concerns.

Classification is another element of the organizational structure within sport for the disabled that contributes to its distinctive culture (Howe & Jones, 2006). Classification is simply a structure for competition similar to the systems used in the sport of judo where competitors perform in distinctive weight categories. Within sport for the disabled, competitors are classified by their body's degree of function, and therefore it is important that the classification process achieves equity in the Paralympic sport practice and enables athletes to compete on a "level playing field" (Sherrill, 1999).

A complex classification system is the result of the historical development of sport for the disabled (Daly & Vanlandewijck, 1999; Steadward, 1996; Vanlandewijck & Chappel, 1996). As far as the

IOC and IPC are concerned, the current classification system used within sport for the disabled detracts from the Paralympic Games as a sport event because it confuses spectators (Smith & Thomas, 2005; Steadward, 1996). Classification is important when considering the issues of integration within mainstream sport contexts because the Paralympic athletes who receive the greatest exposure are in fact the most 'abled,' that is, the least impaired. Other athletes, who are in classes that have a small number of competitors, lack the cultural capital of those who are in larger classes and who are, as a direct result, more culturally competitive.

Integration within Athletics Canada

The move to mainstream track and field athletics within Athletics Canada was preceded by the inclusion of the sport of swimming within the same framework in 1994. In 1997, high performance wheel-chair users, members of the Canadian Wheelchair Sports Association, became part of Athletics Canada. The other national affiliates of the IOSD, namely, the Canadian Cerebral Palsy Sport Association, the Canadian Amputee Sports Association and the Canadian Blind Sports Association, which all continue to be funded by Sport Canada, entered into negotiation with Athletics Canada to have their elite athletes integrated. By 2002, high performance athletes who were the responsibility of these organizations were included officially within the framework of Athletics Canada, though they had become unofficial members of Athletics Canada while negotiations continued with the various disability sport organizations in the late 1990s. One of the obstacles associated with the integration of elite disabled athletes is that each IOSD has numerous classes of competitors.

The advent of a Paralympic Manager within Athletics Canada, in 1999, was facilitated in part because of Sport Canada's desire to see sports integrated across its programs. At this stage, the role and responsibility of the managers was to liaise with Sport Canada primarily regarding funding (carding) for the athletes. The Athlete Assistance Program (AAP) was designed to offset some of the costs of training, but unless the athlete is supported by family members, it does not facilitate full-time athlete status (see Chapter V). New opportunities within high performance sport for the disabled, which reward them for the hours of hard work in the gymnasium and in track and field, represent a coming of age for Paralympic sport.

The adoption of more comprehensive funding for athletes with a disability is also an important step in validating the identities of these individuals as high performance athletes.

Athletes involved within the Para-Athletics Program, however, are not a homogenous group. The desire to organize a high performance program for Paralympic athletes separately from the mainstream suggests that integration is an issue that has not been properly tackled. In the early days of sport for the disabled, divisions amongst Paralympians were often determined by the IOSD of which they were a member. The social world surrounding high performance sport for the disabled was largely demarcated by impairment, so much so that some groups were perceived to be inferior (Sherrill & Williams, 1996). Today the heterogeneity of the group is similar to what would be expected within mainstream athletics where athletes tend to be more sociable with those who engage in similar training practices. In other words, throwers tend to associate more often with other throwers and wheelchair racers tend to do the same. There is, however, a perception within the Paralympic group that some athletes gain the benefits of AAP funding and the support from Athletics Canada while not having to work as hard as others because the classification system advantages some impairment groups (Howe, 2007).

Generally speaking, those athletes with a congenital disability are socialized differently, and many athletes with acquired disabilities feel that this establishes a distinctive culture between these two groups. It is believed by those who have acquired disabilities that the congenitally disabled is not encouraged to train as hard (Howe, 2007). Whether or not this is the case, there is a degree of tension between these two groups of athletes, and this impacts upon whether government financial support is justified. In other words athlete funding should be a perk for those who train well. In essence, a funded athlete should see training as a full-time occupation, in spite of the fact that Sport Canada's AAP funding alone is not enough to sustain an individual with no family, friends or sponsors on which to rely. However, this carries an important responsibility. Receipt of the AAP funding necessarily imposes an obligation on the athlete to devote considerable time to training. In this respect, the athletes who are funded by Sport Canada's AAP and Athletics Canada can be divided by their commitment to performing at their best with all that entails and those who are simply taking the money—often winning medals—because they are in a 'soft' classification. This may be a direct result of many of the athletes being 'products' of the IOSD disability-specific system within athletics where some classes are much less competitive than others (Howe & Jones, 2006).

Many individuals have an expectation that they will be funded, and coaches have been known to petition Athletics Canada to include athletes as part of the AAP plan. This special treatment of some athletes is likely a direct result of the charitable foundation of the IOSD, an ethos that is often in direct conflict with the goals of high performance sport. A lack of communication between the national coaches who are part of the Paralympic program and athletes might be exacerbated by the fact that Athletics Canada only 'looks after' high performance disabled athletes. While Athletics Canada maintains a degree of responsibility for grassroots development in mainstream athletics (Green & Houlihan, 2005), they have no link with potential athletes for the Paralympic program. This can make talent identification problematic, and if the Paralympic program needs to fund a certain number of athletes (or lose the funding) they will return to known athletes who may be a product of the participation model of disability sport.

The image of an athlete with a disability who does not undertake training at the level expected of a high performance athlete can have negative consequences for the organization of Paralympic programs. Structurally, the Paralympic program at Athletics Canada is included within the provision of services but it is clearly not integrated. As mentioned earlier, Athletics Canada appointed a Paralympic Program Manager whose responsibility it was to work alongside the paid head coach selecting the team of national coaches and the athletes for various international competitions. This leads to a situation where all Paralympic athletes are the responsibility of the Paralympic program's head coach and manager.

Athletics Canada is organized broadly into three event areas: endurance, speed and power, and Paralympic. In other words, an athlete with a disability who runs in the 5,000 metre is the responsibility of the Paralympic program. If the Paralympic program were fully integrated, there might be an event area for wheelchair racing, as this is different to running but not an area for Paralympics. Profiled athletes on the organization's webpage are also highlighted by their impairment group. By implication, a javelin thrower with cerebral palsy is not of the same status as his or her 'abled' equivalent. This may represent inclusion but it is a far cry from integration.

The head coach of the Paralympic program monitors the training programs the athlete develops with their personal coach. The fact that the head Paralympic coach, who may have limited experience in some elements of the sport, validates training schedules outside his/her knowledge base might be 'allowing' some athletes to be less than wholly committed to their training. This is a flaw in the current system that may be eliminated through increased funding; however, it certainly should not take away the responsibility of an athlete to action a well-designed training plan.

Following criticism of relatively poor results on the international stage, Athletics Canada underwent an 'independent' review of their Para-Athletics Program (Community Active, 2008) and as a result it has combined the role of the head coach and the Para-Athletics Program leader. This review was undertaken prior to the 2008 Beijing Paralympic Games and, apart from the continuing success of superstar Chantal Petitclerc,[5] results at the Beijing Paralympic Games were relatively poor. The report highlighted the problem associated with the recruitment of high quality athletes, which is of course a big problem but one that also directly impacts upon the 'able-bodied' program at Athletics Canada. The claims that Canada is becoming less competitive in Paralympic Athletics are not only a recruitment issue but the sign that more nations are taking sport for the disabled seriously. It does seem remarkable that the same type of review has not been undertaken in the chronically unsuccessful world of the 'able-bodied' program at Athletics Canada.

Discussion

The success of high profile athletes like Chantal Petitclerc at both the 2004 and 2008 Paralympic Games and the media attention she draws to Paralympic sport should be celebrated (cf. Howe, 2007). But while the public in Canada celebrated Petitclerc's success, there are still problems related to the integration of Paralympic athletes into mainstream Athletics. Petitclerc's triumphant season of 2004 is a good example of this disparity. After victories on both the Olympic and Paralympic stages, Petitclerc was 'honoured' at home by Athletics Canada being jointly made "Athlete of the Year." Petitclerc refused to accept the award she was to share with 100-metre hurdler Perdita Felicien, a world-class athlete and world indoor champion who fell at the start of her final at the 2004 Athens Olympic Games.

Athletics Canada may have been acting appropriately by nominating both an abled and a disabled athlete for the award, but Petitclerc saw it as a snub. She said of the award:

> to me, it's really a symptom that [Athletics Canada] can't evaluate the value of a Paralympic medal—that it's easier to win a Paralympic medal than an Olympic medal. That may have been true 15 years ago. That's not the case any more. (as cited in Wong, 2004, p. 1)

In the events in which Petitclerc competed, the depth of the field was as great as any in able-bodied athletics. At the Olympic Games and other mainstream track and field athletics events there are only ever a handful of likely winners of the top prize. The only difference is that, at the Paralympic Games, particularly in events like wheelchair racing, the winners are drawn from nations that are often the most technologically advanced. While African athletes dominate middle distance running at the Olympic Games, IAAF World Championships and Grand Prix circuit, the need for technology in wheelchair racing means that the winners are typically drawn from westernized nations. The problem according to Patrick Jarvis, former president of the Canadian Paralympic Committee and one of the few former Paralympians in a position of significant power within the Movement, is one of increased competition:

> we get many supportive comments as Paralympians. But as soon as you start to incur in their [able-bodied athletes'] territory, being respected just as equal athletes and you threaten to win some of their awards, a lot are still uncomfortable with [disability]. (Christie, 2004, p. 52)

If the situation had been reversed, and Felicien had won her race while Petitclerc had not won all she contested, would the honour have gone to both athletes? Presumably not.

Athletics Canada is not the only national sport organization that has acted as if integration were an issue to which they only had to pay lip service. The Canadian Olympic Committee (COC) had publicly denounced the Organizing Committee of the 2004 Athens Olympic Games for not allowing three Canadian wheelchair athletes (Jeff Adams, Chantal Petitclerc and Diane Roy) full accreditation (Ewing,

2004). According to Adams (2004) the actions of COC were good but they simply did not realize the gravity of this snub, which flies in the face of the special agreement the IOC has with the IPC (IPC, 2003). Adams believed the COC should have made the following statement:

> I'm sorry, but as Canadians, we simply cannot ask our athletes to comply with your request. It is impossible for us, because of our beliefs, because of our policies, and because of our constitution. If you'd like us to have the athletes removed from the village we'd be happy to do that, and call a press conference to explain why. (Adams, 2004, n.p.)

Whether this sort of direct action would have delivered equitable treatment is anyone's guess. However, since the COC represents a country that, in 1982, as previously mentioned, enacted the *Canadian Charter of Rights and Freedoms*, which includes disability as a prohibited ground for discrimination, this sort of action should have been taken. It is no wonder that high performance athletes with a disability are still today having difficulty becoming integrated into mainstream sport.

In spite of being at the forefront of human rights legislation regarding discrimination on the grounds of disability, integration at all levels of sport is not happening. On November 25, 2003, the Secretary of State for Physical Activity in Sport, Paul DeVillers, announced the creation of a working group to examine the issues related to sport and disability, which ultimately led to the release of the 2006 *Policy on Sport for Persons with a Disability*. As stated earlier, if Sport Canada is working as it should, why has such a policy been launched over two decades after it became unconstitutional to discriminate against people with a disability in Canada?

Let us hope that the 2012 *Canadian Sport Policy* brings Canada closer to *true integration* as there is little in the way of action that suggests the 'able' majority are going to change in order to accept athletes with a disability as equal to athletes without.

Conclusion

To the outsider, the inclusion of Paralympic athletes within the matrix of Sport Canada may be seen as a statement of a progressive nation. Nevertheless, integration within Athletics Canada has not been complete, and as a result this shortfall heightens the social division between the abled and the disabled within high performance sport in Canada. While Athletics Canada has attempted to integrate athletes with a disability by branding them as products of their organization, these actions have done little to address the inequities within the organizations that favour the 'able' athletes. The processes of inclusion, the simple act of including the Paralympic Athletics Program within Athletics Canada has been relatively successful; however, integration, or the intermixing of persons previously segregated, has not.

The inclusion of the Para-Athletics into a mainstream organization like Athletics Canada, in some respect, creates an environment that perpetuates the differences between athletes with and without disabilities. In a sense, the organizations and people in power are catalysts for disablism. Disablism is, according to Miller, Parker, and Gillinson, (2004, p. 9), "discriminatory, oppressive or abusive behaviour arising from the belief that disabled people are inferior to others." Over the last two decades, there have been both national and international legislation passed by governments that has greatly reduced overt disablism. The elimination of overt disablist attitudes makes the lives of impaired people better, opening up opportunities for work and leisure, although some feel there is a long way to go before equity is achieved. As Deal suggested:

> not all forms of prejudice and discriminatory behaviour, however, are blatant and therefore easily identifiable, as subtle forms of prejudice also exist. Therefore any attempt to tackle prejudice towards disabled people must not only focus on overtly discriminatory behaviour but also recognize subtle forms of prejudice, which can be equally damaging. (2007, p. 94)

The disablism that confronts the athletes who are part of the Para-Athletics Program is not blatant but is a subtle form of prejudice. Because of the subtle nature of disablism, it often falls under the radar established by legislation designed to improve the lives of people with disabilities. Disablism can be aversive and is therefore hard to detect, but the establishment of separate and exclusionary policies like the *Policy on Sport for Persons with a Disability* I am hopeful are a thing of the past but we need to vigilant in monitoring the nature of integration practices within Canada to eliminate the potential for human rights violations.

Notes

1. It has been widely accepted within disability studies circles that a person's first approach should be adopted when addressing athletes with a disability, in other words the phrase 'person with a disability' is seen as politically correct. In this paper, I have stuck to this convention except when referring to sport as an institution. I use the term 'sport for the disabled' instead of disability sport because through my research, it is clear that sport provision for the disabled is part of what might be labeled a "disability industry" (Albrecht, 1992; Campbell & Oliver, 1996). As a result, sport for the disabled is exactly what is being discussed in this paper.
2. Athletics Canada is the national sport organization (NSO) for track and field athletics and as such receives core funding from Sport Canada.
3. This is a federation that was launched in September 2004 at the Athens Paralympic Games. It is the result of a merger of two federations, the International Stoke Mandeville Wheelchair Sports Federation (ISMWSF) and the International Organizations of Sports for the Disabled (IOSD) that have been part of the Paralympic Movement since its inception.
4. *No Accidental Champions* is the supplemental document to *Canadian Sport for Life* (also known as the Long-Term Athlete Development Model), covering sport development for athletes with a disability.
5. Chantal Petitclerc retired from high performance international competition following the 2008 Beijing Paralympic Games. In October 2010, Petitclerc became a member at large of the Board of Directors of the Canadian Paralympic Committee (Petitclerc, 2010).

References

Adams, J. (2004, August 25). Follow up to Jeff Adams at the Olympics. Retrieved from http://www.adamsmania.com/archive.php

Albrecht, G.L. (1992). *The disability business: Rehabilitation in America.* Newbury Park, CA: Sage.

Anderson, J. (2003). 'Turned into taxpayers': Paraplegia, rehabilitation and sport at Stoke Mandeville, 1944–56. *Journal of Contemporary History, 38*(3), 461–475.

Bowen, J. (2002). The Americans with disabilities act and its application to sport. *Journal of the Philosophy of Sport, 29*(1), 66–74.

Campbell, J., & Oliver, M. (1996). *Disability politics. Understanding our past, changing our future.* London: Routledge.

Canadian Heritage. (2000). *Sport funding and accountability framework 2000–2005.* Ottawa, ON: Canadian Heritage.

Canadian Heritage. (2006). *Policy on sport for persons with a disability.* Ottawa, ON: Her Majesty the Queen in Right of Canada. Retrieved from http://www.pch.gc.ca/pgm/sc/pol/spt/pwad-eng.pdf

Canadian Paralympic Committee. (2012). *Home. About us. History.* Retrieved from http://paralympic.ca/en/About-Us/History.html

Canadian Sport Centres. (2006). *No accidental champions. Long-term athlete development for athletes with a disability.* Vancouver, BC: Author. Retrieved from http://www.canadiansportforlife.ca/sites/default/files/resources/No%20Accidental%20Champions.pdf

Canadian Sport for Life. (2011). *Welcome to Canadian Sport for Life.* Retrieved from http://www.canadiansportforlife.ca/

Christie, J. (2004, December 11). Spirit in motion: Paralympians rise. *The Globe and Mail*, p. 52.

Cole, B.A. (2005). Good faith and effort? Perspectives on educational inclusion. *Disability and Society, 20*, 331–344.

Community Active. (2008). *Para-Athletics program review—Summary report.* May.

Daly, D.J., & Vanlandewijck, Y. (1999). Some criteria for evaluating the "fairness" of swimming classification. *Adapted Physical Activity Quarterly, 16*, 271–289.

Deal, M. (2007). Aversive disablism: subtle prejudice toward disabled people. *Disability and Society, 22*(1), 93–107.

DePauw, K. (1997). The (in)visibility of disability: Cultural contexts and 'sporting bodies.' *Quest, 49*, 416–430.

Dijkers, M. (1999). Community integration: conceptual issues and measurement approaches in rehabilitation research. *Journal of Rehabilitation Outcome Measurements, 3*(1), 39–49.

Ewing, L. (2004, July 20). Wheelchair athletes can't march in Olympic ceremonies. *Daily News* (Halifax), p. 40.

Green, M. (2004). Power, policy, and political priorities: elite sport development in Canada and the United Kingdom. *Sociology of Sport Journal, 21*, 376–396.

Green, M., & Houlihan, B. (2005). *Elite Sport Development: policy learning and political priorities.* London: Routledge.

Harvey, J. (1988). Sport policy and the welfare state: An outline of the Canadian case. *Sociology of Sport Journal, 5*(4), 315–329.

Howe, P.D. (2007). Integration of Paralympic athletes into Athletics Canada. *International Journal of Canadian Studies, 35*, 133–150.

Howe, P.D. (2008). *The cultural politics of the Paralympic Movement: Through the anthropological lens.* London: Routledge.

Howe, P.D., & Jones, C. (2006). Classification of disabled athletes: (dis)empowering the Paralympic practice community. *Sociology of Sport Journal, 23*, 29–46.

International Paralympic Committee. (2003). *The Paralympian: Newsletter of the International Paralympic Committee.* No 3. Bonn, Germany.

Kelly, M.P. (2001). Disability and community: a sociological approach. In G.L. Albrecht, K.D. Seelman, & M. Bury (Eds.), *Handbook of disability studies* (pp. 396–411). London: Sage.

Labanowich, S. (1988). A case for the integration of the disabled into the Olympic Games. *Adapted Physical Activity Quarterly, 5,* 263–272.

Macintosh, D., Bedecki, T., & Franks, C.E.S. (1987). *Sport and politics in Canada. Federal government involvement since 1961.* Montreal, QC & Kingston, ON: McGill-Queen's University Press.

Miller, P., Parker, S., & Gillinson S. (2004). *Disablism: how to tackle the last prejudice.* London: Demos.

Northway, R. (1997). Integration and Inclusion: illusion or progress in services in services for disabled people, *Social Policy and Administration, 31*(2), 157–172.

Oliver, M. (1996). *Understanding disability: From theory to practice.* Basingstoke, UK: Macmillan.

Oliver, M., & Barnes, C. (1998). *Social policy and disabled People: from exclusion to inclusion.* London: Longman.

Petiticlerc, C. (2010, 13 novembre). *Le Comité paralympique canadien félicite Chantal Petitclerc.* Retrieved from http://www.chantalpetitclerc.com/2011/fr/nouvelles/57-le-comite-paralympique-canadien-felicite-chantal-petitclerc-premiere-athlete-paralympique-feminine-intronisee-au-pantheon-des-sports-canadiens

Ravaud, J-F., & Stiker, H-J. (2001). Inclusion/Exclusion: an analysis of historical and cultural meaning. In G.L. Albrecht, K.D. Seelman, & M. Bury (Eds.), *Handbook of disability studies.* (pp. 490–512). London: Sage.

Scruton, J. (1998). *Stoke Mandeville road to the Paralympics: Fifty years of history.* Aylesbury, UK: Peterhouse Press.

Sherrill, C. (1999). Disability sport and classification theory: A new era, *Adapted Physical Activity Quarterly, 16,* 206–215.

Sherrill, C., & Williams, T. (1996). Disability and sport: psychosocial perspectives on inclusion, integration and participation, *Sport Science Review, 5*(1), 42–64.

Silva, C.F., & Howe, P.D. (2012). Difference, adapted physical activity and human development: Potential contribution of capabilities approach. *Adapted Physical Activity Quarterly, 29*(1) 25–43.

Smith, A., & Thomas, N. (2005). The "inclusion" of elite athletes with disabilities in the 2002 Manchester Commonwealth Games: An exploratory analysis of British newspaper coverage, *Sport, Education and Society, 10,* 49–67.

Sørensen, M., & Kahrs, N. (2006). Integration of disability sport in The Norwegian sport organizations: Lessons learned. *Adapted Physical Activity Quarterly, 23*, 184–203.

Sport Canada. (2002). *The Canadian sport policy.* Ottawa, ON: Department of Canadian Heritage. Retrieved from http://www.pch.gc.ca/pgm/sc/pol/pcs-csp/2003/polsport-eng.pdf

Sport Canada. (2012). *Canadian sport policy 2012.* Ottawa, ON: Department of Canadian Heritage. Retrieved from http://sirc.ca/CSPRenewal/documents/CSP2012_EN.pdf

Steadward, R. (1996). Integration and sport in the Paralympic Movement. *Sport Science Review, 5*, 26–41.

van de Ven, L., Post, M., de Witte, L., & van den Heuvel, W. (2005). It takes two to tango: The integration of people with disabilities into society. *Disability and Society, 20*(3), 311–329.

Vanlandewijck, Y.C., & Chappel, R.J. (1996). Integration and classification issues in competitive sports for athletes with disabilities. *Sport Science Review, 5*, 65–88.

Wong, J. (2004, December 11). Nation builder 2004: Chantal Petitclerc, *The Globe and Mail*, p. F1.

CHAPTER XI

Women in Sport Policy

Parissa Safai, York University

No one can deny that Canadian women have a rich history of participation and leadership in sport and that the current state of Canadian sport—at all levels—involves, and is vitally dependent upon, women as athletes, coaches, volunteers, administrators, and leaders. That said, girls and women in Canada continue to face obstacles to full participation and representation in the Canadian sport system—at all levels and in all capacities—and continue to require formal federal-provincial/territorial policy that advocates and pushes for gender equity in sport (cf. Sport Canada, 2011).

While we must be cautious of the ways in which participation in sport is measured and evaluated (cf. Donnelly et al., 2010), recent statistics from a variety of sources present a mottled picture of participation rates for women in various sport roles. According to the 2009 Canadian Fitness and Lifestyle Research Institute's (CFLRI) monitor on sport participation among adults, approximately 27% of Canadians participate in sports as players, 19% as coaches and assistant coaches, 5% as officials/referees, 3% as leaders and 2% as team managers. As sport participants, CFLRI reports that women participate to a lesser extent (slightly less than 20%) than men (approximately 35%) across a variety of socio-demographic factors (e.g., age, class, educational background, income, etc.) (CFLRI, 2009). This echoes data from the 2005 General Social Survey (GSS) conducted by Statistics Canada that identified a continued large gap between male and female participants in sport (36% versus 21%, respectively) despite its narrowing since 1998 (Ifedi, 2008).

Surprisingly, the 2005 GSS identified some positive trends around women in coaching and women as sport officials. With regard to the latter, the 2005 GSS pointed out that the rates for women as referees, officials and umpires had increased since 1992 such that the ratio of men to women in such roles was 2:1 as compared to 5:1 in 1992. With regard to women in coaching, the 2005 GSS highlighted that over 882,000 women coached in Canada in 2005, up 15% from 1998 and more than four times the total in 1992, whereas the number of men who coached had decreased by 9% (down to 874,000) in the same 13-year span (1992–2005) (Ifedi, 2008). Again, a call for caution is warranted since such statistics do not specify the levels of sport (e.g., community/grassroots versus high performance sport) at which women are coaching, nor does it tell us anything about the quality, including the opportunities or barriers women face, of their experiences as coaches throughout the Canadian sport system. For example, figures from the Coaching Association of Canada (CAC) (2008) show that, within the National Coaching Certification Program, women constitute 29.7% of Canadian coaches with Level 1 certification, 33.9% of those coaches with Level 2 certification, 29.0% of those with Level 3 certification, 20.9% of those with Level 4 certification and only 11.0% of those coaches with the highest level of certification in the country (Level 5). While Canada has sent more female athletes than male athletes to the Olympic Games on two occasions, most recently to the London 2012 Olympic Games, the number of women coaches going to the Olympics remains low (Donnelly & Donnelly, 2012). In the 2008 Beijing Olympic Games, only two of 22 head coaches were women (9%) and 11 of 95 total coaches were women (12%) (CAC, 2008).

In terms of women in sport governance, Canadian Heritage (2009a) reported that only 37% of organizations receiving funding from Sport Canada were headed by women in senior administrative roles and only 19% of Sport Canada-funded organizations have a volunteer governance structure led by a woman (Appendix B, paragraphs 11–12). Both of these figures represent an increase in participation of women in sport leadership roles and yet, much like the other statistics noted above, they also indicate an overall under-representation of women in sport in Canada despite the fact that slightly more than half of all people living in Canada are women.

It should come then as no surprise that the latest policy offering from the federal government, *Actively Engaged: A Policy on Sport for Women and Girls*, both highlights the tremendous improvements for Canadian girls and women in sport over the past few decades and yet retains, as its central objective, the fostering of "sport environments—from playground to podium—where women and girls, particularly as athlete participants, coaches, technical leaders and officials, and as governance leaders are provided with: quality sport experiences; and equitable support by sport organizations" (Canadian Heritage, 2009a, p. 6). No critical examination of Canadian sport policy would be complete without an understanding of policy pertaining to women and sport. An in-depth, comprehensive discussion of the complex history, the current struggles, and the pivotal individuals (e.g., see Keyes, 1989) and groups that have shaped Canadian sport for women falls beyond the scope of one chapter—in fact, volumes have been and can be dedicated to this one sport policy issue alone.

The purpose of this chapter, rather, is to introduce readers to the changing landscape of Canadian sport policy from the 1960s onwards as it has framed and influenced the inclusion (or, at times, the exclusion) and full participation of women in sport in Canada. The focus of this chapter is predominately on federal-level sport policy for women; however, it must be acknowledged that critical action around sport policy for girls and women has occurred (and continues to occur) at the provincial and territorial levels both in response to, and in anticipation of, federal-level developments (e.g., Vail, 1992). This chapter is structured in three main sections and follows Canadian sport policy for women in sport in a fairly chronological fashion although it is important to recognize that the development of sport policy for women in Canada does not follow so neatly or linearly its description here. The first section explores sport policy for women from the 1960s up to, and including, the 1986 *Sport Canada Policy on Women in Sport*. The second section examines the state of Canadian sport for women following the 1986 policy on the Canadian sport system and leading up to Canadian Heritage's 2009 *Actively Engaged*. The final section of the chapter explores theoretical and substantive issues that continue to impact—both negatively and positively—the full engagement of Canadian women in sport.

Starting at Square One? From WAAF to CAAWS and the 1986 *Sport Canada Policy on Women in Sport*

The passage of the Bill C-131, *An Act to Encourage Fitness and Amateur Sport* in 1961 marked the beginning of the federal government's formal involvement in Canadian sport, but it was not until the late 1960s and early 1970s that the federal government "embarked … on a course of direct promotion of what was to become known as high performance sport" (Macintosh & Whitson, 1990, p. 4). The "kitchen table" approach that previously characterized national sport organizations and sport delivery gave way to increasingly bureaucratized, rationalized, evidence-based and corporate models of sport management, in exchange for financial support from the federal government (Hall, 1996). Throughout the 1960s and 1970s, a number of changes marked the transformation of the Canadian elite sport system. For example, a central administrative complex was created to house national sport organizations (NSOs) and multi-sport/service organizations (MSOs), funding for performance-enhancement research increased and, in time, an athlete financial assistance program was created, all in efforts to boost sport performance.

These shifts and developments in the delivery of sport in Canada impacted Canadian women in sport to varying degrees, but to more completely understand the state of sport and sport policy for Canadian women in this same period of time, it is important to understand the gains and losses made by Canadian sportswomen circa Bill C-131. In particular, two key points need to be explicated. The first speaks to the tremendous gains made by women throughout the first half of the twentieth century in sport participation and leadership, particularly through the creation and efforts of the Women's Amateur Athletic Federation (WAAF), while the second speaks to the real losses in opportunity and leadership experienced by women athletes upon the incorporation of the WAAF into the mainstream and male-dominated Amateur Athletic Union of Canada (AAU) by the early 1960s.

Created in 1926—in the wake of first-wave feminism and the feminist breakthroughs of World War I—by such notable Canadian female athletes as Alexandrine Gibb, Marie Parkes, Mable Ray, Ethel Cartwright as well as others, WAAF represented the first national forum for Canadian women to collectively address the sport interests of Canadian women. It was an organization about women's sport that was controlled by women and it focused squarely on encouraging women to fully participate in sport as athletes, coaches and leaders. WAAF members, all of whom were volunteers balancing their personal and work lives with coaching, fundraising and administration, worked tirelessly to secure opportunities for women to compete nationally and internationally (Kidd, 1996). WAAF enjoyed a strong and relatively large membership in Canada, and Canadian women athletes, hand in hand with their international sister athletes, enjoyed tremendous success on the international sport stage. This was, in large part, due to the WAAF's acceptance of the belief that women's sport should be separate from men's sport—a philosophy criticized by some contemporary feminist scholars as reproducing the "dominant, male-privileging sexual division of labour" but recognized by others as an attempt by the women of the interwar period to "forge a new, vigorously active 'womanhood'" (Kidd, 1996, p. 139). It is important to note that this debate between 'separate but equal' and 'sex-integrated' sport for women would be revisited time and time again in Canada over the next 30 years and will be discussed in greater length later in the chapter. Even though the AAU claimed official jurisdiction over women's athletics in Canada since the early 1920s, it never fully or consistently supported the growth and development of women's sport in Canada with the same commitment and dedication as the WAAFers. That noted, due to a variety of factors explored in great detail by Kidd (1996), members of WAAF agreed to amalgamate with the AAU in the early 1950s following World War II.

The consequences of this amalgamation—the loss of focused leadership for women's sport in Canada—were terrible for the development of Canadian sport policy relative to women in the 1960s and 1970s. As Kidd (1996, p. 144) evocatively noted:

> "women's sport run by women" is so utopian an ideal that it cannot be imagined. As a result, girls and women struggle to develop identities of healthy womanhood in a cultural practice largely controlled by males and steeped in discourses of masculinity. In the absence of the sort of vigorous feminist debate about alternatives that the WAAF facilitated, there is little to challenge the naturalization of the male model. That so many women succeed does not discount the enormous contradictions they experience.

During the 1960s and 1970s, when the Canadian sport system was being transformed into a state-directed system of high performance, "women lacked an identifiable leadership to represent their interests and a forum to discuss issues and strategy. Very few women at all participated in the major decisions, and those who did were actively discouraged from speaking from a 'women's point of view'" (Kidd, 1996, p. 144).

It was not until the late 1960s that political attention to women in sport was renewed, albeit through a rather indirect manner. In 1967, a *Royal Commission on the Status of Women* was established and released a report in 1970. The report barely mentioned sport but did acknowledge that girls participated in sport at a much lower rate than boys in school sports and did make two separate recommendations (Recommendations 77 and 78) for further analysis of, and action on, sport for girls in Canada (Government of Canada, 1970). However, no further substantial developments occurred until 1974 (Hall & Richardson, 1982) and the first *National Conference on Women in Sport* spearheaded under the leadership of Marion Lay. At that particular conference, "virtually every woman significantly involved in organizing, coaching, leading and administering sport in Canada was represented" (Hoffman, 1989, p. 28). These sport leaders, such as Petra Burke, Abby Hoffman and Marion Lay, were responsible in large part for the new momentum generated around women's sport in Canada and began to make their voices heard in the Canadian sport system. Ironically, though, the re-initiation of the formal organization of women's sport in Canada occurred almost "as if WAAF's control of women's sports and the networks they created had never existed" (Kidd, 1996, p. 144). Furthermore, with the emergence of second-wave feminism, one of the key differences with this new generation of women sport leaders was a rejection of the 'separate but equal' approach to the provision and delivery of sport for girls and women. This brought some advantages in resources and organization, but also drew criticism since, in contrast to the approach taken by WAAF, once-separate women's programs were "brought under male leadership, and men got most of the jobs created by the expansion in female participation" (Kidd, 1966, p. 144).

The 1974 conference produced numerous recommendations, but as Hoffman (1989, p. 28) noted, the recommendations "were indiscriminately directed to all and sundry without regard to jurisdiction, contradiction among recommendation, priorities, costs, realism, to name a few. There was, in other words, no organizing principle or philosophy underlying the recommendations." The strategies for change that were suggested should not be overlooked but were insufficient in producing action since there were no means to monitor the process or implement the recommendations. This lack of focus contributed, in part, to the lack of further development for women in sport between 1974 and 1980. Even though 1975 was designated as the "International Women's Year" by the United Nations and even though during this time the first-ever Canadian minister of state responsible for fitness and amateur sport was a woman, Iona Campagnolo, "women barely rated a mention" in the Canadian sport system (Hoffman, 1989, p. 28).

It was not until 1980 that the federal government initiated a formal Women's Program within Fitness and Amateur Sport, in large part because the Fitness and Amateur Sport Branch was called to account for its progress on achieving sex equality in sport by the Minister responsible for the Status of Women in Canada (Hall & Richardson, 1982). While this entity also lacked a coherent policy framework, it did contain certain elements never seen before in a federal initiative for women's sport in Canada (Macintosh, Bedecki, & Franks, 1987). Under the thoughtful leadership of Sue Vail (1983), it conducted an important leadership survey that highlighted the under-representation of women sport leaders in Canada, it provided training and internship programs for women in sport management and leadership; it co-ordinated a workshop that eventually led to the creation of a national advocacy organization, to be discussed below; it developed various promotional campaigns on notable women athletes; and it provided seed money to NSOs for projects aimed explicitly at increasing female participation. The program operated for a few years with some success but also some clear limitations as it highlighted the continued ambivalence of the Canadian state towards women in sport. On the one hand, the federal state continued to provide more funds and opportunities for men than women in sport—further legitimating the perception of male superiority in sport—and yet introduced, via a formal women's program within Fitness and Amateur Sport, a means with which to address and attempt to rectify gender inequality in sport (cf. Hall, Slack, Smith, & Whitson, 1991). Part of the continued ambivalence from the government bureaucrats stemmed from the view that gender inequality in Canadian sport was a problem specific to women rather than a structural or systemic problem of the broader sport system. The focus on women as a target population requiring special intervention in isolation of or outside of the existing sport system was a recognized shortcoming among women's sport leaders and advocates (cf. Hoffman, 1989) but it required a few more years before more significant political and policy progress could be initiated for Canadian women in sport.

In addition to the establishment of the Women's Program in Fitness and Amateur Sport in 1980, two significant developments in the early 1980s need to be discussed. The first is the creation of, what is now known as, the Canadian Association for the Advancement of Women and Sport and Physical Activity (CAAWS). The 1981 *Female Athlete Conference*, funded by the Women's Program in Fitness and Amateur Sport, gathered together a small group of sport administrators, federal bureaucrats, physical educators, athletes, coaches and representatives from major national feminist organizations and served as the catalyst for the founding of CAAWS whose purpose was (and is) to explicitly advocate on behalf of women in sport with the intent of making the Canadian sport system gender equitable (Hall, 2003; Robertson, 1995). CAAWS had an explicit feminist agenda that was not unusual given the politics of second wave-feminism at that time. As noted by Vickers (1992, p. 44), "an operational code of the second-wave women's movement in Canada is the belief that change is possible and that state action is an acceptable way of achieving it." This explicit feminist agenda has since been tempered as CAAWS has drifted from its original mission of advancing "the position of women by defining, promoting and supporting a feminist perspective on sport and [by improving] the status of women in sport" to, since the 1990s, providing "leadership and education, and to build capacity to foster equitable support, diverse opportunities and positive experiences for girls and women in sport and physical activity" (CAAWS, n.d.). The nature and consequences of this ideological shift will be discussed in greater detail in the last section of this chapter.

The second significant development of the early 1980s was the incorporation of the *Canadian Charter of Rights and Freedoms* into Canada's Constitution in 1982 (cf. CAAWS, 1994). The Charter provides far-reaching and wide-ranging protection under the law for women and other groups, prohibiting discrimination on the basis of sex, gender or sexual orientation and providing the fundamental freedom of equality to all. Until the establishment of provincial human rights legislation and commissions in the 1970s and the Charter in 1982, there "was little to no recourse for Canadian girls and women who complained of sex discrimination in sport" (Hall, 1996, p. 94). Barnes (2010) (cf. Barnes, 1996 and Hall & Richardson, 1982) outlines a number of sport-related cases of discrimination (specifically the denial of girls and women from playing on boys' and men's sport teams). Arguably the most famous of these cases was that of Justine Blainey in the mid-1980s since her case helped "to legally strike down a discriminatory clause in the Ontario Human Rights Code that specifically exempted membership in athletic organizations, participation in athletic activities, and access to the services and facilities of recreational clubs from its sex equality provisions" (Hall, 1996, p. 94). With the institution of the federal Charter in 1982, there could be no exceptions to its provisions, and thus human rights legislation—and legal action (at times, even just the mere threat of legal action) based on human rights legislation—has been a powerful tool in bringing about change in policy (Corbett & Findlay, 1994; Hall, 1996; Hoffman, 1989).

It became understood over the early 1980s, with the founding of CAAWS and the enactment of the Charter, that it was neither sufficient nor appropriate to simply focus on and treat women as a disadvantaged target group whose condition can be improved exclusively by programs aimed at females. As Hoffman (1989, p. 31) stated:

> it became clear to us by the mid-1980s that we needed a clear policy statement if we were to cross over from a series of programs which focused on particular aspects and problems facing women in sport, to an approach which addressed the basic issue: that is, that the Canadian sport system is fundamentally one which contributes through its very nature to sex inequality in sport. We had to move our target group from females as an isolated group to the overall sport system. Further, we had to acknowledge as well, that much of what we sought to change in sport had its root cause outside of the sport system, and that there were (and are) a number of basic gender equality issues which are bigger than sport that we would have to address in our policy and related programs.

Under Hoffman's leadership, then Director General of Sport Canada, a policy milestone was reached in 1986 with the release of *Sport*

Canada Policy on Women in Sport. The policy represented the federal government's first step in changing the sport system as it made equality of opportunity for women at all levels of the sport system an official goal (Sport Canada, 1986). The policy specifically stated:

> equality implies that women at all levels of the sport system
> should have an equal opportunity to participate. Equality is not
> necessarily meant to imply that women wish to participate in
> the same activities as men, but rather to indicate that activities
> of their choice should be provided and administered in a fair
> and unbiased environment. At all levels of the sport system,
> equal opportunities must exist for women and men to compete,
> coach, officiate or administer sport. (Sport Canada, 1986, p. 10)

The policy document went further than any previous federal statements on the issue by outlining an action-oriented approach and strategy for implementation supported by both the Women's Program and by Sport Canada. It identified a number of areas requiring attention including policy program development; an integrated sport infrastructure; leadership development; high performance competition; participation development; equitable resource allocation; liaison; research; education; promotion; advocacy; and monitoring and evaluation (Sport Canada, 1986).

The importance of this policy in changing the landscape of Canadian sport for women cannot be denied; however, the ability of the policy to effect change was limited by a number of factors. The federal government recognized that gender inequality needed to be resolved but provided little challenge to existing social structures or socio-cultural attitudes that perpetuated structural or systemic inequality or provided little additional funding (a few hundred thousand as compared to the millions spent on amateur sport more broadly) to adequately implement, monitor and evaluate the recommendations made in its policy report (Bell-Altenstad & Vail, 1995; Myers & Doherty, 2007). Furthermore, the policy was intended to be carried out through the NSOs. In the early 1980s, many NSOs created their own women's committees and developed strategies—often unrealistic and undeliverable—with which to increase participation among women (Macintosh et al., 1987). Following the release of the policy in 1986, the federal government through the Women's Program and Sport Canada still encouraged the formation of these committees out of the belief that they could "act as internal watchdogs, develop policy and do more detailed planning on women and sport matters than would otherwise occur" (Hoffman, 1989, pp. 33–34), but the policy itself operated on a voluntary basis as far as the sport organizations were concerned. There was an expectation on these sport organizations but no accountability framework to ensure that they would implement the policy and make a commitment to gender equity (Hall, 1996). There was now policy on women in Canadian sport, but it proved to simply have "no teeth" (Ponic, 2001, p. 59). As will be discussed below, the 1986 *Women in Sport* policy was a landmark moment in the history of women's sport in Canada but it fell short of its proposed aims, and subsequent policy needed to be introduced.

The Second Shift: Moving Towards *Actively Engaged*

The release of the 1986 *Sport Canada Policy on Women in Sport* was a success in the growth and organization of women's sport in Canada but, in general, a very measured one (cf. Doherty & Varpalotai, 2001; Myers & Doherty, 2007). It facilitated the development of some unique initiatives for women in sport; for example, the establishment of a National Coaching School for Women that included both an annual educational program supported by partnerships with various NSOs as well as special three-year coaching apprenticeships for aspiring female coaches (Hall, 1996; Hoffman, 1989). Yet, despite some modest achievements, gender inequality continued to be part of the Canadian sport system. The fallout of the Ben Johnson scandal in the late 1980s included intense introspection of the Canadian sport system by the Dubin inquiry and two recommendations regarding gender equity in his report (Dubin, 1990). A mere two years later, the Minister's Task Force on Federal Sport Policy, *Sport: The Way Ahead* (Minister's Task Force, 1992, pp. 148–152), concluded that "even with an advocacy organization [CAAWS], a federal equity policy, and staffing guidelines to encourage fuller participation by women, little change had occurred over the past 10 years" (as cited in Hall, 1996, p. 94). Rates of participation by female athletes were nowhere close to that of men and, although the number of women among lower and middle-level management had increased, women made "little progress . . . in penetrating the ranks of the senior executive and technical staff in the national sports bureaucracy, or in membership on NSO Board of

Directors and Executive Committees" (Macintosh, 1996, p. 63; see also Hall, Cullen, & Slack, 1989; Whitson & Macintosh, 1989). The report rebuked the sport community for dragging its feet around gender equity and for not working towards equality: "in accountability for public funding, national sport organizations must understand the legal definition and intent of gender equity and implement it through legislation, constitution and policies. NSOs must work toward equality by removing systemic barriers and discrimination" (Minister's Task Force, 1992, p. 152).

The early 1990s marked the many contradictions of the Canadian federal government with regard to gender equity in sport (although it must be acknowledged that the contradictory character of the state around sport and gender equity can be seen before and after this period of time). On the one hand, policies and strategic documents would be produced that positioned the need for gender equality in sport as a top priority while, on the other hand, little was done to ensure the implementation of these policies and/or evaluation of these policies in action. Furthermore, funding for existing programs committed to improving sport for women was either kept to a relative minimum (e.g., funding for the Women's Program was a mere fraction of what was devoted to the entire elite sport system) or was taken away all together.

The removal of state funding was certainly experienced by CAAWS. The decision by the Secretary of State Women's Program to stop all funding for CAAWS in 1989–1990 had tremendous implications for the only major national organization advocating for women in sport and physical activity. Immediately following the loss of funding from the Secretary of State, CAAWS downsized drastically and relied even more heavily on volunteers to fulfil select projects associated with its partnership with the Women's Program—a decision initially made in order to avoid being co-opted by the state and Sport Canada (Robertson, 1995). However by 1991, CAAWS, in an effort to survive, went into an agreement with Sport Canada as a multi-sport/service organization (MSO) that would work with NSOs and other MSOs to assist them in becoming gender equitable. By 1994, CAAWS had moved into the Canadian Sport and Fitness Administration Centre and received its core and project funding from Sport Canada. This had implications for CAAWS' organizational philosophy. While CAAWS initially positioned itself as a feminist organization that promoted sport for women, by 1992, CAAWS had reformulated their mission and vision and shifted towards identifying itself as an organization that advocates for women in sport and physical activity. The distinction here is that:

> the former denotes a more radical feminist perspective in the sense that CAAWS is a women's organization that promotes its aims through sport; the latter represents a distinctly liberal approach that seeks to improve the lot of women already in sport through a sport organization for women. (Hall, 1996, p. 97)

We could speculate at length as to all the factors that may have motivated this shift in vision (e.g., the fear of feminist backlash), but one key factor is the absorption of CAAWS into the mainstream sport system through its Sport Canada funding and physical presence in the Canadian Sport and Fitness Administration Centre (cf. Hall, 2003). Comeau and Church (2010) similarly suggest that while "CAAWS has . . . been successful in promoting sport for women and girls . . . its cooptation has at times influenced the strategies it uses and its abilities to criticize governmental action" (p. 471). Whatever the motivation, CAAWS continued to advocate for girls and women in sport and physical activity, but also took a decidedly more educational and consultative role producing handbooks (e.g., *Towards Gender Equity for Women in Sport: A Handbook for Sport Organizations*), guidelines, research reports, promotional campaigns and awards to highlight the accomplishments of girls and women in Canadian sport.

The contradictory character of the state, with regard to gender equity, can also be seen in the short tenure of the Canadian Sport Council, a now-defunct coalition of NSOs and MSOs that championed the creation of a gender equitable Canadian sport system. Drawing on Kirby (1999), who provided a thoughtful and comprehensive discussion of the Canadian Sport Council including the "building blocks" that went into its formation in 1993, the entire sport system's moment of self-examination following the Johnson positive drug test and the Dubin inquiry opened up an opportunity for those in the Canadian sport community who wanted to push for equitable sport. As she noted:

> when opportunity knocked, women and other marginalized groups in sport were well prepared and conversant with the equity issues. They vigorously sought representation at all levels

of decision-making during their creation and implementation
of the CSC [Canadian Sport Council]. As a direct result of their
readiness, gender equity was identified as a key value of a quality sport system. (Kirby, 1999, p. 57)

Arguably, the most pivotal feature of this coalition was its incorporation of gender equity into its own system of governance; a true
push for women sport leaders and leaders in women's sport. The
Canadian Sport Council maintained that each of its governing and
working committees must have a gender composition of no less
than 40% of one gender and that each delegation of two or more
people attending the Canadian Sport Council general assembly
must include one person from each gender with the overall goal of
50/50 gender representation (CAAWS, 1993; Kirby, 1999). Although
the Canadian Sport Council had tremendous potential to mobilize change, it had a very short lifespan as, by the late 1990s, all of
its funding from the state was removed. Again, on the one hand,
we see the Canadian state responded to the needs of women for
greater opportunity and representation through its initial support
for the Canadian Sport Council while, on the other hand, despite
its own acknowledgement of the chronic under-representation of
women in all facets of the Canadian sport system, the state continued to legitimate male privilege by providing more funding and
opportunity for men (in the case of the Canadian Sport Council, by
withdrawing funding for an initiative that privileged affirmative
action).

Following the release of *Sport: The Way Ahead*, the federal government continued to acknowledge the under-representation of girls
and women in sport in Canada (Sport Canada, 1993). Furthermore,
the federal government continued to address and redress gender
equity through various initiatives, all with varying degrees of success. Even though it was dissolved by the late 1990s, the Canadian
Sport Council was one such initiative as was the movement of
CAAWS into Sport Canada. In a very strong statement of its commitment to gender equity, Sport Canada appointed Marion Lay as the
Program Manager for the Women's Program and provided her with
a clear mandate to examine why the *Women in Sport* policy was not
being fully (or in some cases, even partially) implemented by NSOs
and to provide recommendations to make the policy work (Kirby,
1999; Robertson, 1995).

The 1990s saw continued work on gender equity within Canada and was also witness to pivotal international events specific to gender equity in sport. Canadian women sport leaders have been integrally involved with key international women's sport organizations including the International Association of Physical Education and Sport for Women and Girls (IAPESGW), WomenSport International (WSI) and the International Working Group on Women and Sport (IWG). The first *World Conference on Women and Sport,* held in Brighton, England in 1994, brought together hundreds of delegates—representing governmental and non-governmental organizations, National Olympic Committees, international and national sport organizations and educational/research institutions—from over 80 countries. The conference saw the creation of not only the IWG (see www.iwg-gti.org) but also the first international declaration of global gender equity principles in sport, commonly referred to as *The Brighton Declaration* (1994; cf. Hall, 1996). The declaration was designed to be used as a tool with which to pressure resistant governments and sport organizations to pass equal rights legislation and to ensure opportunity for participation in sport and physical activity to all girls and women. CAAWS was centrally involved in the conference as well as in the development of the declaration.

The declaration was updated and reaffirmed during the second world conference in Windhoek, Namibia, in 1998. The *Windhoek Call for Action* (1998) built on *The Brighton Declaration* and linked it to other international women's rights declarations, particularly the *Beijing Platform for Action and the Convention for the Elimination of All Forms of Discrimination Against Women.* Where *The Brighton Declaration* focused on the principles that underlie inclusive sport for women, the *Windhoek Call for Action* was a call away from statements of principle to action. Action was critically needed in Canada, as identified in the 1999 *Sport Gender Snapshot* (Sport Canada, 1999). While there was some progress in some areas (e.g., access to resources, increase in representation for women on national teams, more equitable training and competing opportunities) for women in sport at the elite level, there remained a "considerable amount of work still to be done to achieve equality for women in sport" (Myers & Doherty, 2007, p. 323). Despite CAAWS's repeated calls for attention among the sport community to such issues as childcare and leadership, officiating and coaching opportunities, the *Gender Snapshot* demonstrated that although some NSOs and MSOs embraced alternative and equitable discourses of gender relations, others continued to rely on dominant inequitable understandings of gender relations (Shaw & Hoeber, 2007).

A key question then becomes: how did the Canadian government take action on gender equity in sport? At risk of skipping over smaller scale but important initiatives, programs and services brought forth through the Women's Program, CAAWS, or through other MSOs (e.g., Coaching Association of Canada; see Strachan & Tomlinson, 1994) throughout the 1990s and into the early 2000s, three key points highlight the action that the Canadian federal government did take with regard to gender equity in sport. The first relates back to the IWG and the decision by the Canadian government to support the organization and to host the 2002 *World Conference on Women and Sport* in Montreal, Quebec (IWG, 2002). This commitment stimulated the government to continue combating gender inequity in two substantial ways—specifically, the incorporation of gender equity principles into Canadian sport policy and federal legislation (rather than in a stand-alone gender equity document) as well as the explicit linking of funding and accountability for NSOs/MSOs to a commitment to equity and access for women.

The release of the *Canadian Sport Policy* (Sport Canada, 2002a), and its follow-up 2002 and 2007 strategic directions documents (Sport Canada, 2002b; 2007), as well as the assent of the *Physical Activity and Sport Act* in 2003 saw the Canadian government explicitly identify the enhanced participation of all Canadians in sport and physical activity as its first of four pillars underpinning the Canadian sport system and the increased participation in sport for all Canadians by 2012 as its first priority. The Act identified the reduction of barriers to participation for all Canadians as one of its principal aims, and, more specifically, the policy (Sport Canada, 2002b, p. 5) highlighted three strategies with which to achieve the reduction of barriers:

Action 1: Develop collaborative strategies to increase the public's understanding of and participation in sport for all;

Action 2: Participate with the Canadian Association for the Advancement of Women and Sport and Physical Activity and provincial/territorial counterparts, where

possible, in the development and implementation of a
Canadian Strategy on Women and Girls in Sport and
Physical Activity; and

Action 3: Undertake initiative to increase opportunities in
coaching, officiating, and volunteer leadership for
women, persons with a disability, Aboriginal peoples,
and visible minorities.

The 2007 strategic directions highlighted progress to date, chiefly the
development of *ACTive: The Canadian Strategy for Girls and Women in
Sport and Physical Activity* (CAAWS, 2007). With the support of Sport
Canada (Canadian Heritage) and Health Canada, and as informed by
The Brighton Declaration (1994) and the *Windhoek Call to Action* (1998),
CAAWS initially developed this national strategy in 2002 with the
specific goal of increasing physical activity and sport opportunities
for girls and women. Following further development and consultation with government officials, sport community representatives, the
Canadian Olympic Committee, the Coaching Association of Canada
and CAAWS, the *ACTive* strategy was approved by federal-provincial/
territorial sport ministers in 2004 and has since been operationalized
in many ways (cf. CAAWS, 2007).

The federal government also demonstrated action around gender equity by implementing an accountability process in 1995–1996
that explicitly identified and linked funding for, and the accountability of, NSOs/MSOs to a commitment to equity and access for
women. Following the winter and summer Olympic cycles, the *Sport
Funding and Accountability Framework* (SFAF) requires NSOs and MSOs
to demonstrate through their policies, programs, procedures, and
practices a commitment to equity and access, notably for women (as
well as for members of other marginalized groups such as persons
with a disability and Aboriginal peoples) as participants, athletes,
coaches, officials, and leaders. The SFAF identifies national standards within the four key areas identified by the Canadian Sport
Policy (excellence, participation, building capacity and interaction)
and the standards describe a set of criteria that will apply across all
organizations, ensuring a consistent minimum level of service. It
is expected that each NSO and MSO provide basic services to meet
or exceed all the identified standards. The only situation where an
NSO or MSO is not required to demonstrate an organization-specific
formal policy on gender equity is where the organization exceeds

40% female participation or representation in all areas (athlete participants, coaches, officials, and leaders). NSOs and MSOs can no longer approach or treat gender equity on a voluntary or haphazard basis in contrast to the approach adopted in the 1980s. The SFAF system has been relatively more successful in encouraging (and at times pushing) NSOs and MSOs to adopt and implement gender equity initiatives because of its 'teeth' (cf. Ponic, 2001)—sport and multi-sport organizations in Canada are now required to address and account for gender equity in their policies, programs, and services in exchange for federal government recognition and funding. This is not to suggest that Sport Canada has been completely successful with regard to the implementation of gender equity within NSOs/MSOs through the SFAF; having a policy and taking action is not the same thing. Although there is better monitoring within the Canadian sport system now than in the past, collecting data in this area remains relatively difficult—some NSOs do not post their gender equity policies in publicly accessible ways (e.g., websites) nor do all NSOs identify gender equity in their strategic plans. Furthermore, not all NSOs require or rely upon Sport Canada funding. While some solid progress has been made with some sport organizations, non-compliance or lack of full compliance remains a feature of some NSOs/MSOs and Sport Canada continues to study (in order to determine the difference between lack of compliance and not meeting the standard due to barriers or other limitations) and strategize around how to address lack of compliance with the national standards.

The 2002 *Canadian Sport Policy* was notable in one additional way—it expressed interest in revisiting and rewriting the 1986 *Sport Canada Policy on Women in Sport*. This initiated a series of consultations with key stakeholders throughout the Canadian sport community and culminated in the release *Actively Engaged: A Policy on Sport for Women and Girls* in 2009 (Canadian Heritage, 2009a). *Actively Engaged* now represents the current acting directive regarding women in sport and reaffirms the government's commitment to a sport system that engages and equitably supports girls and women in a full range of sport roles. The policy operates alongside the 2002 *Canadian Sport Policy* and other Sport Canada protocols such as the SFAF, the *Federal Policy on Hosting International Sport Events,* the *Policy on Aboriginal Peoples Participation in Sport* and the *Sport Canada Policy for Persons with a Disability*. In fact, it is important to acknowledge that—despite the policy's call for increased equity for all Canadians—

specific provisions for equity, gender or otherwise, are not integrated into the *Canadian Sport Policy*; they continue to come in the form of secondary documents such as *Actively Engaged*. In contrast to the 1986 policy, where the focus was predominately on increasing the quantity of women participating in the Canadian sport system, the current policy focuses on—in addition to the provision of (increased) opportunities for participation—the quality of opportunity for participation and representation by women in the sport system. As noted within the policy document, during consultations:

> Stakeholders consistently highlighted the need to "do things differently" to recruit, develop, and retain women in sport, including the potential to re-recruit women into similar or other sport roles after a hiatus, e.g., to raise a family. In contrast to the traditional "build it and they will come" approach in Canadian sport of creating opportunities and expecting uptake, this policy will promote innovative quality sport experiences for women and girls, to not only remove barriers but also to encourage ongoing involvement. (Canadian Heritage, 2009a, Section 3—Context, paragraph 12)

Actively Engaged makes repeated reference to its central objective of fostering the active engagement of women as athlete participants, coaches, officials, and leaders in sport governance. The policy is to be implemented through existing programs and services with intervention focusing on four components:

1. Program Improvement—alignment and refinement of programs and activities to enable sport organizations and other sport system stakeholders to deliver innovative quality sport experiences for women and girls;
2. Strategic Leadership—proactive promotion of complementary measures within other Canadian and international jurisdictions to strengthen quality sport experiences for women and girls through participation in multilateral and bilateral instruments and fora;
3. Awareness—promoting the benefits for individuals and organizations of meaningful involvement of women and girls; and
4. Knowledge Development—expansion, use and sharing of knowledge, practices and innovations concerning the

> sport experiences of women and girls through research and development. (Canadian Heritage, 2009a, Section 6—Policy Interventions, paragraph 1)

Its follow-up Action Plan (Canadian Heritage, 2009b) outlines specific activities to be implemented between 2009 and 2012 as well as the measurement and evaluation strategy to be employed. Again, it may be too soon to tell the sharpness of *Actively Engaged*'s 'teeth' in enacting genuine and sustainable change for girls and women in Canadian sport. The revision and updating of the policy as well as the shift in focus towards the quality of sport experience (as opposed to quantity) holds promise and yet the policy was released without much publicity or promotion within and outside the Canadian sport community (J. Northcott, personal communication, November 2010). Furthermore, while *Actively Engaged* speaks most directly to the pillars of enhanced participation and enhanced excellence (both of which address opportunity and access in sport from playground to podium), critics suggest that it suffers from the same weaknesses as the 2002 *Canadian Sport Policy* (Public Policy Forum, 2010). As one example, commentators point out that integration across all levels of government with regard to sport has been weak even with the identification of enhanced capacity as a key pillar such that one must question whether policy on women in sport has travelled through and across different departments or ministries in government or has remained contained in its own silo? Furthermore, critics point out that the four pillars—while given equal rhetorical support in government documents and missives—are not equally supported in reality such that enhanced excellence remains top priority for government officials (Public Policy Forum, 2010). With regard to women in sport, this results in emphasis on the achievements of female athletes in high performance sports (e.g., the 2010 Vancouver Olympic Winter Games) even though such evidence deflects attention from the reality that a majority of women do not participate in sport as noted in the introduction of the chapter.

The Third Act: Dynamic Change?

The above two sections follow the chronological development of Canadian sport policy for women from the 1960s onwards and are, by necessity, relatively descriptive attempts to map the major events and institutions involved. This final section attempts to more deeply and critically analyze some of the social, political, and historical forces that have shaped policy development in this area and which continue to shape sport policy for women in Canada.

We can easily identify watershed moments in the development of sport policy for women in Canada but, as a whole, policy development in this area has been marked more by incremental change over time than whole-scale revolutions in policy direction and implementation. In large part, this has been a function of the dynamic and changing tensions between different groups, people and organizations—including advocacy groups (e.g., CAAWS), federal-provincial/territorial departments, international governing bodies, key individuals including public figures, sport leaders and activist-scholars—as situated within the broader dynamic and changing social, political, and cultural forces (social movements) over time (cf. Comeau & Church, 2010). Clearly, the same could be noted of policy development in Canadian governance, within and outside of sport, more broadly. This chapter has, on a number of occasions, highlighted the contradictions of the state with regard to policy development and implementation for women in sport and yet, a word of caution is needed: the state is neither a neutral referee between groups nor is the state a homogenous entity that acts only in either-or fashion. As Hall et al. (1991, p. 90) rightly acknowledged:

> the point here is that the Canadian state (and its provincial and local branches) cannot be viewed as a monolithic bloc, nor can we assume that the state acts in a consistent, non-contradictory way. The state itself is site of conflict and struggle as social groups, whether based on gender, class, race, or ethnicity, seek to change or uphold the myriad state policies, agencies, and processes.

Feminist activism in sport and the shift from equality to equity are two sites where we examine tensions that have marked policy development. The predominant feminist approach to sport in Canada has been liberal in nature, with a primary focus on securing equal access for women to sport opportunities long available to men (Hall, 1996; Hoffman, 1989). The 1986 *Sport Canada Policy on Women in Sport*'s central goal was "to attain equality for women in sport" such that "at all levels of the sport system, equal opportunities must exist for women and men to compete, coach, officiate or administer sport" (Sport Canada, 1986, p. 10). This call for increased numbers of women participating in sport at all levels in all capacities (athletes, coaches, administrators, journalists) was consistent with some of the principles of the organized second-wave feminist movement that was starting to emerge in Canada circa the late 1960s and was necessary given the marked quantitative difference in the number of women participants and in the number of opportunities for women in sport (Hall, 1996). However, criticism from some feminist activists followed this approach since many argued that quantitative difference does not necessarily culminate into a fully and genuinely gender equitable sport system (Hargreaves, 1990, 1994). As Lenskyj (2008, p. 102) argued:

> in fact, increased female participation did not necessarily bring with it an increase in leadership opportunities for women; unless organizations adopted an affirmative action policy, new positions were likely to be filled by male applicants who, as a group, were more experienced and qualified for coaching and sport administration than females.

Radical and socialist feminists routinely called (and continue to call) for strategies that go beyond an "add women and stir" recipe preferring those that address the structural and cultural roots of women's oppression in society and in sport. For these advocates, any approach for gender equality in sport that failed and fails to take into account and address the patriarchal nature of sport was and is destined to fail itself. In fact, some argued that patriarchy is so deeply embedded within contemporary sport that it simply cannot be unpacked and that a separate system of sport is required for women (Travers, 2006, 2008).

Clearly, the 'separate but equal' model of sport for women has not been taken up in the contemporary Canadian sport system (cf. Hoffman, 1989). Yet, this does not mean that radical and socialist feminist activism has not had an impact. In demanding that greater attention be paid to inequities arising from "prevailing gendered culture and power imbalances" (Shaw & Hoeber, 2007, p. 194), the policy discourse has shifted from equality to equity. That is, a shift from identifying women as a target group who need to be 'fixed' in order to fit into the sport system towards challenging and changing the social system that perpetuates oppression (Bell-Altenstad & Vail,

1995). The shift towards gender equity recognizes that the provision of equal opportunity or the equal distribution of resources between women and men does not adequately bring about structural change since women begin from a point of disadvantage not experienced by men. As Hoffman (1995, p. 85) urged, "real gains will only be achieved if we take account of the social, cultural, economic and political realities of women's lives beyond sport, and if we endeavour to change those structural and cultural conditions beyond sport that limit sport involvement." This compels us to pay attention to such factors as women's 'double shift,' domestic and family responsibilities, lower incomes and higher poverty rates, since these contribute to barriers to participation in sport by women. We are also compelled to more fully understand interlocking and overlapping dimensions of power and privilege in women's lives. A common criticism among radical feminist advocates is that liberal approaches to gender equity within the state and existing advocacy organizations (e.g., CAAWS) assume "a universal Canadian female" (i.e., white, able-bodied, middle-class, heterosexual) without paying sufficient attention to the "the impacts of systemic racism, classism, ageism, ableism and homophobia on girls' and women's lives. As a result, gains were not evenly distributed across boundaries of race/ethnicity, social class, age, ability and sexuality" (Lenskyj, 2008, p. 102; see also Cranney et al., 2002; Donnelly & Harvey, 1996; Paraschak, 2007, Giles, 2002; Olenik, Matthews, & Steadward, 1995).

The federal government has endorsed the liberal feminist shift towards gender equity such that the 2002 *Canadian Sport Policy*, the 2003 *Act to Promote Physical Activity and Sport* and the 2009 *Actively Engaged* directive speak to not just a continued desire to increase the number of women sport participants but also a commitment to improve the quality of experience and opportunity for women in sport. Paradoxically, while the 2002 *Canadian Sport Policy* explicitly identified women as one of a number of under-represented groups in Canadian sport, requiring intervention in the elimination of barriers to participation, the 2012 *Canadian Sport Policy* makes no such mention. Although the consultation process during the renewal of the policy involved a dedicated round table session on women and sport, the document itself only goes so far as to (albeit repeatedly) state that a major policy objective is the provision of opportunities "for persons from traditionally underrepresented and/or marginalized populations to actively engage in all aspects of sport participation, including leadership roles" (Sport Canada, 2012, p. 9ff).

The *Women and Sport Round Table Summary Report* (Sport Canada, 2011, p. 3) offers more insight into the apparent softening around language related to women and sport as round-table participants expressed concern that:

> equity policies were identified as an area within the sport development delivery system where programming was deemed sufficient. They were concerned that this might suggest that issues for women and girls were no longer a concern of the sport community—that women have reached parity with men and the sport system can move on to other challenges.

In fact, in light of the above concerns, participants at the round table asserted that "women and girls should be specifically referenced and reflected through the language of the policy" (Sport Canada, 2011, p. 4) and that the policy must enforce and reinforce commitment to gender equity: "there was a strong message from participants that Governments should hold funded organizations accountable for gender equity with clearly articulated indicators and consequences for non-performance that are seriously enforced" (Sport Canada, 2011, p. 8). Although it is too soon to tell how 'indicators and consequences' will be articulated in the action plans that emerge from the 2012 *Canadian Sport Policy* document, this will clearly be an important issue. The themes emerging from the round table summary report reproduce the liberal feminist discourse endorsed by government but also, interestingly, reflect some of the broader political and economic shifts. In particular, it is important to note the profit-oriented language in the document:

> Participants pointed out that research has shown that more gender diversity on Boards results in better decision-making and, in the private sector, greater profitability. The private sector has recognized the value of women as leaders, employees and consumers. Participants wondered why sport, which seeks to be leading edge, is lagging behind other sectors in terms of gender representation. (Sport Canada, 2011, p. 4)

Given the global economic downturn of the past few years as well as the federal government's leaning towards fiscal conservatism, such language reflects the political opportunity structures of the times and reminds us to take into account the institutional, cultural and economic factors that act as backdrop to sport policy.

The reasons for the adoption of a liberal approach in Canadian sport are complex; however a key question is whether equity can be accomplished through existing models of governance or through liberal feminism? For liberal feminist sport advocates, "government policy is a viable vehicle for change" since society is not "so mono-lithically patriarchal that at least worthwhile incremental change is impossible" (Hoffman, 1989, p. 31), whereas more radical advocates argue that the long entrenchment of the existing sport system in patriarchy precludes it from the provision of creative, women-centred sport alternatives. According to proponents such as Hall (2002, 2003), Lenskyj (1986, 2003) and Travers (2008), male-defined models of sport remain in need of transformation as the performance ethos, the "authoritarian power structure that demands discipline and obedience and works against political awareness," (Hall, 1996, p. 89) and the Olympic model of 'faster, higher, stronger' privileges the involvement of a select few women willing to assimilate rather than full participation of all women. In general, there is little connection between feminism and gender equity now in the sport movement (Hall, 2002, 2003), and radical feminism has never truly enjoyed the same reception as liberalism in sport, nor have radical feminists truly engaged with sport, often "marginalizing or dismissing sport as unimportant to the real struggles over sexual equality" (Hall, 1996, p. 90). Yet, feminist activism has been important in pushing for atten-tion to, and strategies of change around, gender inequity in sport.

Challenges to gender equity continue to persist in the Canadian sport system. While more women than ever are participating (and winning) in elite international competition, participation rates in physical activity and sport among girls and women more broadly are dropping; women of colour, including aboriginal girls and women, continue to experience severe disadvantage and marginalization; and opportunities for, and the recognitions of, sport for women with disabilities continues to lag behind sport for able-bodied women (Sport Canada, 1999). The chronically limited opportunities and under-representation of women in leadership positions remains a large and overarching obstacle within the Canadian sport system. Despite the initiation of affirmative action programs following the introduction of national and provincial human rights legislation in the 1980s, women continue to be generally under-represented in sport leadership positions (coaching, officiating, and administration) and often remain in low level, less valued positions and with less influence in the decision-making process in the highest levels of sport (McKay, 1997, 1999). With regard to coaching, an increase in women coaches has occurred at participatory or developmental levels since the early 1990s—which, while valuable, are seen as less noteworthy than elite or competitive levels—but the number of women coaches remains less than that of men and the number of women coaches declines more significantly with age, often in relation to such factors as burnout, frustration, low compensation, and the demands of combining family and coaching career (Hall, 2003).

The marginalization of women in Canadian sport organizations may in part be explained by the gendered histories and organizational cultures (e.g., the continuing belief among many that gender equity is a 'woman's issue') of NSOs and MSOs, but it can also be explained by the federal government's lack of consistent attention to, and reinforcement of, gender equity and affirmative action within its own administration (Hall et al., 1989; Hoeber, 2007; Macintosh & Whitson, 1990; McKay, 1999; Shaw & Hoeber, 2007; Whitson & Macintosh, 1989). As Kirby (1999, p. 67) stated, "while commitments have been made within the formal political process, the politics of private interactions [between individual men and women and between gender-equitable and non-gender equitable organizations] have not been addressed." While the pursuit of excellence in international sport has supported the increased participation of women in some areas, it has not been consequence-free and some have argued that the federal government's preoccupation with medal production in international sport events has pushed gender equity, as well as others among its oft-cited equity goals (e.g., bilingualism), to the background (cf. Donnelly, 2008; Kidd, 1996; Macintosh & Whitson, 1990).

The controversy surrounding women's ski jumping in the 2010 Vancouver Olympic Winter Games is an important case in point. To date, the International Olympic Committee (IOC) has excluded women from ski jumping in Olympic competition on the grounds that too few female participants compete in the event internationally (this despite the fact that men's ski jumping suffers the same criticism). In the lead-up to the 2010 Games, over a dozen female ski jumpers filed a law suit against the Vancouver Organizing Committee for the 2010

Olympic and Paralympic Winter Games (VANOC 2010) citing that the exclusion of a women's ski jumping event in the Games constituted a direct violation of the *Canadian Charter of Rights and Freedoms*. The women lost the suit as, "in Sagen v. Vancouver Organizing Committee for the 2010 Olympic and Paralympic Winter Games ("VANOC"), it was found that the decision not to include women's ski jumping had been made by the International Olympic Committee ("IOC") which was not subject to the Charter" (Barnes, 2010, p. 39). In other words, even though the judges felt that the women were being discriminated against, the event was seen as under the jurisdiction and responsibility of the IOC and thus not governed by the Charter. While the federal government has, in the past, been willing to make political statements in connection to high performance sport (e.g., the boycotting of South Africa from international competition during the anti-apartheid movement), this decision was met with relative silence on the part of Canadian political leaders. We must question the willingness of our political leaders and the public to accept such discriminatory policy—in essence, to continue to tolerate sexism in sport—when in direct conflict with the Canadian Charter?

The continued need for an organization such as CAAWS underscores this point. CAAWS has been pivotal in the historical and ongoing struggle for a gender equitable sport system in Canada and has secured a position for itself as a necessary and needed political force in the Canadian sport system. This is particularly critical since, as Hargreaves (1990, p. 301) noted:

> … gaining power is necessary for those who seek change and power comes from organization. For women to become a political force in sport, there must be an organization to attract them to the movement and to gain support to fight and win campaigns.

Yet, commentators have questioned the efficacy and political manoeuvring of CAAWS. As noted above, in constructing itself as the organization for women and sport in Canada, CAAWS has also adopted a less radical approach to its advocacy, positioning itself less as a feminist women's organization promoting its aims through sport and more as an MSO committed to helping the sport community become more gender equitable. In its acceptance of a more liberal feminist orientation inside the Canadian sport system, a key question becomes, "how will CAAWS protect itself from co-optation" (Kirby, 1999, p. 67)? This question is not meant to suggest that CAAWS can no longer contribute to the advancement of gender equity in Canadian sport. CAAWS has played and continues to play a key role in the promotion of gender equitable sport policy and the development of strategic documents (e.g., CAAWS, 1994) in a wide variety of areas—sexual harassment (cf. Barnes, 2010; Kirby, Greaves, & Hankivsky, 2000), organizational cultures, media awareness and promotional campaigns, childcare policies, coaching—but these achievements have not made it impervious to the broader social, political and historical tensions framing and influencing Canadian sport for women.

Conclusion

This chapter introduced readers to the changing landscape of Canadian sport policy from the 1960s onwards in an attempt to outline the dynamic policy events that have framed and influenced—so far—the inclusion (or, at times, the exclusion) and full participation of women in sport in Canada. The rich history of participation and leadership of Canadian women in sport has been shaped by numerous factors—pivotal individuals, important groups, human rights legislation (cf. Donnelly, 2008), the feminist movements, dynamic historical change and the development and implementation of formal government policy. While policy cannot be seen as the only force propelling the advancement of women and sport in Canada, its importance should also not be underestimated. As Hoffman (1989, p. 25) noted, "changes do occur, women do take up new sports, but in the absence of formal mechanisms and institutional and possibly legislative support, the process is long and hard." We continue to strive for gender equity in the Canadian sport system as women sport participants (e.g., athletes, coaches, volunteers, administrators) continue to face obstacles to full participation and representation. Formal mechanisms such as legislation and policy are still needed to push for gender equity in sport; however, such mechanisms cannot succeed without the political will of individuals and groups to adhere, enforce, and be accountable to such interventions (Harvey, 2001; Hoffman, 1995; Macintosh & Whitson, 1990). The history of women in sport policy in Canada is still being written and, if we are serious about gender equity in sport, we can still author new commitment and action to the full engagement of girls and women in sport.

References

Barnes, J. (1996). *Sports and the law in Canada* (3rd ed.). Toronto, ON: Butterworths.

Barnes, J. (2010). *The law of hockey.* Markham, ON: LexisNexis Canada.

Bell-Altenstad, K., & Vail, S. (1995). Developing public policy for women in sport: A discourse analysis. *Canadian Woman Studies/les cahiers de la femme, 15*(4), 109–112.

Brighton Declaration, The. (1994). *The Brighton Declaration on women and wport: Women, sport and the challenge of change conference.* Brighton, UK: UK Sports Council.

Canadian Association of Women and Sport and Physical Activity. (n.d.). CAAWS Strategic framework 2009–2012: Mission and vision. Retrieved from http://www.caaws.ca/e/about/mission_vision.cfm

Canadian Association of Women and Sport and Physical Activity. (1993). *Towards gender equity for women in sport: A handbook for sport organizations.* Ottawa, ON: CAAWS-Canadian Heritage.

Canadian Association of Women and Sport and Physical Activity. (1994). *An introduction to the law, sport and gender equity in Canada.* Ottawa, ON: Author.

Canadian Association of Women and Sport and Physical Activity. (2007). *ACTive: The Canadian strategy for girls and women in sport and physical activity.* Retrieved from http://www.caaws.ca/active/eng/

Canadian Fitness and Lifestyle Research Institute. (2009). *Sport participation in Canada. Let's get active: Physical activity in Canadian communities. 2009 Physical activity monitor: Facts and figures.* Ottawa, ON: Author. Retrieved from http://www.cflri.ca/eng/statistics/surveys/documents/PAM2009Bulletin8-SportParticipationratesofCanadianadults.pdf

Canadian Heritage. (2009a). *Actively engaged: A policy on sport for women and girls.* Ottawa, ON: Her Majesty the Queen in Right of Canada. Retrieved from http://www.pch.gc.ca/pgm/sc/pol/fewom/ws-b-eng.pdf

Canadian Heritage. (2009b). *Actively engaged: A policy on sport for women and girls. Action plan, 2009–2012.* Ottawa, ON: Her Majesty the Queen in Right of Canada. Retrieved from http://www.pch.gc.ca/pgm/sc/pol/fewom/ws-a-eng.pdf

Coaching Association of Canada. (2008). *Coaching Association of Canada's Women in coaching program.* Retrieved from http://www.coach.ca/files/Women-in-Coaching_2008.pdf

Corbett, R., & Findlay, H. (1994 March). *An introduction to the law, sport and gender equity in Canada.* Ottawa, ON: CAAWS.

Comeau, G.S., & Church, A.G. (2010). A comparative analysis of women's sport advocacy groups in Canada and the United States. *Journal of Sport and Social Issues, 34*(4), 457–474.

Cranney, B., Flett, C., Hylland, S., Medorvarski, A., Scherer, S., & Werthner, P. (Eds.) (2002). Special issue: Women and sport. *Canadian Woman Studies/ Les cahiers de la femme, 21*(3), 3.

Doherty, A., & Varpalotai, Λ. (2001). Theory-policy interface: The case of gender equity in sport. *Avante, 7*(1), 32–49.

Donnelly, P. (2008). Sport and human rights. *Sport in Society, 11*(4), 381–394.

Donnelly, P. & Donnelly, M. (2012). *Centre for Sport Policy Studies Research Report. The London Olympic Games: A Gender Equality Audit.* Toronto, ON: University of Toronto.

Donnelly, P., & Harvey, J. (1996, March), *Overcoming systemic barriers to access in active living.* Unpublished report submitted to Fitness Canada, Ottawa, ON.

Donnelly, P., Nakamura, Y., Kidd, B., MacNeill, M., Harvey, J., Houlihan, B., Toohey, K., Kim, K. (2010). *Sport participation in Canada: Evaluating measurements and testing determinants of increased participation.* Report of findings of SSHRC Standard Research Grant No. 410-2006-2405.

Dubin, C.L. (1990). *Commission of inquiry into the use of drugs and banned practices intended to increase athletic performance.* Ottawa, ON: Minister of Supply and Services Canada.

Giles, A. (2002). Sport Nunavut's gender equity policy: Relevance, rhetoric, and reality. *Canadian Woman Studies/les cahiers de la femme, 21*(3), 95–99.

Government of Canada. (1970). *Report of the Royal Commission on Status of Women.* Information Canada.

Hall, M.A. (1996). *Feminism and sporting bodies: Essays on theory and practice.* Champaign, IL: Human Kinetics.

Hall, M.A. (2002). *The girl and the game: A history of women's sport in Canada.* Peterborough, ON: Broadview Press.

Hall, M.A. (2003). Girls' and women's sport in Canada: From playground to podium. In I. Hartmann-Tews & G. Pfister (Eds.), *Sport and women: Social issues in international perspective* (pp. 161–178). London: Routledge.

Hall, M.A., Cullen, D., & Slack, T. (1989). Organizational elites recreating themselves: The gender structure of national sport organizations. *Quest, 41*, 28–45.

Hall, M.A., & Richardson, D.A. (1982). *Fair ball: Towards sex equality in Canadian sport.* Ottawa, ON: Canadian Advisory Council on the Status of Women.

Hall, M.A., Slack, T., Smith, G., & Whitson, D. (1991). *Sport in Canadian society.* Toronto, ON: McClelland and Stewart.

Hargreaves, J. (1990). Gender on the sports agenda. *International Review for the Sociology of Sport, 25*(4), 287–307.

Hargreaves, J. (1994). *Sporting females: Critical issues in the history and sociology of women's sport.* London: Routledge.

Harvey, J. (2001). The role of sport and recreation policy in fostering citizenship: The Canadian experience. In J. Maxwell (Ed.), *Building citizenship: Governance and service provision in Canada* (pp. 23–45). CPRN Discussion Paper No. F/17, September.

Hoeber, L. (2007). 'It's somewhere on the list but maybe it's one of the bottom ones': Examining gender equity as an organizational value in a sport organization. *International Journal of Sport Management and Marketing*, 2(4), 362–378.

Hoffman, A. (1989). Strategies for change: Some thoughts from the Canadian experience. In K. Dyer (Ed.), *Sportswomen towards 2000: A celebration.* Proceedings of a Conference held during Women's Week in Adelaide, South Australia (pp. 25–34). Richmond, AUS: Hyde Park Press.

Hoffman, A. (1995). Women's access to sport and physical activity. *Avante*, 1(1), 77–92.

Ifedi, F. (2008). *Sport Participation in Canada, 2005.* [Statistics Canada Cat. No. 81-595-MIE2008060]. Ottawa, ON: Statistics Canada.

International Working Group on Women and Sport. (2002). *The Montreal Tool Kit*. Retrieved from http://www.iwg-gti.org/past-conferences/montreal-2002/

Keyes, M. (1989). Women and Sport. In D. Morrow, M. Keyes, W. Simpson, F. Cosentino, & R. Lappage (Eds.). *A concise history of sport in Canada* (pp. 230–255). Toronto, ON: Oxford University Press.

Kidd, B. (1996). *The struggle for Canadian sport.* Toronto, ON: University of Toronto Press.

Kirby, S. (1999). Gender equity in the Canadian Sport Council: The new voice for the sport community. In K.A. Blackford, M. Garceau, & S. Kirby (Eds.), *Feminist success stories/Célébrons nos réussites féministes* (pp. 57–70). Ottawa, ON: University of Ottawa Press.

Kirby, S., Greaves, L., & Hankivsky, O. (2000). *The dome of silence: Sexual harassment and abuse in sport.* Halifax, NS: Fernwood.

Lenskyj, H. (1986). *Out of bounds: Women, sport and sexuality.* Toronto, ON: Women's Press.

Lenskyj, H. (2003). *Out on the field: Gender, sport and sexualities.* Toronto, ON: Women's Press.

Lenskyj, H.J. (2008). Women's issues and gender relations. In J. Crossman (Ed.), *Canadian sport sociology* (2nd ed.) (pp. 99–118). Toronto, ON: Thomson Nelson.

Macintosh, D. (1996). Sport and government in Canada. In L. Chalip, A. Johnson, & L. Stachura (Eds.), *National sports policies: An international handbook* (pp. 39–66). Westport, CT: Greenwood Press.

Macintosh, D., Bedecki, T., & Franks, C.E.S. (1987). *Sport and politics in Canada. Federal government involvement since 1961.* Montreal, QC & Kingston, ON: McGill-Queen's University Press.

Macintosh, D., & Whitson, D. (1990). *The game planners. Transforming Canada's sport system.* Montreal, QC & Kingston, ON: McGill-Queen's University Press.

McKay, J. (1997). *Managing gender: Affirmative action and organizational power in Australian, Canadian and New Zealand sport.* New York: SUNY Press.

McKay, J. (1999). Gender and organization power in Canadian sport. In P. White & K. Young (Eds.), *Sport and gender in Canada* (pp. 197–214). Toronto, ON: Oxford University Press.

Minister's Task Force. (1992). *Sport: The way ahead. Minister's task force on federal sport policy.* Ottawa, ON: Minister of Supply and Services Canada.

Myers, J., & Doherty, A.J. (2007). A multidimensional critique of the Sport Canada Policy on Women in Sport and its implementation in one national sport organization. *International Journal of Sport Management and Marketing, 2*(4), 322–343.

Olenik, L.M., Matthews, J.M., & Steadward, R.D. (1995). Women, disability and sport: Unheard voices. *Canadian Woman Studies/Les cahiers de la femme, 15*(4), 54–57.

Paraschak, V. (2007). Doing race, doing gender: First Nations, 'sport' and gender relations. In K. Young & P.G. White (Eds.), *Sport and gender in Canada* (2nd ed.) (pp. 137–154). Don Mills, ON: Oxford University Press.

Ponic, P.L. (2001). A herstory, a legacy: The Canadian amateur sport branch's women's program. *Avante, 6*(2), 51–63.

Public Policy Forum. (2010 May). *The Canadian sport policy: Toward a more comprehensive vision. A discussion paper.* Retrieved from http://www.mhp.gov.on.ca/en/active-living/sport/CSP-ComprehensiveVisionEN.PDF

Robertson, S. (1995). The life and times of CAAWS. *Canadian Woman Studies/les cahiers de la femme, 15*(4), 16–21.

Shaw, S., & Hoeber, L. (2007). Gender relations in Canadian amateur sport organizations: An organizational culture perspective. In K. Young & P.G. White (Eds.), *Sport and gender in Canada* (2nd ed.) (pp. 194–211). Toronto, ON: Oxford University Press.

Sport Canada. (1986). *Sport Canada Policy on Women in Sport.* Ottawa: Fitness and Amateur Sport.

Sport Canada. (1993). *Federal directions in sport: Response to the Minister's task force on federal sport policy.* Ottawa, ON: Minister of Supply and Services Canada.

Sport Canada. (1999). Sport gender snapshot 1997–1998: Survey results report. Ottawa, ON: Minister of Supply and Services Canada

Sport Canada. (2002a). *The Canadian sport policy.* Ottawa, ON: Department of Canadian Heritage. Retrieved from http://www.pch.gc.ca/pgm/sc/pol/pcs-csp/2003/polsport-eng.pdf

Sport Canada. (2002b). *The Canadian sport policy: Federal-provincial/territorial priorities for collaborative action 2002–2005.* Ottawa, ON: Department of Canadian Heritage. Retrieved from http://www.pch.gc.ca/pgm/sc/pol/actn/index-eng.cfm

Sport Canada. (2007). *The Canadian sport policy: Federal-provincial/territorial priorities for collaborative action 2007–2012.* Ottawa, ON: Department of Canadian Heritage. Retrieved from www.pch.gc.ca/pgm/sc/pol/actn07-12/booklet-eng.pdf

Sport Canada. (2011). *Canadian sport policy renewal process summary report: Women and sport round table.* Ottawa, ON: Department of Canadian Heritage. Retrieved from http://www.sirc.ca/csprenewal/documents/2011/women.pdf

Sport Canada. (2012). *Canadian sport policy 2012.* Ottawa, ON: Department of Canadian Heritage. Retrieved from http://sirc.ca/CSPRenewal/documents/CSP2012_EN.pdf

Strachan, D., & Tomlinson, P. (1994). *Gender equity in coaching.* Ottawa: Coaching Association of Canada.

Travers, A. (2006). Queering sport. *International Review for the Sociology of Sport, 41*(4), 431–446.

Travers, A. (2008). The sport nexus and gender injustice. *Studies in Social Injustice, 2*(1), 79–101.

Vail, S. (1983). What the federal government is doing to promote women's sport. *Canadian Woman Studies/Les cahiers de la femme, 4*(3), 75–81.

Vail, S. (1992). *Women in physical activity and sport: Workshop report.* Toronto, ON: Ontario Ministry of Tourism and Recreation.

Vickers, J. (1992). The intellectual origins of the women's movements in Canada. In C. Backhouse & D.H. Flaherty (Eds.), *Challenging times: The women's movement in Canada and the United States* (pp. 39–60). Montreal, QC & Kingston, ON: McGill-Queen's University Press.

Whitson, D., & Macintosh, D. (1989). Gender and power: Explanations of gender inequalities in Canadian national sport organizations. *International Review for the Sociology of Sport, 24*(2), 137–150.

Windhoek Call for Action. (1998). *The Windhoek Call for Action: Second World Conference on Women in Sport.* Ottawa, ON: Sport Canada.

CHAPTER XII

Official Languages and the Canadian Sport System: Steady Progress, Constant Vigilance Needed

Graham Fraser, Commissioner of Official Languages[1]

Canada's language policy applies to all federal institutions and covers many facets of Canadian life, including social and economic development, immigration, transportation and the environment. The policy also addresses high performance sport and the staging of national and international sport events.[2] Both federal support for amateur sport and the federal legislative and administrative framework regarding official languages came into being in the 1960s. There have been a number of points of intersection since that time.

The aim of this chapter is to discuss the intersection between sport and official languages at the Canadian federal level based on the experience of the Office of the Commissioner of Official Languages (OCOL). The chapter presents some of the key points outlined in a chapter written by Commissioner Dyane Adam (2007) for *Jeux, sports et francophonie: L'exemple du Canada*,[3] summarizes lessons learned from the Vancouver 2010 Olympic and Paralympic Winter Games, and provides insights for the future.

Since its creation on April 1, 1970, following the adoption of the *Official Languages Act* in 1969, the OCOL has taken action on several occasions in relation to the Canadian sport system and national and international sport events. Those interventions were intended to foster equality and respect and to ensure that events respect and reflect not only Canada's image, identity, and values, but also the tenants of linguistic duality.

The first section discusses official languages in the Canadian sport system in general. We first examine how the OCOL views the connections between the Canadian sport system and official languages, followed by a brief summary of the laws and policies that govern federal support for the Canadian sport system. The main thrust is a historical overview of official languages in the Canadian sport system from the 1960s to the end of the 1990s.

The second section discusses the OCOL's 2000 study on the Canadian sport system, the follow-up report (published in 2003) and the context in which those publications were released. Continuing the chronological overview, this section focuses on the era in which the *Canadian Sport Policy* and the *Physical Activity and Sport Act* were adopted. Next, it examines the independent study commissioned by the Department of Canadian Heritage, and the action plan adopted by its Sport Canada branch in response to recommendations.

The third section presents the principal linguistic challenges raised by the Vancouver 2010 Olympic and Paralympic Winter Games, and the OCOL's work in that regard. Highlights are presented of the Games' main success stories from a language point of view. The section then sets out a few difficulties that arose during preparations for the Games, as well as shortcomings that tarnished the Games' admirable overall performance in terms of official languages. The chapter concludes with some practical tips for future national and international sport events in Canada, based on the Vancouver experience.

Official languages in the Canadian Sport System

The OCOL and the Canadian Sport System
The Commissioner of Official Languages is a federal ombudsman who reports directly to the Parliament of Canada and is therefore independent of the Canadian government. The OCOL is responsible for upholding Canadians' language rights and investigating alleged breaches of the *Official Languages Act.* The OCOL also promotes linguistic duality and works proactively to help federal institutions meet their language obligations. The OCOL therefore has a dual role of protection and promotion.

In recent years, the OCOL's sport-related interventions have focused primarily on high performance sport at the national and international level, which is under federal government jurisdiction. For the OCOL, there are three aspects to the relationship between the Canadian sport system and official languages. The first two of these aspects are addressed in this chapter:

1. National sport organizations must provide services of equal quality in both official languages to ensure that Canadians who are active in high performance amateur sport have equal chances to realize their potential;

2. National and international sport events are important moments in Canada's national life and opportunities to promote the use and full recognition of both official languages. Therefore, they must properly reflect linguistic duality in terms of the quality and availability of services to participants and visitors as well as cultural expression (e.g., ceremonies, cultural activities);

3. Sports and sport events play an important role in developing the identity of young people in minority language communities. The Canadian Francophone Games and the Jeux de l'Acadie are examples of sport events that combine sport and cultural identity and can foster a strong sense of belonging.

Other considerations pertaining to the place of both official languages in Canadian amateur sport go beyond the federal government's jurisdiction and the scope of this chapter. These considerations include the many aspects of physical activity and 'amateur' sports at provincial/territorial, local and community levels, such as federal-provincial/territorial co-operation in physical literacy and sport participation, all of which are within the scope of the *Canadian Sport Policy 2012* (Sport Canada, 2012).

The Official Languages Act *and the Canadian Sport System*

By enshrining the equal status, rights and privileges of English and French within the *Canadian Charter of Rights and Freedoms*, (Canada, 1982), the Government of Canada has recognized that linguistic duality is a fundamental value in Canadian society. The objective of the *Official Languages Act* is not only to ensure the linguistic equality of both official languages in federal institutions, but also to encourage progression towards the equal status and use of English and French in all aspects of Canadian society.

Under Part IV of the Act, members of the public have the right to receive services from federal institutions in the official language of their choice. Services in the two official languages must be of equal quality in terms of both access and content, no matter which language the person chooses to use. Moreover, Part VII of the Act requires federal institutions to take positive measures to support the development and enhance the vitality of official language minority communities and foster the full recognition and use of both English and French in Canadian society.

The *Physical Activity and Sport Act*, a federal law enacted in 2003, creates a framework for the Government of Canada's actions in this area (Parliament of Canada, 2003). Official languages are an integral part of the Act. Its preamble states that the federal government "is committed to promoting physical activity and sport, having regard to the principles set out in the *Official Languages Act*" (Parliament of Canada, 2003, p. 1). Section 6 of the Act states that the government may "provide financial assistance in the form of grants and contributions to any person, in accordance with Parts IV and VII of the *Official Languages Act*" (Parliament of Canada, 2003, p. 4). This constitutes clear recognition that the Canadian sport system must also help promote both official languages, which are fundamental to our national identity.

Sport Canada, a branch of the Department of Canadian Heritage, co-ordinates the Canadian government's support for high performance sport organizations, elite athletes and national and international sport events. It is important to understand that organizations that receive grants and financial contributions from the Canadian government are not directly subject to the *Official Languages Act* because they are not federal institutions. However, they have substantial language obligations of a contractual nature.

The *Canadian Sport Policy* 2012 stipulates that the Government of Canada is committed to "ensuring access to services in English and French" (Sport Canada, 2012, p. 17). Sport Canada's Sport Funding and Accountability Framework (SFAF) prescribes official languages standards that must be met by national sport organizations (NSOs), multi-sport/service organizations (MSOs) and Canadian Sport Centres/Institutes (CSCs/CSIs).[4]

For its part, the *Federal Policy for Hosting International Sport Events* describes the frequency with which the Canadian government is willing to provide financial assistance for international multi-sport games, international single-sport events, and games for Aboriginal peoples and persons with a disability (Canadian Heritage, 2008). The role of Sport Canada is also to support Canadian applications for such international events. In addition, Sport Canada provides financial assistance for every edition of the Canada Games.

The Canadian sport system is a complex network of non-profit organizations that are financially supported in part by the federal, provincial/territorial, and local governments. These levels of government make an enormous contribution to the physical and administrative infrastructure that underpins our sport system and supports the athletes, coaches, officials and other participants. However, provincial/territorial and local governments as well as the non-profit sector do not fall under the jurisdiction of the *Official Languages Act*, which applies only to federal institutions. As a result, the challenge in terms of official languages is to "overcome structural and jurisdictional compartmentalization in order to enable Canadians to realize their full potential, whatever their official language may be, by practising sports in the language of their choice" (Adam, 2007, p. 28, *translation*).

Overview of Official Languages in Canada's Sport System from the 1960s to the 1990s

The federal government's role in the area of sport and physical activity gradually became more structured starting in the 1960s (Mills, 1998). It was an exciting time for Canada's national identity, with many symbols and policies central to Canadian identity being put in place. The Canadian flag and universal health care are just two examples. The 1960s also gave rise to a complete overhaul of Canada's linguistic framework, in part because of the clear predominance of English and the under-representation of Francophones in the federal public service at the time. In 1963, Prime Minister Lester B. Pearson created the Royal Commission on Bilingualism and Biculturalism, co-chaired by André Laurendeau and A. Davidson Dunton. The Commission was the result of both the increasing self-affirmation of Canada's French language society, particularly in Quebec, and a growing openness to French language and culture among the English-speaking majority and within the federal government (Fraser, 2010).

The Commission travelled across Canada to hear from Canadians and learn more about such topics as socioeconomic status, minority language instruction, learning a second language and bilingualism in the federal administration. It produced a preliminary report in

1965 and a final report, broken down by subject into six volumes, between 1966 and 1970. The Commission laid the foundations for the federal official languages policy framework in general and the *Official Languages Act* in particular. Passed in 1969, the Act established institutional bilingualism at the federal level.

A profound cultural shift took place in the federal public administration following the adoption of the Act, not without certain difficulties. For some people, the changes were revolutionary insofar as they amounted to a major change to the status quo. The 1969 Act, and the official languages policies adopted subsequently by the government, sought to guarantee the individual's right to communicate with the federal government and receive services in the official language of his or her choice, establish a bilingual civil service and support the development of official language minority communities. These three objectives are clearly set forth in the Act, which underwent a complete overhaul when its scope was broadened in 1988.

Official languages were not an integral part of the federal government's role in sport and physical activity at the outset. The first federal statute on fitness and amateur sport, enacted in 1961 and since repealed, did not cover language-related aspects of sport and physical activity. As for the first draft of the *Official Languages Act*, passed in 1969, it did not give the Commissioner of Official Languages much power with respect to non-profit organizations subsidized by the federal government concerning the delivery of services in both official languages. At the time, support for sport organizations was channelled through the National Sport and Recreation Centre, an administrative structure created in the early 1970s. The language obligations incumbent upon these organizations were completely undefined from a legal point of view. The federal administration rarely intervened in their operations, which were carried out essentially in English.

In 1973, the first Commissioner of Official Languages, Keith Spicer, recommended that Canada's Department of Health and Welfare, which provided federal support for the sport system at the time, take the necessary steps to provide equal services in both official languages. His successor, Maxwell Yalden, noted with regret in 1980 that "such work as has been done to counter this splintering effect has made little apparent impact" (Commissioner of Official Languages, 1981, p. 55). The year before, Commissioner Yalden had pointed out that it was vital for the language obligations of non-governmental organizations financed in whole or in part with public funds to be more clearly defined, adding that the real challenge was to help those organizations fulfill their moral and legal obligations under the *Official Languages Act*. He stated: "If those responsible have no more conviction of the importance of third-party dealings than is now the case, polarization of the voluntary sector will not simply happen; they will have helped it along the way" (Commissioner of Official Languages, 1980, p. 48).

The focus on ensuring that organizations subsidized by the federal government delivered services in both official languages in keeping with the spirit of the Act was to take on increasing importance in the following years. Directives issued in 1980 regarding financial assistance to non-profit organizations advised government departments to take official languages issues into account when granting financial assistance. Commissioner Yalden, who found that these directives amounted to "non-advice," recommended that the government require non-profit organizations receiving federal funds and serving both linguistic communities to provide "guarantees that the equal status of the two official languages will be appropriately reflected" (Commissioner of Official Languages, 1981, p. 56).

Shortly after, in 1982, Commissioner Yalden published a language audit of the Fitness and Amateur Sport program of the Secretary of State Department. The audit showed that "Francophone organizations have sometimes been chary of joining national sport organizations because they believe, rightly in many cases, that Anglophones control the decision-making process in these organizations. This perception is often reinforced by very real shortcomings in service in French" (Commissioner of Official Languages, 1982, p. 2). The Commissioner recommended that the branch "adopt a comprehensive official languages policy, define the procedures by which the objectives of the *Official Languages Act* will be promoted, evaluated and controlled in all the activities funded by the branch" (Commissioner of Official Languages, 1982, p. 6).

In 1983, Commissioner Yalden noted that the National Sport and Recreation Centre continued to neglect its language obligations despite the implementation of an official languages program at Fitness and Amateur Sport and the inclusion of language clauses in contracts signed with sport organizations. In 1984, his successor, Commissioner D'Iberville Fortier, stated in his annual report that despite "[a] funding contribution agreement [that came into effect that year] containing a commitment to take better account of the two linguistic communities" and a provision that national sport organizations were to submit official languages plans, less than half of the organizations had submitted such a plan at year's end (Commissioner of Official Languages, 1985, p. 146). Moreover, a special fund put in place to help the organizations meet their language obligations had not been used.

The wind began to turn in the second half of the 1980s, as sport organizations receiving funds from the Canadian government began to improve their performance in delivering services in both official languages. The initiatives designed to help national sport organizations provide higher-quality services in both languages, implemented in 1985, were paying dividends. In the 1988 annual report, Commissioner Fortier pointed to the solid ability of the Fitness and Amateur Sport Branch of the Department of National Health and Welfare to provide services in both official languages. He also noted the branch's "laudable efforts" to "ensure that the national fitness, sport and recreational associations it subsidizes conducted their activities with due regard for official languages matters" (Commissioner of Official Languages, 1989, p. 166). In the same report, however, Commissioner Fortier indicated that he had received some complaints regarding the place of the two official languages at various sport events held during the year.

In 1988, the Parliament of Canada revised the *Official Languages Act* in response to the adoption of the *Canadian Charter of Rights and Freedoms* in 1982. The revised Act maintained the focus on government services in both official languages and broadened the scope of the federal linguistic framework considerably. In particular, it introduced the Canadian government's commitment to promote the full recognition and use of both official languages in Canadian society and to enhance the vitality of linguistic minority communities, namely Anglophones in Quebec and Francophones living in the other provinces and territories.

The OCOL began focusing on national and international sport events in 1989 with the publication of an *Official Languages Act* compliance audit of national and international events (sport events, but also commercial events, cultural events and so on). In fact, Fitness and Amateur Sport's improved performance would raise "new expectations, especially in regard to the bilingual nature of many regional, national, and international sport events that require the co-ordination of partners at several different levels (federal, provincial, local, non-profit organizations and the commercial sector)" (Adam, 2007, p. 33, *translation*).

In the 1989 audit, Commissioner Fortier's proposals included establishing a set of language criteria, including adequate resources for bilingual services, accountability and monitoring, and the active participation of both linguistic communities. In the wake of this audit, the Canadian Parliament's Standing Joint Committee on Official Languages recommended that the government adopt a policy on the use of official languages at national and international popular events. The Treasury Board Secretariat then asked federal institutions to make their financial contributions subject to compliance with the principles of linguistic duality.

Despite the progress accomplished on political and administrative fronts, major obstacles to Francophone participation in the Canadian sport system persisted in the early 1990s. In 1992, the Task Force on Federal Sport Policy, created by the Minister of State for Fitness and Amateur Sport and chaired by J.C. Best, tabled a report that emphasized the persistence of problems related to French-language services and major obstacles to the full participation of Francophones in sport activities (Minister's Task Force, 1992). This result came on the heels of a federal-provincial advisory committee finding that identified, in 1990, numerous deficiencies in the delivery of bilingual services that could pose structural obstacles to the participation of athletes from both language groups (Federal-Provincial Advisory Committee, 1990 as cited in Adam, 2007, p. 35).

In response to the Best Report, the federal government worked with its many partners in the sport community to adopt a new approach to its support of the Canadian sport system. This new approach coincided with a climate of belt-tightening and bringing down public deficits. Significant changes were taking place in public administration just as practices in the field of sport were being transformed, all of which led to a major re-engineering of the Canadian sport system in the mid-1990s.

In 1996, Sport Canada adopted a new Sport Funding and Accountability Framework (SFAF) for organizations receiving public funds. Canadian Sport Centres were also created to group and co-ordinate support services for elite athletes and coaches. During this period, the Canadian government simultaneously adopted

"a 'hands-off' approach to the administration of sport organizations; [clarified] its expectations on social policies, including official
languages; and [cut] funding to sport organizations" (OCOL, 2000,
p. 9). For the organizations in question, these changes posed new
challenges in providing services of equal quality in both official
languages. By way of example, and to demonstrate the scale of
the cuts, the assistance granted by Sport Canada decreased from
CA$ 66.7M in 1987 to CA$ 51.1M in 1997 (Adam, 2007, p. 35). In addition, the common administrative services previously provided by
the National Sport and Recreation Centre were no longer available
as government withdrew from subsidizing common services to sport
organizations.

   In December 1998, the House of Commons Sub-Committee
on the Study of Sport in Canada tabled a substantive report that
examined sport's contribution to the overall Canadian economy
(Mills, 1998). Known as the Mills Report, the document dealt with
the role of the federal government in promoting amateur sport and
participation in sports, as well as sport's contribution to national
unity. Among other elements, the report recommended that "the
Government of Canada ensure the development and delivery of services and programs in both official languages" (Mills, 1998, p. 133).
In a dissenting report, the Bloc Québécois opposed the report's conclusions and affirmed that it ignored "the many difficulties facing
both amateur and professional French-speaking athletes in Canada
and fail[ed] to propose any real measures to remedy the situation"
(Mills, 1998, p. 165).

   In fact, during the sub-committee's work, some speakers cat-
egorically affirmed that French-speaking athletes were being discriminated against in terms of the services available in their language
and the selection of athletes for national teams. The OCOL was also
receiving complaints in early 1998 regarding the Canadian Olympic
Association's ceremony presenting Canadian athletes at the Nagano
Olympic Winter Games, which had taken place solely in English
(Stubbs, 1998). In the same year, a similar incident occurred at a
press conference, held in English only, in connection with the presentation of Canada's flag bearer for the Commonwealth Games in
Kuala Lumpur, Malaysia. In his 1998 annual report, Commissioner
Victor Goldbloom recommended that Canadian Heritage estab-
lish "a mechanism to ensure that when national and international
sporting events are being considered the language aspects be taken

into account before the events are held" (Commissioner of Official Languages, 1999, p. 50).

The conclusions of the Sub-Committee on the Study of Sport in Canada, along with a number of requests made by members of Parliament in the wake of its work, led Commissioner Dyane Adam to launch a special study on the use of official languages in the Canadian sport system as soon as she was appointed in August 1999. During the Sub-Committee's work, "It seemed to some that French-speaking athletes were victims of discrimination in terms of the services provided to them and their opportunities to be selected for national teams" (Commissioner of Official Languages, 2000, p. 58). This study is addressed in the next section.

Impact of the Office of the Commissioner's Study on Official Languages in the Canadian Sport System

The 2000 Study[5]

Official Languages in the Canadian Sports System, published in 2000, was a substantive study based on some 100 interviews with athletes, coaches, sport administrators and researchers, a mail-in survey of athletes and an analysis of parliamentary, government and media documents (OCOL, 2000). Among the study's chief findings were Sport Canada's insufficient bilingual capacity to manage its programs in both official languages, an under-representation of Francophone athletes in national high performance sport and major shortcomings in French services provided by sport organizations financially supported by Sport Canada. In the study, Commissioner Adam made a number of recommendations to Sport Canada, which fell into three main categories:

1. implementing administrative measures to ensure that sport organizations are able to provide an adequate level of service in French;
2. improving the French-language capacity of coaches, managers, and staff; and
3. improving Sport Canada's official language program management, including its bilingual capacity.

The study showed that while the percentage of Canadians who spoke French as their first official language was 24.6%, only 18% of high performance athletes (receiving direct financial assistance from the federal government) stated that French was their first official language. This was a major discrepancy, given that factors determining sport participation rates are quite similar among Francophones and Anglophones (Adam, 2007; OCOL, 2000).

Previous studies had shown that the national team selection process was a major obstacle to the careers of French-speaking athletes; however, at the time of the 2000 study, all signs indicated that the process had become more transparent and fairer. Nonetheless, obstacles posed by conflicts between provincial and national sport organizations, particularly in Quebec, seemed to persist. Although the problem no longer necessarily stemmed from the selection process, its effects were felt strongly in athletes' experiences.

Anglophones were generally satisfied with the language aspects of their sport experience, whereas Francophones signalled various shortcomings, particularly with respect to coaching and services received from sport organizations. The athletes also emphasized the importance of receiving services such as psychological consultations and medical services in the official language of their choice. At the time the study was conducted, for instance, the Canadian Sport Centres in Calgary and Winnipeg provided only English-language services to national teams, while the Canadian Sport Centre in Montreal was able to provide services in both languages.

The fact that many coaches and service providers were not bilingual, along with a lack of cultural sensitivity in some cases, left their mark. Too often, the main obstacle to Francophone participation was the fact that many of the sport organizations financially supported by Sport Canada operated solely in English, had insufficient resources to provide services in French, and still lacked a clear official languages policy.

At the time of the 2000 study, Sport Canada's Sport Funding and Accountability Framework attached little importance to the delivery of services in both official languages. Minimum expectations for the services to be offered were identified in the contribution agreements, but there were major monitoring and follow-up deficiencies by this Canadian Heritage branch. Evaluations focused more on processes (asking, for example, whether an official languages policy was in place) than on results (Were services in fact provided in both official languages?). Although some organizations provided services in both languages and many demonstrated cultural sensitivity, this was far from being the case for all organizations.

Regarding the Government of Canada's support for major sport events, the study concluded that the recommendations made following the 1989 audit on national and international events had, as a rule, been implemented. The study also pointed out that the Winnipeg Pan American Games in 1999 had been a success on the linguistic front "because the organizers planned ahead for linguistic services and committed enough money and human resources to ensure that they could be delivered" (OCOL, 2000, p. 35). Concerning the linguistic aspect of major games, the 2000 study also recommended that Sport Canada ensure the necessary budgets be granted to that end and set clear expectations to be met by recipient organizations.

Canadian Sport Policy, the Physical Activity and Sport Act, and the OCOL's Follow-Up Report

The OCOL's 2000 study was published shortly before the federal, provincial and territorial governments, sport organizations and several other stakeholders began the development of the first *Canadian Sport Policy*. Focusing on participation and inclusivity, the *Canadian Sport Policy* (2002–2012) set expectations pertaining to official languages, specifically by stipulating that sport organizations "provide essential services in English and French for the development of athletes, coaches, officials and administrators" (Sport Canada, 2002, p. 14). It also prescribed that the federal government ensure "access to essential services in English and French" (Sport Canada, 2002, p. 15) and that the provinces and territories should help meet those objectives in their respective areas of jurisdiction. The policy stipulated that "despite past efforts, language-based barriers still exist in the sport system for [F]rancophones, especially at the national team level" (Sport Canada, 2002, p. 8).

In June 2002, the government tabled Bill C-12 on physical activity and sport in the House of Commons. Judging that the bill's official languages provisions were insufficient, Commissioner Adam appeared before the parliamentary committee and made a number of recommendations. Many of those recommendations were included in the *Physical Activity and Sport Act*, which received royal assent on March 19, 2003 (Parliament of Canada, 2003). As Commissioner Adam stated, the bill required certain amendments "because history had shown more than once that in the absence of clear provisions, Canadians' language rights were not respected. The conclusions of the study conducted by the Office of the Commissioner were proof of the fact" (Adam, 2007, p. 45, *translation*). The *Physical Activity and Sport Act* led to the creation of the Sport Dispute Resolution Centre of Canada, which is required to take specific steps to provide services in both official languages. The centre handles a range of disputes, including language-related complaints.

In addition to recommending changes to Bill C-12, the OCOL prepared a follow-up report published in 2003[6] that monitored implementation of the recommendations made in the 2000 study (OCOL, 2003). The follow-up report indicated that three of the 15 recommendations in the 2000 study had been fully implemented by Sport Canada, nine others had been partially implemented and three others had not been implemented. Commissioner Adam deplored the slow pace of change and the lack of a consistent approach—flaws that affected Francophone athletes most directly, since they were required to adapt to the sport system's shortcomings. In addition, the issue of under-representation of Francophone athletes had deteriorated slightly between 2000 and 2003 (OCOL, 2003).

However, some progress had been noted, including improvements to official languages standards, considerable efforts to make many documents available in both languages, and a survey of sport organizations to evaluate the delivery of bilingual services.

In addition to reiterating the recommendations that had not been implemented or had been only partially implemented, the 2003 follow-up report recommended that Sport Canada "undertake an independent study on Francophone participation in sports overall and determine what conditions are conducive for ensuring equal access by both official languages groups to high performance sports" (OCOL, 2003, p. 37).

Athletes and Official Languages: Subsequent Study of the Issue

In response to the recommendation set out in the OCOL's 2003 follow-up report, Canadian Heritage commissioned an independent study on the subject. *Linguistic Barriers to Access to High Performance Sport* was prepared by researchers Mira Svoboda and Peter Donnelly based on the OCOL's methods and findings (Svoboda & Donnelly, 2006). Their study dealt with Francophone and Anglophone participation in high performance sports, barriers to participation, institutional infrastructure, and coaching.

Although it confirmed the findings of the OCOL's 2000 study, the new study did not clearly demonstrate the existence of linguistic barriers for Francophones in high performance sports. However, it did show that the quality of services and support provided to athletes in both official languages was, at times, inadequate, or that such services were not of the same quality in both languages.

Whereas previous studies had primarily identified cases where Francophones bore the brunt of official languages shortcomings in the Canadian sport system, Svoboda and Donnelly's (2006) study also referred to certain situations where Anglophones were most affected. This showed the importance of emphasizing the place of *both* official languages.

Svoboda and Donnelly (2006) made several recommendations, many of which were consistent with the OCOL's 2000 study. Specifically, they recommended that Sport Canada:

- lead by example by ensuring that it has sufficient official languages capacity to interface with client groups in English and French;
- continue its efforts with sport organizations that receive financial assistance from the federal government by focusing on organizations that have been less successful in meeting their language goals, providing them with official languages tools and expertise, and applying any necessary sanctions;
- implement a social marketing program directed at athletes to encourage them to request services in their preferred language once services of equal quality are available in both official languages;
- in collaboration with its partners, expand its knowledge of linguistic barriers at the provincial level and improve partnerships between federal and provincial/territorial stakeholders with the intent to tear down those barriers;
- develop a linguistic profile of coaches; and
- establish strategic alliances with organizations in official language minority communities and develop a pool of volunteers to help integrate athletes living in minority situations.

Sport Canada created an ad hoc official languages committee to advise on its response to the study's recommendations. Based in part on the committee's work, Sport Canada adopted an action plan on official languages for 2008–2012 (Canadian Heritage, 2007). The plan set out the steps already taken and those planned at the time of its adoption for each recommendation made in *Linguistic Barriers to Access to High Performance Sport.* Among the most noteworthy steps, the action plan indicated that sport organizations could be subject to financial penalties "if they do not demonstrate a firm commitment to meeting their contractual obligations with respect to official languages" (Canadian Heritage, 2007, p. 11). On the positive side, however, the action plan described significant progress in Sport Canada's bilingual capacity. At the time of writing, Sport Canada indicated that the vast majority of the measures identified in its 2008–2012 action plan had been implemented. Considerable progress has thus been made since the 1990s, when the Sport Funding and Accountability Framework paid little attention to official languages.

Current Issues

The OCOL had studied the issue of Francophone and Anglophone participation in the Canadian sport system and the availability of French-language services for athletes primarily in response to the lack of data on the subject. Those efforts, in addition to the work since carried out by and for Sport Canada, have supplied relevant data and raised awareness of these issues among Canadian sport system stakeholders.

While the genuine progress made over the years is certainly encouraging, all those working in the Canadian sport system must remain vigilant. For its part, Sport Canada must continue to fulfill its commitments and evaluate what has been accomplished so improvements are lasting.

The Commissioner's 2009–2010 annual report mentioned that, in the run-up to the 2010 Olympic and Paralympic Winter Games in Vancouver, websites of many national sport organizations contained French content that was less than and often of inferior quality to the English. As the OCOL's 2009–2010 annual report pointed out:

> Although these organizations are not subject to the Act directly and their resources for functioning in English and French are often limited, they do have official languages obligations because they receive financial support from Sport Canada's Sport Support Program. Sport Canada has not ensured that these organizations are fulfilling their obligations and providing information of equal quality in English and French on their Web sites. (OCOL, 2010, p. 17)

This problem, which has reoccurred frequently over the past few years, still persists today. In addition, a new variant has arisen with the evolution of the Internet: even when websites do offer content of equal quality in both official languages, social media content (whether it be tweets or videos, for example) generated by organizations on platforms such as Facebook, Twitter and YouTube is not always available simultaneously in both official languages. Sport Canada has an important role to play to monitor progress to ensure equal and prompt access to services and communications in both official languages.

This concludes the short review of the equal use and status of both official languages at Sport Canada and the sport organizations that it financially supports. We will now examine the question of official languages at major sport events, focusing on the Vancouver 2010 Olympic and Paralympic Winter Games.

Official Languages and Major Sport Events: The Vancouver Games

National and international sport events are opportunities to showcase our country, our values and our symbols. Since linguistic duality is both a characteristic and a fundamental value of Canada, it is important to reflect this distinctive trait properly in the services provided to participants and visitors at sport events, and in the associated forms of cultural expression, including ceremonies and cultural activities. All Canadians should see themselves reflected in the image presented to the world.

Vancouver 2010: Raising our Game

As soon as the International Olympic Committee announced on July 2, 2003 that Vancouver had been selected as the host city, the 2010 Olympic and Paralympic Winter Games were destined to be a highlight of Canadian life.[7] In light of the event's scope and past experiences with sports and official languages, the OCOL resolved to make the issue a priority and take action proactively and preventively and then share the lessons learned after the Games. The OCOL's actions were carried out in five phases:

- an initial study published in December 2008 (OCOL, 2008) contained recommendations to help Canadian Heritage and the Vancouver Organizing Committee for the 2010 Olympic and Paralympic Winter Games (VANOC 2010)[8] to fully meet the requirements of the Multi-Party Agreement for the 2010 Olympic and Paralympic Winter Games (Canadian Heritage, 2002) and the *Official Languages Act*;

- an awareness campaign was conducted in early 2009 to help federal institutions incorporate official languages obligations into their planning processes;
- a follow-up report, published in September 2009 examined progress related to official languages at the Games and described obstacles still to be overcome (OCOL, 2009);
- a final report, released in December 2010 evaluated the Games in regard to Canada's official languages and included a number of lessons learned and comments applicable to subsequent major sport events to be held in Canada (OCOL, 2011b); and
- a practical guide to promoting official languages at major sport events held in Canada was published in March 2011 based on lessons learned from the Vancouver Games (OCOL, 2011a).

In the years immediately preceding the Games, the OCOL also took action regarding access to French-language Vancouver Games broadcasts across the country. That action came in response to concerns expressed by a number of parties, including the Fédération des communautés francophones et acadienne du Canada (FCFA). However, the issue of these broadcasts comes with its own specific dynamics and challenges and is beyond the scope of this chapter (OCOL, 2011b).

The Multi-Party Agreement set out specific language obligations incumbent upon VANOC 2010. Those obligations covered most organizational aspects, including services to participants and the general public, all communications and the content of ceremonies. A first for the Olympic Games, the Multi-Party Agreement set out specific language obligations for the organizing committee (Canadian Heritage, 2002).

Major Success Stories

The Vancouver 2010 Olympic and Paralympic Winter Games left an important linguistic legacy. Indeed, according to information gathered by the OCOL,[9] the Games were a great success in terms of public services available on the ground in both official languages. As for the Paralympic Winter Games, they were the first to be entirely bilingual (English and French). The cultural events that preceded the Olympic Winter Games, such as the Cultural Olympiad (spread out over three years) and the Olympic Torch Relay, also reflected Canada's linguistic duality to a significant degree.

VANOC 2010 successfully rose to the challenge of recruiting thousands of bilingual volunteers—nearly 3,000 out of the 20,000 volunteers, according to figures provided before the Games. Generally speaking, this made it possible for both Anglophones and Francophones to have access to information and services in the language of their choice. The bilingual volunteers were easy to identify thanks to their "Bonjour" buttons, and many unilingual volunteers called on the assistance of their bilingual colleagues to provide adequate services, as planned. The announcements and comments broadcast by loudspeakers at the competition sites were made in English and French[10] in the vast majority of cases.

With just a few exceptions, Games signage was bilingual, including the one found on event sites in downtown Vancouver, at Whistler and at Vancouver International Airport. Some national and international sponsors put up signs in both languages. The host cities, Vancouver and Whistler, made a considerable effort to offer services in English and French to the general public, particularly in their signage and by ensuring that the information services and teams of volunteers included bilingual personnel. All these efforts gave Canada's linguistic duality a tangible presence.

VANOC 2010 enjoyed a fruitful cooperative relationship with various partners from the French-speaking community, including the Fédération des francophones de la Colombie-Britannique, the Canadian Foundation for Cross-Cultural Dialogue and the Organisation internationale de la Francophonie. The Advisory Committee on Official Languages, established to advise VANOC 2010 on language-related issues, proved to be a particularly effective organizational mechanism. Moreover, Place de la Francophonie, a cultural showcase held in parallel with the Olympic Winter Games on Granville Island in the centre of Vancouver, was a resounding success. It helped increase the visibility of French in British Columbia by showcasing the vitality and diversity of French culture both nationally and internationally.

In many cases, federal institutions providing essential services (related to health and safety, for example), or services to the travelling public for the Games,[11] also took steps to meet the higher demand for services resulting from the influx of visitors who came to the Games.

A Preparatory Phase with its Share of Pitfalls

As we have just pointed out, the Games were a great success from a linguistic standpoint. Efforts to overcome obstacles encountered in the months and years preceding the Games led to this success. It is important, however, to recognize the shortfalls, which are discussed in greater detail below. It is also important to mention that, during the preparatory phase, several problematic situations arose where VANOC 2010 would have had difficulty complying with the spirit or the letter of its language obligations if corrective action had not been taken.

Concerns about volunteer recruitment and training, signage, cultural activities, and translation and interpretation, among others, were brought to light by a number of parties, including the Standing Committees on Official Languages of the Senate (which published a report and follow-ups on the issue)[12] and of the House of Commons; organizations representing Francophone communities, including the FCFA; and the OCOL.

One of the issues that attracted a great deal of attention from stakeholders, but not necessarily from the media, was the allocation of sufficient resources to translation and interpretation—services for which demand grew constantly as the Games approached. This was a major challenge for VANOC 2010, one that just a few months before the Games compromised its ability to meet the Multi-Party Agreement requirements regarding communications with the general public. For example, it was decided that the biographies of certain athletes would not be translated despite the agreement's provision to the contrary. A number of interested parties had to work very hard to get VANOC 2010 to rectify the situation.

It is important to acknowledge that the difficult economic circumstances at the time led VANOC 2010 to review all expenses, including those related to official languages. Nevertheless, many of the difficulties that arose during the preparatory phase can be attributed to the fact that VANOC 2010's leaders did not necessarily have the official-language "reflex," and as a result, may have underestimated the fundamental importance of official languages to the success of the Games.

The inadequacy of translation and interpretation resources was resolved by means of an additional Government of Canada contribution, which enabled VANOC 2010 to utilize the services of the Translation Bureau, an agency of Public Works and Government Services Canada. Although this last-minute intervention was appropriate under the circumstances, steps should be taken to avoid such situations in the future. According to the OCOL (2011b), translation and interpretation services are essential and should be integrated into the federal government's basic contribution to major sport events.

The Vancouver Games Opening Ceremony: A Window to the World— Almost Entirely in One Language

As indicated earlier, the considerable work accomplished by VANOC 2010 and Canadian Heritage to overcome the obstacles and difficulties that marked the preparatory phase was apparent in every facet of the Games. Nevertheless, certain shortcomings were noted. For example, some announcements were not made in both official languages at certain venues. VANOC 2010 had deployed its bilingual volunteers strategically, an appropriate measure under the circumstances, but it also meant that French services were not available in some locations. In addition, some unilingual volunteers did not follow procedure and refer people to a bilingual colleague. Moreover, the OCOL's on-site personnel were unable to find any souvenir programs in French. It is also regrettable that some sponsors posted information in English only.

As for federal institutions providing key services—including services for travellers as well as health and safety services—many took steps to meet the higher demand for services in both official languages, but only a few monitored the availability of these services in order to ensure that visitors were always provided service in the official language of their choice (OCOL, 2011b).

However, it was the large discrepancy in the use of English and French during the Olympic Games opening ceremony,[13] which was broadcast worldwide, that drew the most attention, casting a shadow over the numerous success stories. While French was noticeably present in the protocol components of the opening ceremony, the near total absence of French in the narrative component[14] raised the ire of many people. After receiving 39 complaints regarding the ceremony's content, the OCOL carried out an investigation and determined that these complaints were founded.

While the ceremony itself included participants from both language groups, French was heard very little outside the strict protocol components. An excerpt of a poem by Quebec author François-Xavier Garneau was translated into English, and the only French-language song came at the very end of the ceremony. VANOC 2010 and Canadian Heritage (which contributed CA\$ 20M to the ceremony) highlighted the Francophone contribution to the ceremony and the addition of visual components representing the Francophonie. In the opinion of the OCOL (2011b, p. 17), "non-spoken performances by Francophone artists cannot compensate for the lack of participation by French-speaking Canadians expressing themselves in their language in song, speeches or in other ways." While recognizing that organizing this type of event is highly complex, the Commissioner:

> deplores the fact that the language clauses negotiated by Canadian Heritage in the contribution agreement were not more explicit regarding both the presence of French in the cultural part of the opening ceremony and the proper representation of official language communities. (OCOL, 2010, p. 43)

Maintaining the Standard Set in Vancouver

Notwithstanding the shortcomings previously mentioned, the Vancouver Games raised the bar in terms of public services in both official languages and co-operation with official language minority communities. In addition to bilingual services, the importance of working with official language minority communities and taking into account their needs in organizing major sport events have become inescapable. This co-operation is included in the *2015 Pan/Parapan American Games Multi-Party Agreement* for the event to be held in the Greater Toronto Area (2015 Pan Parapan American Games, 2009). This constitutes major progress and another linguistic legacy of the Vancouver Games.

Because national and international sport events provide a platform where our two official linguistic communities come together, and because they project Canada's image, these events must uphold the standard set by the Vancouver Games. To aid organizing committees and contributing federal institutions in preparation for upcoming major sport events in Canada, the OCOL offers information, ideas and advice in a practical guide that draws on the Vancouver Games experience (OCOL, 2011a). This section provides a brief outline of the planning steps described in the guide.

It is important for all agreements governing the Government of Canada's financial and logistical assistance to be clear and identify the anticipated results, performance indicators and accountability mechanisms so that signatories have a firm grasp of their official languages obligations.

The role of any federal institution that co-ordinates the Government of Canada's participation in an event is not only to guide the organizers but also to monitor preparations attentively and on an ongoing basis, as well as to take necessary corrective action. It is important for the federal funding agency to provide the organizing committee with advice and expertise on how to meet its language obligations. The federal partner and organizers must define their mutual expectations from the outset. The federal partner must also clearly define what such terms as 'sufficient,' 'adequate' mean from an operational perspective.

A team in charge of official languages, provided with sufficient resources and authority, must be put in place at the beginning of the process. It is also important to establish a language policy that is promoted by senior management as being vital to the event's success. Indeed, the personnel's work to promote Canada's official languages will not be fully effective unless management is firmly committed to presenting a bilingual event. To carry out the necessary follow-up, official languages must be a regular item on meeting agendas. This work will be considerably easier if the organizing committee includes a sufficient number of people who are aware of the cultural sensitivities and references of both language groups. It is also important to ensure that sufficient human and financial resources are available to meet all translation and interpretation needs, including the growing demand as the event approaches.

In terms of public services, an active offer of services must be made in both official languages through a bilingual greeting. Unilingual staff must be familiar with and follow the procedure for contacting a bilingual colleague whenever a member of the public communicates with them in the other official language. It is important to hire sufficient numbers of bilingual personnel to satisfy the demand at every public point of service, at all times. Moreover, planning must include contingency measures to handle unforeseen events and emergency situations.

Cooperating with official language minority communities and taking their needs into account when preparing events has become essential, as indicated above. This co-operation stems from the commitment made by the Government of Canada, as a financial and logistical contributor to the event, to promote their development and enhance their vitality. To ensure the committee takes community needs into account, it must establish a relationship based on dialogue and co-operation with the community. Creating an advisory committee and signing agreements with community representatives are some of the means by which this goal can be met. In any event, it is important to define the roles and expectations of each party at the outset.

To ensure that ceremonies properly reflect Canada's linguistic duality, it is critical that both official languages be used in the spoken and visual aspects of performances. Both languages must be heard beyond the official speeches. However, an adequate representation of linguistic duality in the ceremonies and cultural performances does not necessarily mean a precise half-and-half mix. Rather the balance depends on the situation. It is vital, however, that the clauses governing the government's contribution clearly set out its expectations of the organizers, and that the organizers ensure they are adequately reflecting the cultural richness and diversity of both official language communities.

Language requirements are minimum standards, and responsible organizations are free to exceed these requirements to better serve the two official language communities. Even when the provisions are clear, difficulties related to official languages are not always the result of bad faith. Forecasts may turn out to be in error, for instance. By handling official languages questions in a timely fashion and allocating sufficient resources, it will be possible to prevent situations that could tarnish an event's reputation. Accordingly, planning and follow-up are essential ingredients to ensure success.

Conclusion

Official languages are an important part of the Canadian sport system, just like equitable participation and ethics. In recent decades, major progress has been made in including specific language obligations in agreements governing the federal government's financial contributions to sport organizations and the organizing committees of major sport events. Today, whenever the Government of Canada grants its support to a sport organization or to a committee responsible for organizing a major sport event, it is just as crucial for that support to be paired with clear and comprehensive provisions and close monitoring of their implementation. Official languages success stories are rarely a product of chance. They require understanding, leadership, planning, execution and evaluation, a series of crucial steps illustrated in the OCOL's *Annual Report 2009–2010* as a virtuous circle (OCOL, 2010).

In recent decades, there has been a great improvement in the level of co-operation with official language minority communities and the degree to which their needs are considered. These efforts must be pursued and bolstered, both for major sport events and sport organizations that receive financial support from the Government of Canada. This would be in keeping with the spirit of the *Official Languages Act* and in the best interest of all Canadians.

Canada is showing increasing maturity in implementing federal language policy. However, upholding official languages principles must be a reflex, not an afterthought. Vigilance is required from every stakeholder in the Canadian sport system to avoid situations where one language becomes more official than the other and the fundamental objectives of Canada's language framework are not respected.

Notes

1. The author would like to acknowledge Marcel Fallu of the Office of the Commissioner of Official Languages for his work on this chapter.
2. In this chapter, the term 'international sport events' refers to international events held in Canada.
3. Some sections of this chapter rely on content from Commissioner Adam's (2007) chapter.
4. Note that in this document, the term 'sport organization' refers to the three types of organizations.
5. This section essentially presents the Office of the Commissioner of Official Languages' 2000 study as summarized in Adam (2007).
6. This section essentially presents the follow-up report as summarized in Adam (2007).
7. With this announcement, the Multi-Party Agreement signed by the various levels of government, the host cities (Vancouver and Whistler), and the Canadian Olympic and Paralympic Committees came fully into force.

8. Although VANOC 2010 was not a federal institution subject to the *Official Languages Act*, the Multi-Party Agreement and the contribution agreements signed with the Government of Canada contained specific language obligations. The Department of Canadian Heritage, which co-ordinated the Government of Canada's role in the event, was in charge of ensuring that VANOC fulfilled the language obligations contained in the Multi-Party Agreement governing the Games.

9. The Office of the Commissioner did not carry out systematic monitoring to check compliance. However, the Commissioner was present at the Olympic Winter Games from February 12 to 17, 2010, and other members of his staff also attended. The assessment was completed by means of exhaustive documentary searches and interviews conducted after the Games for the purpose of drafting the final report on the Games.

10. English and French are the official languages of both Canada and the Olympic Movement. However, Canada's official languages requirements applicable to VANOC went further than the Olympic requirements in terms of the presence of French. These language requirements applied just as fully to the 2010 Paralympic Winter Games, even though English is the only official language of the Paralympic Movement.

11. Following the study of the state of preparedness of 11 federal institutions to meet the increased demand for French services in connection with the Games, the Commissioner asked them to monitor their own performance during the Games and to report to it thereafter. Chapter 8 of the *Final Report on the Vancouver 2010 Olympic and Paralympic Winter Games* (which begins on p. 25) presents the information provided by the federal institutions (OCOL, 2011b).

12. Senate of Canada, Standing Committee on Official Languages. *Reflecting Canada's Linguistic Duality at the 2010 Olympic and Paralympic Winter Games: A Golden Opportunity.* 39th Parliament, 2nd Session. http://www.parl.gc.ca/Content/SEN/Committee/392/offi/rep/rep04jun08-e.htm.

13. The opening ceremony of the Olympic Winter Games was held on February 12, 2010 at BC Place Stadium. It is not to be confused with the opening ceremony of the Paralympic Winter Games.

14. The expression 'narrative component' refers to musical performances, choreography and speeches that went beyond strict protocol components, where French was very present as an official language of the Olympic Movement.

References

2015 Pan Parapan American Games. (2009). *2015 Pan Parapan American Games Multi Party Agreement.* Toronto, ON: Toronto 2015 Pan/ Parapan American Games Organizing Committee. Retrieved from http://www.toronto2015.org/assets/files/pdf/multipart-TO2015.pdf

Adam, D. (2007). Les langues officielles et la participation des athlètes francophones dans le système sportif canadien. In J.-P. Augustin & C. Dallaire (Eds.), *Jeux, sports et francophonie: L'exemple du Canada* (pp. 27–50). Talence, FR: Maison des Sciences de l'Homme d'Aquitaine.

Canada. (1982). *Canadian Charter of Rights and Freedoms.* Part I of the *Constitution Act, 1982.* Enacted as Schedule B to the *Canada Act 1982,* 1982, c. 11, (U.K.)

Canadian Heritage. (2002). *Multi-Party Agreement for the 2010 Olympic and Paralympic Winter Games.* Retrieved from http://www.canada2010.gc.ca/ role/gc/mpa/MPA-e.pdf

Canadian Heritage. (2007). *Proposal: Sport Canada 2008–12 Action plan for official languages.* Retrieved from http://www.pch.gc.ca/pgm/sc/pubs/ pda-ap/pda-ap-eng.pdf

Canadian Heritage. (2008). *Federal policy for hosting international sport events.* Ottawa, ON: Her Majesty the Queen in Right of Canada. Retrieved from http://www.pch.gc.ca/pgm/sc/pol/acc/2008/accueil-host_2008- eng.pdf

Commissioner of Official Languages. (1980). *Annual report 1979.* Ottawa, ON: Minister of Supply and Services Canada.

Commissioner of Official Languages. (1981). *Annual report 1980.* Ottawa, ON: Minister of Supply and Services Canada.

Commissioner of Official Languages. (1982). *Official languages audit. Fitness and Amateur Sport program, Secretary of State department.* Ottawa, ON: Minister of Supply and Services Canada.

Commissioner of Official Languages. (1985). *Annual report 1984.* Ottawa, ON: Minister of Supply and Services Canada.

Commissioner of Official Languages. (1989). *Annual report 1988.* Ottawa, ON: Minister of Supply and Services Canada.

Commissioner of Official Languages. (1999). *Annual report 1998.* Ottawa, ON: Minister of Public Works and Government Services Canada.

Commissioner of Official Languages. (2000). *Annual report 1999–2000.* Ottawa, ON: Minister of Public Works and Government Services Canada.

Federal-Provincial Advisory Committee. (1990). *Federal-Provincial Advisory Committee on equal linguistic access to services in sport.* Report submitted to assistant deputy ministers and interested deputy ministers. Ottawa, ON: Author.

Fraser, G. (2010, September 22). *Linguistic duality in Canada and narratives on language: For a different reading of history.* Speaking notes for a presentation at the monthly meeting of the Société d'histoire de Toronto and the Alliance française de Toronto. Retrieved from http://www.ocol-clo.gc.ca/html/speech_discours_22092010_e.php

Mills, D. (1998). *Sport in Canada: Everybody's business. Leadership, partnership and accountability.* Standing Committee on Canadian Heritage, Sub-Committee on the Study of Sport in Canada. Ottawa, ON: Government of Canada. Retrieved from http://www.parl.gc.ca/HousePublications/Publication.aspx?DocId=1031530&Mode=1&Parl=36&Ses=&Language=E

Minister's Task Force. (1992). *Sport: The way ahead. Minister's task force on federal sport policy.* Ottawa, ON: Minister of Supply and Services Canada.

Office of the Commissioner of Official Languages. (2000). *Official languages in the Canadian sports system*, vol. 1. Ottawa, Minister of Public Works and Government Services Canada. Retrieved from http://www.ocol-clo.gc.ca/docs/e/sport1_e.pdf

Office of the Commissioner of Official Languages. (2003). *Official languages in the Canadian sport system: Follow-up.* Ottawa, ON: Minister of Public Works and Government Services Canada. Retrieved from http://www.ocol-clo.gc.ca/docs/e/SportEng.pdf

Office of the Commissioner of Official Languages. (2008). *Raising our game for Vancouver 2010: Towards a Canadian model of linguistic duality in international sport.* Ottawa, ON: Minister of Public Works and Government Services Canada. Retrieved from http://www.ocol-clo.gc.ca/docs/e/vanoc_covan_e.pdf

Office of the Commissioner of Official Languages. (2009). *Raising our game for Vancouver 2010: Towards a Canadian model of linguistic duality in international sport—Follow-up report.* Ottawa, ON: Minister of Public Works and Government Services Canada. Retrieved from http://www.ocol-clo.gc.ca/docs/e/vanoc_covan_2009_e.pdf

Office of the Commissioner of Official Languages. (2010). *Annual report 2009–2010: Beyond obligations, Volume II.* Ottawa, ON: Minister of Public Works and Government Services Canada.

Office of the Commissioner of Official Languages. (2011a). *Organizing a major sporting event in Canada: A practical guide to promoting official languages.* Ottawa, ON: Minister of Public Works and Government Services Canada. Retrieved from http://www.ocol-clo.gc.ca/docs/e/guide_eng.pdf

Office of the Commissioner of Official Languages. (2011b). *Raising our game for Vancouver 2010: Final report on the Vancouver 2010 Olympic and Paralympic Winter Games.* Ottawa, ON: Minister of Public Works and Government Services Canada. Retrieved from http://www.ocol-clo.gc.ca/docs/e/stu_etu_games_jeux_e_02_2011.pdf

Parliament of Canada. (2003). *Bill C-12. An Act to promote physical activity and sport* (S.C. 2003, c. 2). Retrieved from http://www.parl.gc.ca/Content/LOP/LegislativeSummaries/37/2/c12-e.pdf

Sport Canada. (2002). *The Canadian sport policy.* Ottawa, ON: Department of Canadian Heritage. Retrieved from http://www.pch.gc.ca/pgm/sc/pol/pcs-csp/2003/polsport-eng.pdf

Sport Canada. (2012). *Canadian sport policy 2012.* Ottawa, ON: Department of Canadian Heritage. Retrieved from http://sirc.ca/CSPRenewal/documents/CSP2012_EN_LR.pdf

Stubbs, D. (1998, February 7). 'Embarassing' start for COA: Canadian officials virtually ignore French-speaking athletes during team reception. *The Montreal Gazette,* p. D1.

Svoboda, M., & Donnelly, P. (2006). *Linguistic barriers to access to high performance sport—study, 2005.* Toronto, ON: TNS Canadian Facts Social Policy Research. Retrieved from http://www.pch.gc.ca/pgm/sc/pubs/obstacles_linguistiques-linguistic_barriers/obstacles_linguistiques-linguistic_barriers-eng.pdf

CHAPTER XIII

Sport and Social Inclusion

Wendy Frisby and Pamela Ponic,
University of British Columbia

As the quotation below suggests, sport policy makers and researchers have been grappling with what social inclusion means and how to best achieve it:

> Inclusionary and exclusionary mechanisms that influence sport participation and positions of leadership in sport form a complex constellation of interacting factors and dimensions. Changes in the facilitation and organization of sport can enhance an inclusive sport practice, which might also foster social inclusion in broader society. (Elling & Claringbould, 2005, p. 498)

There is also growing recognition that significant portions of the population do not have basic services, opportunities and democratic participation in all spheres of life. We define social inclusion as the process of creating just and equitable systems that facilitate people's choices and opportunities to engage (or not) in a wide range of social and democratic activities, including sport and recreation (Ponic, 2007). While some sport organizations refer to 'inclusion,' we use the term 'social inclusion' to draw attention to the diversity of people in Canada and the broader structures requiring change. As we explain later in this chapter, we think this is important because inclusion might otherwise be interpreted simply as 'opening the doors' or 'providing access' to the existing sport system. Rather, we argue that it is necessary to work collaboratively with those who are currently outside the system to make fundamental changes to sport policies and practices so that more people can benefit from participation in a positive sport environment.

Social inclusion is a highly complex policy arena that requires a number of considerations. For example, it raises questions about what social inclusion means for a variety of people including children living in poverty and their parents, girls and women who participate less in sport than boys and men, persons with disabilities, Aboriginal peoples, Canadian newcomers and racialized minorities, people with disabilities, people with different sexual orientations and the growing number of Canadians who do not participate in sport and physical activity enough to derive health benefits. It also poses implications for sport organizers and policy makers who are expected more than ever before to make sport accessible to historically excluded groups, but have few resources and guidelines on how to do so.

The well-intentioned goal of social inclusion is to create improved quality of life for all persons, regardless of their situations and positions in society. However, "this requires different ideological, political and strategic policy formulations than currently exist" (Pegg & Compton, 2004, p. 5). Such change will be a challenge in a geographically and culturally diverse country like Canada, which has a fragmented sport delivery system (Sport Matters and Public Policy Forum, 2004). In particular, social inclusion cannot be accomplished only by those with power in the sport system in a top-down fashion. Rather, as we will show, it is a process that requires careful negotiation and a fundamental shift in the hierarchical power relations that typically characterize sport policy development.

The purpose of this chapter is to provide an overview of a number of issues that should be taken into account when considering if and how sport in Canada can become more inclusive. We begin by discussing how social inclusion has been defined over time. We then introduce some of the contradictions associated with the concept, along with a discussion of the mechanisms of social exclusion that policies seek to redress. Along the way, we provide examples of how Canadian sport organizations are implementing social inclusion policies. At the end of the chapter, we recommend some promising practices for promoting social inclusion as a starting point for re-envisioning new possibilities for Canadian sport.

History and Definitions of Social Inclusion

Historically, the concept of social inclusion, which originally developed in Europe, had a narrow policy focus on including people in economic activities (Ontario Women's Health Network, 2009). This narrow interpretation has been used to justify coercive welfare-to-work policies to reduce people's dependence on government for social assistance. Researchers have argued that this policy has adversely affected the well-being of some groups in particular, such as single parents who are sometimes forced to work in jobs that do not earn enough to cover the child care expenses incurred when re-entering the workforce (Gurstein, Pulkingham, & Vilches, 2011). Mitchell and Shillington (2005) pointed out that reducing social inclusion policy to a focus on employability ignores the value of unpaid work done in the home and community and obscures inequalities based on gender, class and race in the labour force and other spheres of life. In addition, those who are unable to participate in the workplace for a number of reasons are cast as being deficient in skills and work ethic, stereotypes that work against a sense of belonging, well-being and social inclusion (Reid, 2004). In this way, public policy itself can exclude people in material and other ways, as suggested by Shakir (2005, p. 286) when she asked:

> whether inclusion ought to be a goal of public policy or whether material conditions of contemporary exclusion of some groups in society may in fact be a product of existing public policy, all of which would at least appropriately place the spotlight on public policy as a contested space.

In Canada, the concept evolved more broadly and was initially linked to the disability movement and notions of social accommodation that support public policies attempting to reduce economic, social and cultural disparities. For Richmond and Saloojee (2005, p. 3), "to be included across the different levels of well-being (physical, economic, human, social and political) requires sufficient resources and rights and capacity to participate within the environments and structures of the society in which one lives." Young (2000) argued that social inclusion is fundamentally a social justice issue that is tied to equity, fairness and respect for others. For Donnelly and Coakley (2002), it is a human rights issue that involves the validation and recognition of the diversity of all people's day-to-day experiences and situations.

Since social inclusion is complex, it can mean different things to different people. Ponic and Frisby (2010) found that it had multiple meanings for women living in poverty who were involved in a health promotion project designed to increase their participation in community recreation. The women reported that feelings of acceptance, recognition, belonging, safety and trust were central to their social inclusion in community activities. They also pointed to the importance of relationships based on respect and support, and the crucial role that community organizations with caring staff can play in facilitating their involvement. The women confirmed that a citizen engagement or community development approach that facilitated their input into policy and program development supported their feelings of social inclusion and resulted in activities that better met their needs and interests. The authors concluded that the meanings women on low income associated with social inclusion spanned their own feelings, their relationships with others, their desire to be involved in decision making and their interactions with community organizations. This illustrates the complexities of the concept, yet at the same time provides some helpful guidance to sport and recreation organizers about the dimensions that need to be considered in order to facilitate it.

In addition to the multiple layers of social inclusion, meanings of the concept are not static or linear. The women living in poverty in Ponic's (2007) study reported incidences of feeling both included and excluded at the same time, for example when they were invited to a meeting but then were not listened to during that same meeting. As Elling and Claringbould (2005, p. 501) explained, "because people have multiple social identities, they might often simultaneously experience inclusion and exclusion according to specific social power relations." This contradiction illustrates the complexity of facilitating social inclusion and the importance of paying attention to power imbalances.

Social inclusion is most often conceptualized as being "both a process (i.e., something that is undergoing constant development and is never quite finished) and an outcome (i.e., something that has clearly defined results)" (Sands, 2006, p. 4). That is, social inclusion is something that needs to be planned for and it is also something that can be evaluated. This is an important distinction because as Parnes

(2007) has argued, although numerous benefits like increased social interaction, skill development, and improved health are associated with social inclusion, it is not always clear if these benefits are being actualized in the same ways by all people. According to Frisby (2011), talking directly to excluded groups to determine the conditions under which they would feel included and involving them in determining the criteria used to evaluate success is crucial when striving to develop inclusive communities.

The terms inclusion and social inclusion gained prominence in sport and recreation in the late 1990s (Pegg & Compton, 2004) and is now frequently used. For example, the *Canadian Sport Policy* (2002), which grew out of a consultation process across the country, paid specific attention to "issues of inclusion and equity" (Sport Canada, 2002, p. 7). Enhanced participation, which aims for a "significantly higher proportion of Canadians from all segments of society involved in quality sport activities at all levels and in all forms of participation," is an explicit goal of the *Canadian Sport Policy* (Sport Canada, 2002, p. 16). To achieve this goal, the federal government acknowledges that new initiatives, programs, partnerships and resources must be directed at under-represented groups to reduce barriers, recruit new participants, and reduce drop-out rates (Sport Canada, 2002). Yet, as discussed in other chapters in this book, federal sport policies have been developed for Aboriginal people, girls and women and people with disabilities, but it is not clear whether these policies have had the intended impact. In addition, policies and concrete actions related to other under-represented groups such as the growing number of immigrants, families living on low incomes, LGBT[1] individuals, adults and seniors are lacking. This may be because, in part, the consultation process for the *Canadian Sport Policy* was conducted more with those currently inside the sport system (e.g., athletes, coaches, parents, officials, volunteers and various partners) than those outside of it.

Inclusion is also one of the key policy principles in the new *Canadian Sport Policy* (2012) and is described as occurring when "sport programs are accessible and equitable and reflect the full breadth of interests, motivations, objectives, and the diversity of Canadian society" (Sport Canada, 2012, p. 2). Yet given that sport excellence is also a key goal, one wonders how inclusion can be achieved over the long-term when individuals continue to be cut from teams as they move up the competitive sport ladder? Recreational sport offered at the local level offers an alternative, but program costs are a deterrent for those living on low income. While identifying inclusion as a policy principle is an important first step, much more needs to be done by all levels of government and other organizations working together to more fully achieve it. One such organization is True Sport, a Canadian non-profit organization that is designed to offset the commercialized and overly competitive forms of sport that have arisen in recent decades:

> True Sport is a national movement designed to help sport live up to its full potential as a public asset in Canada. Over 1,400 groups have joined the "True Sport Movement" which is based on values of excellence, fairness, fun and inclusion. (Canadian Centre for Ethics in Sport, 2008, p. 10)

In another example, the Vancouver Organizing Committee for the 2010 Olympic and Paralympic Winter Games Organizing Committee (known as VANOC 2010) developed the following performance objective related to social inclusion:

> Being socially inclusive and responsible means that VANOC considers the needs and interests of its workforce, sponsors and contractors, athletes and members of the Olympic and Paralympic families, as well as our government, First Nations and corporate partners. It also means that we consider the needs and interests of external stakeholders, including communities and non-government organizations (NGOs) affected by our activities. We are particularly aware of the possible impact of our activities on socially or economically disadvantaged groups that traditionally do not benefit from mega-events such as the Olympic Games. VANOC seeks input on our social inclusion programs and activities from our partners and a wide range of stakeholders. When appropriate or possible, we include groups affected by our activities in our decision-making processes. We also adhere to recognized global standards for corporate social responsibility. (Vancouver 2010, 2009, p. 1)

While VANOC 2010 may have gone further in promoting social inclusion than previous Olympic Games, for example by providing some Aboriginal youth with jobs and skills training, the high cost of Olympic Winter Games' tickets meant that only those who could afford them could attend the actual events. Similarly, those working in inflexible, low-paying jobs would not have been able to take time off in order to volunteer. It is also not clear how many people actually benefitted from VANOC 2010's social inclusion efforts and whether benefits were sustained following the Games. While many citizens may have felt temporarily included in the sense of community generated as the Olympic torch run took place across the country or when Canadian athletes won medals, many others were largely excluded from this international sport event.

At a local level, the City of Vancouver developed a Sport for Life Strategy (Vancouver City Council and Vancouver Park Board, 2008, p. 7) with an objective to "build an inclusive sport community where all participants have access to welcoming, safe environments to strive for their desired goals in sport (whether it be for recreation, for self-development, or for excellence)." An overall outcome of the strategy was to "recognise the value sport has in the lives of all Vancouver residents, with the objectives of inclusion of age, gender, ability and ethnicity" (Vancouver City Council and Vancouver Park Board, 2008, p. 7). Some of the challenges to achieving these inclusion objectives and outcomes were identified in their strategic plan. These included: i) the limited interaction and co-ordination among sport organizations, ii) the wide social inequities that exist across the city, iii) inconsistent sport program delivery, and iv) sport programming that is focused on those who are relatively young and already fit (Vancouver City Council and Vancouver Park Board, 2008, p. 12). It is by explicitly identifying challenges like this that steps can be taken for overcoming them.

As you can see, the notion of social inclusion has developed over many years and in different policy contexts. More recently, it is part of a shift towards facilitating broader participation in sport through the increased involvement of historically excluded groups. Social inclusion requires careful consideration if it is to be developed in ways that redress rather than re-create experiences of social exclusion. By considering both the mechanisms that promote social inclusion and exclusion, the possibilities for participation in sport can be broadened so that more Canadians can reap the benefits of an improved and more equitable sport system.

Reasons for Promoting Social Inclusion in Sport

There are many reasons for the rise in social inclusion policies in government and in sport including the learning of skills that contribute to quality of life such as "intra-personal and interpersonal communication, determination, perseverance, confidence, leadership, citizenship, goal-orientation, motivation, and personal satisfaction" (Donnelly & Coakley, 2002, p. 5).

Pegg and Compton (2004) concurred that there is well-documented evidence that inclusive sport and recreation opportunities can contribute to physiological, psychological and social well-being, especially when adequate resources are allocated and when citizens are involved in planning and decision making. Donnelly and Coakley (2002) contended that the benefits are particularly important for children because physical recreation is crucial to their physical, social, motor and emotional development. We add that while most sport inclusion efforts are aimed at children, the benefits are also crucial to youth, adults and seniors especially given the aging of the Canadian population and rising health care costs associated with inactive lifestyles.

Pegg and Compton (2004) argued that neighbourhoods and communities benefit from the learning that occurs through the acceptance of individuals who may differ from mainstream society in their beliefs, backgrounds, customs and abilities. To illustrate this, Canadian Heritage research has shown that participation or volunteering in sport and recreation is a common way that new Canadians get involved in community life (Sport Matters and Public Policy Forum, 2004). This can create spaces for people to become more independent, to learn new skills, and to learn from one another, especially when a community development approach is used that builds sustainable social connections and community partnerships for sharing resources, skills and knowledge (Frisby, Reid, & Ponic, 2007; Vail, 2007). Fostering social interactions between diverse groups of people can also help to dispel myths and assumptions that often result in our fear of differences, rather than a respect for difference. An example of this is the Special Olympics, which has been criticized for segregating persons with intellectual disabilities, as this can be viewed as a form of social exclusion (Storey, 2004). Others argue that segregation can, at times, be a form of inclusion because it does not assimilate people into an existing structure that does not work for them. There is evidence that events like the Special Olympics have raised awareness about the capabilities of persons with disabilities to counter harmful prejudices and stereotypes (Parnes, 2007). Raising awareness can lead to policy changes, such as when the National Deinstitutionalization Initiative in Canada brought about significant changes in how persons with developmental impairments were housed and treated (Hutchison & McGill, 1998). Religious persecution, colonization, homophobia, racism, poverty, ageism and gender inequality are just some of the other areas that can begin to be addressed through effective sport and recreation inclusion policies (Tirone, 2004). What is essential is that a wide range of participation options be made available to accommodate the diverse and shifting interests of people, and this can best be determined by engaging with those outside the sport system. In addition, as Collins (2003) pointed out, sport can rarely yield economic, environmental, health, safety or social benefits acting alone—to be effective, it needs to partner with those promoting other types of social policies.

Mechanisms of Social Exclusion

According to the Canadian Centre for Ethics in Sport (2008, p. 13), "there is a growing gap between the positive benefits Canadians believe sport can provide for their children and their communities and what they are actually experiencing." When people do not have the opportunity for full participation in the economic and social activities of society, they are considered to be excluded (Guildford, 2000). For Labonte (2004), the concept of social exclusion is valuable because it defines disadvantage as an outcome of broader political structures, global capitalism, and social processes rather than as an individual or group trait that make people responsible for their own misfortunes or lack of opportunities.

Despite the rise of 'sport for all policies,' sport in its current form is by nature exclusionary, especially as participants move up the competitive pyramid (Collins, 2003; Donnelly & Coakley, 2002). The skills needed to be successful in sport are not necessarily innate, they may have more to do with the opportunities, encouragement and support available to certain segments of the populations over others. In a True Sport report (Canadian Centre for Ethics in Sport, 2008), the authors acknowledged that sport can play a role in creating and strengthening social ties, connecting people across geographic and ethno-cultural boundaries, and linking disadvantaged people to organizations and services. At the same time, they reported Canadians are concerned about the growing number of people who are excluded from sport, which is partly due to the uneven distribution of resources and facilities, the way sport has become highly formalized and the costs associated with participation (Canadian Centre for Ethics in Sport, 2008). The True Sport report listed a number of issues that Canadians are concerned about including: an over-emphasis on winning, harassment, intolerance, racism and a lack of fair play—all of which foster social exclusion. Donnelly and Coakley (2002) added that sport participants can be abused, bullied or dominated in ways that make them feel alienated, isolated and humiliated. This illustrates that it is important to consider that for some, the decision to avoid participation is not only a matter of individual choice, it is also about how elite sport-based ideologies, tolerance for abuse, and discrimination within the sport culture encourage people to stay away. To illustrate this point further, Allison and Hibbler (2004) found that negative attitudes and stereotypes held by some local recreation management and staff created barriers to serving ethnic minority populations in American cities. Similarly, a study by the Ontario Council for Agencies Serving Immigrants (2006) confirmed that a lack of understanding of the cultural, economic and social circumstances of some communities affect enrolment and ongoing participation in sport and recreation.

Social exclusion is also a function of cultural norms that define the legitimate bodies in sport. For example, Vertinsky, Jette, and Hoffman (2009) documented how females were not allowed to participate in the first Olympic Games and have since had to fight for inclusion in many sports in which only men have traditionally participated. This was because women's bodies were deemed to be too frail and there were fears about injury to their reproductive organs. The lawsuit that female ski jumpers unsuccessfully launched to be included in the 2010 Olympic Winter Games provides a recent example, because some high ranking sport officials used this same rationale along with other arguments to justify the women's exclusion from competition (Vertinsky et al., 2009). It was because of the attention drawn to this issue that women's ski jumping will be included in the 2014 Olympic Winter Games in Sochi, Russia.

Studies in Europe have demonstrated that boys and men, people with higher levels of income and education, ethnic majority groups, heterosexuals and people without physical or mental disabilities are overrepresented in both the participation and leadership of sport (Elling & Claringbould, 2005), and similar patterns exist in other countries around the world. In part, this can be explained by patterns of sport socialization and socio-economic privilege where some youth and adults are not offered similar activities within and outside of the school system and receive differential encouragement from family members, peers, teachers and coaches (Coakley & Donnelly, 2001). Other barriers that limit opportunities that DePauw and Gavron (2005) found in the area of disability sport included a lack of early sport experiences, limited training, a lack of understanding on how to include persons with disabilities in sport and limited access to information, social support and resources.

Discriminatory practices can also lead to social exclusion, for example when girls' athletic teams receive fewer resources than boys' teams or when minority ethnic groups are expected to figure out and fit into the physical cultural practices in their new home country with little or no support or encouragement. Racist, sexist and homophobic comments made on and off the playing field also discourage participation and are rarely adequately addressed by sport leaders (Doherty & Taylor, 2007; King, 2008).

The rise of neo-liberalism in Western governments represents another exclusionary mechanism, as decision making and assessments of program success are increasingly tied to a business- or market-oriented model rather than to social policy (Brodie, 2005). As an example, one of the municipal recreation departments that we and women on low income worked with decided to charge us for using a small, rarely used space for meetings. If the women had not organized and argued that they were essentially working for the municipality for free to increase participation by low income citizens, the municipality may have thought it was making an economically prudent decision by charging a fee even though this would have excluded a group that is least likely to participate in community recreation.

Exclusionary practices in sport are created and re-created by a number of structural mechanisms such as cultural norms, discriminatory practices and economically-driven policies. The ideals of social inclusion are an appealing antidote to such practices for sport organizers and policy makers who are invested in fostering mass participation and more equitable opportunities for involvement.

However, as we discussed earlier, social inclusion is a complex process and requires more than simply 'opening the doors' to everyone. There are a number of challenges and contradictions associated with facilitating it that need to be taken into account to avoid resorting to simplistic solutions that are ineffective and may inadvertently perpetuate social exclusion.

Contradictions with Social Inclusion

There is not always consensus about what the purpose of social inclusion should be, which is due to a number of contradictions associated with the term's use. One of these contradictions has already been discussed, that is, social inclusion and exclusion are not static or polar opposites because they can exist at the same time, shift over time, and from person to person. We agree with Elling and Claringbould (2005, p. 499) that "inclusionary and exclusionary mechanisms are dynamic, often paradoxical and continuously challenged." Three other contradictions that will be discussed here are the following: i) social inclusion can promote assimilation rather than respecting differences, ii) social inclusion is assumed to be beneficial when it may not always be, and iii) it is often those who are already included in sport who are deciding how to include those who are not.

The policy focus in Canadian sport has been on 'access' or 'opening the doors' rather than on social inclusion and sport system change (Harvey, 2001). The problem with this approach is that sport policies and practices that have excluded people in the first place are left unexamined and unchallenged (Labonte, 2004). This can leave responsibility for social inclusion to those who have been historically excluded and require them to figure out how to include themselves into a system that does not necessarily meet their needs. Another danger of 'open the doors' practices and policies is that they promote the assimilation of people, such as Aboriginal people, into the existing sport system instead of creating spaces for different identities and cultures to participate in sport in traditional and non-traditional ways (Paraschak, 2007). Shakir (2005) concluded that social inclusion policy in Canada is flawed because notions of commonality underpin it, and 'difference' is seen as being part of the problem. As King (2008, p. 424) aptly pointed out, sport should reject normalizing processes that assume that excluded groups must become "just like everyone else."

In terms of the second contradiction, Shakir (2005) contended that social inclusion policy has certain assumptions tied to it, for example, that it is 'good' to be included and 'bad' not to be. However, if in fact the sport system is viewed as being flawed in various ways by non-participants, it is possible that exclusion may actually be beneficial to them because they are avoiding the numerous problems with sport discussed earlier in this chapter (Muller, van Zoonenand, & de Roode, 2008). This underscores why Shakir (2005) and others are critical of formulations that position inclusion/exclusion in simplistic and oppositional terms—because this type of thinking draws attention away from the root causes of social inequalities. This ignores how complex social problems such as structural and economic barriers, poverty, discrimination and legal and institutional policies contribute to social exclusion, which imply it is excluded individuals rather than sport and other types of organizations that need to change. Frisby et al. (2007) provided an example of this when they argued that while offering sport programs for free or low cost may encourage more people to participate, it does not address the conditions that lead to a significant portion of the Canadian population living in impoverished conditions in the first place. Arguably, sport organizers would need to work with other social service providers and governments to tackle the poverty issue if a more inclusive society is the ultimate goal (Collins, 2003). However, shifting sport policy towards the promotion of social inclusion more broadly will be difficult because, as Harvey (2001) noted, sport is bounded by its own legitimizing principles, political cultures and forms of governance that have traditionally had a narrow elite competitive sport orientation.

The final contradiction raises the question: Who should be including whom in sport? The traditional approach to sport management assumes that sport professionals know how to include 'others' based on little or no consultation with those who may be very different from themselves (Frisby, Reid, Millar, & Hoeber, 2005). Mitchell and Shillington (2005) reminded us that the process of policy making itself can promote social exclusion if citizens experience a lack of voice in issues that directly affect them. Ironically, it is this top-down, 'expert'-driven approach that reinforces processes of social exclusion by not giving people a say in how they want to be included or in what types of sport opportunities they would like to participate in (Donnelly & Coakley, 2002). In addition, sport organizers and policy makers are often working in neo-liberal environments that prioritize a business-oriented approach that works against social inclusion even when they have policies that appear to promote it. Elling and Claringbould (2005) provided a good illustration of this when they showed how sport organizations can appear to be promoting inclusion when they are really more interested in functional motives such as increasing memberships to raise revenues. The problem with this approach is it is unlikely that sport organizations will be able to retain newly recruited members unless fundamental changes are made to make membership more attractive to the needs of different individuals and groups. The authors suggested that the likelihood for meaningful change is enhanced when sport organizers and policy makers use moral or ethical guidelines as a basis for promoting social inclusion. These include thinking in terms of equal rights (e.g., to sport participation and leadership), equal value (e.g., of different abilities and cultural practices) and equal treatment (e.g., a lack of discrimination). For example, municipal recreation policy makers in Canada could use moral guidelines in their decisions about resource distributions by allocating separate swimming times for Muslim women so they can participate in ways that are culturally appropriate and comfortable to them, which acknowledges that the current approach to public swimming is often discriminatory. Under current neo-liberal thinking and practices, however, this option would only be considered if there were sufficient numbers of swimmers paying fees to justify the costs involved, and therefore the policy would remain exclusionary.

Promising Strategies and Policies for Promoting Social Inclusion

Labonte (2004, p. 117) posed a provocative question related to the strategies needed to promote social inclusion when he asked, "How does one go about including individuals and groups in a set of structured social relationships responsible for excluding them in the first place?" There are now a number of different frameworks that offer promising strategies for promoting social inclusion to redress historically entrenched patterns of exclusion. Drawing upon such tools and frameworks can be helpful for promoting debate, exploration and collective leadership for generating new approaches. Some of these key principles underpinning inclusion frameworks will be briefly reviewed here, but as Ponic (2007) argued, the key is for staff and those desiring to get involved to work together because there is no one approach that will work in every situation. Shakir (2005, p. 210) concurred when she argued that because of the diversity of Canadian society, any static notion of inclusion will inevitably result in assimilation or ongoing social exclusion.

The OCASI (2006) developed and pilot-tested one of the most comprehensive sport and recreation inclusion models we have seen. It was developed after conducting a literature review and obtaining input from immigrant and refugee youth as well as service providers. Their report identified a long list of helpful recommendations for inclusive sport and recreation programs including:

> ... combining educational with sport and recreation activities; introducing sport and recreation activities that immigrant and refugee youth found familiar and popular due to a prevalence in their countries of origin, and the use of these as vehicles to build confidence to learn new sports and recreation activities; boosting parental involvement; developing youth leadership, especially in the areas of officiating and coaching; building collaborative relationships with other service providers; acquiring affordable and accessible space; developing supportive internal organizational structures and top management support; funding and developing strategies for working with funding partners; mobilizing immigrant and minority communities; engaging diverse communities in the youth recruitment activity; training diverse community coaches and people who are skilled in sports; operating under an anti-oppression and anti-racism framework; acquiring transportation for youth; and, where possible, acquiring sportswear for youth. (OCASI, 2006, p. 8)

As indicated in the OCASI recommendations (2006), a starting point in most inclusion frameworks is to engage directly with socially excluded groups to surface the issues requiring attention. This involves discussing how existing policies and practices intersect with people's social and economic circumstances to produce undesirable consequences (Shookner, 2002). Participatory and action forms of research will assist in this regard by generating new knowledge about experiences of social inclusion/exclusion and effective policies and community engagement strategies (Ontario Women's Health Network,

2009). The Working Together Project (2008) on public libraries used a participatory research approach and found that many traditional library policies, such as levying fines for overdue books, worked against the goal of making libraries more accessible. It was by talking directly to non-users in surrounding neighbourhoods that barriers to library use and ideas for overcoming them were identified. Frisby and Fenton's (1998) *Leisure Access Workbook* provided examples of questions that can be adapted or discussed when engaging with socially excluded groups in a recreation or local sport context. Similarly, Ponic (2007) noted in her *Inclusion Tool* that ongoing dialogue is needed from initial brainstorming, to issue identification, through implementation, action and evaluation. It is by working through citizen engagement or community development approaches that communication and trust can be fostered to build relationships that encourage mutual learning and action (Taylor & Frisby, 2010). This requires different approaches to traditional sport program development where staff, management, or sport policy makers talk amongst one another, develop and deliver programs that are convenient for their organization, and then expect people to show up. The problem with this approach is that if people do not attend in sufficient numbers, it reinforces assumptions that they are not interested, which turns attention away from the problems with institutional policies and program delivery methods that may be excluding them.

Developing partnerships amongst community organizations is another key component of social inclusion models and they are often crucial in reaching out to excluded groups to address the issues (Vail, 2007). Important considerations in making partnerships effective in promoting social inclusion include determining the purpose of the partnership, identifying potential partners, determining what the nature of the partnership will be, building partner relations and evaluating the partnership (Working Together Project, 2008). Sport Programs in Inner City neighbourhoods (SPIN) is a unique program in the City of Winnipeg that has partnerships with a number of government agencies and community groups. SPIN targets children between the ages of six and 14 to promote basic skill development, team work, leadership and fair play in a non-competitive environment. This program also tackles some of the barriers facing inner city youth by providing transportation, financial assistance, equipment, leadership and volunteer support which is done in conjunction with program partners.

Engaging community members in sport program planning and policy development is another key dimension of social inclusion frameworks. This requires staff to spend more time working with socially excluded groups and community partners as learners and facilitators rather than acting as experts who should make decisions for them (Working Together Project, 2008). This, in turn, necessitates a paradigm shift in how staff are trained because, as Allison and Hibbler (2004, p. 264) argued, many professionals in our field are "socialized into a seemingly mono-cultural society with social institutions that are predominantly designed to meet the needs of the dominant population." This results in organizations becoming structured around the often hidden but powerful systems that have been set in place by those in power. It is under these conditions that the voices of others are minimized, stigmatized or silenced (Young, 1990). Changing this dynamic requires two-way communication and sensitivity to, and an appreciation of, differences in culture, identities, literacy, language and preferred ways of participating in sport. For example, Frisby (2011) and her colleagues organized a two-day workshop that brought recent immigrant Chinese women together with a range of sport and recreation policy makers and community service providers to discuss how to make policy and programming more culturally inclusive. The women themselves provided over 15 suggestions for changes that would make it easier and more appealing for them and their families to participate, including the production of marketing materials in Mandarin and Cantonese, tours of facilities and having the opportunity to 'sample' some of the programs offered with instructors who can speak their languages.

Making an organizational commitment to change is often recommended, which means that social inclusion policy goals are built directly into planning, policy and sport program design. According to Sands (2006), this requires having a clear vision and obtaining buy-in from decision makers, staff, users and non-users. It also requires building responsibility for social inclusion into job descriptions, the reallocation of resources, and redesigning appropriate reporting and decision-making structures. One of the most important ways that governments and sport organizations can make a commitment is by developing and implementing social inclusion policies (Collins, 2003; Everybody Active, 2009). Policies are a direct reflection of a sport organization's visions and values and provide ongoing guidance to staff, volunteers and the public, even in times of rapid turnover and change. When developed collectively and taken seriously, policies can guide decision making, the reallocation of resources and the development of new approaches to program delivery. A key to effective social inclusion policies is that they should serve as organic guiding principles and be open to improvement, rather than being rigid and carved-in-stone (Working Together Project, 2008). This will provide space for sport organizers and potential participants to work together to accommodate the complexities of the many different situations and circumstances encountered to create more inclusive and adaptable sport cultures.

Ongoing evaluation that involves the celebration of successes and the identification of areas for improvement is another critical consideration. New approaches to evaluation and accountability that encourage innovation, creative thinking and experimentation are tied to social inclusion goals (Sport Matters and Public Policy Forum, 2004). The OCASI (2006) project provided a good example of this that was in keeping with their youth leadership development goals, when youth interviewed staff as part of an evaluation process and helped decide what the end-of-program celebration would be. The key is to use a participatory approach to evaluation that takes both the process (i.e., how are we doing so far) and outcomes (i.e., what did we accomplish) in mind. Conducting evaluations is often crucial to obtaining ongoing support for sport inclusion initiatives and to share the lessons learned with other communities. While process and outcomes can be difficult to measure, it is often a combination of qualitative data (e.g., testimonials from participants) and quantitative data (e.g., the number of new community partnerships created) that help inform ongoing improvements.

Conclusion

As Shakir (2004) argued, social inclusion is not about bringing outsiders into the existing mainstream culture, it is about creating a new and negotiated culture together. A key question that remains is how we re-imagine the Canadian sport system, not by thinking in terms of commonalities that will always exclude some, but instead accepting the diversity amongst us which is based on different historical relations of power and privilege and the right to contest the status quo. As an Australian Public Service Commission document entitled *Tackling Wicked Problems: A Public Policy Perspective* (2007) warned, there is a whole realm of public policy problems that cannot be successfully tackled by traditional narrow approaches. This is because problems like social exclusion are highly complex—there are multiple causes, it is usually interconnected with other social issues, it can rarely be solved by any one organization and there is usually no one clear solution. They contended that innovative and flexible approaches that devolve government to encourage more bottom-up approaches, information sharing and working across organizational boundaries are critical to success. This requires a shift in government–citizen relations where more emphasis is placed on providing citizens with information, more consultation on policy-making and program design, and more active citizen engagement where policy options are proposed through improved two-way dialogue.

Federal, provincial, and local governments in Canada have a key leadership role to play in fostering social inclusion in sport. While this brief summary just 'scratches the surface' in terms of promising social inclusion practices, engaging socially excluded groups to surface the issues requiring attention and to obtain input into program and policy development is very much in keeping with the definition and goals of social inclusion. Developing new partnerships, making an organizational commitment to change, and ongoing evaluation are other key strategies. Reading more about social inclusion tools and frameworks and experimenting with them will help sport organizers and policy makers work collaboratively with participants and non-participants to create more inclusive sport and recreation opportunities across the country. This brief review provides support for Shakir's (2005) contention that having good intentions alone is not enough. Rather, having a long-term focus with a flexible implementation plan is important because 'static quick fixes' are unlikely to be effective in tackling the 'wicked problem' of social exclusion in sport.

Note

1. LGBT stands for Lesbian, Gay, Bisexual, and Transgendered persons.

References

Allison, M.T., & Hibbler, D.K. (2004). Organizational barriers to inclusion: Perspectives from the recreation professional. *Leisure Sciences, 26,* 261–280.

Australian Public Service Commission. (2007). Tackling wicked problems: A public policy perspective. Sydney, AUS: Government of Australia. Retrieved from http://www.apsc.gov.au/publications07/wicked problems.htm

Brodie, J. (2005). The great undoing: State formation, gender politics, and social policy in Canada. In B.A. Crow & L. Gotell (Eds.) *Open Boundaries: A Canadian women's studies reader* (pp. 87–96). Toronto, ON: Prentice Hall.

Canadian Centre for Ethics in Sport. (2008). *What sport can do: The True Sport report.* Ottawa, ON: True Sport. Retrieved from http://www.truesport pur.ca/files/tsreport/TS_report_EN_webdownload.pdf

Coakley, J., & Donnelly, P. (2001). *Inside sports.* London: Routledge.

Collins, M.F. (2003). *Sport and social exclusion.* London: Routledge.

DePauw, K., & Gavron, S. (2005). *Disability sport.* Champaign, IL: Human Kinetics.

Doherty, A., & Taylor, T. (2007). Sport and physical recreation in the settlement of immigrant youth. *Leisure/Loisir, 31*(1), 27–55.

Donnelly, P., & Coakley, J. (2002). *The role of recreation in promoting social inclusion.* Ottawa, ON: Laidlaw Foundation.

Elling, A., & Claringbould, I. (2005). Mechanism of inclusion and exclusion in the Dutch Sports Landscape: Who can and wants to belong? *Sociology of Sport Journal, 22,* 498–515.

Everybody Active. (2009). *Promising practices: Case studies on access and inclusion to recreation.* British Columbia Recreation and Parks Association. Retrieved from www.PhysicalActivityStrategy.ca

Frisby, W. (2011). Promising physical activity inclusion practices for Chinese immigrant women in Vancouver, Canada. *Quest, 63,* 135–147.

Frisby, W., & Fenton, J. (1998). *Leisure access: Enhancing recreation opportunities for those living in poverty.* Vancouver, BC: British Columbia Health Research Foundation Retrieved from www.lin.ca

Frisby, W., Reid, C., Millar, S., & Hoeber, L. (2005). Putting 'participatory' into participatory forms of action research. *Journal of Sport Management, 19,* 367–386.

Frisby, W., Reid, C., & Ponic, P. (2007). Leveling the playing field: Promoting the health of poor women through a community development approach to recreation. In K. Young & P. White (Eds.), *Sport and gender in Canada* (pp. 121–136). Don Mills, ON: Oxford University Press.

Guildford, J. (2000). *Making the case for social and economic inclusion.* Population and Public Health Branch. Halifax, NS: Health Canada, Atlantic Region.

Gurstein, P., Pulkingham, J., & Vilches, S. (2011). Challenging policies for lone mothers: Reflections on, and insights from, longitudinal qualitative interviewing. In G. Creese & W. Frisby (Eds.), *Feminist community research: Case studies and methodologies* (pp. 127–146). Vancouver, BC: University of British Columbia Press.

Harvey, J. (2001). The role of sport and recreation policy in fostering citizenship: The Canadian experience. In J. Jenson, J. Harvey, W. Kimlicka, A. Maoni, E. Schragge, P. Graefe, & J. M. Fontan (Eds.), *Building citizenship: Government and service provision in Canada.* (pp. 23–46). Ottawa, ON: Canadian Policy Research Networks.

Hutchison, P., & McGill, J. (1998). *Leisure, integration, and community.* Toronto, ON: Leisurability Publications.

King, S. (2008). What's queer about (queer) sport sociology now? A review essay. *Sociology of Sport Journal, 25,* 419–442.

Labonte, R. (2004). Social inclusion/exclusion: Dancing the dialectic. *Health Promotion International, 19*(1), 115–121.

Mitchell, A., & Shillington, R. (2005). Poverty, inequality and social inclusion. In T. Richmond & A. Saloojee (Eds.), *Social inclusion: Canadian perspectives* (pp. 33–57). Halifax, NS: Fernwood Publishing.

Muller, F., van Zoonen, L., & de Roode, L. (2008). The integrative power of sport: Imagined and real effects of sport events on multicultural integration. *Sociology of Sport Journal, 25,* 387–401.

Ontario Council for Agencies Serving Immigrants (OCASI). (2006). *OCASI Research on inclusive recreation model for immigrant and refugee youth: Provisional model.* Toronto, ON. Retrieved from http://www.ocasi.org/index.php?catid=130

Ontario Women's Health Network. (2009). *Inclusion research handbook.* Toronto, ON. Retrieved from http://www.echo-ontario.ca/echo/en/echos-work-in-strengthening-communities/inclusion-guide.html

Paraschak, V. (2007). Doing race, doing gender: First Nations, 'sport' and gender relations. In K. Young & P.G. White (Eds.), *Sport and gender in Canada* (2nd ed.) (pp. 137–154). Don Mills, ON: Oxford University Press.

Parnes, P. (2007). Sport as a means to foster inclusion, health and well-being of people with disabilities. In *Report for the Sport for Development and Peace International Working Group (SDP IWG) Secretariat* (pp. 124–157). University of Toronto, Faculty of Physical Education and Health. Retrieved from http://iwg.sportanddev.org/data/htmleditor/file/SDP%20IWG/literature%20review%20SDP.pdf

Pegg, S., & Compton, D.M. (2004). Creating opportunities and ensuring access to leisure and recreation services through inclusion in the global community. *Leisure/Loisir, 28*(1–2), 5–26.

Ponic, P. (2007). *Embracing complexity in community-based health promotion: Inclusion, power and women's health.* Unpublished doctoral dissertation, University of British Columbia, Canada.

Ponic, P., & Frisby, W. (2010). Unpacking assumptions about 'inclusion' in community-based health promotion: Perspectives of women living in poverty. *Qualitative Health Research, 11,* 1519–1531.

Reid, C. (2004). *The wounds of exclusion: Poverty, women's health and social justice.* Edmonton, AB: Qualitative Institute Press.

Richmond, T., & Saloojee, A. (Eds.) (2005). *Social inclusion: Canadian perspectives.* Halifax, NS: Fernwood Publishing.

Sands, J. (2006). *Everybody's welcome: A social inclusion approach to program planning and development for recreation and parks services.* Vancouver, BC: Social Planning and Research Council of BC and the BC Recreation and Parks Association.

Shakir, U. (2004). Role of settlement houses and neighbourhood centres. Retrieved from http://inclusion.ifsnetwork.org/role.index.asp

Shakir, U. (2005). Dangers of a new dogma: Social inclusion or else …! In T. Richmond & A. Saloojee (Eds.), *Social inclusion: Canadian perspectives* (pp. 203–214). Halifax, NS: Fernwood Publishing.

Shookner, M. (2002). *An inclusion lens: Workbook for looking at social and economic exclusion and inclusion.* Halifax, NS: Population and Public Health Branch Atlantic Region.

Sport Canada. (2002). *The Canadian sport policy.* Ottawa, ON: Department of Canadian Heritage. Retrieved from http://www.pch.gc.ca/pgm/sc/pol/pcs-csp/2003/polsport-eng.pdf

Sport Canada. (2012). *Canadian sport policy 2012.* Ottawa, ON: Department of Canadian Heritage. Retrieved from http://sirc.ca/CSPRenewal/documents/CSP2012_EN.pdf

Sport Matters and Public Policy Forum. (2004). *Investing in Canada: Fostering an Agenda for Citizen and Community Participation.* Ottawa, ON: Department of Canadian Heritage.

Storey, K. (2004). The case against the Special Olympics. *Journal of Disability Policy Studies, 15*(1), 35–42.

Taylor, J., & Frisby, W. (2010). Addressing inadequate leisure access policies through citizen engagement. In H. Mair, S. M. Arai, & D.G. Reid (Eds.), *Decentring work: Critical perspectives on leisure, social policy, and human development* (pp. 30–45), Calgary, AB: University of Calgary Press.

Tirone, S. (2004). Evening the playing field: Recreation in a low-income Canadian community. *Leisure/Loisir, 28*(1–2), 155–174.

Vail, S.E. (2007). Community development and sport participation. *Journal of Sport Management, 21,* 571–596.

Vancouver 2010. (2009). Social inclusion and responsibility. Retrieved from http://www.vancouver2010.com/en/sustainability-and-br-aboriginal-pa/social-inclusion-and-responsibility/-/30822/qs93wq/index.html

Vancouver City Council and Vancouver Park Board. (2008). Sport for life strategy. Retrieved from http://vancouver.ca/ctyclerk/cclerk/20081014/documents/a7.pdf

Vertinsky, P., Jette, S., & Hoffman, A. (2009). Skierinas in the Olympics: Gender justice and gender politics at the local, national and international level over the challenge of women's ski jumping. *Olympika, 18,* 25–56.

Working Together Project. (2008). *Community-led libraries toolkit.* Vancouver, BC. Retrieved from www.librariesincommunities.ca

Vancouver City Council and Vancouver Park Board. (2008). *Vancouver Sport for Life—Vancouver Sport Strategy,* Vancouver, BC.

Young, I.M. (2000). *Inclusion and democracy.* Oxford, UK: Oxford University Press.

Conclusion

Jean Harvey, University of Ottawa and
Lucie Thibault, Brock University

This book fills the need for a renewed overall examination of sport policy in Canada since the publication of Macintosh, Bedecki and Franks's (1987) text entitled *Sport and Politics in Canada. Federal Government Involvement Since 1961*. Moreover, this book offers the most comprehensive analysis of Canadian sport policy that has ever been published. Indeed, by bringing together the finest scholars in the field under this collective project, this book provides a broad selection of detailed assessments of the most salient aspects of Canadian sport policy both past and present. The general *Canadian Sport Policy* along with specific policies covering anti-doping (see Beamish's Chapter VII), sport event hosting (see McCloy and Thibault's Chapter VIII), Aboriginal sport (see Forsyth and Paraschak's Chapter IX), sport for people with disability (see Howe's Chapter X), sport for girls and women (see Safai's Chapter XI), and official languages in Canada's sport system (see Fraser's Chapter XII) have been addressed in the book. As well, issues relating to multi-level governance mechanisms (see Harvey's Chapter II), international development through sport (see Kidd's Chapter III), high performance sport (see Kikulis's Chapter IV), athlete development and support (see Thibault and Babiak's Chapter V), sport participation (see Donnelly's Chapter VI), and social inclusion and sport (see Frisby and Ponic's Chapter XIII) are extensively discussed. In essence, the sheer complexity of sport policy in Canada is fully covered in this book.

At a time when the new *Canadian Sport Policy* (CSP) has just been launched, this book is both timely and valuable in that it not only provides extensive analyses of early and more recent developments and issues related to this policy, but also identifies new opportunities and potential pitfalls that already face policy makers and other stakeholders with regard to its implementation.

In the last two decades, government involvement in sport and physical activity has increased steadily and reached new levels in terms of the breadth of policies and programs put in place to support high performance athletes. To a much lesser extent, policies have also been implemented to encourage and support mass participation for Canadians and to promote the inclusion of disadvantaged constituencies, girls and women, Aboriginal peoples, the disabled, linguistic minorities and low income families. After a decade of cutbacks in the 1990s, Sport Canada's budget has increased significantly, more support has been offered to high performance athletes and coaches, tax deductions have been made available for children's participation in sport and physical activity, and so on. Moreover, significant amounts of federal funds have been devoted to the organization and hosting of the 2015 Toronto Pan and Parapan Am Games, the 2010 Olympic Winter Games in Vancouver, as well as other major sport events, such as the IAAF World Championships in Edmonton in 2001 and the FINA World Aquatics Championships in Montreal in 2005, public investments that resulted in new and expensive sport infrastructures, mostly for the benefit of professional athletes and/or high performance athletes. The federal government is not the only level of government that has invested large amounts of public funds in sport over that period. As discussed in Harvey's chapter (Chapter II), provincial and local governments have also invested significantly in this area. They are indeed the foremost providers of public funding for sport. All in all, it can be argued that, over the last two decades, sport in Canada has benefited from major increases in public funding by successive governments, which have demonstrated a sustained interest in providing Canadian athletes with the means to develop and compete successfully on the international scene and win increasingly costly medals, ostensibly winning international prestige for their country abroad and, similarly, pride, unity, and identity for Canadians at home.

However, during the same period, increased interest in mass participation sport remained limited to general statements of commitment to the issue while in reality very limited material investment in terms of dedicated programs and sport infrastructure at the local level (i.e., where sport participation really occurs) actually occurred. Therefore, as shown by Kikulis (Chapter IV) and Donnelly (Chapter VI), while Canadian high performance athletes have continued to strive for medals internationally, overall sport participation among Canadians has been declining, regardless of the type of metrics chosen. Moreover, even though mechanisms of intergovernmental collaboration have been put in place, and bilateral agreements have been signed between the federal, provincial and territorial governments, the amounts of dollars involved pale in comparison to the overall spending in high performance sport. Despite the efforts of the 2002 *Canadian Sport Policy* to bring the issue of sport participation to the forefront of awareness with a dedicated objective, the attainment of the participation objective is not among the list of the successes of this policy. The 2012 CSP, however, further addresses the issue, broadening the scope of sport covered by the policy to include four spheres: introduction to sport, recreational sport, competitive sport, and high performance sport. Moreover, the 2012 CSP breaks new ground insofar as it envisions a wider role for sport in Canadian society, in particular through community sport.

The first set of issues is related to sport funding. After a massive injection of funds by governments into the economy to offset the 2008 economic downfall, sport, like almost all policy areas, has entered an era of high turbulence. For the most part, the federal, provincial and territorial governments are now focusing on deficit reduction and have moved toward, at least at the federal level, reducing the overall size of government. The vision for the 2012 CSP broadens the role sport is meant to play in the next 10 years in order to make Canada a leading sport nation. More precisely, increased funds and infrastructures will be imperative to achieve the policy goals set for increased physical literacy, better access to the introduction to sport and recreational sport and improved competitive and high performance sport opportunities. Indeed, increased financial resources will have to be funneled through bilateral agreements between the federal and the provincial and territorial governments if the federal government is to fulfill the role it set out in the 2012 CSP. Yet, this CSP refers to renewed partnerships both as a means to achieve the wider role of sport and to indirectly access increased funding for sport through resource sharing with other government departments. It calls for increased funding of sport by the private sector at the same time as it calls for "sharing and economizing resources" (Sport Canada, 2012, p. 2) through "innovative public–private funding models . . . for the ongoing development of sport" (Sport Canada, 2012, p. 20). In short, it will be challenging to reach for the vision and goals of the 2012 CSP in a context of increasingly scarce public funding. For example, from where will the funds needed to offset the huge deficit in community sport infrastructure originate? How will programs such as Own the Podium and national sport organizations continue to be funded, as the corporations that sponsored them in the context of the 2010 Vancouver Olympic and Paralympic Winter Games and the 2012 London Olympic and Paralympic Games are either reorienting their marketing strategies or are dealing with fewer resources to invest in sport programs, events and athletes as the economy stagnates? Will the state take up the slack?

Dedicating sufficient public funding for sport is not the only leadership challenge for governments in realizing the 2012 CSP vision. Increasingly, governments ". . . can no longer govern alone, as they once did. This makes it increasingly risky to propose big initiatives" (Lenihan, 2012, p. 25). People do not defer anymore to the authority of state elites; citizens want to be involved, consulted and want processes to be transparent (Lenihan, 2012). Policy building requires taking into consideration the often divergent interests of a growing number of disparate stakeholders, making it difficult for governments to propose and implement innovative policies. Yet, the development of the 2012 CSP followed an extensive consultation process, albeit mostly limited to the sport and physical activity field, and called for engagement by all concerned stakeholders in the development of the new policy. Implementation of the policy will require renewed and sustained engagement on the part of interested stakeholders, as well as the willingness of governments to assume the leadership to realize the vision. New information technologies and social media will continue to remodel the interactions between citizens, stakeholders and governments.

Since the International Year for Sport and Physical Education (2005), sport for development has become a major trend in sport. As Kidd has explained (Chapter III), Canada has played and continues to play an important role in this area. The 2012 CSP calls for an increased Canadian role at the international level. The 2012 CSP also paves the road for sport for development within Canada. Huge inequalities still exist in Canadian sport; improving opportunities and overall inclusion as discussed by Frisby and Ponic (Chapter XIII) are the the greatest challenges for sport in Canada in the decade ahead.

While this book has focused on the challenges and issues relating to sport policy in Canada it is vital to underscore that Canadian sport policy is substantially influenced by developments at the international level. As a participant country in the Olympic Games, Canada's sport policy is increasingly subjected to the dictates of the IOC and International sport federations. Two examples include Canada's anti-doping policy, which is subject to WADA's anti-doping code, and a specific stringent law (Bill C-47, *The Olympic and Paralympic Marks Act*) had to be passed by the Government of Canada to protect the IOC trademarks during the Vancouver Olympic and Paralympic Winter Games. Other events on the international sport scene will likely influence Canadian sport policy in the future, especially with regard to hosting policy and the promotion of human rights in the world through sport. New social movements are indeed active at the international level, for example, working toward 'greener' games and more environmentally sensitive sport events, calling for action against countries with poor human rights records and fighting against corruption in the highest spheres of international sport (Harvey, Horne, & Safai, 2009).

As noted at the outset of these closing remarks, this book offers the most comprehensive interpretation of sport policy in Canada published to date. However, it does not cover everything. For example, it does not address government support of professional sport. It mostly focuses on sport policy at the federal level. More research on sport policy at the provincial/territorial and local government levels is needed. This book provides a detailed introduction to sport policy in Canada and a thorough assessment of the issues and challenges of that policy, providing a valuable reference both for policy makers and sport policy scholars in Canada and abroad.

References

Harvey, J., Horne, J., & Safai, P. (2009). Alterglobalization, global social movements, and the possibility of political transformation through sport. *Sociology of Sport Journal, 26,* 383–403.

Lenihan, D. (2012). *Rescuing policy: The case for public engagement.* Ottawa, ON: Public Policy Forum.

Macintosh, D., Bedecki, T., & Franks, C.E.S. (1987). *Sport and politics in Canada. Federal government involvement since 1961.* Montreal, QC & Kingston, ON: McGill-Queen's University Press.

Sport Canada. (2012). *Canadian sport policy 2012.* Ottawa, ON: Canadian Heritage. Retrieved from http://sirc.ca/CSPRenewal/documents/CSP2012_EN.pdf

About the Contributors

(in alphabetical order)

Katherine Babiak is Associate Professor in the Department of Sport Management at the University of Michigan. Her research interests include the role and impact of sport in society; in particular, how sport institutions allow for social development in areas such as philanthropy, governance, policy, sustainability, and diversity and equity. Most of her work centres on these issues at the organizational level and she has explored these issues in the professional sport setting as well as Olympic and community sport. Her work has appeared in publications such as *Journal of Sport Management, Journal of Business Ethics, Sport Management Review, International Journal of Sport Policy and Politics*, and *Nonprofit and Voluntary Sector Quarterly.*

Rob Beamish is Head of the Department of Sociology at Queen's University. His research centres on high-performance sport, the sociology of the body, and specific issues related to work, labour, and classical and contemporary social theory. In addition to numerous articles, book chapters, and encyclopedia entries related to social theory and sport sociology, Rob is author of *Fastest, Highest, Strongest: The Critique of High-Performance Sport* (co-authored with Ian Ritchie); *Sociology's Task and Promise: The Classical Tradition and Contemporary Sociological Thinking;* and *Steroids: A New Look at Performance-Enhancing Drugs.*

Peter Donnelly is Professor in the Faculty of Physical Education and Health at the University of Toronto and Director of the Centre for Sport Policy Studies. He has served as Editor of the *Sociology of Sport Journal* and the *International Review for the Sociology of Sport* and served two terms as General Secretary of the International Sociology of Sport Association and a term as President of the North American Society for the Sociology of Sport. He has published widely in the area of sociology of sport and recently led a research team to devise strategies to measure sport participation.

Janice Forsyth is Director of the International Centre for Olympic Studies and Assistant Professor in the School of Kinesiology, Faculty of Health Sciences at Western University. Her primary research area is in Canadian sport history, with a specific interest in contemporary Aboriginal sport practices. Recent projects include Aboriginal people and Olympic Games; sporting experiences of Tom Longboat Award recipients; sports and games at residential schools; and Aboriginal women, work, and sport. She is a member of the Fisher River Cree First Nation, Manitoba.

Graham Fraser is a highly respected journalist and author. During a long and distinguished career that has straddled the language divide, Graham has reported on issues affecting Canada and Canadians, including cultural and foreign policy; constitutional debates; and provincial, national, and international politics. Graham has written five books *Fighting Back: Urban Renewal in Trefann Court* (1972), *Playing for Keeps: The Making of a Prime Minister* (1988) and *Vous m'intéressez: Chroniques* (2001). His latest book, *Sorry, I Don't Speak French* (2006) helped stimulate renewed public discussion of language policy in Canada. Graham's 1984 book *PQ: René Lévesque and the Parti Québecois in Power* which deals with Québec language policy was nominated for the Governor General's Literary Award for non-fiction.

Wendy Frisby is Professor and Associate Director of Community and Student Development, School of Kinesiology, University of British Columbia. Her areas of expertise include social inclusion and equality, poverty, interculturalism, and community-based health promotion. Most of her work has utilized a feminist participatory action research approach that directly involves community members in all phases of the research process. She has received several research grants including funding from the Social Sciences and Humanities Research Council of Canada and the Canadian Institutes of Health Research. Her work has been published in several book chapters and journals such as *Journal of Sport Management, International Journal of Sport Policy and Politics, Qualitative Health Research, Canadian Journal of Public Health, Quest, Action Research,* and *European Sport Management Quarterly.*

Jean Harvey is Professor and member and former director of the Research Centre for Sport in Canadian Society at the School of Human Kinetics, University of Ottawa. His main research interests are sport policy and sport in the context of globalization. His research has been supported by the Social Sciences and Humanities Research Council of Canada and published in various peer-reviewed journals. He is also the co-editor (with Hart Cantelon) of *Not Just a Game: Essays in Canadian Sport Sociology* (1988), co-editor (along with Robert Young) of *Image-Building in Canadian Municipalities* (2012), and co-author of *Sport and Social Movements: From the Local to the Global* (2013) published by Bloomsbury.

P. David Howe is Senior Lecturer in the Anthropology of Sport in the School of Sport, Exercise and Health Sciences at Loughborough University He is currently also Vice-President of the International Federation of Adapted Physical Activity (IFAPA). David holds a visiting professorship at Katholieke Universiteit Leuven, Belgium. Trained as a medical anthropologist, he authored *Sport, Professionalism and Pain: Ethnographies of Injury and Risk* (Routledge, 2004) and *The Cultural Politics of the Paralympic Movement: Through the Anthropological Lens* (Routledge, 2008).

Bruce Kidd is Warden of Hart House and Professor of kinesiology and physical education at the University of Toronto. He has published extensively on the political economy of Canadian and international sport, most recently co-editing *Olympic Reform Ten Years After* (with Heather Dichter) and *Forty Years of Sport and Social Change, 1968–2008: 'To remember is to Resist'* (with Russell Field). He has served in many roles as a sport policy advisor and voluntary sport leader. He currently chairs the Commonwealth Advisory Body on Sport, the Maple Leaf Sports and Entertainment Team Up Foundation, and the Selection Committee of Canada's Sports Hall of Fame. He is an honorary member of the Canadian Olympic Committee.

Lisa M. Kikulis is Associate Professor in the Department of Sport Management at Brock University. Her research interests bridge the broad field of policy and organizational studies. She examines the social, political, and organizational contexts and their impact on sport policy and its implementation by and through government and non-government organizations with a particular focus on citizen engagement, community development, and the relationship between public and private interests. She also has an interest in qualitative methodology and has begun exploring narrative inquiry and reflexive methodology. Her current sporting practice involves running and yoga.

Cora McCloy is Research Officer and Faculty Liaison at the Centre for Teaching Support and Innovation at the University of Toronto. Her dissertation focused on federal sport event hosting policies with an emphasis on amateur sport legacies for a range of stakeholder groups. Cora has published this work in historical journals and in national and international conference proceedings. Her interest in exploring hosting benefits for the amateur sport system stem in large part from her own experiences as an elite athlete and as a coach to a wide range of participants from community-level recreation programs to varsity sport.

Victoria Paraschak is Associate Professor at the University of Windsor. Her research examines the experiences of marginalized groups in sport, with a particular focus on Aboriginal peoples and their physical cultural practices, including related recreation and sport policy analysis. She has combined this research background with practical workshops with Aboriginal delegates that address their sporting realities, as well as strategic planning with sport and recreation organizations in the Northwest Territories. She has published a variety of chapters addressing Aboriginal peoples' experiences in sport, along with articles in journals such as *Sociology of Sport*, *Avante*, *Sport History Review*, and *Ethnologies*.

Pamela Ponic is Researcher at the BC Centre of Excellence in Women's Health (BCCEWH). She completed her Canadian Institutes of Health Research-funded postdoctoral training at BCCEWH and the School of Nursing, University of British Columbia, in 2011. Her doctoral research, funded by the Social Sciences and Humanities Research Council of Canada, focused on social inclusion in community recreation for women living in poverty. Pam's most recent work is exploring trauma-informed approaches to physical activity for marginalized women. She has published in journals such as *Violence Against Women*, *Qualitative Health Research*, and the *Canadian Journal of Public Health*.

Parissa Safai is Associate Professor in the School of Kinesiology and Health Science in the Faculty of Health at York University. Her research interests focus on the critical study of sport at the intersection of risk, health and healthcare. This includes research on sports' "culture of risk", the development and social organization of sport and exercise medicine, as well as the social determinants of athletes' health. Her work has been published in such journals as the *Sociology of Sport Journal*, the *International Review for the Sociology of Sport*, *Sport History Review*, and the *Canadian Bulletin of Medical History/Bulletin canadien d'histoire de la médecine*.

Lucie Thibault is Professor at Brock University. Her areas of expertise include sport policy, globalization of sport, and organizational theory as it applies to sport and leisure organizations. She also investigates the Canadian government's role in sport and athlete involvement in the governance of sport. Her research has been funded by the Social Sciences and Humanities Research Council of Canada and has appeared in such publications as: *Journal of Sport Management, European Sport Management Quarterly, Journal of Sport and Social Issues, International Journal of Sport Policy and Politics,* and *Leisure Studies.* Lucie has also published numerous book chapters.

Index

relations, 86–88; history, 72–77, 81; monitoring and evaluation, 84–88; overview, 69–72, 408–9; policy framework, 81–83; power relations, 72, 84, 87–88; Right to Play, 70–71, 77, 79, 82–83, 89; sport as social intervention, 86–87; 'sport for good,' 72–75, 87, 89n4; UN initiatives, 82–83, 88–89; UN Millennium Development Goals, 69, 79, 82, 84; Victoria Declaration, 75–76. *See also* health education

Sport for More, 61

Sport Funding and Accountability Framework (SFAF), 108–14, 192–93; agreements, 114; assessment, 110, 111t–113t, 192–93; background, 106–8; eligibility, 109–10; funding, 108–10, 114; funding decline, 108t–109; gender equity, 333–34; high performance sport, 109–10, 114; history, 19, 25; and LTAD, 110, 130, 133; official languages, 354, 359–60, 362, 366; participation, 192–93

Sport Gender Snapshot, 331–32

Sport in Canada (1998). *See* Mills Report

Sport Leaders Abroad, 88

Sport Medicine Council of Canada, 229–30

sport officials and gender, 318

Sport Participation Research Initiative (SPRI), 193–94

Sport Participation Strategy 2008–2012 (2008), 189–92, 194–96, 198

Sport Schools in Canada, 132–33

Sport Support Program (SSP), 105–6, 366

Status of the High Performance Athlete reports, 159, 160, 163, 165, 166

Steadward, Robert, 298, 300, 305–06, 339

substances, doping. *See* doping in sport

Summative Evaluation of the Department of Canadian Heritage's Sport Hosting Program (2003), 253–54

Svoboda, Mira, 23t, 364–65

swimming, 112t, 209n15, 296, 306, 394

Targets for Athlete Performance and the Sport System (2004), 120

Tenasco, René, 270

tennis, 112t, 209n14

Tewksbury, Mark, 126

Thibault, Lucie, 165–66, 168, 416; on athlete development, 147–76; on history of federal policy, 11–35; on hosting policies, 243–65; on sport policy, 1–8, 405–10

Toronto: facilities, 209n15; Pan/Parapan (2015), 2, 55, 135, 372; participation, 203–4; sport academies, 133; Sport Institute, 135, 151

Toward 2000: Building Canada's Sport System (1988), 224–25, 229–30

track and field: team *vs.* individual sports, 188. *See also* Athletics Canada

transgendered people. *See* sexual orientation

Trudeau, Pierre Elliott, 13, 16t, 70, 98, 190

True Sport, 168, 200, 386, 389–90

Trupish, Adam, 123–24

under-represented groups: and CSP, 59, 284, 339–40, 385; official languages, 361, 362, 364, 365; participation, 195–96; social inclusion, 385, 406. *See also* Aboriginal sport; immigrants; low-income people; people with disabilities; race/ethnicity; seniors; social inclusion; women and girls in sport

UNESCO, 180, 234

United Kingdom: LTAD model, 132, 140n5; social class and elite athletes, 187; sport academies, 133; sport for development, 76; UK Sport, 77, 127. *See also* Olympic Games, 2012, London

United Nations: Millennium Development Goals, 69, 79, 82, 84; sport for development and peace (UNOSDP), 82–83, 88–89

United States: Aboriginal sports, 281–82; Cold War and sports, 185,